GREAT SPORTING HEADLINES

INTRODUCED BY
IAN WOOLDRIDGE

COLLINS
8, GRAFTON STREET,
LONDON, W1
1984

PRODUCED BY NUTSHELL LIMITED
FOR WILLIAM COLLINS SONS AND CO LIMITED
LONDON · GLASGOW · SYDNEY · AUCKLAND
TORONTO · JOHANNESBURG

PRINTED IN GREAT BRITAIN BY WILLIAM CLOWES, BECCLES, SUFFOLK
TYPESETTING BY ECLIPSE GRAPHICS, LONDON
ORIGINATION BY CENTRAL REPRODUCTION, LONDON
PRODUCTION BY MAIN TITLES ASSOCIATES, LONDON

COMPILED AND DESIGNED BY STANLEY GLAZER
RESEARCH BY THE JOHN FROST HISTORIC NEWSPAPER SERVICE
ADDITIONAL RESEARCH BY
DOUG GARDNER (SPORTFAX), ANDREA BONNER AND ANNE-MARIE EHRLICH
EDITED BY ANDREW TAYLOR

NEWSPAPERS REPRODUCED FROM THE
JOHN FROST HISTORIC NEWSPAPER SERVICE,
THE BRITISH LIBRARY AND THE ILN LIBRARY

INTRODUCTION
BY
IAN WOOLDRIDGE

Two things strike you forcibly as you journey almost a century back into the world's sporting archives. The first is that there is little so ephemeral as fame won in the arena. The second is that sporting eras, like governments, get the Press they deserve.

I suppose, in the first instance, that my own trade of sportswriting is principally to blame. We are fans and often friends of the fleeting heroes we write about and we are incorrigibly trigger-happy with words like 'immortal'. The truth is, of course, that for every legendary figure like Donald George Bradman or Muhammad Ali there are a dozen Ian Bothams and Frank Brunos. It is a small sadness of these fascinating pages that they confirm that the poor woman who flung herself beneath the king's horse during the 1913 Derby had far greater impact on history than any jockey who ever lived.

The second noticeable factor is that the gradual erosion of good manners on the field of play has been matched by a growing hostility between journalist and sports performer and administrator. The obsequious reporting of Edwardian England has given way to newspaper witch hunts into the private lives of sports stars. Just look, on the front page of the *Daily Mirror* on June 2, 1914, at the great C B Fry standing rigidly to attention before his sovereign at Lord's Cricket Ground. And then remember that on the same turf, more than half a century later, as Queen Elizabeth II was being introduced to the Australian Test team, one Dennis Lillee suddenly leaned towards her, whipped out pen and paper and said, 'D'yer reckon I could have yer autergraph?'

Two elements above all are responsible for the quite dramatic changes in the newspaper chronicling of sport. Money and television.

The pre-eminent sports star in tennis, golf, boxing, skiing, even athletics, is now capable of grossing £1 million in a year. He is backed by professional merchandisers who need the media to exploit his commercial potential. The minions of the media, with mortgages to meet, do not necessarily believe this is an equable arrangement. If the sportsman wants to be a showbiz star then he must accept the showbiz rules — which are that his sex-life, his drinking habits and all other personal predilections are front-

**If the sportsman wants to be a
showbiz star then he
must accept the showbiz rules**

page property. There was an unwritten rule, when I was travelling with Test cricket teams as recently as the 1960s, that while you could criticise unmercifully a man's performance on the field, you never mentioned his activities — mostly innocent but on rare occasions bizarre in the extreme — off it. That rule no longer applies and television more than the perennial Fleet Street circulation war is responsible for it.

Television was the death-knell of romantic — and romanticised — sportswriting. Just as Sir Neville Cardus's awesome elegies about a strokeless innings by Maurice Leyland would now be seen by millions as the product of an incandescent imagination, so would the exaggerated and even fabricated excesses of the popular press be dismissed for the sheer fiction they often are. Now the nation, even the world, sees for itself — and sports journalism has been forced onto another tack.

The tabloids, particularly, have turned to the provocative columnist and the investigative reporter to counter the challenge of TV. Now 'newsmen' as well as sportswriters are assigned to Test cricket tours, Wimbledon and the Olympic beat. Their charge is to cover the ground that television cameras cannot reach. Descriptive writing has given way to the dressing room exposé. The critique has been replaced by the player's 'quote'. Both sport and sportswriting have radically changed since the day in 1932 when a covey of Australian journalists approached the English cricket captain, Douglas Jardine, and asked him to name his team for the following day's opening Test in Sydney. Jardine was outraged. 'What business is that of yours?' demanded the haughty Wykehamist. 'And anyway, I never speak to the Press.' His unrevealed team did the speaking for him. They scored 524, beat Australia by ten wickets and set fire to what was to become the infamous Bodyline Tour.

Bodyline was to signal a third development clearly traced in the historic headlines which fill these pages: the full-scale invasion, never mind intrusion, of politics into sport. Adolf Hitler, Jimmy Carter, Johannes Balthazar Vorster, Margaret Thatcher and the grim geriatrics of the Kremlin were all to play their roles in dragging sport from its leisured acres at the back of the papers into screaming front-page headlines.

Abused by politicians, torn asunder by terrorists, plundered by commercialists and occasionally ill-used by the Press, sport has somehow survived it all. At its worst it remains a welcome substitute for war even if, as you progress through this book, you could sometimes scarcely tell the difference.

1
THE GOLDEN AGE

William Gilbert Grace, country doctor, cricketer and eminent Victorian, epitomised the Golden Age of sport. In his athletic lifetime, which defied a massive girth and spanned an incredible 43 years, he represented Empire, Queen and unquestioned British supremacy at all things. Indeed only the Queen commanded greater idolatry. Grace's was the most familiar male face in the land and his arrogance, in the circumstances, was seen as an endearing trait. When adjudged lbw early in his innings before a large crowd at Blackheath, he addressed the umpire thus: 'Listen, you damned fool, they haven't come here to see you make a fool of yourself. They've come to see me bat.' And bat on he did. Naturally he wasn't at home the day his wife gave birth to their second child. He was batting at Grimsby and scored exactly 400.

Muscular Christianity and benevolent bullying were the cornerstones of this era in sport, which lasted until the Kaiser's guns blew it to perdition on the Somme and Passchendaele. Quite who first nominated it the Golden Age is open to question. So, too, is the carat value of the gold concerned for, in hindsight and on closer inspection, it was as tarnished as any other. Just as no-one dreamed of delving into the murky waters of Victorian sexuality, so no-one questioned the anomaly of the heroic amateur, Dr W G Grace, receiving a little matter of £8,835 — worth probably £200,000 by today's spending standards — as an outright gift from an admiring nation. That the average cricket professional then earned £2 a week for a 24-week season bothered no-one except the threadbare wives and shabbily shod kids of the cricket professionals concerned. But, then, while Grace was batting, Karl Heinrich Marx was still struggling with *Das Kapital* in the reading room of the British Museum just down the road from Lord's.

It must also amuse the modern international cricketer, who seems to play about ten Test matches every year, that the good doctor's Test record for England — in the longest career there ever will be — amounted to scoring precisely 1,098 runs at an average of 32.29 and taking just nine wickets. It may have been

The truly golden aspect of the era was that sport was developing for the enjoyment of the masses

nice of him to spare the time, but golden it was certainly not.

The truly golden aspect of the era was that sport was developing for the enjoyment and entertainment of the masses. On April 17, 1888, in the Royal Hotel in Manchester, worthy men with high wing-collars and *Coronation Street* accents met to tackle the shambles of a rising game called soccer. Within five years they were meeting again to decree that no player should earn from it more than £140 per calendar year. Professionalism was already getting out of hand but the birth of the Football League signalled the blossoming of soccer into the world game.

On an afternoon in June, 1894, in the amphitheatre of the Sorbonne University of Paris, a totally unathletic French nobleman named Pierre de Coubertin addressed an equally unathletic assembly on a matter dear to his heart. The world, he suggested, would be a safer, better place if, every year in four, the youth of many countries could assemble to meet one another in the friendship of sporting contests. He argued so passionately that he won the day. He failed to avert two catastrophic world wars, but he did give birth to the Olympic Games.

The first Olympics since AD 393 were staged in Athens in 1896. The fourth Olympics were held in Shepherd's Bush, West London, in 1908. The British royals, despite pouring rain, turned out in force for the opening ceremony. They were back in force to witness poor Dorando Pietri, of Italy, stumble and fall three times on the track as he tried to urge his exhausted body towards the finish line of the marathon. At one point well-meaning doctors rushed to help him and in so doing guaranteed his disqualification. 'Seldom, if ever,' recorded *The Graphic*, the posh sixpenny illustrated weekly, 'has there been a more dramatic finish to a great athletic contest.'

The Queen was so moved that she presented Dorando with a special trophy. Carrier pigeons and crude telegraphs bore the tear-jerking story to the corners of the world. The Olympics were on the map; the great cult of marathon running was born.

The *Daily Mirror*, then circulating 960,000 papers a day at one halfpenny a copy, probably did not realise at the time that its gloriously trivial front page on Friday June 19, 1914, was virtually a valedictory tribute not so much to a Golden Age as to a way of British life that was never to return. Then, as now, Royal Ascot was famed for its outrageous millinery. Then, as now, there was perverse delight in reporting that 'the French horse, which was favourite, was unplaced'. But what the page radiates is an aura of privilege, a peep-show of the upper classes at play in

days of endless sunshine at the heart of an empire on which the sun never set at all. Seven weeks later the guns of August opened up, millions died and the disillusioned survivors were to return to question everything.

At Wimbledon, dear little Lottie Dod had parked her bicycle against a tree while she popped inside to win the women's singles title at the age of 15 years and 10 months, while out in the Solent the longest-running and most bitter of all sporting sagas — ironically the only one which links the Golden Era with the present day — was at another argumentative height. Was *Constitution* a fitter yacht than Thomas Lipton's *Shamrock III* to cross the Atlantic and fight America for the America's Cup? Despite the fearful embarrassment of having had his mate, King Edward VII, on board when he dismasted his earlier *Shamrock II*, the old tea magnate was again chosen to be Britain's seafaring champion. No luck. Leading America's *Reliance* in the final race, poor Sir Thomas got lost in the fog and failed to find the finish line.

America had first won the America's Cup, in the presence of Queen Victoria, off Cowes, Isle of Wight, in 1851.

It will remain one of the joys of my life that 132 years later I was privileged to be in Newport, Rhode Island, when a foreign challenger finally wrenched that trophy back from the New York Yacht Club after one of the dirtiest campaigns that sport has ever known. That *Australia II* did it to the strains of *Waltzing Matilda* was mildly mitigated by the fact that its owner, Alan Bond, had been born a working-class Londoner. Somehow it finally laid the Golden Age to rest.

2
THE CULT OF PERSONALITY

In the high summer of 1922 an American named Walter Hagen arrived at Sandwich, Kent, to compete with 224 others in the British Open Golf Championship. No-one quite knew what to make of him. He was wearing a flamboyant bespoke suit of the kind that was soon to be adopted by Al Capone's hit-men. He

At Wimbledon, Lottie Dod parked her bicycle against a tree while she popped inside to win the singles title

sported an exotic buttonhole. He chatted, hands in pockets, to peers, knights of the realm, pretty ladies and caddies and then, around lunchtime, strolled off to his hired Rolls Royce to picnic from a hamper provisioned with champagne and smoked salmon sandwiches. This, he maintained to those curious enough to question such bizarre behaviour, was the only thing he could do. He was a *professional* golfer. And professional golfers in Britain, whose social status ranked with that of gamekeepers, gillies, army corporals and chauffeurs, were not permitted to eat in the clubhouse. He was not, you understand, *criticising* the system. He was merely making alternative arrangements.

Walter Hagen, despite a third round 79, won the 1922 British Open. He also won the British Open in 1924, 1928 and 1929. He established a terrific rapport with the Press. He was always available for interview, never short of a newsworthy story. Returning to his hotel in the small hours before a critical final round, he was approached by a reporter who said, 'Mr Hagen, do you know your opponent has already been in bed for three hours?' 'Just tell me one thing,' replied Hagen. 'Is he sleeping?'

Walter Hagen revolutionised sport by introducing the cult of the personality. It was not a swift process, particularly in Britiain where feudalism had been an accepted way of life for considerably more than 1,000 years. But by 1934 it had had its effect. Two *Daily Mirror* headlines in the space of eight days that year provide the evidence.

On June 30 — now double the price at one penny — the *Mirror* splashed its front page with the headline 'Cotton Ties up the Americans'. The following Saturday, sport expropriated the front page again: 'Perry World Tennis Champion'.

Born only 17 miles distant in Cheshire, Henry Cotton, golfer, and Fred Perry, tennis player, weren't two of a kind at all. Henry, son of a prosperous cotton-spinner whose middle-class outlook decreed a public school education for his heir, chose professional golf despite the social pitfalls. Like Hagen, he travelled by limousine, lunched courtesy of Messrs Fortnum and Mason and cultivated the inmates of *Burke's Peerage*. In tennis Fred, born the son of a pioneer Socialist MP in industrial Stockport, had a much rougher time. Tennis was amateur, Fred was a working-class lad in need of readies and the powers that were regarded him as a rough-neck. While his tremendous victory in the 1936 men's singles at Wimbledon, the first home win for 25 years, was hailed by the nation, it was less than

graciously acknowledged by the All England Club. They didn't actually present him with a commemorative necktie. They left it over the chair in his locker room.

Though it was to take yet another world war to rid sport of these nasty snobberies, Cotton and Perry had blazed a trail into the public's affection. They were great charismatic champions. Cotton was to win the Open title twice more just as Perry was twice more to win Wimbledon. They had much of Walter Hagen about them and to both these pioneers today's affluent and socially accepted sports stars owe more than most of them understand or acknowledge. They had put a price on prowess at sport and paved the way to the bank for its first millionaires.

Cricket, run by an oligarchy from an ivory tower in London NW8, was much slower to give an inch to its belowstairs performers. Of course, it was to reap the whirlwind many years later when Kerry Packer, though hardly from the same high motives as Wilberforce, took the game's parsimonious slavers to the High Court and massacred them on the point of restraint of trade. It was one of the most foolish actions ever defended in law but cricket's reluctance to acknowledge the dawn of the 20th century was, if you weren't personally involved, one of its more endearing characteristics. Lord Hawke's personal intervention to the Almighty — 'Pray God no professional will ever captain England' — received such a sympathetic hearing in the celestial committee room that it was all of 1953 before Len, later Sir Leonard, Hutton was elevated from the professional ranks and allowed to have a go at the reins. That he proceeded to captain England 23 times without ever losing a series did nothing to placate the traditional die hards. They regarded him as an opportunist with an accent wholly unacceptable in the drawing rooms well south of Pudsey.

Actually, cricket had no right to take such highly moralistic postures, since its starring role in the greatest sports story between the two world wars revealed a capacity for physical brutality, duplicity and treachery second to none. The campaign was the Bodyline Test series between England and Australia in the southern hemisphere summer of 1932-33.

As a forthcoming film will no doubt accentuate, the cult of personality — though not a penny was at stake — has never been so clearly defined as in the meeting between Donald George Bradman, the man born to humiliate English cricket, and Douglas Robert Jardine, the Scotsman elected to stop him. This entire book could be devoted to the subject if it weren't for

Cotton and Perry had blazed a trail into the public's affection. They were great charismatic champions . . .

one amazing fact. The British Press ignored the story until it was far too late.

Today, a huge Press retinue travels with touring Test teams. In 1932 only three permanent correspondents were attached to Jardine's campaign. One of these, Bruce Harris, was predominantly a tennis writer and another, Pelham Warner, reporting for the then *Morning Post,* was actually *manager* of the side. When the tour exploded — Jardine's strategy of using a battery of very fast bowlers to intimidate batsmen and frequently hit them guaranteed that it would — a powerful English Press campaign might well have put a stop to it. Unfortunately Harris was too unsure of his cricket knowledge to take a firm moral stance. Disgracefully Warner, perhaps to conceal his lack of control over a captain with a near paranoic hatred of Australians, largely brushed the story under his blotting pad.

So the grim theatre of Bodyline, invented by Jardine to halt the huge-scoring Bradman right in his tracks, was played out to the carnage of its final act. By then the governments of both countries had been drawn into the conflict and, at one juncture, Australia even threatened to secede from the Empire. When a scapegoat had to be found, Harold Larwood's protests that, as an ill-paid professional, he had only bowled to orders fell on diplomatically deaf ears. Larwood was broken on the wheel of cricket's uneasy conscience. Douglas Jardine never conceded he had acted unethically. Pelham Warner received a knighthood. Bradman recovered his nerve, took terrible vengeance against subsequent English teams and emerged, arguably, as the greatest single sports personality of the inter-war years.

Americans will probably protest that Joe Louis, the boxer, or Jesse Owens, the athlete, are more suitable nominees. Perhaps, but Louis begat Muhammad Ali and Owens was erased from the record books by Carl Lewis. Bradman begat no-one and only retirement finally lifted the scourge from those burdened to bowl at him.

3
THE ULTIMATE FRONTIER

Was there ever a machine more beautiful than that which appeared on the *Daily Mirror's* front page of February 25, 1932? And has any photograph more swiftly chilled the blood than that which dominated the *Daily Express* on January 5, 1967? In the first a suave, relaxed Sir Malcolm Campbell sits at the wheel of *Bluebird* after screaming down Daytona Beach at 267 miles per hour. The second horrifyingly records the death of his son as another *Bluebird* somersaults at 310 miles an hour and carries Donald Campbell, aged 46, to the black depths of Coniston Water. They span a courageous era of accomplishment, they illustrate grand obsession, they recall days of rejoicing in triumphs in which we had no part and mourning for men we never met. The brave loners out there on the ultimate frontiers have made a noble contribution to the world's front pages. Is it my imagination, or are they becoming fewer?

There are, of course, fewer mountains left unclimbed, no oceans left to navigate single-handed and the next great uncharted territories are out there beyond the moon. Maybe we have seen the best of comprehensible record breaking.

The Campbells, father and son, were in the headlines altogether for slightly more than 42 years. Sir Malcolm broke the land speed record nine times — raising it from 146 mph to 301 mph — between 1924 and 1935. His son broke both the land and water speed records three years before he was killed trying to push frontiers back still further in a 13-year-old boat.

I never met Donald Campbell but I have an Australian friend, Graham Ferrett, who was his site manager for his record bids both at Lake Ayre in Australia and on Coniston Water. On the evening of January 3, 1967, Ferrett and two colleagues were playing cards with Campbell to pass the nervous hours before the morning dash down Coniston. Ferrett tells the story: 'Suddenly Donald turned over a card. It was the Queen of Spades. He stared at it, then held it up and laughed.' Fourteen hours later he was dead.

**Harold Larwood was broken on the wheel of cricket's uneasy conscience . . .
Pelham Warner received a knighthood**

Romantic single-handed seafaring brought the best out of Fleet Street's photographers but the worst of hackneyed clichés out of its tabloid writers. Sir Francis Chichester, 64 and a life-long adventurer, was instantly hailed by the *Daily Mirror* as the Old Man of the Sea and Naomi James, to the *Daily Express*, appeared to be a 'sailor extraordinary' suffering from some malaise known as 'long-distance loneliness'.

Perhaps their heroics are out of place in a volume essentially about sport, but I include one journey on the ultimate frontier which, I am happy to say, was to sweep even Mr Molotov's May 1954 offer of sweet detente between the Soviet Union and the rest of the world out of the banner headlines. What was unknown to him as he made his hypocritical speech in Geneva was that on the cinder track of Oxford University a young medical student was running a mile in under four minutes.

That barrier had been worrying athletes for many of the 79 years since Walter Slade clocked 4 minutes 24.5 seconds in 1875. Walter George brought it down to 4 minutes 19.4 in 1882 but it took another 55 years for Sydney Wooderson to lower it to 4 minutes 6.4 seconds at Motspur Park, Surrey. Then, while the rest of the world was recovering its breath from a little matter called World War Two, a neutral Swede named Gundar Haegg slashed it down to 4 minutes 1.4. And there is stood, unviolated, for another nine years.

What was so admirable about the achievement on that damp and unpropitious evening at Oxford was that it was not accomplished by any of those dead beat 'athletics scholarship' students whose presence at seats of learning is the bane of genuine students with brains. The assault on the four-minute mile was a plot, let us make no bones about that, but the plotters were rounded men who did not believe that sport was the be-all and end-all of life. Bannister, elected to make the last-lap glory assault, was already on the first rung of his career as one of the world's most eminent neurologists. His first pacemaker, Chris Brasher, was to head into a distinguished career in journalism and television. His second pacemaker, Chris Chataway, was to go into television, become a Cabinet minister and then turn to banking. Sport was a hobby, an adjunct to life.

Bannister went over in 3 minutes 59.4 seconds. The job was done. They showered, packed their bags, celebrated and got on with living.

Now every Tom, Steve and Sebastian can run a sub-four-minute mile. Almost 400 have stormed through the barrier. None has ever experienced the glorious emotion of Bannister out there on the frontier that chilly, unforgettable night.

4
AVAILABLE HEROES

Belles époques are in the eye of the beholder. For this beholder, despite continued rationing and school dinners, the immediate post-Hitler years were times of continual magic, frustrated only by vain attempts to look like Keith Miller, sweep like Denis Compton and wrong-foot a full back with the scarcely perceptible body-feint which was the trade mark of the great god, Stanley Matthews.

But there was more to it than that. If you stood four-foot-ten on the terraces at Arsenal or Southampton they lifted you and passed you over 20 rows of cloth-capped heads until you were down peering through the railings. There was no violence off the field and very little on it. The war was over. There was a peace to celebrate. Probably the most vibrant cricket ever played was in the Victory Tests of 1945. Pilot Officer K R Miller, just back from aerial night-fighter combat over Germany, hit a century on his first appearance at Lord's and, later that season, struck a ball on to the roof of the commentary box above the England dressing room. It was, in carry, an even bigger blow than that by Albert Trott in 1899 which remains the only instance of a six clearing the pavilion. Miller didn't give a damn. He was alive. A generation of schoolboys tried to emulate his sheerly dramatic walk to the wicket, throwing his hair back, dragging on his batting gloves with his teeth and grinning at the prospect of the duel to come.

Against Miller England pitted their own champion, Denis Compton. Two of a kind. No adversaries ever gave such little quarter on the field or were such inseparable companions off it. They enjoyed drink, women and horse racing. Gloriously, they emblazoned sport.

Though accurate statistics are not available I will wager much that more schoolboys were beaten for truancy in the summer of 1947 than in any other academic year. Six of the most painful were but a puny price to pay for having merely *glimpsed* Compton on his way to 3,816 runs and 18 centuries in that single season, records that will never be approached again. His autograph that year, though worth ten of any others, was never swapped. Frequently Compton sacrificed half his lunch interval to sign

Compton and Miller . . . no adversaries ever gave such little quarter on the field or were such inseparable companions off it

them, instructing us — for I was one of them and have the piece of paper still — to form an orderly queue in front of him at the pavilion gate. There was a disciplined exuberance about it all and a magic, too, for these were available heroes.

It wasn't that England reigned supreme. In soccer, surely, we were still monstrously patronising the ballet dancers of the Continental forward lines, but in cricket we were crushed in Australia in the winter of 1946-7 and had to wait seven more years for the glorious scene recorded by the *Illustrated London News* of August 29, 1953. D C S Compton had just hit the winning run and the Ashes had been won for the first time since Jardine's scorched-earth policy called Bodyline.

Somehow the joy didn't depend on winning. There seemed no particular virtue in basking in reflected glory. In golf and tennis this was just as well. After Max Faulkner took the British Open title and the £350 prize money that went with it at Portrush in 1951 no Briton won it again until Tony Jacklin in 1969. Wimbledon was to be annexed by Americans and Australians but there was no sense of deprivation, only acclamation for each successive champion. There was grace under pressure out there on the Centre Court and there was mourning worldwide when poor Maureen Connolly, perhaps the most gracious of them all, died of cancer at the cruel age of 35.

The sheer nightmare prospect of being host city to an Olympic Games in the closing quarter of the 20th century never occurred to London in 1948. Blitz-scarred but unbowed, the austerity capital of the winning side merely improvised its way unapologetically to a glittering success. There were notable absentees, of course, since war wounds do not heal that quickly, but the number of competing nations, 59, and athletes, almost 4,500, were both Olympic records. Since new housing was the obvious priority no-one dreamed of erecting elaborate Olympic Villages. Competitors were housed in schools and ex-service huts at Uxbridge. Among them was the now Madame Monique Berlioux, the formidable executive director of the International Olympic Committee, who then was swimming for France. 'Each morning,' she recalls, 'we were handed a package of three sandwiches and two apples and led off to some rather battered buses to go and represent our countries. No-one complained. It would never have crossed our minds. Those were the most glorious days of our lives.'

Wembley was packed with 80,000 spectators daily. It was almost precisely the same number as the television sets that then existed in the entire country and what those who could see did see was Olympic history. For the first time a woman, the

Netherlands sprinter and hurdler Fanny Blankers-Koen, emerged as the unrivalled personality of the Games. Back home they erected a statue to her but her bank statement reflected nothing of her headline-catching success.

It was money, the lack of it, the greed for it, the underhanded dealing with it, the constant pressures and occasional corruption created by it, that brought this beautiful époque to an end. There were to be still more emotional scenes on those same Wembley acres 18 years later, with Bobby Moore holding aloft the surprisingly small and modest trophy that signifies a nation's supremacy in world soccer. But by then a new and more lowering age of sport was dawning.

5

THE TARNISHED IMAGE

In the summer of 1968 in a restaurant just outside Oxford a South African businessman named Tienie Oosthuizen offered Basil D'Oliveira £4,000 to declare himself unavailable for England on their imminent tour of South Africa. By the standards of the cricket pay structure of the period, it was a very large bribe. D'Oliveira, born a South African Cape Coloured but by then a naturalised Englishman, refused it. He was chosen for the tour. The late and unlamented J B Vorster then made a speech in Bloemfontein, the heartland of apartheid, declaring D'Oliveira an unacceptable guest. England's cricket authorities took the South African prime minister at his word. They cancelled the tour completely. South Africa, expelled from the Olympic movement, expelled by FIFA, the world football family, had lost its last cricketing friend. Politics and sport, despite the efforts of honest people and the protests of the naive, and because of the machinations of professional agitators, are now interwoven. There can be no escape.

When American president Jimmy Carter led a Western boycott of the 1980 Moscow Olympics — unsuccessfully supported by a British prime minister who was legally defied — he begat the retaliatory Communist bloc boycott of the 1984 Olympics in Los Angeles. Already many black nations had boycotted the 1976 Olympics in Montreal. The only winners

**Politics and sport, despite the efforts
of honest people and the protests
of the naive . . . are now interwoven**

Ian Wooldridge, Montreal Olympics 1976

were the newspapers, whose dramatic headlines, for days on end, recorded the latest twists and nuances of a bulletless war. But was it so bulletless? At the 1972 Olympics in Munich, Black September Arab terrorists had burst in and murdered Israeli athletes before they themselves died on a pyre of burned out helicopters.

A new dimension — the use of globally televised sport as the stage of protest — frustrated the once simple, often altruistic business of sports promotion. On the medallists' rostrum as early as the 1968 Mexico Games two Americans, Tommie Smith and John Carlos, raised black-gloved hands in sinister demonstration. They were pawns of the Black Power movement that threatened, and briefly achieved , civic violence within the United States. Smith, at one stage the holder of nine world sprint records, was broken by it. Ironically Carlos, the more militant of the two, recanted and was appointed to high executive office at the Los Angeles Olympics. By then, however, 'security' was an established word in the glossary of sporting terms. It took 17,500 police and military to 'secure' the Los Angeles Games at a cost ten times greater than was needed to run the entire London Olympics of 1948. There was no chance that the initial concept of the movement, the quadrennial gathering of the world's youth to establish international goodwill and lasting friendships, could survive in what even the gaudiest banners could not disguise as high-wired concentration camps. The Olympics are still about glittering high performance but it is sorrowful to record that they are now best enjoyed on television, half a world away from the action.

For more than half a century sport on the front pages of the world's Press had signified achievement or the triumph of the human will but — more reflecting the ugliness and recalcitrance of the world than through any shortcomings of its own — those headlines were to change. The new vocabulary was ban, boycott, blacked, riot, wrecked, rumpus, truncheons, tear-gas, thugs and death. Britain's name was blackened across Europe by the train of hooligans who attached themselves to football teams and pillaged their drunken progress through towns and cities. There will be many who share my misgivings that my own trade of journalism, by according acres of space to their brutish behaviour, has done nothing to help the cause.

There was no shortage of thrilling new performers. On May 22, 1966, Henry Cooper won the whole front page of the *Sunday Mirror* to himself for surviving six rounds against Muhammad Ali, a man so brilliant and outrageous that *Time* magazine was to conduct a poll proving him a more instantly recognised figure throughout the world than any prelate, president or entertainer. Pele's crown in soccer was handed down to Diego Maradonna, middle-distance running was annexed by Steve Ovett and Sebastian Coe, golf rode from a middle-class recreation to a huge spectator sport on the broad shoulders of Arnold Palmer, the man who foreswore caution and always went for broke. Then Jack Nicklaus arrived to drive the final green at St Andrews in all four rounds of a British Open Championship to inform Scots that even religions don't stand still. Lester Piggott was no new performer. He just breakfasted on the usual cigar and rode anywhere, except into the sunset.

It was at Wimbledon, so long the high temple of impeccable behaviour, that we saw the trend. Rod Laver, then Bjorn Borg,took the rough with smooth — expressionless geniuses only beaten, respectively, by age and boredom. Evonne Goolagong brought a sunrise smile, a touch of unpredictable battiness and the most glorious intuitive backhand you ever saw. Christine Evert-Lloyd controlled herself and the match from the baseline. But then all were swept out of the headlines by the two greatest players ever seen. Few now will question that John McEnroe and Martina Navratilova answer to that description. Many will ask if the abrasiveness of one and the overt pursuit of money that induced the other to dismiss more than £90,000 of Wimbledon prize money as chickenfeed is actually worth it? The answer will probably determine to which generation the reader belongs. McEnroe's reformed behaviour in 1984 may have come too late to repair the damage he inflicted on a whole new breed of impressionable imitators. Navratilova, attended by a retinue not noticeably smaller than the Queen of Sheba's, complains that the crowds are instinctively against her without realising that this tends to be the fate of relentless multi-millionaires.

True sport hardly attains the headlines at all these days. It is played on the village green, it is lost in the head-bobbing tidal wave of some mega-marathon, it is back there with some tail-ender in an Olympic run, it is rigidly preserved by world hockey. The rest is business, open to exploitation, ruled by relentless pressure, tainted by occasional corruption, disfigured from time to time by cheating. It is why Carl Lewis made minimally five million dollars from the Los Angeles Olympic Games. It is why Mary Decker's distress was so awful to witness when she fell on that same track. Her business life was over in the time it takes to tear up a huge endorsement cheque.

So be it. Sport gets the Press it deserves. It always has.

Laver and Borg took the rough with the smooth — expressionless geniuses only beaten by age and boredom

THE GRAPHIC

AN ILLUSTRATED WEEKLY NEWSPAPER

No. 1,239—Vol. XLVIII.]
Registered as a Newspaper

SATURDAY, AUGUST 26, 1893

THIRTY-TWO PAGES

PRICE SIXPENCE
By Post 6½d.

Luncheon-hour on the first day, the reception at the pavilion : W. G. Grace (not out, 63) and A. E. Stoddart (not out, 71)

ENGLAND *VERSUS* AUSTRALIA AT THE OVAL

THE ALL-ENGLAND LAWN TENNIS CHAMPIONSHIPS.

MRS. HILLYARD, WINNER LADIES' SINGLES FOR FIFTH TIME.   MISS C. COOPER, CHALLENGER (THREE TIMES WINNER).   MRS. HILLYARD.

MR. H. S. SMITH, CHALLENGER GENTLEMEN'S SINGLES.

MR. R. F. DOHERTY, WINNER GENTLEMEN'S SINGLES FOR THE FOURTH SUCCESSIVE TIME.

TOTTENHAM HOTSPURS v. SHEFFIELD UNITED.

THE DRAW AT SYDENHAM BEFORE A RECORD CROWD.

BEFORE THE UNITED GOAL.

THE TOTTENHAM BACKS STOPPING A SHEFFIELD RUSH.

THE "SPURS" GET AHEAD WITH THEIR SECOND GOAL EARLY IN THE SECOND HALF.

Cameron passed back to Brown, who shot past Foulke. A minute later Sheffield equalised.

THE THIRD TEST MATCH AT SHEFFIELD—AUSTRALIA BEATS ENGLAND BY 143 RUNS.

R. A. Duff (25 and 1).   Victor Trumper (1 and 62).
ABOUT TO START THE COLONIALS' SECOND INNINGS.

A. C. MACLAREN, THE ENGLISH CAPTAIN, WHO MADE MORE RUNS
THAN ANY OF HIS MEN.

CLEMENT HILL, WHOSE FINE THIRD INNINGS SCORE OF 119,
PRACTICALLY DEFEATED THE MOTHER COUNTRY.

GILBERT JESSOP, THE SECOND TOP SCORER FOR ENGLAND.

AFTER five successive draws, a test match has been definitely decided in England. That is satisfactory, but it is about the extent of the satisfaction which last week's game at Sheffield provides to the cricketers of this country. The play at Birmingham on May 29, 30, and 31 engendered bright hopes; but, inasmuch as we had all the luck on that occasion, we were fairly well satisfied with the empty honour of a moral victory. We wanted to beat the Australians fairly and squarely; the opportunity was provided at Sheffield; and it was lost. The Colonials won by 143 runs, so that, on the series of five games, they became, in the language of the golfer, one up with two to play, with very prospect of at least developing the impregnable position of "dormy" by effecting a draw at Manchester on July 24, 25, and 26. England, of course, may yet secure the rubber by winning the two remaining matches; but this one defeat at a critical time has driven far away the regained laurels which appeared to be nestling in the offing.

Probably the Australians had some luck in winning the toss, for Sheffield was never a good-wearing pitch. It has certainly improved out of all knowledge during recent years, but it were none too well on the occasion under notice, and, on Saturday, gave considerable assistance to such bowlers as Noble and Trumble, although less skilful trundlers would probably have got little out of it. However, it was quite time that the Australian captain's luck changed. In the twelve preceding test matches he had only won the spin of the coin on three occasions. The Australians' first innings of 194 was by no means brilliant. S. F. Barnes, the Lancastrian, introduced into the team at the last moment, bowled so well at the start that only a gallant display by the tail men brought the total so close to 200. England had every chance of securing the lead; and, when 100 runs had been scored for three wickets, the prospects were bright, considering that so many good batsmen were to follow. A mistake, however, was undoubtedly made in not appealing against the light, which was distinctly bad, when three wickets had fallen for 100 runs. The result was that F. S. Jackson and C. B. Fry were sent back for an addition of two runs,

F. S. Jackson.   A. C. Maclaren.
ENGLAND, LED BY JACKSON AND MACLAREN, TAKE THE FIELD FOR AUSTRALIA'S SECOND INNINGS.

THE AMERICA CUP.

SCENES ON THE RELIANCE DURING HER LAST TRIAL WITH CONSTITUTION, BEFORE HER SELECTION TO MEET SHAMROCK III.

Close work.

Taking in the foresail.   *Hoisting the mainsail.*

Mr. Edgar Seligman is here shown engaged in a bout with Herr August Petri, which he won.

FENCING : GERMANY v. ENGLAND

The exhibition on the opening day by a team of Danish ladies evoked much enthusiasm.

AN EXHIBITION BY DANISH LADIES

The Duke of Sparta, as President of the Games, facing King George and the other Royal personages, delivered an inaugural address.   The competitors ranged themselves in a solid group behind him in front of the Royal seats.   Photo supplied by Stanley and Co.

THE OPENING CEREMONY : THE DUKE OF SPARTA INAUGURATING THE GAMES

King George walked with Queen Alexandra, and King Edward followed with Queen Olga.

THE ARRIVAL OF THE ROYAL PARTY

This race was won by the English pair, J. Matthews and A. Rushen, who are here shown riding second

THE TANDEM BICYCLE RACE : THE THIRD LAP

THE MEETING OF THE WORLD'S ATHLETES : THE OLYMPIC GAMES IN THE STADIUM AT ATHENS

The King Opens the Olympic Games

The Olympic Games in the Stadium at Shepherd's Bush were opened by the King in person, to a fanfare of trumpets and the hearty cheering of the international competitors. Undeterred by the bad weather, a number of Royal personages were present at the opening ceremony, and in the Royal Box there were assembled, besides the King, the Queen, Princess Victoria, the Prince and Princess of Wales, Princes Edward and John of Wales, the Duke and Duchess of Connaught, the Crown Prince and Princess of Sweden, and the Duke and Duchess of Sparta. The scene in the Stadium is the subject of one of our supplements.

The Royal Party Watching the March Past from their Box in the Stadium

DRAWN BY W. HATHERELL, R.I.

THE GRAPHIC

AN ILLUSTRATED WEEKLY NEWSPAPER

The entire contents of this paper, both Illustrations and Letterpress, are copyright.

No. 2018.—VOL. LXXVIII.
Registered as a Newspaper

SATURDAY, AUGUST 1, 1908

WITH SUPPLEMENT

PRICE SIXPENCE
By Post, 6½d.

Seldom, if ever, has there been a more dramatic finish to a great athletic contest than that of the Marathon race on Friday of last week. Every seat in the Stadium was filled, and 100,000 spectators, among them the Queen and other members of the Royal Family, awaited the coming of the victor. At last, heralded by a roar of cheers, Dorando, of Italy, made his appearance. Even as he entered he staggered and reeled in complete exhaustion, and before he could complete the final lap he fell three times. Meanwhile, a group of people had rushed on to the track, and, though he at last struggled to the tape, their assistance caused him to be disqualified, the race being allotted to the next man, Hayes of America. The Queen, however, presented a special cup to Dorando in honour of his pluck. Our photograph is by Kodak Limited, who took a number of pictures of the race.

The Tragedy of the Marathon Race : Dorando, Utterly Exhausted, Entering the Stadium First, Only to Lose

THREE PAGES OF DERBY DAY PICTURES. (1, 8, and 9.)

LONDON: THURSDAY, MAY 27, 1909.

One Penny

Registered as a Newspaper.

G. 501.—Vol. LXXVIII.

THE CROWN DERBY.

THE KING WATCHES MINORU COMING IN.

HIS MAJESTY'S MINORU RECEIVING A GREAT OVATION ON ENTERING THE WEIGHING-IN ENCLOSURE
AFTER WINNING THE DERBY—THE FIRST IN HISTORY WON BY A SOVEREIGN—AT EPSOM YESTERDAY.

("Daily Graphic" Photograph.)   (See page 7.)

PICTURES OF THE BIG FIGHT

ILLUSTRATED

SPORTING BUDGET

AND BOXING RECORD

No. 893.] [Registered at the G.P.O. as a Newspaper. SATURDAY, JULY 16, 1910. For Transmission in Great Britain and Canada.] [PRICE ONE PENNY.

JACK JOHNSON'S GOLDEN SMILE.

The above characteristic picture of the world's champion boxer shows him in happy mood after defeating Jim Jeffries. Johnson is now in New York, where he is undergoing a six months' tour. Although he possessed a fine set of teeth, Johnson a little time ago had these extracted, and in their place now wears a set made of pure gold.

DAILY SKETCH.

No. 1,323.—THURSDAY, JUNE 5, 1913. LONDON: 46-47, Shoe-lane, E.C. MANCHESTER: Withy-grove. Telephones—Editorial and Publishing: 6676 Holborn. Advertisements: 10,782 Central. [Registered as a Newspaper.] **ONE HALFPENNY.**

HISTORY'S MOST WONDERFUL DERBY: FIRST HORSE DISQUALIFIED: A 100 TO 1 CHANCE WINS: SUFFRAGETTE NEARLY KILLED BY THE KING'S COLT.

Miss Emily Davison. The woman falling to the ground. The King's horse, Anmer, falls on his jockey. Herbert Jones.

Yesterday's Derby was extraordinary. Not only was Craganour, the favourite, disqualified after finishing first, the race being awarded to Aboyeur; a suffragette ran across the course at Tattenham Corner and seized the bridle of the King's horse. The King's horse and jockey were thrown to the ground, while the woman was nearly killed. The extraordinary photograph seen above was taken by the *Daily Sketch* a second after the horse and the woman fell to the ground.

Between Them, Winners of the Open Golf Championship Fourteen Times.

REPRODUCED FROM MR. CLEMENT FLOWER'S PAINTING, "THE CHAMPIONS." COPYRIGHT OF 'GOLF ILLUSTRATED," LTD., WHO ARE PUBLISHING A LARGE COLOUR PLATE OF THE PICTURE.

THE TRIUMVIRATE: J. H. TAYLOR. JAMES BRAID. AND HARRY VARDON.

With the great Open Championship tournament upon us, one of the chief questions of the moment in the golfing world is whether the famous triumvirate will assert itself again. No group of players in any game has ever carried all before it as these three great golfers have done in the last twenty years, when, among them, they have won the Open Championship fourteen times—Braid and Vardon five times each, and Taylor four times. But last year they received a check; the winner was Ray. Only four times previously since 1893 in years wide apart had they ever received any such check, and three of those four reverses that they sustained were at Hoylake. They have never won the Open Championship at Hoylake, though they have taken it on every other championship course. Will they now regain the distinction that they lost last year? If they do not they will for the first time in their history have let two years go by without success, and people will think that the Triumvirate fails at last. But their effort has to be made at Hoylake!

Collision Recalling the Empress of Ireland Disaster: Pictures.

The Daily Mirror

LATEST CERTIFIED CIRCULATION MORE THAN 960,000 COPIES PER DAY

No. 3,324. | Registered at the G.P.O. as a Newspaper. | FRIDAY, JUNE 19, 1914 | One Halfpenny.

EXTREMES IN FASHIONS MEET AT ASCOT: THE "EYEGLASS GIRL" WHOM THE PEOPLE THOUGHT WAS A SUFFRAGETTE.

Finish of the Gold Cup, won by Mr. Fairie's Aleppo. Willbrook was second and Junior third. The French horse, Bruleur, which was favourite, was unplaced.

Not a bird but a hat, and a very smart one, too.

Her butterfly sunshade was original. | Cavalier cape and a Charles II. hat. | The masculine girl with her eyeglass and stick.

Despite the fact that she was surrounded by women wearing striking toilettes, an American girl was able to rivet attention on herself at Ascot yesterday. But for her coat and skirt—and these were tailor-made—she might have borrowed her get-up from her brother's wardrobe. The straw hat, the collar, the tie, the eyeglass, the walking-stick, and even the way she dressed her hair, all helped towards the masculine effect, and people were heard to murmur "Suffragette."—(*Daily Mirror* photographs.)

THE DAILY MIRROR, Wednesday, June 24, 1914.

Well-Known Actors Beat Drums at a Garden Party: Pictures.

The Daily Mirror

LATEST   CERTIFIED   CIRCULATION   MORE   THAN   **960,000**   COPIES   PER   DAY

No. 3,328.   Registered at the G.P.O. as a Newspaper.   WEDNESDAY, JUNE 24, 1914   One Halfpenny.

OUR SPORTS-LOVING KING WATCHES THE CENTENARY MATCH AT LORD'S AND CHATS WITH THE RIVAL CAPTAINS.

Lord Hawke presents J. W. H. T. Douglas (wearing pads) and C. B. Fry to his Majesty.   The Prince is chatting with Mr. F. E. Lacey, the M.C.C. secretary.

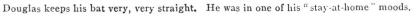

Douglas keeps his bat very, very straight.   He was in one of his "stay-at-home" moods.

Hobbs bowled by his clubmate Hitch.

Lord's, the most famous cricket ground in the world, is celebrating its centenary with a match between the eleven which did so brilliantly in South Africa and the Rest of England.   Lord's is, of course, the headquarters of the Marylebone Cricket Club, which shyly hides its identity under the famous initials of M.C.C.   During the afternoon the King visited the ground, accompanied by the Prince of Wales, who celebrated his twentieth birthday yesterday.   *(Daily Mirror photographs.)*

THE DAILY MIRROR, Friday, July 17, 1914.

"Pamela Chetwynd," Our Great Summer Serial, Begins To-day.

The Daily Mirror

LATEST CERTIFIED CIRCULATION MORE THAN 1,000,000 COPIES PER DAY

No. 3,348.   Registered at the G.P.O. as a Newspaper.   FRIDAY, JULY 17, 1914   One Halfpenny.

"GUNBOAT" SMITH DISQUALIFIED IN THE SIXTH ROUND OF THE GREAT CHAMPIONSHIP CONTEST WITH CARPENTIER.

Carpentier ducks, but fails to avoid a right swing.   Smith about to deliver the blow which led to his disqualification and which gave Carpentier a barren victory.

Smith about to deliver the foul blow, taken from another angle.

Smith sent to the boards. He was down for nine seconds.

Carpentier is the world's white heavy-weight champion. The great contest, however, had a most unsatisfactory ending, "Gunboat" Smith being disqualified in the sixth round. Carpentier slipped to his knees and the onrushing Smith was unable to pull up before he had struck his opponent.—(Daily Mirror photographs.)

FINAL WEEKS OF £7,000 FILM CONTEST—See Page 5

SUNDAY·PICTORIAL

SALE MORE THAN DOUBLE THAT OF ANY OTHER SUNDAY PICTURE PAPER

No. 424. | Registered at the G.P.O. as a Newspaper. | SUNDAY, APRIL 29, 1923 | [24 PAGES] | Twopence.

WEMBLEY STADIUM STORMED BY EXCITED CUP FINAL CROWDS

A striking aerial photograph of the scene at Wembley Stadium yesterday after the gates had been closed. All accommodation is packed, spectators flood the playing pitch, while thousands clustered outside are clamouring for admittance.

One of four daring souls who climbed a drain-pipe to secure an entrance at the back of the lofty covered stand.

Police holding back would-be spectators at the entrance to the tunnel leading to the pitch.

Police arriving by motor-van at the ground in response to a call for reinforcements.

The crowd swarming over the closed turnstiles heedless of the instruction to "Pay Here."

The most amazing Cup final on record was won by Bolton Wanderers yesterday, when they defeated West Ham United by two clear goals at the Empire Stadium, Wembley. The start was delayed for three-quarters of an hour by the most extraordinary scenes. The gates were closed with thousands still waiting for admission, though the spectators within had broken through to the running track around the ground and invaded the playing pitch itself. The crowd outside rushed the ground, clambering over the turnstiles, and made the confusion even greater. With the arrival of the King, mounted police managed to get the pitch just clear. Pictures of play on page 24.

SUZANNE'S OWN STORY OF "WONDERFUL WIMBLEDON"

DAILY SKETCH

No. 5,367. Telephones {London—Museum **9841.** / Manchester—City **6501.**   LONDON, TUESDAY, JUNE 22, 1926.   [Registered as a Newspaper.]   ONE PENNY.

DRESSING FOR THE PLATFORM

LADY DUFF-GORDON

To - morrow

THE KING'S HANDSHAKE FOR SUZANNE

The King shaking hands with Mlle. Suzanne Lenglen yesterday at the opening of Wimbledon's jubilee fortnight of lawn tennis.   He was accompanied by the Queen. who presented jubilee commemoration medals to winners of the various championships since the inception of the All-England Club.—(Daily Sketch.)

Mrs. Godfree (Kitty McKane) making obeisance to the Queen.   She was champion in 1924.—(Daily Sketch.)

H. W. Austin, the brilliant young Cambridge player (left), in play against B. R. Lawrence, whom he defeated in the first round of the gentlemen's singles. Lord Cholmondeley (second from left) was also victorious, his victim being F. Bryans. France suffered a reverse in the defeat of P. Feret by Baron de Kehrling, the Hungarian star (right). The other picture shows Mlle. Lenglen dealing with a high return in the exhibition match in which she partnered Miss Ryan against Mrs. Godfree and Miss Bouman.—(Daily Sketch.)

TWO KILLED, 11 INJURED IN AIR LINER CRASH IN FOG

DAILY SKETCH

HOW THE KITCHENER FAKE BEGAN

No. 5,417. Telephones {London—Museum **9841**. {Manchester—City **6501**. LONDON, THURSDAY, AUGUST 19, 1926. [Registered as a Newspaper.] ONE PENNY.

CROWD'S WILD RUSH AFTER TEST MATCH VICTORY

How the excited crowd at the Oval yesterday rushed across the ground to cheer the English eleven on their great victory over the Australians in the final Test Match. Unprecedented scenes of enthusiasm were witnessed, the crowd for a long time clamouring for speeches from favourite players.

GENE TUNNEY.

The Des Moines Register

DES MOINES, IOWA; FRIDAY MORNING, SEPT. 23, 1927.

JACK DEMPSEY.

TUNNEY WINS

Ruth Hits No. 56

YANKEES EQUAL LEAGUE RECORD FOR GAMES WON

Bambino's Drive Permits Teammates to Win by 8-7 Tally.

New York, Sept. 22 (A.P.)—The Yankees tied the American league record for games won in a single season today by defeating the Tigers by 8 to 7 for their 105th victory. That feat was accomplished by the Boston Red Sox in 1912. Detroit took the lead with a three run drive in the ninth only to have Babe Ruth plant out his fifty-sixth homer in the New York half with Koenig on base to decide the contest.

Lou Gehrig established a new major league record for driving in runs when he sent two across to raise his total to 172. Ruth formerly held the record with 170 in 1921.

Flynn Asks Reversal of the Verdict

Count Too Long; Will Appeal to Comish.

Soldiers Field, Chicago, Sept. 22 (U.P.)—Leo Flynn, manager of Jack Dempsey, declared immediately after tonight's fight in which Tunney was given the decision over Dempsey, that he would appeal to the Illinois boxing commission for a reversal of the decision.

PIRATES DIVIDE DOUBLET WITH NEW YORK CLUB

Kremer Baffles Giants in Opener, Winning by 5 to 2.

Pittsburgh, Sept. 22 (A.P.)—The Pirates retained their three and one-half game advantage over the Giants today by dividing a doubleheader with the New York before 40,000 fans, the largest crowd to witness a National league engagement in this city.

CHAMP TAKES COUNT; RISES, BATTERS RIVAL

Gains Decision Over 10 Rounds As Mammoth Throng Watches.

Chicago, Sept. 22 (U.P.)—Here are some interesting statistics on the Tunney-Dempsey fight at Soldier field tonight:

Purse, $1,450,000.
Tunney's share, $1,000,000.
Dempsey's share, $450,000.
Gate (estimated), $2,800,000.

BY DAMON RUNYON
(Copyright, 1927, by Universal Service.)

Soldiers Field, Chicago, Ill., Sept. 22.—Down on the canvas for a count for the first time in his boxing career, sniffing the resin dust there, with the murderous old Manassa man glowering over him with evil intent, Gene Tunney, the fighting marine, got up and carried on to victory against Jack Dempsey tonight.

Gene Tunney Says—

Tonight I kept a promise that I made with myself a year ago at Philadelphia.

I won the world's heavyweight title then by boxing. I retained it tonight by fighting. I pledged myself that I would beat Dempsey this time—beat him so decisively that there would be no doubt in anyone's mind as to my right to the heavyweight championship of the world.

Jack Dempsey Says—

My ring career came to its end tonight when my dreams of regaining the title ended in defeat.

I bow to Gene Tunney—a better fighter and a great champion.

I have no excuses to offer, no alibis. But I am at this moment confused as to how long was the count that Tunney got when I flattened him in the seventh round.

Peterson Is Victor Over New York Foe

Okun Loses to Denver Mauler.

TUNNEY 'ENJOYS' NEW SENSATION

Knocked Off Feet for First Time in Life.

BOUT ATTRACTS 150,000 FANS

Receipts Are Estimated at $2,800,000.

Big Ring Mix Draws Many Celebrities

Movie Stars, Capitalists All Are Present.

EVERY DAY IS NEW YEAR'S DAY, By EDGAR WALLACE—P.6

SUNDAY·PICTORIAL

SALE VASTLY IN EXCESS OF ANY OTHER PICTURE PAPER IN THE WORLD

No. 720   Registered at the G.P.O as a Newspaper   SUNDAY, DECEMBER 30, 1928   Twopence

£750 PICTURE PUZZLE

AUSTRALIA'S GREAT RECOVERY IN THIRD TEST MATCH AT MELBOURNE

A section of the great cricket ground at Melbourne, where the third Test match is being played. The overflowing grandstand gives an idea of how the ground is packed. It certainly does not suggest that cricket is dead.

HUNTING-DEATH OF FORMER M.F.H.

J. S. Ryder, who scored 111 not out

Jardine, who caught Woodfull (Tate bowling), as well as Hendry and Kippax.

A. F. Kippax batted brilliantly to make a century. He and Ryder scored a run a minute.

After a poor start, Australia made a good recovery at Melbourne in the third Test match and scored 276 runs for four wickets. Kippax and Ryder were the heroes of the innings. The big hitting so excited the crowd that they got into the arena and held up play. The spectators numbered 63,217, a new world's record for a cricket match.

Mr. William Wroughton, of Melton Mowbray, a former master of the Pytchley Hunt, was killed yesterday while out with the Belvoir.

BOY BATSMAN WHO MAKES NO MISTAKES: By M. D. LYON

DAILY SKETCH

INCORPORATING THE DAILY GRAPHIC

No. 6,626. | [Registered as a newspaper.] | SATURDAY, JULY 12, 1930. | ONE PENNY.

LAST DAY £1,200 PUZZLE

BRADMAN'S 100 BEFORE LUNCH—& A NEW RECORD

Don Bradman, who yesterday in the Test Match at Leeds beat R. E. Foster's Test Match record score of 287. Australia's boy batsman scored a century before lunch and at the close was 309 not out, the tourists' total being 458 for 3.—(Daily Sketch.)

Bradman signalling with his bat his acknowledgment of the roars of cheering that greeted his 200th run.—(Daily Sketch.)

Another picture of the man who has been described as a run-making machine. Here he is hitting a ball from Leyland. —(Daily Sketch.)

The 200th run came from a ball from Dick Tyldesley. Bradman starting on the run.—(Daily Sketch.)

The wonder batsman slips—but the ball was safely out of the way. —(Daily Sketch.)

Chapman tosses his lucky coin—

—and finds Woodfull has called right. —(Daily Sketch.)

MORE SUCCESSES FOR BOUVERIE

Daily Mirror

THE DAILY PICTURE NEWSPAPER WITH THE LARGEST NET SALE

No. 8,817 | Registered at the G.P.O. as a Newspaper. | THURSDAY, FEBRUARY 25, 1932 | One Penny

KNIGHT'S SON IN SUIT FOR BREACH

Wireless on Page 14

BLUEBIRD'S 267 m.p.h.

RECORD OF 254 m.p.h. BY MALCOLM CAMPBELL

Sir Malcolm Campbell, who yesterday attained a land speed of 267.459 m.p.h. and set up a record of 253.968.

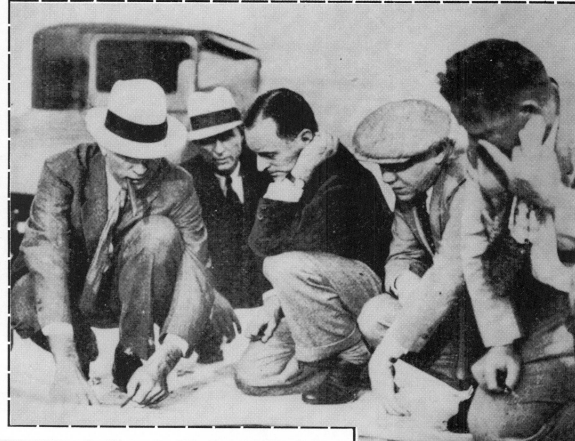

An examination recently by Sir Malcolm Campbell and engineers of a map of the Daytona Beach Course, Florida, where yesterday's triumph for British motoring was achieved.

Sir Malcolm Campbell in the all-British Bluebird on Daytona Beach during his present visit.

The land speed record made by Sir Malcolm Campbell yesterday beats by over 8 m.p.h. his last year's record of 245.736 m.p.h. set up on the same beach. The amazing speed of 267 m.p.h. was attained on the first of his two thrilling dashes over the measured mile. Still Sir Malcolm is not satisfied and intends to make a fresh attempt to-day. Since last year's record the Bluebird has been overhauled and rebuilt, having been fitted with a more powerful Napier engine, one of approximately 1,500 h.p.

NEW GALLIPOLI DISCLOSURES—P. 5

Theatre & Cinema Guide: P. 14

DAILY MIRROR

THE DAILY PICTURE — NEWSPAPER WITH THE LARGEST NET SALE

YOUNG COUPLE'S VAIN DASH TO GRETNA

No. 8,867 — Registered at the G.P.O. as a Newspaper. — MONDAY, APRIL 25, 1932 — One Penny

Wireless on Page 16

FILM PROVES THE BALL WAS OUT OF PLAY

NEWCASTLE'S LUCKY EQUALISER IN CUP FINAL

SOUND BAND ON FILM

LINESMAN

REFEREE

LINESMAN

FAMOUS FRENCH GENERAL HONOURS 29th DIVISION

General Gouraud, Military Governor of Paris, saying good-bye to the Rev. G. Wooley, V.C., after a memorial service at Eltham, S.E., yesterday, to the 29th Division. Field-Marshal Sir Claud Jacob also attended.

A cutting from the Movietone film of the Cup Final, which shows without a shadow of doubt that the ball had gone out of play before Boyd centred for Allen to score Newcastle's equaliser. The white lines indicating the angles of vision of referee and linesmen demonstrate that they were badly placed to judge the exact position of the ball. This goal put a fresh face on the match, Arsenal being henceforth dominated. See other Wembley pictures on page 24.

OLIVE PEARCE, aged fifteen, of Salisbury, for whom a broadcast appeal was circulated on Saturday. She was still missing yesterday. It is thought she may be in the company of a youth of seventeen.

The Sketch

No. 2058. — Vol. CLIX.   WEDNESDAY, JULY 6, 1932.   ONE SHILLING.

SMILING — AND SHINGLED : MRS. HELEN WILLS MOODY.

The name of "Helen Wills" no longer figures in the list of entrants at Wimbledon, but it's of no consequence, for everyone knows that "Mrs. F. S. Moody" means the famous U.S.A. player, who is still "Helen Wills" to so many "fans"! This year she has had her long hair cut, and wears it in a shingle.

Mrs. Moody is an artist as well as a lawn tennis player, and in this issue we reproduce one of her landscapes in full colours. Her animated expression and charming smile are characteristic, for the nick-name of "Poker-face" is not really very well deserved— as everyone who actually knows Mrs. Moody must realise.

CAMERA PORTRAIT BY DOROTHY WILDING.

The Sun
NEWS ~ PICTORIAL
WITH WHICH IS INCORPORATED
THE MORNING POST

DAILY AT DAWN

No. 3177. | Registered at the G.P.O., Melbourne, for transmission by post as a newspaper. | MELBOURNE: MONDAY, NOVEMBER 21, 1932 | (28 Pages) | 1½d.

54,000 See Bradman Bat Against England

BRADMAN WAS THE CHIEF ATTRACTION for a great crowd of 54,000 at the M.C.G. on Saturday. A section of the packed outer stands is shown above. Left: Woodfull staggered by a fast rising ball from Larwood, which struck him over the heart. Lower: Bradman gets Voce away to leg for a single. Right: O'Brien bowled by Larwood for 46. In reply to England's 282, an Australian XI. had scored 216 for nine when stumps were drawn.

Daily Mirror

THE DAILY PICTURE NEWSPAPER WITH THE LARGEST NET SALE

No. 9,210   Registered at the G.P.O. as a Newspaper.   THURSDAY, JUNE, 1, 1933   One Penny

'WOMEN ARE CHEATS'
—PAGE TEN

WIRELESS PAGE 22   AMUSEMENTS PAGE 8

HYPERION WINS FASTEST DERBY

Lord Derby's Horse Breaks All Time Records—Sick Trainer Unable to See Triumph

THE KING AND QUEEN AT EPSOM

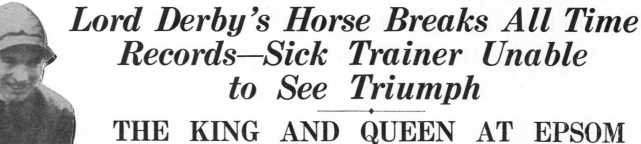

The Earl of Derby's beam of delight after his Hyperion had won the Derby yesterday. Right, his handshake of congratulation for the jockey, T. Weston, as he was taking Hyperion's rein for the leading-in and as the Stanley House travelling head lad, Bill Newman, patted him on the back. See also pages 16 and 17 and the back page.

TRAVELLING FASTER THAN ANY HORSE HAS RUN IN A DERBY, **HYPERION** YESTERDAY WON FOR LORD DERBY HIS SECOND SUCCESS IN THE CLASSIC RACE FOUNDED BY AN ANCESTOR. HIS PREVIOUS WINNER WAS SANSOVINO IN 1924.

Sir Hugo Cunliffe Owen's **KING SALMON** was second, Mr. Victor Emanuel's **STATESMAN** third, and Lord Durham's **SCARLET TIGER** fourth. The starting prices and jockeys were:

Hyperion (6-1) .... T. Weston
King Salmon (7-1) .... H. Wragg
Statesman (20-1) .... B. Carslake
Scarlet Tiger (18-1) .... A. Wragg

The King and Queen and many other members of the Royal Family were at Epsom. After the race Lord Derby was congratulated by the King.

Bookmakers Lose

By a trick of fate Hyperion's trainer, the Hon. George Lambton, who is over seventy years old, was prevented by a leg injury from attending the race.

Thus he missed one of the triumphs of his life.

As Scarlet Tiger was placed fourth and Thrapston fifth, Mr. Lambton was responsible for three of the first five.

Hyperion is the second Derby winner trained by Mr. Lambton and the second ridden by T. Weston.

The result was unpopular only with the bookmakers, who were badly hit.

35 m.p.h. WINNER

Hyperion averaged a speed of over thirty-five miles per hour, winning the race in 2 minutes 34 seconds. This was two-fifths of a second faster than the previous record for the race, shared by Call Boy and Felstead, which were successful in 1927 and 1928.

It was an immensely popular victory, as the colt had been one of the leading fancies for the race, and wound up favourite.

A great roar greeted Lord Derby as he stepped on to the course to lead in his winner.

HEATHMAN

(Our Newmarket Correspondent)

gave HYPERION

He was almost swept off his feet as he went through the narrow gateway into the unsaddling enclosure with Mrs. George Lambton, the trainer's wife, close behind him.

Lord Derby's face was wreathed in a big smile, and from time to time as he stood and watched his horse he could be heard chuckling.

All the time from the seething crowd came intermittent roars.

Hyperion's owner seemed unsettled by his great reception, and all he could say was, "Thank you so much. It was a great victory, and I have always had faith in the colt."

After the excitement had died down Lord Derby's first thought was for his trainer.

"Could there possibly be a greater tribute to a trainer than Hyperion was to Mr. Lambton to-day?" he asked.

(Continued on page 3)

20,000 CROWD CHEERS HOBBS' 196th CENTURY

HOBBS hitting out at the Oval to-day in his bid for his 196th century.

Big Surrey Stand After Losses in Leg-trap

From J. A. H. CATTON

Surrey's first three wickets fell for 42 runs, but Hobbs and Gregory then put on 149, and Hobbs completed his 196th century.

THE Oval presented a cheering sight to-day to the lovers of cricket, who hear and read so many jeremiahs about the lack of popularity of the summer game. There was a complete ring of humanity, and deep in rank before mid-day, to see Surrey bat against Notts. The circle was a study in white, all the male spectators having removed their coats.

The attack was opened by Voce, his fellow bowler being Butler. Butler is a tall stripling who bowls right hand at a good pace, but it is doubtful whether he makes the most of his height. The batsmen began to place the ball to leg for small contributions, but in the fifth over Hobbs was hit high on the thigh by a ball from Voce.

Only six overs had been bowled for 8 runs when Carr switched his fielders round to Voce for his leg theory stuff. There were three men at short leg with a mid-on, but there was a short slip, a cover point, a mid-off and a deep third man. This was a modified form of the much discussed attack, and in Voce's second over Sandham was struck by a ball under the armpit. He was out to the last ball of this same over, for he made a one-hand stroke and was caught by Arthur Staples at short leg.

Squires made a brief stay, for with four runs added by Hobbs—three to leg off a no-ball—he was caught by Carr at fine leg behind the wicket. Barling made a few shots to leg that encouraged the hope that he would stay. Meanwhile, Hobbs was progressing, although he dropped his bat in playing a ball from Voce.

The Third Victim

At 41 Carr brought back Butler and relieved Voce. The move was successful, for with a single added by Hobbs Barling gave a catch to Carr, still in the same position. The board showed three wickets down for 42, and each of the departing batsmen had fallen into the leg-side trap. At this crisis Gregory appeared, and when Gunn and Harris took over the bowling the 50 was telegraphed, Hobbs having made more than half the runs from the bat.

The sixth bowler introduced was Sam Staples with the total 70, and his brother Arthur went on at the other crease. This change provided Hobbs with some runs, chiefly to the on, and the batsman advanced his figures to 51 with the total 92 after he had batted an hour and 40 minutes. Then Arthur Carr reverted to leg theory with Voce at the Vauxhall end, and Gunn bowled from the Pavilion crease.

Gregory evoked a cheer when he crashed a ball between the cordon of leg fielders to the boundary. Then Voce bowled a wide—so wide that the ball rattled the pavilion rails. The umpire signalled four, four wides according to law, and up went 102—a measure of success that prompted Gregory to hit another four to leg. At luncheon the total was 108, Hobbs being 54 and Gregory 22.

After an over from A. Staples, Voce continued his leg-theory attacks. Hobbs went steadily along, while Gregory was very accurate in placing to leg off each bowler, until he introduced a variation, for he scored ten in one over from Staples, including an on drive and a pull.

A ball from Voce hit Hobbs inside the left knee, and some of the crowd were incensed, but Hobbs drove the next ball past cover-point to the boundary.

Voce's bowling provoked the crowd to shout "Take him off." The last ball of an over Hobbs placed to mid-wicket, and dashed for a single as he finished the stroke. Voce fielded the ball with alacrity and threw down the middle stump, but Gregory was well home. Butler was tried in place of Voce, and in his second over he got rid of Gregory, who placed a catch in the hands of Harris at very short square leg. The wicket added 117, Gregory playing really well.

Hobbs, then 78, was joined by McMurray. Both excelled, the latter in defence, and Hobbs in his judgment of the ball and the variety of his strokes. Gunn and Sam Staples were called up, and Hobbs scored eight in an over. These strokes took him into the nineties, but he did not delay, for with a square leg hit to the ropes he completed his sixth century of the season and the 196th of his career.

McMurray brought the 200 on the scoreboard and the new ball was at once taken by Voce, but every delivery in his first over was played for runs—13 in all—mostly to Hobbs, who scored one of his fours by a fantastic flick over the heads of the fielders behind the wicket to the pavilion rails.

The bowling was changed without effect until Gunn was called on at 238. Hobbs tried to drive his first ball, but he gave a catch to mid-off, and was out for 133 after batting 3 hours and 50 minutes. He hit 12 fours and never gave a real chance.

Allom joined McMurray, and at tea the total was 250 for 5 wickets.

Surrey Idol's Feat Delights Shirt-Sleeved Spectators

Ames and Ashdown Put On 155 for Fifth Kent Wicket at Canterbury

A crowd of over 20,000 shirt-sleeved spectators at the Oval to-day stood and cheered Jack Hobbs for a full two minutes when he completed his sixth century of the season and the 196th of his career. Hobbs and Gregory retrieved a bad Surrey start.

Ames and Ashdown did the same for Kent at Canterbury, where they added 155 together after four wickets were down for 39.

SHIRT-SLEEVED crowds watched this second day of the holiday cricket. At the Oval practically every man of a big crowd had removed his coat and was content to sit and grill in the heat while Hobbs steadily built up yet another century.

Hobbs was very wary of a leg trap set by the Notts bowlers, Voce and Butler, but Sandham, Squires and Barling all were victims of it, and three Surrey wickets were down for 42 before Gregory became a reliable partner for Hobbs. Together they put on 149. Hobbs went on to score 133 before being caught by Butler, off Gunn.

Kent, replying to a Hampshire score of 344 at Canterbury, made an even worse beginning, for they lost four wickets for 39. Ames and Ashdown then held the fort and the stand eventually realised 155 runs. Ames completed 2000 runs for the season.

The Yorkshire score at Leeds reached 296, and Bowes did his side a good service by getting rid of both Watson and Tyldesley with only 27 scored. Leyland disposed of Paynter before the interval, but Hopwood played very soundly.

At Worcester the crowd barracked the umpires because of two l.b.w decisions in favour of the Essex bowlers.

Ames Reaches 2000 And Ashdown Hits A Century

Kent went through a bad period of 40 minutes at Canterbury, Freeman, who was Saturday's stopgap, Todd, and Woolley falling for the addition of 27 to the 12 made for Marriott's loss against Hampshire's 344.

Ashdown played well, and Ames came out in his best form, with the result that 83 more runs came without loss before lunch. Ames was careful to play himself in, but with 3 to the off he got the 20 necessary to complete his season's 2000, and then without any undue risk he bludgeoned the bowling. His off-drive and cuts were brilliant. Ashdown excelled in cutting. He completed 50 out of 93, and claimed 66 out of 122 at the interval.

Ashdown and Ames got on top of the bowling after lunch. Palmer was twice hit to the boundary by each batsman in consecutive overs, Ashdown scoring the first 13 runs, and then Ames following with 14, which made him 51 in 90 minutes. Both men showed very fine form, treating both Palmer and Kennedy with great severity, and runs came regularly at two a minute.

When Brown at the second attempt held a hot drive at mid-off Ames had scored 79 out of 157 in five hours. This splendid display of hard driving and cutting included twelve fours. Ashdown went to 102 with a beautiful off-boundary from Baring, the total then being 220 when the innings had lasted three hours and 20 minutes. Valentine, after driving Boyes to the off boundary, on drove Kennedy for six and went on scoring freely.

PETERS WINS SYDNEY FIGHT

SYDNEY, Monday.

Showing superior strength and experience, Johnny Peters, the Battersea boxer, beat Dal Costa (New South Wales) on a technical knockout in the fifth round of a bout billed for fifteen rounds here to-night. Costa was down once in the third and twice in the fourth round. Peters scaled 8st. 12lb. and his opponent 8st. 7lb.—Reuter.

Tommy Rogers, of Willenhall, beat Tommy Hyams, of King's Cross, in the fifth round of a 15-round contest for the Southern Area featherweight boxing championship at Wolverhampton this morning.

New Golf Club for A. H. Padgham

To Join J. Randall as Professional at Sundridge Park

A. H. Padgham, who for a considerable time has been associate professional with Jack Rowe at Royal Ashdown Forest, has been appointed professional, in partnership with Jack Randall, to the Sundridge Park Golf Club, Kent.

Padgham, who is 27 years of age, was the winner of the Professional Golfers' Association £1040 tournament (match play championship) in 1931, and won the Irish Open Championship and the Roehampton tournament last year.

He was a member of the successful British Ryder Cup team which defeated the United States at Southport this year. In the top singles match he lost to Gene Sarazen.

Randall has been many years with the Sundridge Park Club, which now possesses two courses.

Macaulay Takes Three Smart Catches

At Leeds to-day Yorkshire added 24 runs for their two outstanding wickets. They batted 6½ hours for their total of 296. Lancashire suffered two early shocks, losing Watson at 7 and Tyldesley at 19 to catches at third slip, Macaulay's one-hand effort which dismissed Tyldesley being very smart. Hopwood and Paynter steadily carried the score to 50, when the latter fell to a third catch by Macaulay just on lunch time.

Yorkshire h[illegible] substitutes fielding during the morning for Verity and Holmes, unwell, and Hawkwood had a runner when he went in to bat for Lancashire after lunch. Hopwood, who so far had been the only batsman to play the bowling at all confidently, took two fours in one over from short-pitched balls by Leyland. Subsequently by a beautiful leg glance from Bowes for four Hopwood reached a chanceless 50.

Hawkwood, after an unsteady opening, also batted well and 100 appeared after 2¼ hours. Hawkwood made several fine drives, and a late cut from Rhodes and the batsmen now seemed well on top of the bowling. In an effort to separate the batsmen both Macaulay and Rhodes tried leg theory bowling, and slowed the scoring, which had become rather brisk. It did not, however, greatly trouble the batsmen.

Sussex Declare and Their Bowlers Get Busy

As was expected, the Sussex captain declared his side's innings closed at Saturday's huge total of 512 for three, and on a perfect Hove wicket bowlers appeared to be at a considerable disadvantage. Yet in the beginning matters went badly for Middlesex, Lee leaving at 26 and Price 10 runs later. Shortly after 50 had been passed, as the result of 70 minutes' steady batting, Hearne was leg-before. Then followed a valuable stand between Hendren and G. O. Allen, although Allen was fortunate to be missed when one, a rather difficult chance to mid-off from Wensley's bowling. Altogether the fourth wicket partnership produced 56 runs in just under an hour before Allen was cleverly taken at the wicket.

Hendren began quietly after lunch, but soon completed his 50, made out of 87 as the result of an hour and three-quarters very steady batting. Shortly before the interval, when his score was 46, he gave a sharp chance at the wicket off Tate, which Cornford just got to but failed to hold. For a time Hendren monopolised the scoring, for Hulme could do little against Tate and Cornford, and after nearly half an hour's batting had scored only a single. Then he became more like his real self, twice driving Cornford to the boundary.

There appeared every likelihood that Hendren and Hearne would bring about a big improvement in the fortunes of Middlesex, but the advent of Jas. Langridge for Tate at 161 effected a separation, Hulme being easily stumped two runs later. Further disaster befell the visitors when Hendren was dismissed, the sixth wicket falling at 177.

Worcester Crowd Barracks the Umpires

Essex did not close their innings at the overnight total of 455 for nine. Thanks largely to Pope they added another 22 runs, and again Worcestershire had a formidable aggregate piled up against them. Brook was the only bowler who met with reasonable success, but his wickets this season have cost nearly 50 runs each. His leg breaks are nothing like so accurate as they used to be. Sheffield at the wicket showed remarkable dexterity when dealing with Farnes's deliveries.

By lunch Worcester had lost C. F. Walters and the Nawab of Pataudi for 85 runs, Farnes taking both wickets through catches at the wicket.

Worcestershire had the best batting side on paper they have put into the field this season, but the show they were making was in no way convincing. Farnes had the first four wickets, and he is in outstanding form this season. He never attempted to bowl at the pace that Nichols was showing, but varied his pace and pitch skilfully, and bowled to his field admirably. It was a really curious field, too, for at one time he had four slips, backward point, a short cover-point, and only a short mid-on the other side of the wicket.

There was some foolish barracking, when at 112 and 116 respectively both Gibbons and Fiddian Green were the victims of leg before decisions. There was a big crowd present for Worcester, and they can scarcely rank as a well-informed aggregation. They shouted offensive remarks at the two white-coated officials for the next half-hour. Considering the strength of the Worcestershire batting on paper they had given a rather poor show. However, Quaife and Martin at least showed resolute cricket.

Another South African Soccer Player for Liverpool F.C.

Leslie Dewar, a young South African full-back, who has been signed on by Liverpool F.C., arrived in England to-day.

Dewar was 17 when he played for Rhodesia against an F.A. eleven captained by J. Seed. He is a scratch golfer, a good cricketer and has played representative water-polo.

Liverpool already have two South African players on their books—Gordon Hodgson, the international forward and Lancashire cricketer, and A. J. Riley, the goalkeeper.

THE CRICKET SCORE BOARD

(Later Scores on Back Page)

SURREY v. NOTTINGHAMSHIRE

At THE OVAL (Second day).

NOTTINGHAMSHIRE

First innings (Keeton 129, Staples (A.) 100) ...379

SURREY

Hobbs, c Butler, b Gunn	133
Sandham, c Staples (A), b Voce	7
Squires, c Carr, b Voce	0
Barling, c Carr, b Butler	4
Gregory, c Harris, b Butler	43
McMurray, not out	24
M J C Allom, not out	8
Extras	33
Total (5 wkts)	252

KENT v. HAMPSHIRE

At CANTERBURY (Second day).

HAMPSHIRE

First innings (Mead 87; Freeman 5 for 120) ...344

KENT

Ashdown, b Boyes	106
C. S. Marriott, c Boyes, b Baring	2
Freeman, c Mead, b Baring	2
Todd, c Kennedy, b Baring	0
Woolley, c Boyes, b Kennedy	14
Ames, c Brown, b Boyes	79
B H Valentine, not out	58
C H Knott, not out	10
Extras	13
Total (6 wkts)	284

DERBYSHIRE v. WARWICKSHIRE

At DERBY (Second Day).

DERBYSHIRE

Storer, c Smart, b Hollies	39
A F Skinner, c Smart, b Paine	50
Townsend, not out	172
Worthington, c and b Paine	40
Pope (A V), c Croom, b Collins	23
G R Jackson, b Sanders	21
L B Blaxland b Paine	64
Elliott, b Paine	9
Armstrong, st. Smart, b Paine	6
Mitchell, not out	6
Extras	18
Total (8 wkts)	*448

* Innings declared closed.

Bowling: Paine 5 for 115, Sanders 1 for 39, Hollies 1 for 105, Collin 1 for 58

WARWICKSHIRE

Kilner, lbw, b Worthington	6
Croom, b Mitchell	18
Bates, b Copson	2
R E S Wyatt, not out	93
Santall, c Elliott, b Copson	19
Collin, b Copson	1
Paine, run out	7
Barber, c Elliott, b Mitchell	9
Smart, b Copson	17
Sanders, not out	10
Extras	3
Total (8 wkts)	185

LEICESTERSHIRE v. NORTHANTS

At LEICESTER (Second day).

NORTHAMPTONSHIRE

First innings (Bakewell 192) ...299

LEICESTERSHIRE

Shipman, c Bellamy, b Matthews	12
Berry, c Bellamy, b Matthews	63
Armstrong, run out	4
Wiggington, b Partridge	3
Geary, b Jupp	5
E W Dawson, b Jupp	5
Sidwell, lbw, b Matthews	11
Astill, b Jupp	48
B J Packe, c Bakewell, b Jupp	12
Marlow, lbw, b Thomas	0
Smith, not out	0
Extras	6
Total	169

WORCESTERSHIRE v. ESSEX

At WORCESTER (Second day).

ESSEX

L G Crawley, b Martin	49
Cutmore, b Perks	19
Taylor, b Brook	17
O'Connor, hit wkt, b Brook	47
Nichols, b Martin	9
Eastman, lbw., b Brooks	100
D R Wilcox, c Quaife, b White	90
Pope, c Fiddian-Green, b Perks	49
Sheffield, c Nichol, b Gibbons	2[illegible]
Smith, c Bull, b Brook	40
K Farnes, not out	5
Extras	23
Total	477

Bowling: Brook 4 for 92, Perks 2 for 93, Martin 2 for 65, White 1 for 91, Gibbons 1 for 17.

WORCESTERSHIRE

C F Walters, c Sheffield, b Farnes	34
Gibbons, lbw, b Smith	47
Nawab of Pataudi, c Sheffield, b Farnes	0
Nichol, c O'Connor, b Farnes	17
Bull, b Farnes	0
C A Fiddian-Green, lbw, b O'Connor	11
B W Quaife, c Eastman, b Farnes	37
Martin, not out	43
White, c Nichols, b Eastman	0
Brook, not out	12
Extras	11
Total (8 wkts)	212

YORKSHIRE v. LANCASHIRE

At LEEDS (Second day).

YORKSHIRE

Holmes, c Watson, b Sibbles	20
Sutcliffe, lbw, b Parkinson	18
Mitchell, lbw, b Parkinson	45
Leyland, c Duckworth, b Booth	7
Barber, c Duckworth, b Sibbles	81
A B Sellers, b Hopwood	19
Verity, st Duckworth, b Hopwood	22
Wood, c Sibbles, b Booth	31
Rhodes, st Duckworth, b Watson	16
Macaulay, not out	13
Bowes, run out	0
Extras	24
Total	296

Bowling: Hopwood 2 for 51, Parkinson 2 for 59, Booth 2 for 51, Sibbles 2 for 62, Watson 1 for 17.

LANCASHIRE

Hopwood, not out	83
Watson, c Macaulay, b Bowes	2
Tyldesley, c Macaulay, b Bowes	1
Paynter, c Macaulay, b Leyland	14
Hawkwood, not out	63
Extras	9
Total (3 wkts)	172

GLOUCESTERSHIRE v. SOMERSET

At BRISTOL (Second day).

GLOUCESTERSHIRE

Sinfield, c Young, b Lee (J)	36
Barnett, b Hazell	111
Hammond, c Luckes, b Wellard	40
B H Lyon, c Luckes, b Lee (J)	51
Dacre, lbw., b Lee (J)	5
B O Allen, run out	0
Neale, b Young	10
Goddard, c Wellard, b Young	1
P G Van der Gucht, not out	31
Parker (C), c Seamer, b Young	9
G W Parker, b Lee (J)	56
Extras	17
Total	367

Bowling: Lee (J) 4 for 91, Young [illegible] for 76, Hazell 1 for 89, Wellard 1 for 94

SOMERSETSHIRE

Lee (J), not out	32
E F Longrigg, c Sinfield, b Goddard	62
C C Case, not out	9
Extras	5
Total (1 wkt)	108

SUSSEX v. MIDDLESEX

At HOVE (Second day).

SUSSEX

Bowley, c Hulme, b Lee	283
Langridge (Jn), lbw, b Sims	195
Parks (J), c Enthoven, b Sims	5
Cook, not out	2
Langridge (Jas), not out	10
Extras	17
Total (3 wkts)	*512

*Innings declared closed.

Bowling: Sims 2 for 122, Lee 1 for 90

MIDDLESEX

Lee, b Tate	10
Price, c Langridge (Jn), b Parks (J)	15
Hearne, lbw, b Wensley	12
Hendren, b Wensley	79
G O Allen, c Cornford (W), b Tate	23
Hulme, st Cornford (W), b Langridge (Jas)	19
H J Enthoven, lbw, b Langridge (Jas)	8
N Haig, c Cook, c Langridge (Jas)	41
Sims, not out	22
Watkins, not out	23
Extras	11
Total (8 wkts)	263

GLAMORGAN v. WEST INDIES

At SWANSEA (Second day).

GLAMORGAN

First innings (W G Morgan 69, Davies (D.), 57, Every 51) ...295

WEST INDIES

C A Roach, b Mercer	70
I Barrow, b Davies (D)	22
G Headley, lbw, b Mercer	89
G C Grant, c Jenkins, b Davies (E)	2
O C Da Costa, c Davies (D), b Clay	66
B J Sealey, not out	46
C A Merry, b Davies (E)	6
E Achong, c Brierley, b Davies (E)	9
Extras	13
Total (7 wkts)	323

LORD'S SCHOOLS v. THE REST

At LORD'S

THE REST

T R Garnett, b Turner	6
N S Mitchell-Innes, b Darewski	0
R H Angelo, run out	85
H T Bartlett, c Napper, b Brocklebank	19
D G Boussild, c Napper, b Hotchkiss	39
D F Mendl, lbw, b Brocklebank	47
P F Judge, lbw, b Brocklebank	35
P Singleton, b Brocklebank	9
M A Matthews, c Burns, b Morrison	4
G Ballence, not out	9
C D Beaumont, b Turner	2
Extras	12
Total	261

Bowling: Brocklebank 4 for 45, Turner 2 for 70, Darewski 1 for 47, Morrison 1 for 30, Hodgkin 1 for 18.

LORD'S SCHOOLS.

M Tindall, not out	18
N S Hotchkin, not out	8
Total (no wkt)	26

THE DAILY MIRROR, Saturday, June 30, 1934

Broadcasting - Page 22

Daily Mirror

THE DAILY PICTURE NEWSPAPER WITH THE LARGEST NET SALE

WIMBLEDON STARS' THROAT TROUBLE

No. 9,545   Registered at the G.P.O. as a Newspaper.   SATURDAY, JUNE 30, 1934   One Penny

COTTON TIES UP THE AMERICANS

The 'Open' Won for Britain

RECORD OF 283 EQUALLED

After winning the Open Golf Championship at Sandwich yesterday, with a score that has never been bettered, Henry Cotton, the 27-year-old Englishman, revealed that he had nearly been beaten—by indigestion!

The new champion won with an aggregate of 283 for seventy-two holes, and tied with the record created by Gene Sarazen, the American, two years ago.

Cotton's feat is a triumph of attention to detail. He has beaten the Americans at their own game of hard training

For years he has practised, practised, practised until he mastered every stroke to perfection. He has kept himself in first-class physical condition He even went to America to study their methods.

Thus Cotton, a native of Holmes Chapel, Cheshire, brought up in Dulwich, London, and for the past two years professional at the Waterloo Club, Brussels, became champion golfer.

His was the first English win in the Open for eleven years.

Syd Brews, the South African champion, was second with 288, and Alfred Padgham, of Sundridge Park, third with 290. MacDonald Smith and Kirkwood, from America, and Dallemagne, the Frenchman, came next with 292 each.

Success—and Tragedy

Shortly after he finished in second place Brews received a cable that his mother had died.

He was almost overcome with grief at the moment of the greatest golfing achievement of his life.

When he stepped up to receive his prize his eyes were flooded with tears. Brews's wife took his arm and assisted him away.

Cotton had made the championship a certainty by the end of the third round, and he was being acclaimed champion before he had struck a ball in the final test. Only a golfing miracle, it was contended, could deprive him of the crown of the game.

He had a lead of ten strokes from Joe Kirkwood, a start in magnitude never before enjoyed by anyone setting out in the supreme stage.

But the miracle nearly happened. A gale of wind sprang up from the Channel and Cotton, affected too by the tense struggle of four days, made errors and slips in putting. By the ninth hole he had expended forty strokes.

S. F. Brews

For the next three holes Cotton took fifteen strokes, but he rallied and finished the round in 79.

As Cotton holed out his putt on the last green cheers broke out, and he was carried shoulder high to the pavilion.

"I was nearly beaten by indigestion," Cotton said after he had been released by his admirers.

"I had a very heavy lunch and every time I pivoted for a shot I felt the effects of it. I was more easy after playing twelve holes and then felt more like my old self."

P.S.—This, according to Reuter, is America's opinion of Cotton: "What a man!" Just that.

E. M. Wellings describes the play on page 26.

Henry Cotton, the British golfer, with his championship cup and (above) chaired at Sandwich after his victory. He is the first Englishman to win the golf open championship since 1923.

Miss Ellen Tuck French and (right) Mr. John Jacob Astor, the twenty-one-year-old millionaire, who are to be married to-day.

LORRY LOAD OF FLOWERS FOR BRIDE

Millionaire Groom is "Somewhat Nervous"

FORMER FIANCEE

NEWPORT (Rhode Island, U.S.A.), Friday.

A lorry-load of white flowers, palms and ferns is being sent from the estate of Senator W. H. Vanderbilt, second cousin of the bride, to decorate the quaint old church of Holy Trinity here at to-morrow's fashionable wedding of Mr. John Jacob Astor, the twenty-one-year-old millionaire, and Miss Ellen Tuck French, grandniece of the Dowager Lady Cheylesmore.

A somewhat nervous bridegroom, in an interview to-day, revealed that about 200 guests had been invited.

150 Presents

He said that his mother, who is now the wife of the Italian boxer, Signor Enzo Firmente, has announced her intention of attending the wedding.

About 150 presents, including works of art, forty-eight silver plates and several silver coffee sets, have already been received by the couple.

The Lohengrin and Mendelssohn wedding marches will be the principal musical items on the programme.

It is still not known whether or not Miss Eileen Gillespie, Mr. Astor's former fiancee and the best friend of the bride—by whom she was superseded in Mr. Astor's affections—will be present at the ceremony.—Reuter.

Daily Mirror

THE DAILY PICTURE — NEWSPAPER WITH THE LARGEST NET SALE

DRASTIC NEW WATER LAWS NEXT WEEK

No. 9,551 — Registered at the G.P.O. as a Newspaper. — SATURDAY, JULY 7, 1934 — One Penny

PERRY WORLD TENNIS CHAMPION
Title Comes Home After 25 Years

MISS ROUND'S CHANCE TO-DAY

Fred Perry, of Ealing, London, by beating J. H. Crawford at Wimbledon yesterday by 6-3, 6-0, 7-5, brought back to England, after 25 years, the Blue Riband of Tennis—the Wimbledon Men's Singles—and became the world's leading tennis star.

It was last won for England by A. W. Gore in 1909, when Perry was a newly-born babe!

AFTER the match had been won, Perry said: " I don't think I have ever played better, and I don't think I ever will again."

Crawford said: "He played magnificently. England couldn't have found a better champion."

And England to-day stands a chance of winning also the women's singles.

Miss Dorothy Round, who has been playing on the top of her form lately, meets Miss Helen Jacobs this afternoon for the title.

WON TWELVE GAMES IN SUCCESSION

BY A SPECIAL CORRESPONDENT

Perry played the most amazing tennis in beating Crawford, the holder, in three straight sets.

Its equal has probably never been seen.

He reeled off twelve games in succession—the equivalent of two love sets—after being 1—3 behind in the first set.

The match is fully described by H. E. Lainson Wood on page 26.

Since the late A. W. Gore relinquished the singles title to A. F. Wilding in 1910, it has been the exclusive property of Australians, Americans and Frenchmen.

Its return to the home of its birth puts England once more on the top of the tennis world.

We already hold the Davis Cup, the world's team championship. Now we have the supreme individual honour.

Perry, the son of an ex-Socialist M.P., was born at Stockport (Lancs) in 1909.

And only the pleas of a few experts persuaded his father, at long last, to give him a chance at tennis.

(Continued on page 3)

F. J. Perry rushing forward after his victory to take J. Crawford's extended hand

Lady Burghley with her son John, who is now dead, and daughter Davina.

F. J. Perry playing in the match which made him champion yesterday.

DEATH OF LD. BURGHLEY'S HEIR

Father and Mother at Baby Son's Bedside

Lord Burghley, M.P., the world-famous athlete, and his wife suffered a sad bereavement yesterday in the death of their thirteen-month-old son, the Hon. John William Edward Cecil.

He became dangerously ill at the beginning of the week, developing tubercular meningitis.

Famous doctors fought desperately to save the frail life, but it was realised from the beginning of the illness that there was only a slender chance of recovery.

Lord and Lady Burghley were at the bedside when their son died.

"His end was peaceful," Lady Burghley said later.

The child was born on June 1 last year at the London home of the Duke of Buccleuch. His mother, a daughter of the Duke, as Lady Mary Theresa Montagu - Douglas - Scott, married Lord Burghley, the Marquis of Exeter's heir, at the Church of St. Clement Danes, Strand, in 1929.

Many royal gifts were received by the bride, who is a goddaughter of the Queen.

At the son's christening last year water brought from the River Jordan was used, and the baby wore the historic robes in which his father, grandfather and great-grandfather were christened.

There is another child, Lady Davina Cecil, aged three. Lord Burghley, who is twenty-nine, is M.P. for Peterborough and a world-famous athlete.

Lord Burghley.

While at Magdalene College, Cambridge, he was the winner of the Oxford v. Cambridge 120 yards hurdles and the 220 yards hurdles in 1925, 1926 and 1927, being president of the Cambridge University Athletic Club during the 1926-27 season.

He was the winner of eight British championships and of the Olympic 400 metre hurdles in 1928.

THE WEATHER
Cooler Tuesday night and Wednesday; Wednesday fair

Columbus Evening Dispatch

OHIO'S GREATEST HOME DAILY

Wirephotos
Associated Press
International
News Service

VOL. 66, NO. 35. *** Telephone—MAin 1234 TUESDAY, AUGUST 4, 1936. 22 PAGES PRICE In Greater Columbus, One Cent; Elsewhere . . . . . Two Cents

OWENS SETS TWO MORE OLYMPIC MARKS

Sanity Hearing May Be Given Grocery Owner Who Slew Wife

CHARGE OF FIRST DEGREE MURDER IS PLACED AGAINST JAMES KISH

QUESTIONING KISH AT POLICE HEADQUARTERS

CAUSE OF THE QUARREL

MRS. CARRIE KISH
(Pictured Shortly After Wedding)

JAMES KISH—"She said, 'Kish Bros.' and I plugged her."

A quarrel over the name of their $35,000 grocery business at 3375 Indianola avenue led James Kish to kill his wife in the bedroom of their home at 976 Carpenter street, Monday. Kish wanted to call the business "Kish & Sons," and his wife insisted on "Kish Bros." The gun used in the killing was obtained by Kish when he was in the oil fields years ago. Kish is pictured as he was questioned at police headquarters. Left to right are Detective W. D. Austin, Policeman Clarence Wolf, Kish and Detective Sergeant Cole.

Relatives Blame Mental Condition for Slaying; Scoff at Grievances.

A son, and two relatives of James Kish, age 48, of 976 Carpenter street, Tuesday, branded as imaginary grievences the statements Kish related to police as being the causes which led to his slaying of his wife, Carrie, Monday night.

Newspapermen were refused admission to the Kish home, but over the telephone, William Edward, age 24, eldest son of Kish, attributed his father's actions and words to his mental condition.

Son Tells Story

"For the last five years," he said, "he has been abusive to mother.

"It reached such a point that we had to sell out one grocery and when we opened the new store we knew we couldn't have him around.

"We were willing to take care of him, but because of his mental condition, it was impossible to reason with him."

Asked if his father's statement that the sons had beaten him four times were true, the young man, a captain in the Ohio National Guard replied:

"He was so abusive to mother that I did slap him several times. I did it to protect mother."

Relatives Agree

The relatives who joined in claiming Kish was mentally ill were Louis Laposh of Cleveland, who married a sister of the dead woman, and J. M. Yacso of Cleveland, who married a sister of Mr. Kish.

"I can say this," exclaimed Mr. Laposh, "you won't find any two better boys than those two. I could tell a whole lot but it isn't my place to. Anyone can tell you what was wrong. He had been drinking too much lately. He wasn't right. You could tell that by the look in his eye."

Quarrel Over Selection of Name For New Store Is Blamed for Shooting.

A first degree murder charge was filed, Tuesday noon, against James Kish, age 48, grocer, arrested Monday night, for the fatal shooting of his wife, Carrie, age 45, during an argument in an upstairs bedroom of their home at 976 Carpenter street.

The suspect, whom police quoted as confessing the act, saying, "I feel more satisfied than ever before," will be arraigned in police court. Wednesday.

Despite his admissions, the man, proprietor of a $35,000 grocery business at 3375 Indianola avenue, indicated he will enter an innocent plea pending employment of and consultation with an attorney.

The murder charge was lodged by Detective Sergeant Charles Cole.

May Test Sanity

Meantime, the possibility arose that the prisoner may be subjected to a sanity hearing before his case reaches the grand jury.

County Prosecutor Don Hoskins, informed that relatives believe the man unbalanced, said:

"If it is thought advisable later, a sanity hearing will be held. The grand jury does not report until the last of the month. If the sanity hearing is held, it will probably be before the grand jury goes into session."

The prisoner's purported confession was made several hours after his flight from the home in a truck and his subsequent capture by Patrolmen Clarence Wolfe and Wayne Miller who recognized the truck at Greenlawn avenue and High street and forced Kish to the curb.

The timely arrest, Detective Sergeant Cole reported, may have prevented another slaying.

"Kish told me," the sleuth related," that he was en route north to the home of a former business

CONTINUED ON PAGE 6, COL. THREE

Candidates' Free Beer Custom Frowned Upon

HAMILTON, OHIO, AUG. 4.—(AP).—Someone besides the candidates will have to provide the free beer—if any—at Butler county Democratic political rallies.

The county Democratic executive committee in a resolution adopted last night frowned on the custom of having candidates supply free beer.

Akron Balloon Winner Of Special Contest

TOWANDA, PA., AUG. 4.—(INS).—Safe and rested after their thrilling match race from Cleveland had ended in adjoining counties of this northern tier mountain area, two teams of balloon pilots packed and prepared their silken gas bags for shipment westward today.

The apparent winners in the close flight from the Cleveland Exposition grounds, Frank Trotter and John Ricker, were to bring their Goodyear X into Towando from nearby Leraysville today. They landed in a Bradford county meadow 18 miles east of here.

About 50 miles to the west, Milford Vanik and Anthony Fairbanks, pilots of the Great Lakes Exposition, landed and spent the night at Wellsboro.

$10 Per Month Hike Is Made For Pensions

Annual Increase of $10,000,000 Ordered.

EFFECTIVE AT ONCE

Checks for August To Be Mailed This Week.

An annual increase of approximately $10,000,000 in pensions paid to the aged, was ordered by Gov. Martin L. Davey, in a letter to Henry J. Berrodin, chief of the division of aid for the aged, Tuesday.

Mr. Berrodin, said that steps would be taken immediately to provide for the increase in pension checks for August.

He asserted that his division would certify the increases to the state auditor later this week with the possibility that the auditor could send out the August pension checks either Thursday or Friday.

The governor's recommendation, will raise the average monthly award for $15.10 to $25.10

The proposed increase will bring Ohio's bill for aid for the aged to approximately $26,000,000 a year, one half of which is received in federal grants from the social security board.

Governor Davey wrote that the "remarkable performance" of the Ohio liquor department and the social program of the federal government makes possible the increase.

The Social Security board granted Ohio a total of $1,846,864, Tuesday, as the federal government's share of expenditures in caring for the aged from July 1 to Sept. 30.

Lewis and Aides Placed on Trial

Bitterness Added to Internal Labor Quarrel.

WASHINGTON, AUG. 4.—(AP)—Charging that strong arm threats were used to force trade unionists into the John L. Lewis camp, the prosecution today pressed the "trial" of Lewis and 11 other American Federation of Labor chiefs, accused of rebellion.

John P. Frey, a federation official who is seeking to have the A. F. of L. executive council adjudge Lewis' Committee for Industrial Organization guilty of insurrection, announced he would present documentary evidence that men had been threatened with beatings to induce them to vote for industrial unionism.

"I will prove that meetings were packed," Frey added.

This charge, voiced before the council gathered in a stuffy Washington office for the second day of the "trial," added new bitterness to the internal quarrel in the A. F. of L.

Lewis and his committee remained adamant in their stand that in a mass production industry workers should generally be organized into one big industrial union, regardless of craft divisions. This has aroused the ire of craft union leaders dominating the A. F. of L. council, several of whom seemed determined to suspend the Lewis faction from the federation.

Lewis, president of the United Mine Workers, and his associates are leaders of more than 1,000,000 trade unionists.

Jesse Owens in Berlin This Morning

Picture Rushed to City by Radio and Wirephoto

This radiophoto from Berlin shows Jesse Owens, Olympic 100-meter champion, who broke the Olympic broad jump record, this morning, with a leap of 25 feet, 4 47-64 inches, in action in a qualifying jump today. The photo was radioed from London to New York and transmitted by a (AP) Wirephoto to The Dispatch.

Burglar Starting To Pen Tries to End Life

MARIETTA, OHIO, AUG. 4.—(AP).—A convicted burglar, who had pleaded with Common Pleas Judge David H. Thomas to send him to the electric chair, tried today to kill himself.

Sheriff Arthur H. Mackey said A. E. Frost, 42, slashed his throat with a razor blade as deputies started with him to Ohio penitentiary. The guards took Frost to Memorial hospital here.

Sentenced last week to serve five to 30 years for burglary, Frost told Judge Thomas he would rather die in the electric chair than serve so long in prison.

CIVIL SERVICE TO BAN DAVEY'S MAILING LIST

The state civil service commission, Tuesday, issued a ban on the activities of the Davey administration seeking to compel members of the classified service to write personal letters to their friends urging the re-election of Gov. Martin L. Davy.

In a letter to heads of various state departments, W. B. Francis, chairman of the civil service commission, pointed out that numerous court decisions and opinions of the attorney general "have definitely determined that such procedure constitutes political activity" and is in "violation of the provisions of the civil service laws of Ohio."

In calling the attention of departmental heads to the provisions of the state law, the commission asserted that "any political activity, whether Democratic or Republican, will be prohibited among classified employes of your department."

It had been reported that employes of the department of liquor control had been requested to write personal letters to eight of their friends citing the necessity for the re-election of Gov. Martin L. Davey.

BLAST KILLS FOUR

ROME, ITALY, AUG. 4.—(AP).—Explosion of a munitions factory at Orbetello today was reported to have killed at least four persons.

MAYOR THINKS SWIFTLY, HANDWRITING SHOWS

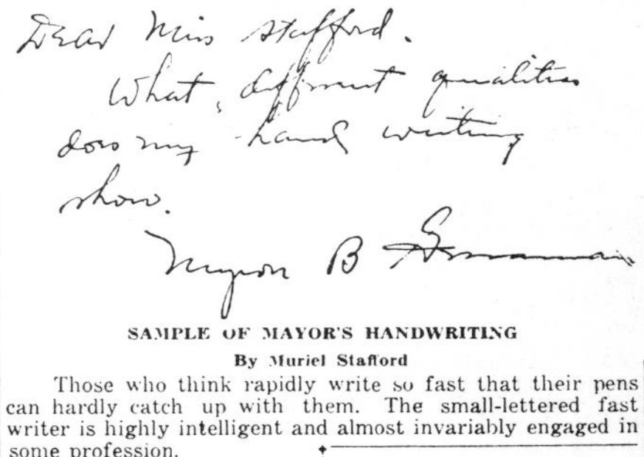

SAMPLE OF MAYOR'S HANDWRITING

By Muriel Stafford

Those who think rapidly write so fast that their pens can hardly catch up with them. The small-lettered fast writer is highly intelligent and almost invariably engaged in some profession.

Yesterday I had the pleasure of analyzing Mayor Gessaman's handwriting. He writes the typical professional handwriting of the highest type.

Notice that some of this handwriting seems to be almost scribbled it is written in such haste. It just flies along. Illegibility is usually a good sign rather than the opposite as so many persons

CONTINUED ON PAGE 6, COL. TWO

MAYOR GESSAMAN AND MISS STAFFORD

Boy Dies When Fishing Pole Hits Power Line

BRADFORD, PA., AUG. 4.—(AP).—Seven-year-old William Owens, swinging his fishing pole above his head, touched an electric power line. The shock knocked him from the bridge on which he stood into the water. He was dead before spectators recovered the body.

Buckeye Star Scores Win In Broad Jump

Previous Records in 200-Meters and Leap Fall.

HELEN STEPHENS WINS

Hardin of U. S. Team Cops 100-Meter Hurdle Title.

BERLIN, AUG. 4.—(AP).—A fresh assault on the record book, with Jesse Owens once again capturing the major share of the honors, today featured the third day of the Olympic track and field competition.

The Ohio State Negro all-around star won the broad jump title, following up his earlier triumph in the 100-meter sprint.

Owens won his second title of the eleventh Olympiad with a leap of 8.06 meters, 26 feet, 5 21-64 inches, shattering the previous record of 25 feet, 4¾ inches made by Edward Hamm in the 1928 games.

The tan thunderbolt from Ohio State twice clipped one-tenth of a second from Eddie Tolan's Olympic mark of 21.2 seconds in the

first two trials of the 200-meter event, and then twice bettered the Olympic standard in the running broad jump.

Owens qualified in the morning with a leap of 24 feet, 5¼ inches, and then in the afternoon, on his first two tries, did 25 feet, 4 47-64 inches and 25 feet, 9 27-32 inches in succession.

His first afternoon jump also shaded the record of Hamm by approximately one centimeter in the metric list.

Helen Stephens of Fulton, Mo., broke into the spotlight again, capturing the 100-meter championship in 11.5, beating the old mark by four-tenths of a second for the second time in two days. However, her winning time was one-tenth of a second slower than her smashing victory in yesterday's semi-final trials.

Packard, Robinson In

While all this was going on, Uncle Sam qualified all his entrants for the 200-meter semi-finals, Matthew (Mack) Robinson of Pasadena, Calif., and Bobby Packard of Rockford, Ill., making the grade along with Owens.

However, the Americans lost one member in the 400-meter hurdle semi-finals as Dale Schofield of Provo, Utah, was beaten for third place by Christos Mandikas of Greece in a "photo-finish."

Glenn Hardin of Greenwood, Miss., won the 400-meter hurdle championship.

Gisela Mauermayer of Germany captured the women's discus throw championship with a toss of 47.63 meters, 156 feet, 3⅜ inches, shattering the Olympic record of 133 feet, 2 inches set

CONTINUED ON PAGE 6, COL. ONE

Fleeing Prisoner Caught by Police

Two Injured in Frantic Downtown Chase.

Central police station was almost depopulated, two officers were injured and traffic was thrown into a wild tangle in Front street, Tuesday morning, with the escape of a prisoner and his eventual capture by a dozen policemen.

The prisoner, Harold Thompson, age 26, Grove City, held for investigation in connection with several robberies in the university district, broke loose from Detective Charles Loudenslager as the two men waited for an elevator on the first floor of police station.

Detective Loudenslager shouted a warning as Thompson headed for a stairway. Intercepted at the head of the stairs by two men, Thompson fell down a full flight of stairs. Dashing out on the lawn in front of the building, he was caught by Lieut. Earl Heise, head of the vice squad. Lieutenant Heise and Thompson wrestled on the grass but the prisoner again broke loose. As he left the lawn

CONTINUED ON PAGE 6, COL. TWO

CONTINUED COOL

Continued cool weather is in store for Columbus Tuesday and Wednesday, according to Weatherman W. H. Alexander. The mercury probably will not exceed its Monday peak of 90 degrees Tuesday or Wednesday.

DAILY SKETCH

FRIDAY JUNE 24 1938 Head Office: 200 Gray's Inn-road W.C.1 'Phone: TERminus 1234

Schmeling Battered by Louis

Picture of Louis' Swift Victory—By Radio From New York

Evidence of Max Schmeling's swift and decisive defeat by Joe Louis—these striking pictures, which were radioed from New York to London, show the dramatic incidents of the world-title fight—one of the shortest in history—at the Yankee Stadium, New York.

Above: Struggling to rise, Schmeling seems finished, while Louis, menacing as ever, is motioned away by the referee.

Schmeling rose, but knocked down again (right) for a count. Louis standing over his prostrate body waiting for him to rise.

Left: Feet high in the air, and bouncing heavily on the mat, Schmeling goes down for the last time, throwing his hand helplessly across his face. It is possible this fall caused Schmeling to enter hospital with an injured hip.

CHARM OF THE PAST

The charm of a Victorian wedding has been caught once again in this DAILY SKETCH picture. The happy couple alighting from the coach and four are Miss Aileen Duprez and Mr. Percival Robinson, who were married at Chelsea Old Church.

Mac Is Back

Popular broadcaster "Uncle Mac" (Mr. Derek McCulloch) going back smiling to Broadcasting House yesterday after the road accident in April which cost him his left foot.

STOP PRESS NEWS

TWO DIE IN ARAB-JEW CLASH

Two Arabs killed and seven Arabs and three Jews wounded in clash at Tel-Aviv.

One Jew stated to be dying.

Printed and Published by The DAILY SKETCH and SUNDAY GRAPHIC Ltd. 200 Gray's Inn-road London W.C.1 (Telephone: Terminus 1234)—FRIDAY JUNE 24 1938

Sunday Pictorial

March 10, 1946.

No. 1,617

TWOPENCE

EILEEN
Her Story—on Page 5

The Most Horrible Game Ever Played

33 KILLED AT A CUP TIE—AND THEY WENT ON PLAYING FOOTBALL

The Twisted Bits Of Iron Caused It

The conscience of the nation will be shocked this morning by the news that while 33 people lay dead, mangled and suffocated and 500 injured were being treated, the Bolton v. Stoke Cup-Tie game yesterday continued to its end as though nothing had happened.

500 WERE INJURED

THIRTY-THREE spectators, one of them a woman, at the Bolton Wanderers football ground, were trampled to death or suffocated and 500 injured when two crush barriers collapsed under a seething weight and sent thousands surging downward in a terrible, irresistible wave of fighting and struggling humanity.

The disaster was caused by thousands of gate-crashers, who broke through the outside fences and forced the crowd, already a record of nearly 70,000, helplessly forward.

A quarter of an hour after the start of the game the jammed crowd began to sway bodily towards the pitch.

A waist-high crush wall, built to keep crowds back, collapsed under the tremendous weight and hundreds were shot down a slope, to be trampled on by the oncoming mass. On and on went the chaotic rush, and finally two iron crush barriers bent and cracked.

People tumbled and fell to death and injury knowing that they were trampling on other human beings and could not avoid it. Those at the front were swept in their hundreds on to the pitch.

The referee stopped the game and the players pushed their way to the dressing-rooms, but after 26 minutes, on police advice after the pitch had been cleared by mounted men, play was resumed.

The players had little idea of the extent of the tragedy. Nor had half the people in the ground, and they roared and cheered the game.

And all the time dead bodies were being pulled out from helpless piles of half-conscious injured people. The dead were carried away to the mortuary, scores of severely crushed people were taken to hospital, and hundreds were treated where they lay.

Last night Bolton women besieged the mortuary, terrified lest they should recognise their missing menfolk, and there was a vast, tearful crowd outside the infirmary.

THE WHOLE STORY IS TOLD IN FULL ON THE BACK PAGE.

These few bent pieces of steel bars tell the story of the disaster. They are the remains of one of the two crush-bars that broke as the crowd surged forward to end in a pile of screaming humanity. The bars were forced out of their concrete bed by the stampede.

★

REFEREE of the match and the man who gave the decision to play on was Mr. G. Dutton, of Warwick, and he explained that he was advised to continue the game by the police.

"After the barrier broke, a police officer asked me if I would get the players into the dressing room until some order could be restored," he said.

"The police officer told me some people were dead, but I did not tell the teams. I called the two captains and told them to get the players into the dressing room. When order had been restored on the field, I gave the players instructions to resume."

The players did not know the extent of the disaster.

F. Steele, the Stoke centre-forward, said: "Mr. Dutton came into 'he dressing-room and told the players, 'I have been asked by the Chief Constable of Bolton to request you to carry on with the game.' That was the first we knew.

"When we were going on the field, Baker, the outside left, and Pettit, inside right, were stopped by a man, who got hold of them and said: 'It is a crime for you to carry on with the match.'"

Nor did thousands of the onlookers know of the extent of the disaster. When play was resumed there was all the usual cheering and excitement of a Cup-tie.

WHAT WE THINK—P. 4

Why?

THE people of Bolton who were outside the ground were unaware of what had happened until the match was over.

Then, as they saw the crowd streaming away from the match they refused to believe rumours that a disaster had occurred in the middle of the game.

When the facts were confirmed and the news began to spread, Bolton was amazed and shocked.

The vicar of the town, Canon W. J. H. Davidson, told the "Sunday Pictorial": "Although I do not know all the circumstances, I am appalled that the game should have gone on afterwards.

"I should like to know why, and unless there was a very good reason, I can only condemn such a decision.

"The human thing to have done would have been to stop the game and send the people home."

Aug. 25, 1946

Sunday Pictorial

No. 1,641   Twopence

Special article—p. 4: by
J. B. PRIESTLEY

SALUTE TO A HERO

TEN yards after breaking the tape in his last—and greatest—international race, Sydney Wooderson collapsed, dead beat, in the arms of a masseur. This picture, taken as he was being helped from the track, reached London last night. Sportsmen from twenty-one nations flung hats in the air and cheered as the little, bespectacled Englishman raced to become European 5,000 metres champion in a killing spurt that nearly killed him.

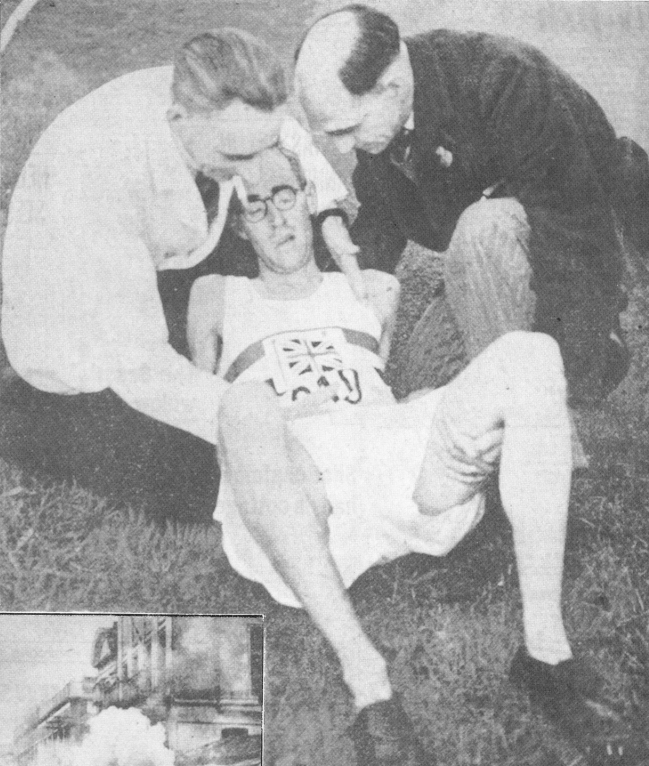

India Riot: First Pictures

From Calcutta, last night, came the first pictures of the tragic happenings in India, where nine battalions of troops had to be used to quell Moslem-Hindu riots which caused over 2,000 deaths.

The picture below translates these "disturbances" into terms which the war has taught Britain to understand.

Here police are using tear gas bombs to break up a Moslem attempt to set fire to a Hindu temple, the building on the right.

Other pictures are on Pages 6 and 7:

ALL THE CUP FINAL PICTURES
Pages 12 and 13

Sunday Graphic

No. 1,673   (E)   SUNDAY, APRIL 27, 1947   A KEMSLEY NEWSPAPER   TWOPENCE

CHARLTON'S CUP AT LAST!

AFTER four Cup Finals in five years, Charlton have won the F.A. Cup at last. On the shoulders of goalkeeper Bartram (left) and Croker, Don Welsh, Charlton captain, carries it off in triumph. Match-winning goal-scorer Duffy (Charlton's top scorer in the Cup this year) got the base of the Cup as a consolation prize—and was nearly chaired off the field himself.

Dutch housewife wins Games Double: Maureen Gardner beaten, but shares record

FASTEST WOMAN IN THE WORLD IS AN EXPERT COOK

Mrs. Blankers-Koen (Holland), on the extreme right, and Maureen Gardner (Britain) in the next lane take the first hurdles together.

'I shall train my two children to be athletes as well'

By JACK MILLIGAN

A 30-year-old blonde mother of two children has captured the hearts of Wembley's Olympic crowds.

She is Mrs. Fanny Blankers-Koen, the Dutch girl who yesterday won the 80 metres hurdles in an eyelash finish with Maureen Gardner, the 19-year-old Oxford ballet dancer.

Both their times were 11.2 seconds—a new world record.

Unique record

This amazing Dutch athlete, who holds the world record for the high jump, long jump and 100 metres, has thus gained an Olympic double, first woman ever to achieve the feat.

But, at home she is just an ordinary housewife. She is an expert cook and darns socks with artistry.

She is married to her former coach, 40-year-old J. Blankers, who once won an A.A.A. hop, step and jump title.

Her greatest love next to racing is housework. She is an early riser, drinks three litres of milk a day and trains two hours each morning.

Mrs. Blankers-Koen won't retire from the track after her Olympic conquest—she hopes to win the 200 metres to-day.

"I will probably keep on doing some athletics because I like it so much," she told me. And she intends to train her

children age 7 and 2½ for athletics.

Maureen Gardner, shyest girl in the Games, who most people thought had beaten the Dutch wonder girl, is more excited about September 11 than about her record-breaking run.

Kiss for Maureen

It is her wedding day. She is getting married to her coach, Geoff Dyson, who ran on to the track and kissed her after she had given the best performance by any Briton.

Yet there was a time when she thought she might not be fit to run. When she knocked over a hurdle on Tuesday, she banged her knee which now sports a big bruise. "Fortunately it didn't trouble me," she said. "What did trouble me though was nerves."

Coach Dyson says . . .

Speaking as the A.A.A. Chief Coach, Mr. Dyson scorned the prevalent notion that Britain is losing in the Games because her athletes lacked stamina through the food shortage.

"What Britain needs," he said, "is athletic training, particularly in the schools, where, for the most part, athletics are ignored.

"There are lots of Maureen Gardners in the country and lots of first-class men."

The sensational finish of the Women's 80 metres hurdles is shown here through the official photo-finish camera. At top Fanny Blankers-Koen (Holland) breaks the tape with Maureen Gardner (G.B.) placed second, and Shirley Strickland (Australia) (bottom) setting a problem for the judges. The attendance of 80,000 broke the Wembley record for the third successive day.

Passengers landing at Blackbushe, Surrey, yesterday after a free flight from Paris in a Mercury Airlines Dakota.

'Pirate' plane comes in

MR. MORRIS KERNEY, 36-year-old Managing Director of Mercury Airlines, is willing to fly passengers from London to Paris, and back, for nothing.

Mercury Airlines, of Johannesburg, flew a regular service from London to Johannesburg — until the Government stepped in. The Civil Aviation Act reserved all scheduled airline business in Britain to State-owned lines.

At 1.25 p.m. yesterday, a Mercury Airlines silver-and-orange Dakota touched

down at Blackbushe airfield. The nine passengers had flown from Paris to London for nothing.

Passengers flying by Mercury Airlines from Britain to Johannesburg and back pay the fare only for the stages between Paris and South Africa. Thereby, Mr. Kerney contends, the airline is not "plying for hire and reward" in Britain.

A Ministry spokesman said last night that if the regulation was not complied with they would have to consider what action to take.

To-day's Programme

ATHLETICS
Wembley Stadium

10.30: Decathlon, 110 m.
11.30: Decathlon, Long Jump.
3.0: 400 m. Semi-final. Decathlon, Putting the Shot.
3.30: 200 m. (Women) First Round.
4.0: Decathlon, High Jump.
4.15: 3,000 m. Steeplechase Final.
4.45: 400 m. Final.
5.0: 200 m. (Women) Semi-final.
5.30: Decathlon, 400 m.

BASKETBALL: Harringay, three sessions.

FENCING: Palace of Engineering, Wembley, two sessions.

FOOTBALL: Second Round, 6.30.

HOCKEY: Preliminary Rounds, 6.0.

ROWING: Henley, a.m. and p.m.

SWIMMING: Empire Pool, Wembley, three sessions.

WRESTLING: Earl's Court, two sessions.

YACHTING: Torquay.

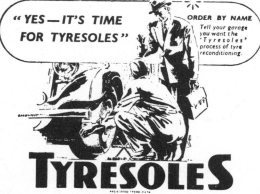
OLYMPIC RESULTS

110 METRES HURDLES

World record: F. G. Towns (U.S.) and F. Wolcott (U.S.), 13.7sec. Olympic record: F. G. Towns (U.S.), 14.1sec.

SEMI-FINAL—(First three in each heat qualify for Final). Heat 1: C. Dixon (U.S.), 14.2sec.; 1; P. Gardner (Australia), 14.5sec.; 2; H. Lidman (Sweden), 14.6sec., 3. Heat 2: W. F. Porter (U.S.), 14.1sec. equals Olympic record), 1; C. L. Scott (U.S.), 14.2sec.; 2; A. U. Triulzi (Argentina), 14.6sec.; 3.

FINAL—W. F. Porter (U.S.), 13.9 sec. (New Olympic record), 1; C. Scott (U.S.), 14.1sec.; 2; C. K. Dixon (U.S.), 14.1sec. 3. (Scott and Dixon equalled old Olympic record.) A. Triulzi (Argentina), 14.7sec., 4; P. J. Gardner (Australia), 5; H. Lidman (Sweden), 6.

400 METRES

World record: R. Harbig (Germany) and G. Klemmer (U.S.) 46sec. Olympic record: W. A. Carr (U.S.) 46.2sec.

FIRST ROUND (first two in each heat qualify for second round)—Heat 1: J. R. Reardon (Eire), 48.4sec.; 1; M. Racine (Yugoslavia), 50.5sec., 2. Heat 2: H. H. McKenley (Jamaica), 48.4sec.; 1; R. Larsson (Sweden), 49.2sec., 2. Heat 3: Z. Sabolovic (Yugoslavia), 49.9sec.; 1; K. Lundqvist (Sweden), 50sec., 2. Heat

4: V. G. Rhoden (Jamaica), 48.4sec., 1; D. V. Shore (S. African), 48sec., 2. Heat 5: J. Lunis (France), 48.8sec.; 1; F. Alnevik (Sweden), 50.2sec., 2.

Heat 6: D. Bolen (U.S.), 50.1sec., 1; J. L. Battram (Australia), 50.8sec., 2. Heat 7: L. C. Lewis (G.B.), 48.4sec., 1; B. Vade (Norway), 49.6sec., 2. Heat 8: M. G. Whitfield (U.S.), 48.3sec., 1; W. Roberts (G.B.), 48.8sec., 2. Heat 9: A. S. Wint (Jamaica), 47.7sec., 1; P. Schwetta (France), 48.8sec., 2. Heat 10: M. J. Curotta (Australia), 49.1sec., 1; R. Costa Ramos (Brazil), 49.2sec., 2. Heat 11: P. G. Guida (U.S.), 49sec., 1; D. Pugh (G.B.), 49.5sec., 2. Heat 12: H. Kunnen (Belgium), 50sec., 1; R. M. McFarlane (Canada), 50.6sec., 2.

SECOND ROUND (first three in each heat qualify for Semi-Final)—Heat 1: M. G. Whitfield (U.S.), 48.5sec., 1; V. Rhoden (Jamaica), 48.6sec., 2; R. Lewis (G.B.), 48.8sec., 3. Heat 2: A. S. Wint (Jamaica), 47.7sec., 1; M. J. Curotta (Australia), 47.9sec., 2; D. V. Shore (S. Africa), 48.3sec., 3. Heat 3: J. G. W. Nankeville (G.B.), 3min. 55.8sec.; 2; J. Barthel (Luxemburg), 3 min. 56.4sec., 3. Heat 4: G. Bergkvist (Sweden), 3min. 51.8sec.; 1; M. Hansenne (France), 3min. 52.8sec.; 2; S.

Heat 3: H. H. McKenley (Jamaica), 48sec., 1; G. J. Guida (U.S.) 48sec., 2; R. Larsson (Sweden), 48.8sec., 3. Heat 4: D. B. Bolen (U.S.), 48sec., 1; J. Reardon (Eire), 48.5sec., 2; R. McFarlane (Canada), 48.4sec., 3. D. C. Pugh (G.B.) eliminated.

1,500 METRES

World record: G. Haegg (Sweden) and L. Strand (Sweden), 3min. 43sec. Olympic record: J. Lovelock (New Zealand), 3min. 47.8sec.

FIRST ROUND (First three in each heat qualify for Final)—Heat 1: L. Strand (Sweden), 3min. 54.2sec., 1; E. A. Jorgensen (Denmark), 3min. 54.2 sec., 2; D. A. Gehrman (U.S.), 3min. 54.8sec., 3. Heat 2: W. F. Slijkhuis (Holland), 3min. 52.4sec.; 1; V. Cevona (Czechoslovakia), 3min. 55sec., 2; D. S. Johansson (Finland), 3min. 54sec., 3. (D. O. Wilson (G.B.) was eliminated). Heat 3: Henriksson (Sweden),

Garay (Hungary), 3min. 53sec., 3. (R. A. Morris (G.B.) was eliminated.)

THROWING THE JAVELIN

World record: Y. Nikkanen (Finland), 258ft. 2½in. Olympic record: M. Jarvinen (Finland), 238ft. 6½in.

FINAL: K. T. Rautavaara (Finland), 228ft. 10½in., 1; S. A. Seymour (U.S.), 221ft. 7¼in., 2; J. Varszegi (Hungary), 219ft. 11in., 3; E. M. Vesterinen (Finland), 216ft. 2in., 4; O. Maehium (Norway), 214ft. 5½in., 5; M. B. Biles (U.S.), 215ft. 9½in., 6.

M. Chote (G.B.) and M. Dalrymple (G.B.) failed to qualify for final.

80 METRES HURDLES (Women)

World record: C. Testoni (Italy) and F. Blankers-Koen (Holland), 11.3sec. Olympic record: T. Valla (Italy), 11.6 sec.

FINAL—F. Blankers-Koen (Holland), 11.2sec. (New World and Olympic record), 1; M. Gardner (G.B.), 11.2sec (also equals World record), 2; S. B. Strickland (Australia), 11.4sec., 3; Y. Monginou (France), 4; M. Oberbreyer (Austria), 5; L. Loniska (Czechoslovakia), 6.

Continued on Page 7.

THE ILLUSTRATED LONDON NEWS.

The World Copyright of all the Editorial Matter, both Illustrations and Letterpress, is Strictly Reserved in Great Britain, the British Dominions and Colonies, Europe, and the United States of America.

SATURDAY, AUGUST 21, 1948.

THE CLOSE, AT WEMBLEY STADIUM, OF THE 14TH, AND MOST SUCCESSFUL, MODERN OLYMPIAD, MR. EDSTRÖM HAS HANDED THE OLYMPIC FLAG TO THE LORD MAYOR OF LONDON AND THE FANFARE IS ABOUT TO SOUND.

The 14th Modern Olympiad closed on August 14. The white Tribune of Honour was placed before the Royal Box (occupied by the Duke of Edinburgh, the Duchess of Kent, Princess Juliana of the Netherlands and Prince Bernhard) and the flags of the fifty-eight competing nations arranged behind it. Mr. J. Sigfrid Edström, President of the International Olympic Committee, speaking from the Tribune, referred to the ties of brotherhood and friendship formed between the 6000 athletes who had fought nobly and with honour. After announcing the end of the Games, he handed to the Lord Mayor of London, Sir Frederick Wells, for safe keeping until it goes to Helsinki in 1952, the Olympic flag of embroidered satin. A fanfare of trumpets and a salute of guns sounded, and the choir (centre background, behind the massed bands of the Guards) sang the Olympic hymn while the flag in the arena was lowered and the flame extinguished before the march out began. The Games not only set up a record for attendance and receipts (estimated at £500,000), but have been remarkable for the excellence of the organisation and absence of incidents.

Daily Mirror

WED JULY 11 1951

1½d

No. 14,824

Registered at G.P.O. as a Newspaper

FORWARD WITH THE PEOPLE

Cheers—and tears—as Turpin wins for Britain

By TOM PHILLIPS

A tired Robinson leans heavily on Turpin during the fight.

TWENTY thousand Britons cheered at Earls Court, London, last night as the hand of a young English lad was raised in victory in one of the most dramatic moments in sporting history—Randolph Turpin, 23, of Leamington, had defeated the hitherto invincible Sugar Ray Robinson, of America, and won the world middleweight championship on points over 15 rounds.

And their cheers resounded around the British Isles as listeners-in everywhere heard the result.

What a great moment it was! Some of us were in tears at the ringside as Mr. Eugene Henderson, the referee, unhesitatingly gave his verdict.

And in the dressing-room there was even greater drama, for Mr. George Middleton, Turpin's manager, was crying unashamedly, and so were Randolph's brothers, Dick and Jackie, and his sparring partners, Mel Brown and Ted Morgan.

As soon as Turpin could tear himself away from the mobbing which the enthusiastic crowd had given him, he went straight to Robinson's dressing-room and said: "Sorry, Sugar." Robinson grasped his hand and replied: "Don't worry, Randy. You were real good like I thought you were."

Robinson took his defeat like a great sportsman. "Randy was a better man than I tonight," he told me. "It was a tough fight, if not my toughest. Randy sure can punch."

'No Alibis'

George Gainford, Robinson's manager, said: "No alibis. He was beaten. That's all there is to it. There's always the return fight, for which contracts were signed in the event of Turpin's winning. This is due to take place in New York on September 26."

At the end of the fight Turpin looked down and said to me: "Tom, come into the ring. Thank you for your faith in me, all through."

I always believed in him when other people had said Turpin should wait twelve months before meeting

Continued on Back Page

Sugar's wife (right) and sister watch.

RIGHTS OF WIVES INQUIRY ORDERED

A ROYAL Commission is to consider if any legal changes should be made in the property rights of husbands and wives DURING MARRIAGE and after divorce.

This was revealed in the Commons yesterday by Mr. Attlee, the Premier, in announcing the setting up of the Commission—promised by the Government in May—to investigate the law on marriage and divorce.

In looking into the property laws, the Commission, said Mr. Attlee, would "have in mind the need to promote and maintain a healthy and happy married life and to safeguard the interests and well-being of children."

The Commission—headed by Lord Morton of Henryton, 63, law lord, married, with one daughter—will consider also whether any alterations should be made in the law prohibiting marriage to certain relatives.

A legal expert said that a married woman could, of course, own separate property. But there were, he added, many points which remained to be cleared up.

These points included:

Should a wife have the legal right to some part of her husband's income as pin money?

And what about the actual ownership of money in a banking account to which both husband and wife have contributed?

Should a deserted wife have the right to remain in her home if her husband was the legal tenant? At present, if a tenant-husband does not pay the rent after leaving his wife, she can be turned out.

Christine, 7, found strangled in picnic spot

CHRISTINE
Missing with her doll since Sunday

THE body of Christine Butcher, 7, who had been missing from her home in Windsor since Sunday, was found in Home Park, near Windsor Castle, just before ten o'clock last night. She had been strangled. Two men visitors to Windsor, taking a short cut across the park, found the body in the long grass a mile and a quarter from her home.

The men ran to the Windsor Police Station, and within a few minutes police officers, led by Detective-Superintendent Walter Crombie, of the Berkshire C.I.D., were searching the grass for clues.

The child's body when found was covered by her blue mackintosh. She had been interfered with, a police officer stated last night.

The place where the body was found is on a favourite walk along the River Thames from Windsor. Normally on a Sunday afternoon hundreds of people would be picnicking there.

Before Christine's body was found, her mother, Mrs. Barbara Butcher, told the Daily Mirror: "I had warned Christine against going anywhere with a man or woman she didn't know. I even told her, 'Little girls who get lifts in cars are sometimes found murdered. You promise you won't do it?' She promised she never would."

LOVE AFFAIR OF BOY, 15, AND AN EX-ACTRESS

Mrs. DIANA STUART

AN ex-actress, aged forty-nine, and a mother, aged twenty-seven, both allowed a grammar-school boy of fifteen to make love to them after he had been drinking port, a court was told yesterday.

Former musical comedy artist Patricia Frances O'Rourke, a widow, whose address was given as a Torquay hotel, and Diana Valerie Stuart, of Teignmouth-road, Torquay, pleaded guilty before Torquay magistrates to indecently assaulting the boy.

Mrs. Stuart's lawyer told the court: "She says the advances were from him, and that after she had been at his home a few days, he was always hanging around her, trying to kiss her and so forth.

"From the way he behaved it would seem neither of these women was the first to be implicated by this boy. He has said he likes older women and has boasted of his association with them. He looks at least eighteen."

Detective-Inspector John Upward said Mrs. O'Rourke was staying at the boy's home at the time and the incident occurred after celebrations last Christmas, when the boy had been drinking port.

The inspector said Mrs. O'Rourke told the police: "The boy started making love to me. I did not entice or encourage him, but at the same time I did not attempt to resist him."

In the case of Mrs. Stuart, the inspector said the boy alleged she made advances to him. She agreed she did not resist him.

In a statement, Mrs. Stuart had said: "He is only fifteen, but he acts like someone much older."

The matter came to the notice of the police, the inspector added, when Mrs. Stuart's husband consulted solicitors about getting a divorce.

Mrs. O'Rourke's solicitor, Mr. H. A. T. Coles, said all the family had been drinking, and the boy, "incensed by port, made certain advances which were not repulsed.

"In normal circumstances I am sure they would have been," said Mr. Coles.

A probation officer said Mrs. Stuart had a "dear little girl of three," and her husband were now reconciled.

Both women were put on probation for a year.

The same magistrates afterwards formed a

Continued on Back Page

Golden SUNDAY PICTORIAL for the Queen

June 7, 1953   No. 1,994   Twopence-halfpenny

And the QUEEN SAYS—

AFTER YOU, SIR GORDON!

1

GORDON
2. The Queen
3. Pink Horse

2

Gayest and biggest crowd greeted the Royal party

3

Not so gay —the bookies. One firm paid out £300,000

SHAKE! Full story and more pictures in Page 10 and Back Page

The Queen, a gallant loser, shakes hands with Gordon Richards, the gay winner.

Peter Wilson reports the transformation of Little Mo
GIGGLE GIRL NOW QUEEN OF THE COURT

LITTLE MO
Last year a giggle girl with bounce

TWENTY-TWO months ago in Boston I met a bouncy, puppy-fatted apricot-coloured schoolgirl, who at sixteen was representing America in the Wightman Cup.

I christened her then "The Giggle Girl"—for she could not say a single sentence without fizzing over like damp sherbert—and the name stuck.

Yesterday I saw that same girl, Maureen Little Mo Connolly, on the Wimbledon Centre Court at eighteen, the youngest defending champion of this century.

And what a change in her. She came on to court wearing a vivid green jacket, decorated with a big white M. C.

There was a matching green ribbon in her blonde hair, and as she posed for the battery of photographers at the net there was that tremendous infectious smile which illuminates her whole face like a piece of Coronation floodlighting.

THERE WAS POISE AND EVEN SOPHISTICATION WHICH HAD TURNED "THE GIGGLE GIRL" INTO "THE QUEEN OF THE COURT."

Her First Romance

Besides poise she had acquired many things in those months. A horse as a gift from the proud citizens of her native Californian town San Diego. A ring from the young American naval man who is the first hint of romance in her life.

She had acquired lawn tennis titles as well like ordinary girls of her age pick up bargains at a sale.

The U.S. championships twice, the Australian title six months or so ago and only a few weeks back I saw her romp through the French Championships on that red frying pan of a court at Auteuil.

THAT MADE HER THE FIRST WOMAN IN THE HISTORY OF THE GAME TO HOLD THE FOUR MAJOR TENNIS TITLES OF THE WORLD AT THE SAME TIME.

When she walked on to court yesterday the smile went to be replaced by that sergeant major stride and that nodding pecking trick which looks so like a chicken eating corn off a plate

Now she was the ruthless killer, the fighter without mercy. Her opponent, brunette Dora Killan, from South Africa, must have felt as she were trying to stop a circular saw with her bare hand.

Even allowing for the comparative weakness of the opposition. I cannot ever remember a display of such controlledly ferocious hitting from ANY woman at Wimbledon—and it's twenty-four years since I saw my first final.

Little Mo swept through the first set in eleven minutes and the second in nine minutes. With the exception of the fifth game in the first set, when she served three double faults, it was impossible to criticise her game. It was perfection.

WHEN SHE HAD BLASTED DORA KILIAN OFF THE COURT, 6—0, 6—0, THE KILLER TURNED INTO A NICE KID AGAIN.

And a Smile Again

On came the smile and you could see how this girl who has mesmerised the tennis fans of the world last week went out to my colleague C. M. Jones's house, insisted on helping with the washing up, and was happiest sitting on the bed and playing with Jimmy's children.

Dora revealed to me that before her game with Little Mo, Maureen did her best to comfort her. "Don't be nervous. Just hit the ball in the usual way. It's only a game."

"She was perfectly sweet to me throughout," said Dora.

A GREAT PLAYER—A GRAND GAL.

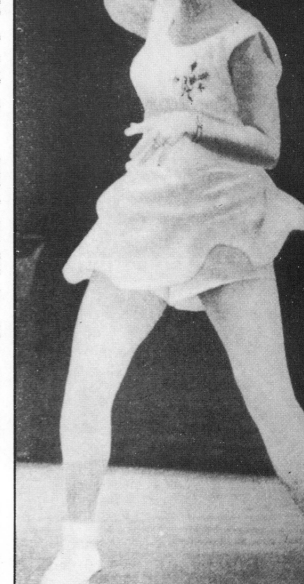

★ **LITTLE MO** ★
At Wimbledon yesterday a ruthless Queen of the Court as she sweeps to a 6—0, 6—0 victory over Dora Kilian of South Africa in twenty minutes.

Hart fails in a great fight

MARK HART, the Croydon heavyweight, was outpointed by Lloyd Barnett (Jamaica) over eight rounds at Mile End Arena last night.

Mr. J. Onslow Fane, chairman of the B.B.B. of C., sat at the ringside. His visits to this type of boxing are as rare as the great performance these two heavyweights staged.

He saw Hart climb from the canvas in the first, second and sixth rounds after counts of nine, when most boxers would have cried "enough" after taking the looping right-hand punch that Barnett threw on every occasion.

He also saw Hart stage a comeback in the seventh and eighth rounds — a comeback that almost gained him the verdict.

But Barnett's earlier straight left-hand boxing, coupled with the knock downs, had given him too great a lead for Hart to wipe out in the last stages of this exciting fight.

PAT GIVES A TEST HINT

WHAT incentives West Ham had to beat Wimbledon last night. They needed to pull back twelve points to get into the London Cup Final against Harringay. Then, with Bert Roger signed from New Cross, riders had to drive like whirlwinds to keep their place.

And like whirlwinds the team men rode—that accounts for the 69—38 defeat of Wimbledon, which gave West Ham a 115—96 aggregate win.

For young Pat Clarke, who is determined to break into the England team, it was a great night. Unbeaten, scoring seventeen points with an England selector looking on, his name must have gone on the short list of candidates.

Heats 5 to 9 sank Wimbledon. West Ham outscored them 25 to 5, and with only Ronnie Moore and Geoff Marden showing normal form, they were beaten from then on.

Don Perry, match winner for Wimbledon on Monday, again rode well, taking five points from three rides.

There was an exciting last heat home win for St. Austell, who beat Rayleigh 42—40 in their Southern League match. The star was Jackie Gates, who clinched the victory—and scored eleven points.

CHALLENGE MATCH.—Southampton 39 (E. Rawlins 10, E. Brecknell 8), Coventry 45 (C. New 10, L. Hewitt 10).
NORFOLK SHIELD (1st Leg).—Great Yarmouth 49 (B. Baker, R. Reeves 12), Norwich 35 (F. Rogers, B. Bales 9).
LONDON CUP SEMI-FINAL (2nd Leg).—West Ham 69 (P. Clarke 17, J. Young 16), Wimbledon 38 (R. Moore, G. Marden 10) (West Ham win on aggregate: 115—96).
SOUTHERN LEAGUE. — St. Austell 42 (J. Gates 11, K. Monk J. Yates 9), Rayleigh 40 (G. Jackson 12, M. McDermott 9).

NOW SKIPPER JOINS NEW CLUB

IRISH-BORN Eric French, skipper of the disbanded New Cross team, has been signed by Wembley for £1,600.

Already this season Wembley have paid £2,500 for Brian Crutcher to strengthen their team. Like Crutcher, French is an English international.

French, 39, was a Wimbledon rider in 1938. After the war, New Cross picked him from the pool of riders.

Evening Standard

40.166

TUESDAY, JUNE 30, 1953 ●● Three-halfpence

ENGLAND'S GREAT FIGHT
Watson, Bailey in fine stand

TOWARDS THE 200

From BRUCE HARRIS: Lord's, Tuesday

England 173 for 4 this afternoon here in the second Test against Australia—a brave recovery from the calamitous three wickets for 12 runs which opened the venture last night.

AUSTRALIA: First innings
Hassett 104, Davidson 76,
Harvey 59; Bedser 5—105,
Wardle 4—77   346
Second innings (Miller 109,
Morris 89, Lindwall 50;
Brown 4—82)   368
ENGLAND: First innings
(Hutton 145, Graveney 78,
Compton 57; Lindwall
5—66)   372
                Second innings
L. Hutton, c Hole, b Lindwall   5
D Kenyon, c Hassett, b Lind-
wall   2
T. Graveney, c Langley, b
Johnston   2
D Compton lbw, b Johnston   57
W Watson, not out   80
T E Bailey, not out   36
        Extras   15
        Total (4 wkts)   173
Fall of wickets: 1—6, 2—10,
3—12, 4—73.

WE BUY MORE SOVIET CRAB

Britain is to sell about £973,000 of cured herrings to Russia and in return will buy from the Soviet canned salmon and crab to the value of £1,090,000, under a new trade pact announced this afternoon. (See Page Two).

SIR GORDON IS THIRD

In his first race as a knight

Gordon Richards, who was knighted by the Queen at Buckingham Palace to-day, afterwards flew to Newmarket.

His first mount, Tintinnabulum, finished third in the Hare Park Handicap.

As Sir Gordon left the investiture a Palace policeman, Sergeant Junemann, congratulated him and, returning thanks, Sir Gordon said: "Watch me in the third race."

Sir Gordon rode Blood Test in that race the Bottisham Stakes. It was unplaced.

In the big race, the July Stakes, Sir Gordon's mount, Princely Gift, was beaten into second place by Darius in a photo-finish.

See the Londoner's Diary—PAGE FOUR.

2 American women reach Wimbledon semi-finals

Two American women, challengers for the title held by Maureen Connolly, reached the semi-final of the Wimbledon singles this afternoon.

Miss Shirley Fry and Miss Doris Hart, a former champion, who won in straight sets, are expected to be joined in the last four by Miss Connolly.

The fourth place will be taken by the winner of the match between Britain's lone hope, Miss Angela Mortimer, and another American, Mrs. Dorothy Knode.

Miss Fry beat another American, Miss Julie Samp-

son, 6—4, 6—2, and Miss Hart knocked out the Hungarian, Mrs. Koermoczi, 7–5, 7–5. Prince Philip was at Wimbledon this afternoon.

FRED PERRY reports the tennis. PAGE FIFTEEN.

In this rally the hero was a Yorkshireman. Willie Watson, who combined with Denis Compton in the morning in a stand of 61, and then, when Compton was out for 33, with Trevor Bailey in another stand far passed the half century.

Could we win? Time was against us, for with two and threequarter hours 188 runs were still required.

Could we draw? The chances were better, but still not bright.

Prince Philip arrived just before play began. He watched the match until 1.15.

Plenty of room

There was plenty of room to-day for everyone wanting to attend the obsequies of the Test match.

That slip catch by GRAHAM HOLE which ended LEN HUTTON'S innings last night may well have cost his country and ours £5000. A solemn thought for the young man.

First objective was to avoid the record low total in a Test match by England against Australia. This was 45 at Sydney in 1886-87. The lowest of which we had ever been guilty in England was 52 at The Oval five years ago.

Lindwall bowls

There were plenty of empty seats when LINDWALL wound himself up for his new onslaught to-day, directed against Compton, three not out, and Watson two not out. The attendance was about 5000.

For the first half-hour the two batsmen played Lindwall and his opposite number Johnston with fair comfort though without advancing the score far.

Watson, who scored 61 for Yorkshire at Sheffield against an Australian attack which included both these bowlers, took a two and a single off the first over from Lindwall and just afterwards drove Johnston very surely for four. These runs took him ahead of Compton, whose only run.

● Back Page, Col Four

The Queen, who returned overnight from Scotland, arrives at London Airport this afternoon to say goodbye to the Queen Mother and Princess Margaret before they left by Comet for Rhodesia. The Queen wears a rose-pink patterned dress, a small hat to match, black shoes and gloves.

The Queen Mother and Princess Margaret turn and smile as they go aboard the Comet.

THE QUEEN AT AIRPORT TO SAY FAREWELL

Evening Standard Reporter

The Queen and Prince Philip watched from the roof of a lounge at London Airport this afternoon as a Comet jetliner flew off, taking the Queen Mother and Princess Margaret to Rhodesia.

CHURCHILL IN GOOD SPIRITS

The Marquess of Salisbury, the new Acting Foreign Secretary, told the House of Lords to-day that Sir Winston Churchill was "in his usual good spirits."

At Chartwell to-day, Lord Cherwell, the Paymaster-General, was the guest at lunch of Sir Winston. Lady Churchill and Mrs. Anthony Beauchamp were also there.

Sir Winston spent the morning in bed working on Cabinet papers.

▲ Page Two, Col. Three

The Queen Mother and Prince Margaret had driven along the Great West Road to the airport past thousands of girls from factories and offices who lined the roadway to cheer.

The Queen and Prince Philip arrived a few minutes later and the Queen's standard was broken from the flagstaff in front of the waiting-room.

The Queen wore a rose pink patterned dress with a small hat to match and black shoes and gloves.

Princess Margaret was in a full-skirted light blue coat. Close to her left shoulder was a sprig of white heather. She wore a small round beret-type

CHEER LAST NIGHT'S SENSATIONAL RECORD-BREAKERS

BEN HOGAN.
With his cup last night.

HOGAN

'I feel like 60,' says Ben after winning the Open golf title with wonder rounds of 73, 71, 70, 68

From George Harley, Carnoustie, Friday

BEN HOGAN, tough little Texan wonder-golfer, gained a stupendous victory in the Open Championship here today — suffering from a heavy cold and after a night of little sleep.

Yet, playing in intermittent drizzle, Ben mastered his cold, his weariness, the formidable 7,200-yard course and many of the greatest golfers in the world by finishing with superb rounds of seventy and sixty-eight for a total of 282.

For hours a quadruple tie seemed probable, but Hogan's final course record round of sixty-eight shattered local dreams of a play off tomorrow.

He finished four strokes ahead of the gallant Dai Rees (seventy-three and seventy-one), American amateur Frank Stranahan (seventy-three and sixty-nine), Australian Peter Thomson (seventy-one and seventy-one) and Argentinian Toni Cerda (sixty-nine and seventy-one).

Tomorrow Hogan and his wife Valerie fly to Paris for a much needed holiday. The American champion has played golf every day since March 1 and admits that he is a very tired man. But he will keep a promise to play an exhibition in Paris for American Servicemen stationed in France.

He will not play in the Ryder Cup match with Britain in October, and will decide next year whether or not to return to defend the Open title.

"I've been travelling for nineteen years and have got a lot of mileage on me." he said. "I'm forty, but right now I feel like I'm sixty

"Quitting the game? No. sir. Why should I? I'm just getting where I started out to get when I was twelve."

Hogan's opinion of the course: "Extremely tough . . . you need radar to play some of those blind shots." His opinion of the enormous galleries: "Just wonderful. They sure are appreciative and the stewards did a great job."

Hogan's growing mastery of the course is reflected in his score: 73, 71, 70, 68. But he had staggered the crowds in the morning by taking six at the 17th, where he three putted after bunker trouble.

Flying Home

Stranahan, who shared the brief record of 69 with Cerda, is flying home to marry Ann Williams, a fashion model, next Friday. This millionaire's son might have taken home a wonderful wedding present but for the unbeatable Ben

HOW THEY FINISHED

B. HOGAN 73, 71, 70, 68—282.
F. STRANAHAN 70, 74, 73, 69—286.
D. J. REES 72, 70, 73, 71—286.
P. THOMSON 72, 72, 71, 71—286.
A. CERDA 75, 71, 69, 71—286.
287—R. de Vicenzo; 290—S. L. King; 291—A. D. Locke; 292—P. Alliss, E. C. Brown; 294—F. Daly; 295—M. Faulkner; 296—A. Lees.

SPEEDWAY RESULTS

NATIONAL LEAGUE—Div. 1. Bristol 39 (Bradley 11, Salmon 7) Wimbledon 45 (Moore 12, Mardon 9).

World Championship.—At Motherwell. Leading scorers: R Mountford Birmingham, 12; D. Forsberg, Sweden, 11; S. Pramberg, Sweden, 11; Graham Warren, Birmingham, 10; Ron Clarke, Odsal, 10.

At Leicester.—O. Nygren, Sweden, 14; L. Williams, Leicester, 13; K. McKinlay, Glasgow White City, 13; H Edwards, Belle Vue, 11.

TOUR DE FRANCE

JAN NOLTON, Holland, won stage eight of the Tour de France cycle race, covering the 214 miles—Nantes to Bordeaux—in 9h. 56m. 40s.

Van der Stockt, Belgium, was second—9h. 58m. 6s.—and Marcel Dierkens, Luxembourg, took third place.

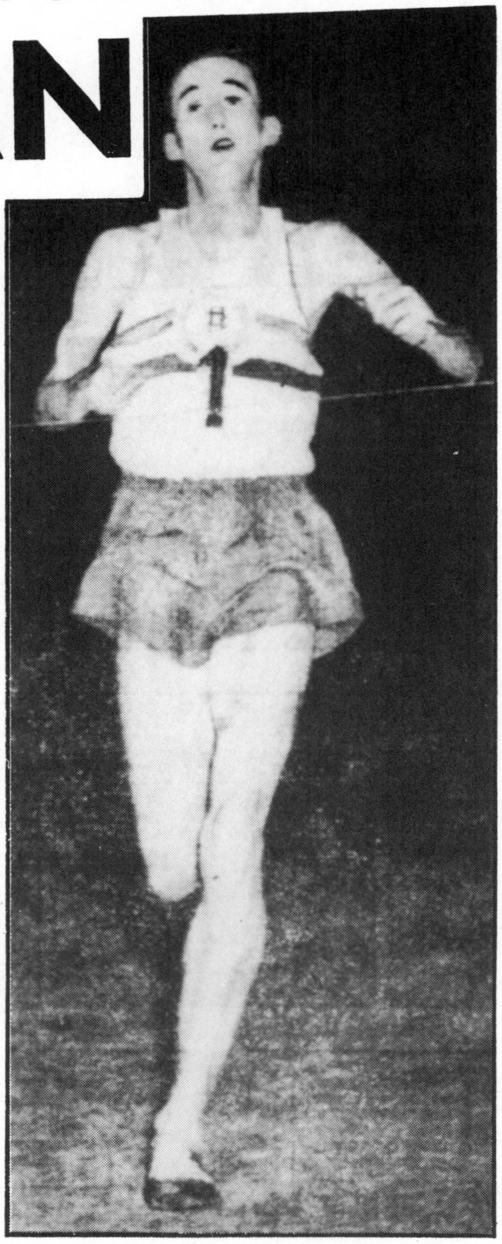

Gordon Pirie breaks the tape after his record-smashing six miles last night.

PIRIE

'It was easy,' says Gordon after smashing the world's six-mile record by 11.4 seconds

"DAILY MIRROR" REPORTER

GORDON PIRIE, 22, the Surrey bank clerk, was tucked up in bed last night as the first British athlete to break a world running record for fifteen years, and he is dreaming of another one today.

A few hours before, at the White City, in the A.A.A. championships, he ran six miles in 28m. 19.4s., 11.4s. faster than the record of the Flying Finn, Heino, in 1949. And at the close of this terrific performance Pirie said, "It was easy."

A heavy cold made it doubtful whether he would be able to compete in the championships. His parents, on holiday in the North of England, returned home to Coulsdon, especially to look after him and get rid of his cold.

Chanting All the Way

Thousands of school children invited to go along and see British athletics, cheered Pirie for the twenty-four laps chanting, "Come on, Gordon."

Twice an announcer had rebuked them for shouting but no one cared as Pirie ticked off the miles as accurately as clockwork.

His lapping was remarkably even. A car driver could not have been more regular for this is how the six miles went:

First mile: 4m 42s.; Second: 4m. 37.8s.; Third: 4m. 42.8s.; Fourth: 4m. 42.6s.; Fifth: 4m. 49s.; Sixth: 4m. 45.2s

Not content with last night's achievement, he is going for a second title today — in the three miles, which holder Chris Chataway is not defending.

The time of Frank Sando in second place was 28m. 47.2s., a fifth of a second inside Pirie's existing British record—yet he finished 200 yards behind. Third was Ian Binnie, of Scotland.

COUNTY TABLE

	P	W	L	D	Nd	1st Inns Ld. L.	1st Inns Ld. D	P
Middx	16	7	2	5	1	1	4	116
Sussex	14	6	3	5	0	1	4	92
Glam	15	7	2	5	1	0	2	92
Surrey	14	6	3	5	0	0	3	84
Lancs	13	5	1	5	2	0	3	72
Hants	14	5	3	6	0	1	2	72
Leics	15	4	4	7	0	3	3	72
Gloucs	13	4	2	6	1	0	3	60
Warwk	15	3	4	7	1	0	6	60
N'hnts	15	3	0	9	2	0	4	58
Derby	14	4	4	4	2	1	1	56
Worcs	14	4	6	3	1	1	1	56
Essex	15	1	4	10	0	0	6	36
Yorks	13	1	3	7	2	0	5	32
Notts	14	2	4	7	1	1	1	32
Som'set	17	2	11	3	1	0	0	24
Kent	15	1	9	4	1	1	1	20

Middlesex and Northants 6pts each for tie

TV and Radio

TELEVISION

1.15 England v. Australia. 3.15 Aqua View. 3.25 Athletics: A.A.A. Championships. 4.30 England v. Australia. 6.30-7.0 Children: Gordon Gets Going: The Appleyards. 7.15 Week's Newsreels. 8.25 Interlude. 8.30 "Stand By To Shoot." 9.0 Test Match. 9.15 Evening Alfresco. 10.30 News.

HOME

6.30 Organ 7.0 News 7.15 Record Roundabout 7.50 Lift Up Your Hearts! 8.0 News. 8.15 Revue Orchestra. 9.0 Braden 9.30 Bernard Monshin Rio Tango Band 10.15 Service. 10.30 Music While You Work. 11.0 Records to Remember 11.55 Star Bill.

1.0 News. 1.10 Riders of the Range 1.40 Burl Ives (records). 1.55 Cricket scoreboard. 2.0 Tottenham Citadel Salvation Army Band. 2.30 Oscar Rabin Band 3.0 Northern Orchestra. 4.0 Plays: "The Question of Latin": (4 23 app.) "Young Leonardo." 5.0 Children

6.0 News 6.25 Those Were the Days! 7.15 In Town Tonight 7.45 Week in Westminster 8.0 Variety Playhouse.

9.0 News 9.15 Play: "The Corn is Green," by Emlyn Williams. 10.45 Lighten Our Darkness 11.0 News

LIGHT

9.0 News. 9.10 Children's Choice 9.55 Five to Ten. 10.0 Organ. 10.30 Music While You Work 11.0 Welsh Orchestra. 11.45 Parliament. 12.0 Frank Weir Orchestra. 12.30 England v Australia 1.35 Meyer's Ensemble (records). 1.45 Listen on Saturday. 2.0 Variety Orchestra 2.20 Going Places. 4.15 RAMC Band 4.45 England v Australia. 5.0 Jazz Club 5.30 A.A.A Championships. 5.45 England v Australia. 6.35 Organ. 7.0 News. Newsreel 7.30 Archers. 8.30 Music for Everybody

10.0 News. 10.15 England v. Australia. 10.20 Ted Heath Music. 11.0 Record Rendezvous 11 56 News.

THIRD

6.0 Szymanowski 6.45 Summer Pasture. 7.50 Boyd Neel Orchestra. 8.35 Talk. 8.55 Orchestra. 9.35 Reading. 10.25 Kentucky Sings 10.55 Anthology 11.25 Tregian's Anthology.

MIDLAND

3.0 Peter Ustinov (records). 3.10 Tribute in Sound. 5.25 West. 6.15 News 6.25 Sport.

NORTH

3.0 Out and About. 5.0 Children 6.15 News

N. IRELAND

2.0 Ravenhill Temperance Flute Band. 2.20 Interlude (records). 3.0 North. 3.30 Cricket: Ireland v. Scotland. 4.0 North 5.0 North 6.15 News. 7.15 Variety. 7.30 Ulster Sports Report.

SCOTTISH

3.0 Folk Dances 3.30 N. Ireland. 5.0 Children. 6.15 News. 6.50 Scottish Dance Music 7.20 Story. 7.35 Scots Songs 10.45 Prayers.

WELSH

5.25 West 6.25 News. 6.35 Newyddion. 6.45 Welsh. 7.0 Llangollen Musical Eisteddfod

WEST

11.30 Hampshire v Somerset. 2.30 Hampshire v. Somerset. 5.25 Children. 6.25 Sport.

The rain has him worried

From ROSS HALL
Old Trafford, Friday.

THERE must be easier ways of earning free board and lodging than skippering a side batting first at Manchester when there is only ninety-three minutes' play on the second day.

I don't envy Lindsay Hassett. He has more to worry about tonight than Len Hutton.

O.K., Australia, with 221 on the board for the loss of only three wickets, look to be very nicely placed. Against defeat, perhaps. But what about trying to force a victory?

Hassett can't afford to declare at his present score. Yet there are only three days' play left,

He could go on till lunch time tomorrow, build up his score to 350 and then declare. But what happens to Hassett if England—going in to bat with the conditions still against the bowler, a treacherous run up and a wet ball—bat through to Monday night and a formidable total?

Australia would be left to bat on the fifth day, and on what could be a bad enough wicket to make 150 runs assume gigantic proportions. No, Mr. Lindsay Hassett had good cause tonight to think the same about Manchester's weather as the disappointed thousands of spectators.

THE SECOND DAY'S PLAY

AUSTRALIA—First Innings

Hassett, b Bailey	26
Morris, b Bedser	1
Miller, b Bedser	17
Harvey, not out	105
Hole, not out	66
Extras	6
Total (3 wkts)	221

Bowling: Bedser 2 for 60, Bailey 1 for 83, Wardle 0 for 53, Laker 0 for 19.

To bat: De Courcy, Davidson, Archer, Lindwall, Hill, Langley.

Fall of wickets: 1—15, 2—48, 3—48.

ENGLAND. — Hutton (capt.), Edrich, Graveney, Compton, Watson, Simpson, Bailey, Evans, Laker, Wardle, Bedser.

ROSEWALL'S SHOCK DEFEAT

Ken Rosewall, 18, Australia, was beaten in the singles semi-final of the Swiss tennis championships by Vladimir Skonecki, Poland, 6—0, 6—2, 0—6, 1—6, 6—3.

SANDOWN, MANCHESTER WINNERS

SANDOWN, Going good.

2.0—**MARGARIS** (J. Wilson, 100-8), 1; **Devoted** (Sirett, 11-2), 2; **El-Bee-A** (Piggott, 7-1), 3. 7 ran. 3 l, 4. Also: Lexicon (6-4 f) Honest Joe, Corn of the Cob, Cottonblossom. Tote: 32/3; 13/7, 11/6: forecast £20 8/9.

2.30—**BLARNEY STONE** (L Piggott, 13-8), 1; **High Principle** (Rickaby, 11-2), 2; **Upton Court** (Carter, 33-1) 3. 9 ran. ½ l, 6. Also: Gulliano, Pirate II, Toreno, Connemara, Ticatica II, Perpetual Kip. Tote: 5/1; 2/11, 4/2, 15/3.

3.0—**TUDOR HONEY** (E Mercer, 10-1), 1; **Ozbeg** (Gdn Richards, 6-4 f), 2; **Fair Risk** (Gosling, 9-2), 3. 6 ran. 2 l, ½. Also: Ever-Ready, Prudence, Arabis. Tote: 29/3; 7/7, 3/3: forecast 69/9.

3.30—**MOUNTAIN KING** (E. Smith, 7-4 f), 1; **Friseur** (Gdn Richards, 2-1), 2; **Brolly** (Rickaby, 100-30), 3. 4 ran. 3 l, sh hd. Also: Victory Roll. Tote: 5/8: forecast 12/7.

4.0.—**GUYS AND DOLLS** (J Sirett, 4-1), 1; **Blazing** (J Mercer, 7-2), 2; **Queen's Bench** (Durr, 5-2) 3. 4 ran. 5 l, ½. Also: Poeticus (6-4 f). Tote: 10/4; forecast 31/1.

4.30.—**RED INK** (W Rickaby, 3-1), 1; **Saucy Boy** (Wilson, 3-1), 2; **Fairikos** (Fordyce, 11-2), 3. 4 ran. 2 l, ½. Also: King's Beeches (11-8 f). Tote: 7/3; forecast 18/11.

Tote Double: £32

MANCHESTER: Going soft on top.

6.45—**FLEET LANE** (P Povall, 11-2), 1; **Clive** (evens f), 2; **Brunnell's Verdict** (20-1), 3. 8 ran. ½ l, 6. Tote: 10/-; 2/10, 2/4, 9/11.

7.15—**SYLVAN** (D Smith, 2-7 f), 1; **Black Vein** (100-7), 2; **Devondellah** (5-1), 3. 5 ran. 2 l, 4. Tote: 2/3; forecast 7/8.

7.45.—**LEPIDOPTIC** (W Snaith, 11-4 f), 1; **Star Lyon** (7-2), 2; **Durham Castle** (7-2), 3. 7 ran. 3 l; 1. Tote: 7/4; 4/9, 5/11; forecast 38/10.

8.10.—**STONE FOX** (J. Etherington, 100-30), 1; **Quiver II** (100-8), 2; **Hoosharar** (10-1), 3. 11 ran. ½ l, same. (Spring Day 3-1 f) Tote: 8/11; 4/1, 11/2, 5/6.

8.35—**NELL GWYNNE** (W Snaith, evens f), 1; **Sirelis** (9-4), 2; **Wild Honey** (9-2), 3. 6 ran. 3 l, 5. Tote: 4/7; 2/6; 2/11; forecast 9/7.

9.0.—**PARAKEET** (Sime, 6-4 f), 1; **Primette** (9-4), 2; **Mavourneen** (4-1), 3. 7 ran. 3 l; same. Tote: 5/8, 3/2, 3/5; forecast 11/4.

Tote double: £4/7/-.

CRICKET SCOREBOARD

NOTTS v. NORTHANTS. At Nottingham. **Notts** 245 and 17 for 0. **Northants** 286 (Dooland 4 for 91). **Abandoned as a draw.**

WARWICK v. SURREY. At Birmingham. **Warwick** 257 and 133 (Loader 4 for 45, Surridge 3 for 54). **Surrey** 151 and 99 (Pritchard 5 for 48, Grove 4 for 31). **Warwick won by 140 rurs.**

DERBY v. KENT. At Chesterfield. **Derby** 300 for 3 dec. **Kent** 146 for 3 (Fagg 87). **Drawn.**

WORCESTER v. LANCS. At Worcester. **Lancs** 291 for 8 dec (Perks 4 for 119). **Worcester** 234 for 6 (Richardson 67; Tattersall 3 for 72). **Drawn.**

LEICESTER v. SOMERSET. At Leicester. **Somerset** 248 and 221 (Buse 67; Walsh 4 for 42). **Leicester** 379 for 7 dec (Hall 3 for 101) and 91 for 3 (Hall 3 for 27). **Leicester won by 7 wkts.**

YORKS v. GLOUCESTER. At Sheffield. **Yorks** 330 for 4 dec. **Gloucester** 97 (Foord 5 for 33, Illingworth 3 for 4) and 29 for 2. **Drawn.**

TODAY'S MATCHES

Manchester.—England v. Australia. 11.30-6.30. **Colchester.**—Essex v. Lancs. 11.30-6.30. **Gloucester.** — Gloucester v. Glamorgan. 11.30-6.30. **Portsmouth.** — Hants v. Somerset. 11.30-7. **Blackheath.**—Kent v. Surrey. 11.30-6.30. **Ashby-de-la-Zouch.** — Leicester v. Derby. 11.30-7. **Northampton.**—Northants v. Warwick. 11.30-6.30. **Worthing.**—Sussex v. Worcester. 11.30-6.30. **Bradford.**—Yorks v. Middlesex. 11.30-7. **Nottingham.**—Notts v RAF. 11.30-7.

THE ASHES REGAINED AFTER TWENTY YEARS: COMPTON AND EDRICH MAKING THEIR WAY THROUGH VOCIFEROUS HERO-WORSHIPPERS TO THE PAVILION AT THE OVAL ON WEDNESDAY, AUGUST 19.

Never can the Oval have seen greater expressions of enthusiasm than those called forth by Compton's winning hit to the boundary which at just before three on the afternoon of August 19 brought the Ashes—last won in Australia in 1932-33 —back to England in the first victory in England against Australia since 1926. Excitement over the fifth and final Test Match of 1953 had mounted during the afternoon, and with the score at 127, only five runs were needed to win. A single

by W. J. Edrich brought Denis Compton facing A. R. Morris, with only four runs needed. Shouts enjoined him to hit a six, and off the fifth ball he hit a four. The match and the Ashes were England's — and the huge crowd made a rush for the Pavilion. Edrich and Compton had to run the gauntlet of vociferous hero-worshippers, who shouted, tried to slap them on the back, or pat them on the head as they raced down the narrow lane which police managed to keep clear for them.

B

DAILY EXPRESS

No. 16,805 | FRIDAY MAY 7 1954 | CONTROLLING SHAREHOLDER LORD BEAVERBROOK | Weather: Mainly fine | Price 1½d.

EXPRESSMAN Peron's police hold Buenos Aires man — **BANNISTER** The mile 'shrinks' to 3 mins. 59.4 secs. — **GENEVA** Molotov says to Eden: 'Let's get together' — **BEVAN** 'Nonsense' he shouts at Mr. Attlee

AT LAST—THE 4-MINUTE MILE

THIS IS IT—THE DREAM OF ATHLETES COMES TRUE . . . BUT FIRST, SOME BREATH

BANNISTER DOES IT

English victory beats world

Express Staff Reporter

THE dream of world athletes through the years was achieved yesterday by an Englishman — 25-year-old Roger Bannister, who became the first man on earth to run a mile in under four minutes.

His feat at Oxford last evening—against a 20-mile-an-hour cross-wind—was equal in dramatic achievement to the crashing of the sound barrier in the air.

Bannister's time, officially recorded, was **3MINS. 59.4SECS.**—beating the world record of Sweden's Gundar Haegg by 2secs.

Lap 1 : 57.5 secs.

It happened at his old university track—he is now a student at St. Mary's Hospital, Paddington—and 45 minutes before the attempt, it had been called off.

It was to be Bannister's first race this season and his first attempt at the four-minute mile. And it was a cold, damp evening with lightning streaking far off.

The flag of St. George, flying on nearby St. John's Church, was fluttering in a stiff wind.

Bannister looked at the flag looked at the sky—and went back to his dressing-room "It would be stupid to try it today," he said

Twenty-five minutes later he came out again. He looked up at the flag of St. George—the wind had dropped a bit. There was a double rainbow over the church. Bannister said : **"RIGHT. I'LL TRY IT."**

Lap 2 : 60.7 secs.

What was he trying? Experts had said it was impossible. Way back in 1886 Britain's Walter C. George had made the world gasp with a mile in 4mins. 12.7secs.

After half a century of improved techniques, Britain's Sydney Wooderson clipped the time to 4mins. 6.4secs. And then in 1945 Gundar Haegg got it down to 4mins. 1.4secs.

For nine years those 1.4secs. had tantalised the world's athletes. Santee was trying hard in America and Landy in Australia—and Bannister wanted to put Britain there first

For the past three weeks he had been sitting for examinations.

But **"RIGHT, I'LL TRY IT,"** he said at six o'clock last evening.

Lap 3 : 62.3 secs.

He lined up with Chris Chataway and Chris Brasher for the A.A.A. against Oxford University—in an utterly English scene.

No tension. A couple of thousand people thinly lining the track. Straw-hatted boys lounging under golf umbrellas.

And then : First lap—57.5secs. Second lap—1 minute 58.2secs. Third lap—3 minutes 0.5secs. Could he do it? The fourth lap in under 59.5secs.?

He didn't know then how fast he was running. But he ran the lap in 58.9secs.—and ran straight on into the almanacs of glory.

He finished fighting for breath, his head rolling with fatigue—and as he broke the tape, he fell headlong into waiting arms.

He was unconscious—and so the last man at the track to realise his success.

Lap 4 : 58.9 secs.

The crowd cheered and cheered. Bannister then murmured feebly: "Did I do it?" And then he stumbled off to thank everybody who had helped.

He said last night : "This has been overrated. The important thing is to run against competitors—not against the clock."

But no such modest view was taken by his parents, who went at the last minute to see him run—or by his fellow-athletes.

Gordon Pirie, Britain's other hope, said in Bonn : "Gosh, that's fantastic! Can I beat it? I don't know"

Sydney Wooderson said : "It is absolutely wonderful. I always thought he would be the first to do it."

Australia's **John Landy**, training in Finland, said : "This is great, great, great. He's a great runner."

Gundar Haegg, whose record was broken, said in Norway : "I fancied Bannister to do it."

Mr. Dan Ferris, secretary of the U.S. Amateur Athletic Union, said "Delighted. He's a great athlete."

And last night the flag of St. George fluttered still more proudly over St. John's Church, Oxford.

● Bannister, first man to beat the four-minute mile, breaks the tape. . . . There was electricity along that side-line. . . . He was fighting for breath, his head rolling with fatigue—but his stride was superb.

YES, I MIGHT DO EVEN BETTER

By ROGER BANNISTER

—as told to a Daily Express Reporter.

I HAVE never felt so good in all my life and I am so glad it took an Englishman to do this thing before America's Wes Santee and the other chaps got down to it.

When I got into the last bend this evening I wasn't thinking of anything in particular. I just couldn't think. I saw the tape faintly ahead, put everything into getting there and that was the last I knew about it.

You know I think people have been frightened of this four-minute record. It has been rather like the sound barrier. Now it has been broken and I am sure other people will break it too.

I think in a way that the wind may have cut me down by two or three seconds and that I might make even better time in the future.

It was not until late today that I decided to try for the mile record because of the bad weather but if you wait for the right weather in this country you wait a long time.

However, when I found I had broken the record I went off with friends to Vincent's Club at Oxford and had a pint of shandy.

Two peaks

Then I was rushed off to London and here I am. All I have had to eat since I ran the race is two sandwiches.

I think there could be a great race between Landy of Australia and Santee and myself.

Races against opponents do not tend to produce so fast a time because you are watching their tactics.

I am looking forward to doing well at the Empire Games at Vancouver this summer and at the games in Berne.

I have enjoyed every minute of running and it has given me wonderful opportunities for travelling. But I regard my medical career as more important.

Even today, if I'd considered the weather absolutely hopeless I would have waited to try another day. I feel that there are two peaks in my training this year.

One is the four-minute mile, and then there are the Empire Games.

I don't really know if anybody would be interested if I reduced my time for the mile.

I feel that the increment by which records are broken will steadily diminish. Instead of records being broken by seconds it will be a matter of tenths of seconds.

I would, in fact, be more interested in beating Santee alone than in achieving a faster time for the mile.

His problem

And slim, six-foot, fair-haired Roger Bannister said this to a TV audience from Lime Grove—just over two hours after the 6 p.m. race :—

THE main problem was the weather. We were worried about the very strong winds which might slow us down so much that we would not be able to run it under four minutes. I particularly wanted someone from this country to do it.

We set off with our plans fairly uncertain to run very hard, and then if the wind did not tire us too much then I was going to see if I could try to do it under four minutes.

I have been training with Brasher during the last three months.

Brasher set off and set the pace for the first half-mile. He reached the first lap in just under 60 seconds. In the third lap Chataway took over and reached the three-quarter mile in a shade over three minutes.

Tired

So I had to try to take over from them and do the last lap in about 59 seconds.

I was not really certain I was doing it, and I was tired, and it was not possible to assess the speed as accurately as you could earlier in the race.

I was particularly happy that the occasion should have been at Oxford where I ran my first mile ever in 1947, when I was second.

I did a time of just over five minutes.

It went big in New York

Bannister was big news in the New York newspapers. It was the leading report on the sports page of the New York Post. And the New York World Telegram devoted three columns to the achievement.

DID I DO IT?—HE GASPED

● Bannister, eyes closed, has a support-escort. He was the last to know he had made sports history.

● *In the duffel coat : Bannister's adviser, Franz Stampfl. On the right : George Truelove, A.A.A. team manager.*

A little party

Roger Bannister arrived at the Royal Court Theatre in Sloane-square as the audience was leaving last night. He strode through, unrecognised, and ran up a staircase to a club over the theatre.

He was joined at a table by a tall fair girl in an off-the-shoulder green gown. They sat talking and watching the dancing.

The debate continued . . .

AT the Oxford Union Society's debate last night a motion was put forward that the House should adjourn for 3 minutes 59.4 seconds in honour of Bannister's achievement. There were loud cheers, but the president, Mr. Raghavan Iyer, an Indian, said the motion could not be accepted as no notice had been given.

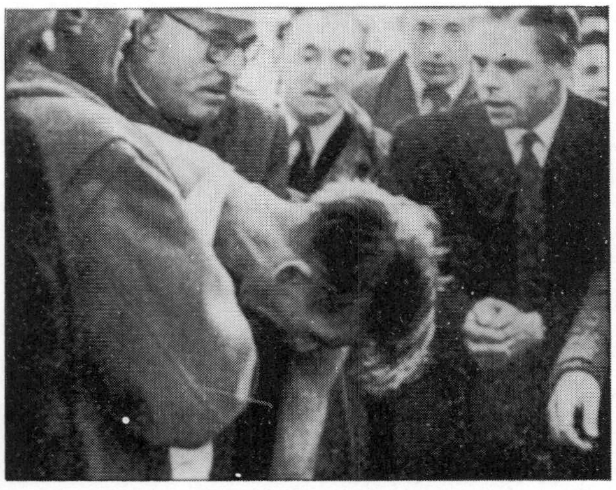

● A man clasps anxious hands. And Bannister, completely exhausted after his terrific effort, doubles up to regain breath.

'Nonsense' shouts Bevan at leaders

Express Political Correspondent

MR. ANEURIN BEVAN shouted "Nonsense" last night when Socialist leaders gave reasons for postponing the "free-for-all" inquiry into Mr. Morrison's attack on him.

Mr. Morrison—in a magazine article—has accused Mr. Bevan of losing seats for the party.

This personal attack caused many moderates in the party to demand an immediate meeting of all Socialist M.P.s to discuss Mr. Morrison's defiance of the rules.

But last night the party leaders, who have agreed to such a meeting, got it postponed until May 19—*a day after* the executive meets.

The idea

The timing of the special meeting made the Bevanites angry because they believe that the executive—*on the day before*—will issue orders to curb them.

Last night Mr. Attlee explained that such an idea had not occurred to him.

He said the meeting could not be held next week because there was no suitable room available—and it would clash with other engagements.

This brought shouts of derision from the Bevanites. Afterwards one said : "There are 1,100 rooms in the Houses of Parliament—more than enough even for all our splinter groups."

All-night search for boy, 4

BONN, Thursday. — Hundreds of Cameron Highlanders, military police, and German police staged an all-night search of the woods around Luneburg to find a missing four-year-old British boy—Ian Frazer, son of Corporal P. Frazer, of the Cameron Battalion. His body was found in a pond just outside the city—drowned when he fell from a boat.—Express News Service.

More at work

Unemployment in Britain last month touched its lowest level for six months. There were 316,600 out of work on April 12—60,000 fewer than in April last year, and 150,000 fewer than in April 1952.

Homes in a hurry

New houses were being completed in Britain during March at an all-time record rate of over 404,000 a year. Total for the month was 33,709 highest since the war.

Visit cancelled

The Duchess of Gloucester, who was to have gone to Northern Ireland today for two days, cancelled the visit last night because of influenza. She acted on medical advice.

DAILY EXPRESS MAN ARRESTED AGAIN

BUENOS AIRES, Thursday. Mr. John Comben, staff correspondent of the Daily Express, was arrested today for the second time in a year.

He was put in the Villa Devoto prison in Buenos Aires, charged with sending news to London "which is inconvenient to the Argentine Republic."

On May 28 last Mr. Comben was released after 35 hours' detention during which he was questioned about his residence permit.

An apology for an "unfortunate mistake" was given later. Comben then reported to the Daily Express the incidents he had seen in prison knife fights and a suicide attempt.

It is understood that the charge now preferred against him relates to that story.

Later Mr. Comben was released. No date was fixed for the hearing. Express News Service.

Round-up (cont'd.)

CAIRO, Thursday. Twenty more army officers, making a total of 45, have been arrested for "plotting".—A.P.

BE FRIENDS SAYS MOLOTOV

Talks with Eden go smoothly

From DEREK MARKS: Geneva, Thursday

A "LET'S-GET-TOGETHER" offer was made by Mr. Molotov to Mr. Eden at a dinner which the Foreign Secretary gave for the Soviet delegates to the Geneva conference last night.

This morning, in accordance with Allied practice, Mr. Eden sent a report of what went on at the dinner to General Bedell Smith, leader of the U.S. delegation, and France's Foreign Minister, M. Bidault.

'EASIER'

Mr. Eden told them that Mr. Molotov was in his most friendly mood and had suggested it was much easier to deal with Britain than America

Why, asked Mr. Molotov, did not Britain and Russia get together to settle outstanding world problems?

All sides rate the dinner as the most friendly which British and Russian diplomats have had since the war.

Mr. Eden and Mr. Molotov quickly reached decisions on procedure to be followed when talks

PAGE TWO, COL. FIVE

3 a.m. LATEST

3 WARSHIPS SEEK PLANE

HALIFAX, Nova Scotia, Thursday. — Three warships sped tonight to a point off Halifax where a naval plane with four people aboard was believed to have crashed into the sea.—A.P.

CENtral 8000

REQUIEM REPORT

Magyars chant songs of victory over the 'Masters'

ENGLAND (SEVEN DOWN) R.I.P.

Broadis goal stops slam

HUNGARY 7 ENGLAND 1

From DESMOND HACKETT: Budapest, Sunday

THIS is not so much a report as a requiem to mourn the passing of England's football greatness. It is the sad story of a team ruthlessly and scientifically dissected and strewn around the People's Stadium to-day. It is the grim news of England's greatest-ever international defeat.

It was all done to the inspiring music of a 90,000-voice choir.

They chanted in an ecstasy of joy as their heroes beat us unmercifully and, worst of all, with laughing, nonchalant ease.

It was an experience England paid too much for in the last bitter seconds.

This is something when you realise that the Hungarians whipped in nine goals in 30 minutes in the first half, then easily slammed down on the shooting trigger and merely coasted to a goal in four minutes in the second half.

HOPEFUL

Record-making

Scotland beat England 7 2 at Glasgow in 1878. Scotland beat England 6 1 at the Oval in 1881 but never before has an England team been beaten by such a margin as 7—1.

'Your forwards went for a siesta'

From GIANNI BRERA

— Sports reporter with the Gazzetta Dello Sport Milan, Italy, who gives a neutral view of the game.

WHEN I saw you play Hungary at Wembley I think then that England wish learn the lesson that her football is no longer in fashion. But you learn nothing. You try to beat this Hungarian team with the same technique that failed you so dramatically at Wembley. That does not make sense to me.

QUOTES

● We came with a very experimental side and it simply was not good enough. England does not have the outstanding players it used to have — and this is particularly true of the defence. — England team manager WALTER WINTER-BOTTOM

● It was a clean game and they really deserved to win. They have a great team — England skipper BILLY WRIGHT

● The re-orientation between Hungary's forwards is perfect. The Hungarians are forced to switch so very smash to intercept. They split in any — England centre half SYD OWEN

● We admired the spirit of the English team. They fought enthusiastically even after the sixth goal. Bill Wright is a great sportsman — Hungarian team manager GUSTAV SEBES

TRAINING SYSTEM IS AT FAULT

From FERRY WIMMER

Top-ranking Austrian sports writer who also gave his verdict on the England-Hungary game in November

WHEN I wrote for you on Hungary's 6 3 victory in England last November I did not expect that an England team could twice be beaten so badly by the same plan.

ONE MAN'S JOB

Overheard

● An aye, there's only one thing left we'll have to teach the Europeans how to play cricket.

● As a Scotsman and a neutral I sympathise entirely with the English.

● What do you expect with none of us Irish in the English team.

● Why don't they send Chelsea to Hungary? They'd sort them out.

Uruguay centre sent off

[cartoon caption:] THE H-BOMB   7-1   HUNGARY

PERSONALITY PARADE

EDITED BY SYDNEY HULLS

Rona wins match in four jumpers

LAST ball of the match... one wicket to fall time-tanned but frozen New Zealanders crouched round the wicket.

Cold Pirie

GORDON PIRIE broke another record when he won the Surrey mile in 4mins. 16.6secs. at Motspur Park.

Clear view

Cotton-picking

Ken's double

School 'cert'

Success!

Sherpa Mahmood

SPORTS SUMMARY

ASSOCIATION

CRICKET

PEACOCK BOOSTS THE FAVOURITE

By THE SCOUT

"THE nicest, kindest, most sensible horse I have ever had through my hands and the best." That is Harry Peacock's opinion of Derby favourite Rowston Manor.

The big chestnut colt, accompanied by James Curtis who rides him in most of his work, will leave Richmond for Epsom next Sunday.

INTENSIVE WORK

ONE DOUBT

James Curtis, in charge of Rowston Manor, prepares to give the favourite his morning exercise at Middleham, Yorkshire.

FIFTY ACE CYCLISTS RIDE IN TOUR

By RONALD WHITE

FIFTY star British and Continental road-racing cyclists will battle out the Daily Express £1500 14-day Tour of Britain starting on Whit Sunday, June 6.

THE SCOUT RACE CARDS   LAWN TENNIS on Page 7

FA must give the 'B' team jobs to experienced men

By BOB PENNINGTON

ENGLAND'S "B" Boys, beaten by the "B" teams of Yugoslavia (2 1 last week) and Switzerland (2-0 on Saturday), flew back to London yesterday, shamed and humiliated.

Arsenal to play in Russia

Arsenal have agreed to play two matches in Russia in October the first visit by a Football League club to the Soviet Union.

AUSTRALIAN SOCCER

Greyhound hints

Sports diary

JAEGER WEEK END

casual
comfortable
correct

Blazer, double-breasted, navy ...
Single-breasted ...
Sports Shirts, jersey slash-neck. Striped & plain ...
Slipovers ...
Slacks, self-supporting ...
Worsted ...
Casual Jackets in many different tweeds, from £7.15
The famous '51' Socks ... 6/6

Go to your nearest Jaeger

THE GAMBOLS

by BARRY APPLEBY

DIRK STOREY

by GEORGE DAVIES

DAILY Mirror

MON AUG. 9 1954

1½d FORWARD WITH THE PEOPLE

No. 15,779

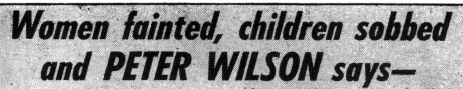

I FELT DIRTY AND ASHAMED

WEDNESDAY IS POOLS DAY

START the football pools season right. This WEDNESDAY IS POOLS DAY in the "Daily Mirror."

It will mark the start of a great, NEW Pools Service conducted by Longsight, the best and brightest of newspaper experts.

Each Wednesday throughout the football season he will give SPECIAL forecasts, selections and hints to help YOU win dividends.

Starting on Wednes-day with the Scottish matches which get the pools season under way, the Special Pools Service will include:

● New ideas for landing BIG dividends.

● COMPLETE forecasts with past results.

● Details of sequences.

● And Longsight's special selections for the Treble Chance, Results, Three Draws, and Aways Pools.

COUNTESS, 20, KILLED IN FALL FROM CLIFF

TWENTY-YEAR-OLD Irene, Countess Blucher died after falling 60ft. from a cliff at Pleinmont Guernsey, yesterday.

The countess, on hol'day from Germany, was climbing a 300ft. cliff when she fell 40ft. on to a ledge, then 20ft. to a beach covered with boulders.

Two ambulance men were lowered with ropes but they could not take the unconscious girl to the cliff top.

They called an ambulance crew at the cliff top on their walkie-talkie radio and the marine ambulance Flying Christine was rushed from St. Peter Port eight miles away.

The Flying Christine took the countess off the beach, but she died as the boat returned to harbour.

THIS is the fantastic scene as Jim Peters collapses near the end of the Empire Games twenty-six-mile marathon race in Vancouver. Officials gape team-mate John Savidge, kneeling (right), looks on anxiously... and in the background (left) a woman is led away, unable to watch as Peters staggers and sways—to the wrong finishing line. In the stands woman fainted, children sobbed, even tough men found the ten minutes of horror hard to stomach.

It was a sight that made PETER WILSON write: "I NEVER WANT TO SEE ANOTHER MARATHON RACE IN WHICH SOMEONE — ANYONE — CAN'T STEP IN AND SAY THAT THIS IS NO LONGER SPORT." Wilson's great story of the amazing marathon drama, which starts below, prompts us to print this headline—

WAS THIS SPORT?

From PETER WILSON, Vancouver, Sunday

SPORT can be heroic or routine. It is sometimes superlative and occasionally shabby.

You can thrill to it or yawn through it. But it should never revolt you, make you squirm, force you to close your eyes and feel dirty and ashamed, as though you had paid a black market price to be a 'privileged' spectator at a public execution.

That was how I felt yesterday at the Empire Games in Vancouver when we had the Everest and the Hades of Sport. The Everest was, of course the mile race with regal Roger Bannister beating eagle-beaked John Landy of Australia, and for the first time in athletic history two men splintering the four-minute barrier. (Bannister 3m 58 8s,. Landy 3m 59 6s.)

Yet this record-breaking epoch - making athletic superlative was within a few minutes wiped from the memory of the 32,573 fans who crowded Canada's Empire Stadium by one of the most gut - wrenching spectacles I have ever had to sit through—in or out of sport.

IF YOU ARE SQUEAMISH, DON'T READ ON I'm going to tell you about the end of the marathon race—a finish which had women fainting in the stands, children sobbing and tough men wanting to be sick—and that is the literal truth. Picture the scene:

It's a blazing hot day and down the hill winding through the wooden

Continued on Page 15

DAILY EXPRESS

No. 17,125   MONDAY JUNE 13 1955   Weather: Mainly fine, showers   Price 1½d.

I SAW IT ALL reports Basil Cardew from Le Mans disaster circuit

RACE CASUALTIES OVER 150

DIAGRAM SHOWS THAT SPLIT SECOND BEFORE A CAR STOOD ON ITS NOSE

HAWTHORN PULLS INTO THE PITS · MACKLIN PULLS OUT TO PASS HAWTHORN · FANGIO · LEVEGH'S CAR STRIKES MACKLIN'S, EXPLODES, AND ITS ENGINE TEARS INTO THE CROWD

HAWTHORN WINS

'Most tragic day of my life'

From BASIL CARDEW
LE MANS, Sunday.

MIKE HAWTHORN won the 24-hour "race of death" at Le Mans today in a British Jaguar at a record 107.09 miles an hour.

Second was another British car, an Aston Martin, and third another Jaguar.

It was a race that cost 77 spectators their lives and 77 others more or less serious injury when a German Mercedes somersaulted at 180 miles an hour into an enclosure.

Said Hawthorn when he stopped to the chequered black and white end-of-race flag : " It was the most tragic race of my life. It could have been my greatest."

147 minutes

It was in the warm, bright evening sunshine of yesterday when the race was only 147 minutes old that the moment of the first horror arrived.

I saw it all.

This race is a carnival occasion every year for a quarter of a million French people and some thousands had paid to watch the race from an enclosure near the pits.

Down the narrow—too narrow—winding road approaching the pits came the rising snarl of a group of cars. Faster, faster.

Men in shirtsleeves looked over the heads of girls in gay summer prints craning forward to see who was leading.

'Les Anglais'

They murmured : " Les Anglais," for there came two cars in the racing green of Britain—26-year-old Mike Hawthorn in a new D type Jaguar and 36-year-old Lance Macklin in an Austin-Healey.

Hawthorn slowed and was pulling in to his pit on the right to hand over to his co-driver, Londoner Ivor Bueb.

And then the spectators saw the silver Mercedes driven by 50-year-old Pierre Levegh of France streaking up at 180 miles an hour to pass the smaller and slower car of Macklin.

He pulled to the left to pass Hawthorn. It was then I saw the Mercedes touch the rear end of the Austin-Healey.

Macklin went into a terrifying broadside skid for 100 yards. But hardly anyone was watching him.

Every eye was on the fantastic sight of the Mercedes rising up on its streamlined nose and sailing upside down over the Austin-Healey which was spinning dizzily like a demented roulette.

Like rocket

The Mercedes tore on into the enclosure, airborne still, mowing down people in the enclosure like a sweeping scythe.

The car's wheels and components parts burst among the crowd like grape shot. The petrol tanks exploded and rained down fire.

The impact wrenched the engine from its mountings and it shot onwards like a rocket, cutting people down in its path for 50 yards.

What was left of the car finished up on the track again burning.

Macklin got out of his car unhurt, but Pierre Levegh lay dead not far from where the first impact took place.

Fade out . . .

It is not possible to describe the scenes in the enclosure. French TV cameras were faded out. Newsreels cut.

Violent death and terrible injury had been visited in the twinkling of an eye on numbers uncountable.

What followed is fragmentary.

I saw an Englishman run over from the pits and try to get into the enclosure. Gendarmes stopped him. He was seeking a friend. A gendarme pushed him back but the Englishman was insistent. A policeman knocked his fist and knocked the Englishman cold.

Jack Diamond, of St Margaret's-road, Edware, Middlesex, and John Loxley of Lechmere-crescent, Worcester, were among those killed.

Two other Britons, 23-year-old John Chapman and Victor William Thomas Sanders of Brunston, Northants, were injured.

Doctors, including two Britons who would not give their names ignored the dead. There were —

▶ PAGE TWO, COL. FIVE

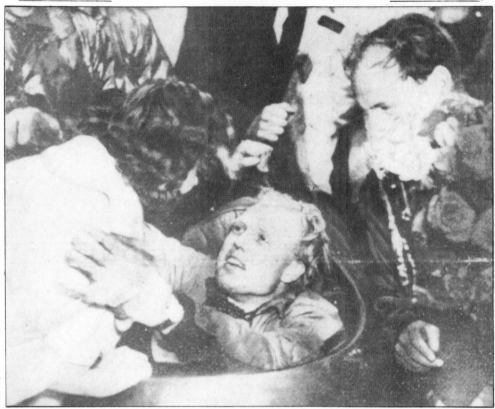

THE RACE IS WON AT RECORD SPEED—AND HAWTHORN GETS A KISS

SCOUTS GIVE FIRST AID TO THE INJURED

● In the public enclosure a few minutes after the accident . . . the injured lie on boards, the only stretchers available. Grim, taut-faced Scouts move among them, giving first aid where they can.

MISSING GIRL: A FATHER ACCUSED

Express Staff Reporter

THE 10-year-old missing girl for whom there was a nation-wide search—and whose picture was shown on TV on Saturday—was found dead in a lonely bluebell wood yesterday.

Blond - haired Evelyn Patricia Higgins had been missing from her home in Lowther - street, Coventry, since last Wednesday.

Then, through heavy rain early yesterday, C.I.D. men raced in patrol cars to 44-acre Shawbury Wood, Warwickshire.

The wood—a remote beauty spot and picnic paradise on the outskirts of Pillongley village—is eight miles from Coventry.

Torches used

Helped by torches in the pale half-light of dawn the gumbooted detectives began to dig in a bluebell-spotted vale.

Soon, from a grave beneath a silver birch tree, they lifted the missing child's body.

Later, 42 - year - old Ernest Charles Harding, a bricklayer, was charged with the girl's murder.

Harding, burly, 5ft 6½in. tall lives in Lauderdale-avenue, Coventry. He is married with a daughter aged 21 and an 18-year-old son.

He will appear in court at Coleshill, Warwickshire, today.

Union bosses are arrested

SINGAPORE Sunday.—The Singapore Government tonight ordered the arrest of all trade union leaders concerned in a general strike of 70,000 workers planned for tomorrow over a wages dispute. Four union leaders have been arrested so far. Army units have been alerted and squads of armed police are ready to stop possible riots.

Four public school boys expelled

Four boys all aged 14 have been expelled from a £234-a-year public school, Kelly College at Tavistock, Devon. Other boys have been barred from the town unless accompanied by their parents.

Troops fight locusts

TRIPOLI, Sunday. A thousand British troops are helping to fight a locust plague that has stripped 6,000 acres of vines and fruit trees in Tripolitania.—A.P.

Mail soldier killed

Ian Wing, aged 21, the driver of an Army lorry carrying mail, was killed last night when it hit a wall near Batley, Yorks.

PAY LEAP-FROGGING MUST STOP

SIR BRIAN WARNS

By TREVOR EVANS

IN a new move to end the rail strike, Sir Brian Robertson, chief of the British Transport Commission, asked Mr. Baty, the strikers' leader, for an assurance this week-end.

Sir Brian wants Mr. Baty to promise that if he gets an agreement he will not start "leap-frogging" with fresh demands should differential increases be granted to some other grades in the N.U.R.

Sir Brian and the Transport Commission feel they have been generous in the proposals they announced at the week-end to the surprise of Mr. Baty and his colleagues in the A.S.L.E.F.

The commission makes three major concessions.

IT DROPS its earlier proposals for classifying drivers into two grades.

IT IS PREPARED to introduce mileage payments to footplate crews which would mean extra money for firemen as well as drivers.

AND WAGES . . .

IT IS WILLING to examine the basic wages in the driver grade, particularly in respect of the highest rated drivers and motormen.

So Sir Brian has conceded the all-important principle of differential payment to the highest rated drivers and motormen.

And why not to firemen as Mr. Baty pleads ? Simple because Sir Brian has accepted a differential payment on the basic rates Mr. James Campbell and the N.U.R. will have more justification to demand as a differential the same other grade of railwaymen.

Sir Brian is trying to keep down these consequential demands.

ASCOT: July 12-15 new date?

By CLIVE GRAHAM (The Scout)

THE Jockey Club Stewards will meet today to confirm the provisional new dates for Royal Ascot—July 12-15.

Postponement of this week's fixture became certain when, on Saturday, there was obviously no hope of a settlement of the rail strike by midday today.

The Queen's approval has been sought for the new dates, which do not clash seriously with her long list of official duties.

By July 12 the Queen and Prince Philip will have returned from their state visit to Norway at their annual stay at Holyrood-house, Edinburgh.

If for some reason the greeting cannot be held on the dates now set the fixture will be cancelled.

Coming back . . .

Parcels up to the normal 15lb limit can now be posted in London for any part of the capital. The 8oz limit on letter mail will have more justification packed post covering the whole count goes up to 15lb.

4.30 a.m. LATEST

HUNT FOR BOY

Police searching bombed-out open spaces in London today for Anthony Horrell, aged seven, missing from his home in Guilford-road.

'SPIES' SEIZED

Two U.S.-trained spies reported captured after parachuting into Rumania.

PILGRIMS DIE

Three people killed and 13 injured when bus carrying pilgrims crashed into church near Mexico City.

CENtral 8000

500 attack cardinal's house

Express Staff Reporter

BUENOS AIRES, Sunday.—A mob of 500 tonight fired shots and threw stones at worshippers outside the Roman Catholic cathedral in Buenos Aires.

They then broke into the residence of Cardinal Copello and smashed windows. Casualties are not yet known.

The mob shouted slogans supporting President Peron's move to cut the power of the Church.

Yesterday thousands of Roman Catholic demonstrators invaded Parliament, tore down the flag and smashed windows of pro-Government newspapers.

Boy drowned

The nine-year-old son of Detective Sergeant Leslie Stewart of Abingdon police was drowned yesterday when he fell in the Thames there.

More for radio men

About 2,500 radio officers in the Government's signals station have been awarded pay increases of £28 a year, backdated to January 1, 1953.

England's ASHES!

1-28
2-55
3-114
4-124
5-130
6-130
7-181
8-198
9-203
10-205
HARVEY
BURKE
CRAIG
MACKAY
MILLER
ARCHER
McDONALD
BENAUD
LINDWALL
MADDOCKS

Ten Little Aussie Boys Lakered in a Row

10 FOR 53

By FRANK ROSTRON: Manchester, Tuesday

THE Old Trafford clock nears 5.30, umpire Frank Lee lifts his finger . . . out goes Len Maddocks . . . Jim Laker has done it again, another 10-wicket rout of the Aussies.

England had won by an innings and 170 runs. England had retained the Ashes, but the fans could think only of Laker and his unique feat.

As the wickets began to tumble after lunch the crowd's earlier anxiety was replaced by suspense—suspense for their hero, Laker.

As Big Jim loped up to the crease, methodically mowing through the Aussies, there was one question . . . and one growing hope: *"Can Jim do the lot again as he did for Surrey at the Oval?"*

He was such a hero, alike with elderly business men in the pavilion and shrilly screeching schoolboys scampering excitedly all round the ground, that the other players became like chorus nonentities acting as a backcloth to a great star.

Even Tony Lock, the other half of the famous Surrey mowing machine, lashing away at the other end with his left-arm spinners, was just a supporting player.

SUCH SUSPENSE . . .

As Laker's total of victims mounted there was a perverse suspense about Lock too. Ironically, they began to watch the menace of Lock's biting spinners with fear—fear that he might take a wicket and interrupt a history-making spell.

At five o'clock, when Richie Benaud, after a stubborn stay of just over an hour and three-quarters, stretched out to grope for a ball that broke sharply past his bat, Laker had taken his eighth victim of the innings.

The cheers were followed by a hubbub of chatter as statisticians portentously told their neighbours: *"Jim has equalled the 42-year-old record of old Sydney Barnes."*

When Johnson came in to join Ray Lindwall it had ceased to be a Test match. It had become a personal drama with every man, woman and child around the area identifying himself with Laker.

"One more . . . one more," the old men prayed as unashamedly as the schoolboys gnawing at their autograph books. How they danced to their feet in the hundred shouting when Lindwall stabbed a Laker off break into the hungry hands of Lock in the familiar leg trap.

HE'S DONE IT

"Laker again! Laker again. By gum, lads! It's a world record," called a group of portly Lancashire business men, their pipes long since converted to tobaccoless dummies, even forgiving Surrey's Laker his Yorkshire birth.

Out came last man Maddocks. There was the silence of unspoken prayers again. Could Jim get the final wicket to complete the fairy tale?

Each ball Lock bowled was an agony. Every spectator seemed to be a traitor to England hoping no wicket would fall. Then the ball was thrown to Laker again. With his second ball Laker spun another of those biting turns. There was the thudding "plop" as the ball struck Maddocks's pad plumb in front of the stumps.

OUT! ALL 10 FOR LAKER. TEN FOR 53 AND 19 FOR 90 IN ALL.

Then they ran, scampering joyfully, past the mildly protesting police. They ran in their hundreds to acclaim their hero and set up the chant "Laker, Laker . . . we want Laker."

It was a perfect finish, the happy ending to a cricket fairy story. Even the sporting Australians were happy about it all and went to the England dressing-room, one by one, to take blushing Jim affectionately by the arm as he puffed with embarrassment at a cigarette.

But earlier all this had seemed most unlikely. The wicket, which fortunately for Laker and England livened up under the rays of the afternoon's sun, was lifeless in the morning.

Right until lunch Ian Craig and Colin McDonald were comfortable and confident.

But the sun broke through the clouds, literally and metaphorically, for England at lunch time when Australia were 112 for two.

A quarter of an hour after the restart Laker at last beat the vigilant Craig, who had defied England for over four and a quarter hours spread, like McDonald's innings, over four days.

McDonald defied Laker until 4.35 when his magnificent innings of 89 ended in his being caught in that lucrative leg trap by Alan Oakman. He had batted over six and a half hours.

Then came the final suspense chapter and the dramatic finishing touches to Laker's day of cricket history.

INJURY HOODOO HITS 5 STARS

By BOB PENNINGTON

ONLY 18 days until Soccer takes over from Jim Laker and Co., and already a mounting casualty list in unlucky London makes it certain that at least five top-liners will be missing.

PETER SILLETT, England and Chelsea back, was told by a specialist yesterday that he will be unable to resume training for at least a month.

Sillett enters hospital tomorrow for an operation to remove "foreign bodies" from his knee, leaving manager Ted Drake to start the season with two bright, but inexperienced young backs, Wally Bellett and Dick Whittaker.

KEN HEWKINS, Fulham's star South African goalkeeper, has also broken down in training with an ankle injury.

Hewkins, £2,500 capture from Clyde, sees a specialist on Friday. Fulham are worried. The injury is a legacy from last season and has shown little improvement after three months complete rest.

Hawkins' breakdown halts the transfer of 21-year-old reserve keeper Brian Ronson to Southend. Ronson's transfer forms were awaiting posting when Hewkins reported: "My ankle's gone again."

Fulham worry

BEDFORD JEZZARD, England and Fulham centre forward, arrives back from the South African tour on Friday with his club worried over this confirmed medical report: *"Left ankle bone united after break. Ankle ligaments severely damaged."*

"He will be out of football until at least Christmas," said general manager Frank Osborne. "Damaged ligaments can take months to heal."

JOHN BOND, West Ham's right back, who was injured in South Africa, will be out until September. Bond was flown home with his left knee in plaster, but is making a quick recovery.

VIC GROVES, Arsenal's England-class leader, gives this latest verdict on his fight back to fitness after a double cartilage operation: "The knee goes well . . . but don't expect to see me in action during the first few games."

PLAYING TIME

The Test was scheduled for 30 hours play—six per day. Here is the actual play day by day:

	Hours	Mins.
Thursday (all day)	6	—
Friday (all day)	6	—
Saturday	—	20
Monday	1	0
Tuesday	4	45
Total	18	5

THE LAUGH'S ON CRAIG

Laker laughs . . . as patient Craig is l.b.w.

Sports summary

ASSOCIATION

Olympic Games Qualifying Competition [illegible]

ATHLETICS

Oslo [illegible]

LAWN TENNIS

Stazenger Professional Tournament [illegible]

NETBALL

[illegible]

SPEEDWAY

National League [illegible]

U.S. BASEBALL

National League [illegible]

American League [illegible]

RECORDS AHOY!

. . . by Laker

- **LAKER** sets up a new bowling record in all first-class cricket history by taking 19 wickets in a match. Previous record: 17. Previous Test best: 17 for 159 by S. F. Barnes for England against South Africa, 1913-14.
- **LAKER** becomes the first bowler in Test history to take all 10 wickets in an innings.
- **LAKER** is the first bowler in first-class cricket history to take all 10 wickets in an innings twice in the same season.
- **LAKER** equals Surrey colleague Alec Bedser's record of 39 wickets in an England-Australia Test series. Bedser took his 39 (average 17.48) against Australia in 1953. Laker's 39 have cost 9.07 runs each.

S. F. Barnes (England) holds the world Test record with 49 (average 10.93) against South Africa in 1913-14.

- **LAKER** has now taken 51 wickets for 484 runs (average 9.49) aainst the Ausgtralians this year in four Tests and the Surrey match in May.

. . by England

- England's victory was the first by either side in a Test at Old Trafford since 1905.
- It is the first time England have won two matches in a home series since that year.

JOHNSON STOPS FOR SAWDUST

TV-VIEWERS were mystified when Ian Johnson held up play to consult the umpires.

The crowd, thinking he was playing for time, gave the slow handclap.

Johnson explained afterwards: "I was troubled by loose sawdust. The wind was blowing it into our eyes.

"Benaud once had to draw away just as he was about to receive the ball and I had the same bother.

"I asked the umpires whether it would be possible to have the sawdust swept away."

SCOREBOARD

ENGLAND.—First Innings 459 (D. Sheppard 113, P. Richardson 104, C. Cowdrey 80).

AUSTRALIA.—First Innings 84 (J. Laker 9—37).

Second Innings

C. McDonald c Oakman b Laker	89
J. Burke c Lock b Laker	33
R. Harvey c Cowdrey b Laker	0
I. Craig lbw Laker	38
K. Mackay c Oakman b Laker	0
K. Miller b Laker	0
R. Archer c Oakman b Laker	0
R. Benaud b Laker	18
R. Lindwall c Lock b Laker	8
I. Johnson not out	1
L. Maddocks lbw Laker	2
B 12, lb 4	16
Total	205

BOWLING: Statham 16-9-15-0; Bailey 20-8-31-0; Laker 51.2-23-53-10; Lock 55-30-69-0; Oakman 8-3-21-0.

FALL OF WICKETS: 1—28, 2—55, 3—114, 4—124, 5—130, 6—130, 7—181, 8—198, 9—203.

HERE LIE THE AUSSIES OF '56 SKITTLED BY LAKER FOR NEXT TO NIX

ARTHUR MORRIS

Now build on men like Craig

MANCHESTER, Tuesday.—They should rename the Stretford end at Old Trafford LAKER'S END. For it was from there that he took all his 19 wickets in the fourth Test.

England have proved conclusively that on a turning wicket they hold the ace. . . . Not that every one turned up trumps.

Though we had a slowly drying wicket here today, with the sun beating on it, Tony Lock, who bowled 55 overs in the Australian second innings, did not take a wicket.

I am afraid he did not bowl well and, without detracting from Laker's wonderful performance, there is no doubt that Jim was helped somewhat through his spin confederate being off target.

STILL HOPE

Australia must not be downhearted at this defeat by an innings and 170 runs.

There is still a chance of squaring the series even if the Ashes cannot be won back before 1959.

They can be consoled by the thought that all the tough breaks have gone against them in this series.

They were terribly unlucky to be trapped on so many successive turning wickets—either from there being too much or too little moisture in the pitch.

But they will have learned much and can put the experience gained to good use.

Jimmy Burke, Richie Benaud, and—on the final day especially—Colin McDonald and Ian Craig have come on a lot.

It will be to players such as these that Australia must look to tip the balance once more in their favour.

For the moment England are right on top—and most deservedly so.

A lot of hard things have been written, spoken, and thought during this match. Thank goodness it has not affected the relations between the two teams.

IAN'S TRIBUTE

The first person to shake Jim Laker's hand — the hand that had tumbled Australia to defeat with 10 wickets—was Ian Johnson.

And don't forget that, though losing, the Australians themselves scored a victory.

They batted nearly five hours today and nearly eight in all on a rain-affected wicket. . . . Proving that on a "turner" they are not quite the novices some people seem to think after that collapse on Friday's dusty strip.

Ian Craig was a success in his first Test against England. He has found that concentration which has been lacking.

This talented youngster has experienced a tough baptism to the big stuff, and should be all the better for it.

Craig (38) and Colin McDonald (89) fought so well. After Craig went all Australia's hopes rested on McDonald—until Laker's second ball after tea had him caught in the leg trap.

Then nothing could stop the superb Laker bowling England to victory with 65 minutes to spare.

Yes, this fourth and vital Ashes-deciding Test will belong in cricket history to Jim Laker.

Championship table

Points awarded	P.	W. 12	L. —	D. —	1st inns lead in match Lost 4	1st inns lead in match drwn. 4	Pts —
Surrey (1)	18	11	5	2	1	2	144
Lancashire (9)	19	10	1	8	0	6	144
Northants (7)	20	7	3	10	1	6	112
Yorkshire (2)	20	7	6	7	3	5	10[illegible]
Gloucester (12)	19	8	6	4	1	1	104
Middlesex (5)	21	8	9	8	0	2	104
Derbyshire (8)	21	7	5	9	0	5	98
Glamorgan (16)	21	6	6	7	2	4	[illegible]
Hampshire (3)	18	9	4	5	1	4	[illegible]
Worcester (15)	19	7	2	9	0	2	[illegible]
Sussex (4)	19	5	7	6	2	4	84
Essex (14)	20	4	9	6	5	3	82
Notts (11)	19	4	4	10	1	6	80
Somerset (17)	20	4	12	3	3	1	74
Leicester (6)	19	3	11	4	1	3	62
Warwick (9)	19	3	9	7	2	2	53
Kent (13)	20	3	9	7	1	2	48

Figures in brackets indicate 1955 positions.

IT'S THE L-MENACE PLUS BEDSER

By PAT MARSHALL

PITY the Australians. Straight from the Test debacle at Manchester they face bogey man Jim Laker again today.

And they meet him at the Oval where big Jim took ten for 88 when Surrey beat the Aussies in May.

There is no let-up for Laker and Tony Lock. They are included in a Surrey side which is out for a double over the Tourists.

And this time the "L" boys will have the assistance of another Aussie bogey-man—Alec Bedser, who missed the first match because of fibrositis.

The Australians face a Surrey now going flat-out for their fifth successive County championship.

Surrey swept to a 109 runs win over Essex yesterday with over two and a half hours to spare. This victory puts them level on points with Lancashire—and Surrey have a game in hand.

Only Essex resistance yesterday came from former Cambridge blue Charles Williams, who hit a stylish 42, and Young Geoff Smith, who twice hit leg-break bowler Derek Pratt into the pavilion for 6.

Essex were set to get 256 to win in five and a half hours. But they found the leg-cutters of Alec Bedser, the off-spin of his twin, Eric, and the flighted leg-breaks of Pratt quite beyond them.

Joan Poole leads women's tour

Joan Poole (London) won the third stage of the women's Tour de France cycle race yesterday.

She covered the 42 miles to Thiers in 2hrs. 6min. 56sec. Three seconds behind was Milly Robinson (Leeds).

Joan Poole leads the general classification with 6hrs. 24min. 20sec., and Milly Robinson is second in 6hrs. 24min. 23sec.

Johnson outboxes Scottish champ

Frank Johnson, the former British light-weight champion, made a good start to his welter-weight career when he scored a six rounds win over Scottish champion Jimmy Cross at West Hartlepool last night.

The referee stopped their scheduled eight rounds contest to save Cross from further punishment.

TEST MATCH AVERAGES

ENGLAND—Batting

	Inns	Not out	Runs	Highest inns	Aver.
[illegible]					

Bowling

	Overs	Mdns	Runs	Wkts	Aver.
[illegible]					

AUSTRALIA—Batting

	Inns	Not out	Runs	Highest inns	Aver.
[illegible]					

Bowling

	Overs	Mdns	Runs	Wkts	Aver.
[illegible]					

CRICKET SCOREBOARD: LAST DAY

Surrey v. Essex

[illegible]

Warwick v. Hants

At Birmingham — Drawn. Hampshire (4 pts).

HAMPSHIRE. First Innings [illegible] 8 dec (J Gray 115, R Marshall 89).

WARWICK. First Innings [illegible] (R Spooner 76, D Shackleton 7—54).

Second Innings [illegible]

Leicester v. Middlesex

[illegible]

Derbyshire v. Notts

[illegible]

NOTTINGHAM. First Innings 265 (R Simpson 74). [illegible]

Gloucester v. Worcs

At Bristol. Gloucester (12 pts) won by 131 runs.

GLOUCESTER. First Innings [illegible] (D Young 53, R Berry 5 [illegible]). Second Innings 204 [illegible]

WORCESTER. First Innings 64 [illegible]. Second Innings 95 [illegible]

Yorks v. Glamorgan

[illegible]

Somerset v. Kent

[illegible]

TODAY'S GAMES

[illegible]

Northants v. Sussex

At Northampton. Drawn. Northampton (4 pts).

SUSSEX. First Innings 206 (G Tribe 5 [illegible]).

NORTHAMPTON. First Innings [illegible]

N. Wales v. Lancs

[illegible]

Clifton v. Tonbridge

CLIFTON. First Innings [illegible] (Bernard 36, Foster 5 [illegible]). Second Innings 103 [illegible]

MINOR COUNTIES

At Barrow. Lancashire II 247 for 7 dec [illegible] Cumberland 144 for 8 (R Talbot 54). [illegible]

At High Wycombe. Oxford 144 and 218 for 7 dec (D Rickard 5 [illegible]). Buckinghamshire 151 for 4 dec and 144 for 4 (D Laitt 5 [illegible]). Drawn.

* Denotes County Amateur

DOG WINNERS AND HINTS

DAGENHAM. [illegible]

ROMFORD. [illegible]

WALTHAMSTOW. [illegible]

WIMBLEDON. [illegible]

NORWICH. [illegible]

OXFORD. 7.30 Uplands Breeze [illegible]

SLOUGH. [illegible]

HAWKEYE'S FANCIES

[illegible]

OTHER SELECTIONS

[illegible]. Kilbroney Dom. 8.40. Hot Pace (nap). 9.5. Bright Spell. 9.40. [illegible]

[illegible]. —7.30. Overtime. 7.45. Happy Attraction (nap). 8.0. Rubhill Blackbird. 8.20. [illegible] Wish.

[illegible]. 8.1. Dandy Lad. 8.30. Leading [illegible] (nap). 8.34. Pimfield Cross. 9.12. April Again.

[illegible] Park). 7.45. [illegible] Count. 8.15. Denver Comrade [illegible]

THE GAMBOLS . . . by Barry Appleby

This is the life
COME ALONG, GEORGE, YOU'RE WANTED FOR THE HOTEL TENNIS TOURNAMENT — AND THE SWIMMING GALA — AND THEN THERE'S THE PING-PONG
AND THE INTER-HOTEL CRICKET ON THE BEACH — DON'T SIT THERE SNOOZING
YOU CAN DO THAT AT THE OFFICE

Printed and published by Beaverbrook Newspapers Ltd, Fleet-street, London, E.C.4, Great Ancoats-st, Manchester, 4, and Albion-st, Glasgow, C.1.

OLYMPIC SPECIAL

HOW FOUL CAN THE GAMES GET!

After the brawl was over. . . . Hungarian Ervin Zador, blood running down him, leaves the pool.

Melbourne, Thursday.

I'D like to leave Melbourne now, please.

I'm a sports writer. I love sport. But I don't think there's much sport left in these 16th Olympic Games.

I don't like them any longer. IN FACT I THINK THEY STINK !

But it is my job to tell you what is happening—and plenty happened in the swimming pool here today.

During the water polo match, which the Hungarians won 4—0, a Russian hit a rival, Ervin Zador, such a vicious and violent blow over the right eye that it split his brow and stained the water red.

Hungarian officials and reserve players stood on the side of the pool screaming abuse at the Russians.

New "Australian Hungarians" joined in the uproar.

KICK, BITE

Five policemen and swimming officials rushed to the pool

Russian players swam to the scene of the incident and smiled at the demonstrators.

Twenty - one - year - old Zador, after being treated by ambulance men, said he would stay in Australia after the Games.

And as a summing-up of the second half, let me quote the Melbourne Argus front page story, which ends:

"It was kick, bite and gouge by both sides in a session that would have done credit to an all-in wrestling match."

All right, I know that water polo is probably the most filthy game there is

PETER WILSON

CABLES:

'I'd like to leave now'

and if that were all—well it wouldn't matter. But that isn't all.

Look, I'm a sports writer and I'd like to quit these Games — Games? that's a laugh —right now.

For why ? Well, let's go over to the fencing in the fashionable Melbourne suburb of St. Kilda.

By ill luck a Russian met a Hungarian in the individual sabre competition.

Every time the Hungarian scored there was rapturous, almost hysterical, applause from the crowd.

Every time the Russian registered t h e r e were boos and catcalls.

The jury were mainly American and several times during the various bouts Kouznetsov, the Russian fencer, covered his face with his hands in protest against their decisions.

Still he didn't forget to congratulate his Hungarian opponent even when he looked most disgusted with the jury's decision.

THEY LAUGHED

On the public address system an announcer asked the crowd for silence, only to be met with derisive laughter.

Look, I'm a sports writer. It's my job and my life and my love. These Games are getting so grimy. Please let me pack up now.

In the afternoon diving judges were booed because the crowd thought unfair marks were being given to a Russian girl.

At night it was much worse in the men's high diving.

There was a Hungarian and a Russian judge and claims were made that neither would raise his score card until all the other judges had voted.

There were bitter accusations that the Hungarian judge had coached his own country's competitors between the dives.

There were even more vitriolic charges that a Russian woman judge had been marking the Americans low and the Russians high.

The Americans, who have won this event since the 1928 Olympics, claimed, "It's not a true result."

Their coach, Karl B. Michael, has put in a protest to the International Amateur Swimming Federation.

Their two divers, Gary Tobian and Dick Connor, both from California, were as upset as the winner, Joaquin Capilla, twenty-seven-year-old Mexican.

'DISGUSTING'

CAPILLA said: "The marking was disgusting. It made the competition ridiculous.

"The judges let national feeling get the better of them."

TOBIAN said: "I agree. If I thought diving was going to be reduced to this, I'd give it up."

CONNOR added: "It is the worst competition I have ever been in. It was a battle of the nationalities of the judges."

Look. Look. Look ! I'm a sports writer. I don't want to get mixed up in this. I'll throw in the towel, I'll call it a day, call me a quitter if you like, but this isn't my idea of sport.

Now over to the Olympic village, the "dream camp" which was supposed to be the Utopia of brotherly love.

The Hungarian section of the village was a sad place tonight.

Three Hungarian women gymnasts and one Yugoslav woman weight-putter are among eleven athletes who have disappeared from this high-wire enclosed "paradise."

Athletes sat around in groups talking in church whispers.

Some still wore a black ribbon across the Hungarian flag on their track suits.

Officials said that about sixty per cent of the men were married—and because of that they would return to Hungary.

And just to end off the saddest Olympic day since

the racial hatred time of "Hitler's Games" in 1936, there is a smear report from Sydney.

British and American athletes are accused of behaving like hooligans after the British Commonwealth-U.S.A. match there yesterday.

It was admitted that a glass had been thrown at a party held at the Coogee Hotel — near Sydney's world-famous Bondi Beach

A taxi-driver said: "Athletes, carrying beer, tried to bend metal street-signs,"

dived nude into the sea and sounded the shark bell alarm."

The people for whom I am most sorry are our Australian hosts

It is not their fault that the Games seem to be deteriorating into a squalid carnival of political pressure groups and Olympic oafs.

But I repeat: I'm a sports writer and I want nothing of these last twenty-four hours. EXCEPT RELIEF FROM THEM.

★ OLYMPIC RESULTS ★

SWIMMING

100 METRES BACKSTROKE

FINAL.—1, D. Thiele (Australia), 1m. 2.2s. (Olympic record): 2, J. Monckton (Australia), 63.2s.; 3, F. McKinney (U.S.), 64.5s.; 6, Dean Sykes (G.S.) 65.6s.

200 METRE BREAST-STROKE

FINAL.—1, M. Furukawa (Japan), 2m. 34.7s. (Olympic record): 2, J. Yoshimura (Japan), 2m. 36.7s.; 3, K. Ishchenko (U.S.S.R.)

HIGH DIVING

FINAL.—1, K. Capilla (Mexico), 156.6pts.; 3, G. Tobian (U.S.), 152.41; 3, R. Connor (U.S.), 149.79.

WOMEN'S 4 X 100 METRES RELAY

FINAL.—1, Australia, 4m. 17.1s. (world record): 2, U.S., 4m. 19.2s. (also beat world record): 3, S.A., 4m. 25.7s.; 8, Britain (Frances Hogben, Judy Grinham, Margaret Girvan, Pearne Ewart), 4m. 35.8s.

WOMEN'S HIGH DIVING

FIRST ROUND (Highest 12 scores continue in second round

for remaining two dives)—1, Paula Jean Myers (U.S.), 52.96; 2, R. Gorokhovskaia (U.S.S.R.), 52.64; 3, T. Karachachiants (U.S.S.R.), 52.19; 4, P. McCormick (U.S.), 51.28; 5, J. Irwin (U.S.), 50.81; 6, B. Hanssen (Sweden), 50.48; 7, N. Darrigrand (France), 50.02; 8, K. Jigalova (U.S.S.R.), 49.22; 9, Ann Long (G.B.) 49.15; 10, K. Tsutani (Japan), 48.45; 11, Charmian Welsh (G.B.), 46.55; 12, H. Hirose (Japan), 46.15.

WATER POLO

FINAL POOL. — Hungary 4, U.S.S.R. 0; Yugoslavia 2, Italy 1.

LOSERS ROUND (Places from seven downwards).—Australia 3, Singapore 2; Britain 11, Singapore 5; Rumania 4, Australia 2; Britain 5, Rumania 2.

CYCLING

1,000 METRES TIME TRIAL

FINAL.—1, L. Faggin (Italy), 69.8s.; 2, L. Foucek (Czech), 71.4s.; 3, A. Swift (S. Afr.), 71.6s.; 5, Alan Danson (G.B.), 72.3s.

1,000 METRES SPRINT

FINAL.—1, M. Rousseau (France); 2, G. Pesenti (Italy); 3, R. Ploog (Australia); 4, W. Johnston (N.Z.).

2,000 METRES TANDEM

FINAL.—1, Australia; 2, Czech; 3, Italy; 4, Britain (Peter Brotherton, Eric Thompson).

HOCKEY

FINAL.—India 1, Pakistan 0. Play-off for bronze medal.—Germany 3, Britain 1 (J. Conroy) Final Placings.—1, India; 2, Pakistan; 3, Germany; 4, Britain.

FENCING

SABRE (INDIVIDUAL)

FINAL.—1, R. Karpati (Hungary), 6—1; 2, J. Pawlowski (Poland), 5—2; 3, L. Kouznetsov (U.S.S.R.).

GYMNASTICS

WOMEN'S PARALLEL BARS

FINAL.—1, A. Keleti (Hungary), 18.966 pts.; 2, L. Latynina (U.S.S.R.), 18.83; 3, S. Mouratova (U.S.S.R.), 18.58; 86, Pat Hirst (G.B.), 16.266.

RON'S CHANCE

Ron Stockin gets his first game of the season in Cardiff City's team against Blackpool tomorrow. Cliff Nugent switches to inside left and Gerry Hitchens leads the attack.

HOW THEY STAND

	MEDALS			
	Gold	Sil.	Br.	Pts.
Russia	35	29	30	597
U.S.A.	31	24	14	465
Australia	11	7	14	181
Germany	5	9	6	189
Hungary	7	7	5	165
Britain	5	7	10	153
Italy	7	7	6	147
Sweden	7	4	5	129
Japan	4	9	4	120
France	3	4	5	93
Rumania	3	5	4	83
Finland	3	1	11	66
C'k'slov'kia	1	3	5	48
Poland	1	4	3	44
Turkey	—	2	2	46

Table includes medals won in Equestrian events at Stockholm.

Daily Mirror

FRI FEB 7 1958

2½ FORWARD WITH THE PEOPLE ✦ No. 16,843

SOCCER AIR TRAGEDY

Manchester United plane crashes

21 dead

THE END The chartered Elizabethan airliner in which the Manchester United team was travelling home lies shattered in a snowfield near Munich. The pilot, Captain James Thain, escaped alive from the smashed nose

AN Elizabethan airliner—on charter to Manchester United football team, the fabulous "Busby Babes"—crashed on take-off at Munich Airport, Germany, yesterday, and plunged the world of Soccer into mourning.

Twenty-one men — among them some of the brightest stars in British football—died.

Seven Manchester United players who died were:

Roger Byrne (Capt.), Tommy Taylor, Mark Jones, Eddie Colman, Billy Whelan, David Pegg, Geoff Bent.

Also dead was ex-England goalkeeper and sports writer Frank Swift.

In hospital, fighting for his life, was manager Matt Busby.

Not far from him ace centre half Jackie Blanchflower lay with a broken pelvis.

Twenty-three of the 44 passengers survived.

Among the dead was Archie Ledbrooke, the Mirror's famous Northern sports writer. His last story is on Page 21.

● THE CRASH—Story and pictures Back Page and Page 5.
● THE TEAM in the Tragedy—See Centre Pages.

**Blackest Day of All—By Peter Wilson
See Page 23**

THE BEGINNING This picture was taken when the team, accompanied by sports writers, boarded the plane at Manchester on Monday. Left to right, with known survivors marked with asterisk: Jackie Blanchflower*; Billy Foulkes*; Walter Crickmer, secretary; Don Davies, Manchester Guardian; Roger Byrne, captain; Duncan Edwards*; Albert Scanlon* — just visible behind Scanlon is Frank Swift, News of the World; Ray Wood*; Dennis Viollet*; Archie Ledbrooke, Daily Mirror; Geoff Bent; Mark Jones and Alf Clarke, Kemsley Newspapers.

Daily Mirror

MON OCT 20 1958

2½ FORWARD WITH THE PEOPLE ✦ No. 17,060

RACE OF THE CENTURY DRAMA

Moss wins—MIKE is the CHAMPION

From PETER STEPHENS, Casablanca, Sunday

BRITISH racing ace Stirling Moss won the "race of the century" at Casablanca, Morocco, today with a breathtaking victory over his British rival Mike Hawthorn.

But Hawthorn took second place—and that was enough for HIM to win the world racing drivers' championship.

This was the last Grand Prix of the season—and Hawthorn's final aggregate of forty-two points was **one better** than Moss's total.

Moss had hoped to wipe out Hawthorn's points lead with this one race and win the title.

As admirers crowded round them after the race Moss shook hands with Hawthorn and said wryly: "You got it after all, you old so-and-so."

The race was marred by two accidents. Fair-haired Stuart Lewis-Evans, of Britain, driving a Vanwall, skidded on a patch of oil and spun off the track.

He crawled out of the blazing car and ran along the track, his clothes in flames. A helicopter took him to hospital.

Last night doctors at the hospital said that Lewis-Evans's condition was grave.

They said burns covered three-quarters of his body.

In the other accident French driver Francois Picard and Oliver Gendebien of Belgium were injured when their cars crashed. Picard was said to have several broken bones.

Always Led

Hurling his British Vanwall around the track Moss led from start to finish in the 249-mile race.

But Hawthorn was always close behind, trailing in second or third

AND BRITON CRASHES

position in his flame-red Italian Ferrari.

Moss's average speed was 116.4 miles per hour—and he set up a lap record with a blistering 119.3 m.p.h.

His time for the race was 2h. 9m. 15s. Hawthorn's time was 2h. 10m. 39.8s. Phil Hill, of America, was third in a Ferrari.

Later Hawthorn celebrated his championship in CHAMPAGNE with his pit crew. He is the first Briton to win the title since it was introduced in 1950.

Moss, a teetotaller, drank to his race victory with—a FRUIT JUICE.

Juan Fangio, of Argentina, who was the previous holder of the championship —he has retired from racing—said tonight: "British drivers have come back into the racing limelight."

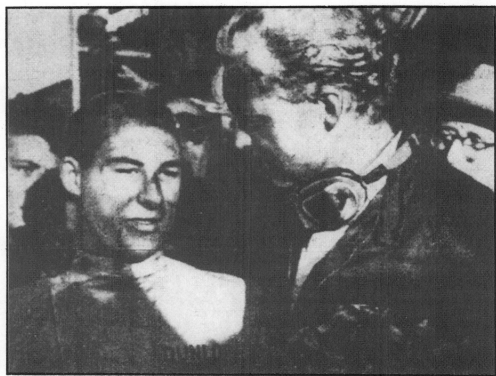

● Stirling Moss (left), who won the race, congratulates Mike Hawthorn, who was second — but who scored enough points to give him the world racing drivers' championship.

Shirley Sanders and Robert Kardell pictured after their Hollywood wedding.

A 'BRAIN' PICKED THE BRIDE

HERE comes the bride, in Hollywood —the first to be chosen by an ELECTRONIC BRAIN.

Each week personal details of applicants are fed into, and sorted by, the "cupid with coils" on the television show "People are Funny." The machine chooses couples who seem to be best suited to each other.

But only one couple out of thirty-five have so far taken the machine's advice. Shirley Sanders and Robert Kardell, both twenty-six.

They are pictured here after their wedding yesterday.

Following them are the bride's sister Karen and television star Art Linkletter, who introduced them to the "brain."

Shirley and Bob won £7,000 on the show and a "bonus" honeymoon in Honolulu.

Big match night

REAL champs!

By BILL HOLDEN
Eintracht 3, Real Madrid 7

THE Hampden Roar, the most impressive sound in British Soccer, rose again and again last night to salute our superiors.

Real Madrid, the Spanish maestros beat Eintracht of Germany to win the European Cup for the fifth time.

LOOKING ON were top managers from Stan Cullis (Wolves) and Bill Nicholson (Spurs) downwards.

LOOKING IN were millions of TV fans who must have been just as impressed as the lucky people on the Hampden Park terraces.

And every one must have realised just how far our standard falls below this super show.

The film of this final should be hired by every club in Britain.

It should be shown and studied from now until our players begin training for next season.

Because this was the brilliant stuff which must come to Britain—the home of Soccer—if we are to retain any pretensions to modern-day greatness.

But it is worth remembering that the two men most responsible for Real Madrid's victory are not Spanish.

Centre forward Di Stefano was imported from the Argentine, and inside left Puskas is an exiled Hungarian.

IBBOTSON BEATEN

Derek Ibbotson, the four-minute miler, was beaten by twenty yards by Basil Heatley, English cross country champion, in a 5,000 metres race at Hampden Park, Glasgow, last night.

Shock Lead

Di Stefano began playing a triple role—defender, schemer and striker. He took command of his team after outside right Kress flashed the underdog German team into a shock nineteenth minute lead.

Screaming for more endeavour, Di Stefano tongue-lashed his side to glory.

Outside right Canario responded with a pass from which Di Stefano equalised. Then the winger slammed in a shot which German 'keeper Loy could only parry and Di Stefano ran in to smash a second goal.

On the stroke of half-time Puskas came into the game as a force for the first time, and scored a goal that was worth all the pesetas he gets paid . . . because it clinched victory.

Penalty

Nine minutes after the interval Puskas made it 4—1, with a penalty, which I thought was a harsh decision. He completed his hat-trick in the sixtieth minute and set off a fantastic scoring spree when he got Madrid's sixth goal in the seventieth minute.

Two minutes later German centre forward Stein jiggled through to score. Another minute and Di Stefano notched his hat-trick with Madrid's seventh goal.

And again within a minute, Stein made it 7—3.

But the real measure of the brilliance of this match was there were so many heart pounding incidents it would still live in the memory even if it had finished without ANY SCORE!

Start of a hat-trick

Di Stefano, in white, throws up his hands in triumph as he scores Real Madrid's second goal—the first of his personal hat-trick.

AROUND THE SCOREBOARD

Worcs v Kent
WORCESTER.—With first innings wickets standing. Kent lead by one.

WORCESTER—First Innings
Horton, c Leary, b Ridgway 1
Headley, c Leary, b Dixon 59
Richardson, run out 0
Kenyon, b Halfyard 19
Spencer, c Jones, b Halfyard 22
Dews, c Catt, b Jones 5
Standen, c Catt, b Brown 2
Booth, c Catt, b Brown 6
Slade, lbw, b Brown 0
Coldwell, b Halfyard 7
Flavell, not out 0
Extras 15
Total 136
Fall of wickets: 1-3, 2-11, 3-44, 4-100, 5-120, 6-126, 7-128, 8-129, 9-132.
Scoring rate: 2.09 per over.
Bowling: Ridgway 10-3-24-1; Brown 16-8-34-3; Halfyard 22-11-43-3; Jones 12-9-10-1; Dixon 8-1-10-1.
KENT.—First Innings: 137 for 4 (Richardson 37) at 2.82 per over
Today: 11.30-7.

Warwick v Hants
BIRMINGHAM.—With nine first innings wickets standing. Hants need 189 for lead.

WARWICK—First Innings
Gardner, b Heath 1
Horner, c Sainsbury, b Heath 4
Stewart, lbw, b Shackleton 0
Smith, c Horton, b Shackleton 2
Cartwright, c Marshall, b Heath 33
Townsend, c Gray, b Shackleton 0
Atkins, lbw, b Pothecary 1
Howard, c O'Linn, b Pothecary 35
L. Coghlan, b Fellows-Smith 4
Brodie, c Waite, b Fellows-Smith 9
Hurd, not out 0
Extras 7
Total 103
Fall of wickets: 1-16, 2-17, 3-17, 4-24, 5-92, 6-95, 7-178, 8-209, 9-215.
Scoring rate: 7.12 per over.
Bowling: Shackleton 36-15-48-3; Heath 36-2-6-88-5; Pothecary 25-6-62-2; Fellows-Smith 16-1-6-26-2; McKinnon 18-5-50-1.
SOUTH AFRICANS.—First Innings: 11 for 1.
Today: 11.30-6.30.

Glam v Derby
LLANELLY.—With eight first innings wickets standing. Derby need 189 for lead.

GLAMORGAN—First Innings
Parkhouse, run out 72
Hedges, c Berry, b Jackson 9
Pressdee, c and b Rhodes 24
Walker, c Hall, b Smith 55
Watkins, b Rhodes 55
Wooller, c Lee, b Jackson 36
McConnon, c Dawkes, b Jackson 0
Evans, J., b Jackson 0
Evans, D., lbw, b Jackson 0
Burke, c Stephenson, b Langford 0
Shepherd, not out 0
Extras 10
Total (9 wkts dec.) 339
Fall of wickets: 1-23, 2-118, 3-138, 4-206, 5-251, 6-257, 7-233, 8-257, 9-339.
Scoring rate: 2.56 per over.
Bowling: Biddulph 26-6-82-1; Jackson 20-5-52-6; Buxton 12-5-29-0; Berry 29-13-49-0; Smith 20-5-60-1.
DERBY.—First Innings: 47 for 2.
Today: 11.30-7.

Oxford Univ v Lancs
OXFORD.—With seven first innings wickets standing. Oxford lead by 62.

LANCASHIRE—First Innings
Pullar, c Smith, b Sayer 12
Barber, run out 9
Wharton, c Pataudi, b Corran 22
Grieves, b Corran 0
Marner, c Baig, b Corran 64
Booth, b Corran 12
Clayton, c Smith, b Corran 5
Greenhough, b Corran 17
Higgs, c Drybrough, b Corran 8
Hilton, c Drybrough, b Sayer 1
Tattersall, not out 0
Extras 3
Total 103
Fall of wickets: 1-13, 2-34, 3-49, 4-50, 5-63, 6-72, 7-87, 8-96, 9-101.
Bowling: Sayer 19-3-49-2; Corran 24.5-9-48-7; Burki 6-2-9-0.
OXFORD UNIV.—First Innings: 165 for 3 (Burki 52 not Pataudi 42 not).
Today: 11.30-7.

Camb Univ v S Africans
CAMBRIDGE.—With nine first innings wickets standing, the South Africans need 182 for lead.

CAMBRIDGE UNIV.—First Innings
Kirby, b Adcock 5
Fredericks, c Waite, b Adcock 64
Lewis, c Waite, b Pothecary 55
Willard, b Adcock 0
Morris, b Pothecary 1
Rose, lbw, b McKinnon 0
Aikins, lbw, b Pothecary 9
Howard, c O'Linn, b Pothecary 35
L. Coghlan, b Fellows-Smith 4
Brodie, c Waite, b Fellows-Smith 9
Hurd, not out 0
Extras 7
Total 192
Fall of wickets: 1-13, 2-109, 3-109, 4-125, 5-136, 6-159, 7-168, 8-181, 9-187.
Bowling: Adcock 18-6-35-3; Pothecary 19-4-51-4; Fellows-Smith 16.1-6-26-2; McKinnon 18-5-50-1.
SOUTH AFRICANS.—First Innings: 11 for 1.
Today: 11.30-6.30.

Yorks v Somerset
HULL.—With nine first innings wickets standing. Somerset need 321 for lead.

YORKSHIRE—First Innings
Stott, c Palmer, b Whitehead 74
Taylor, c Stephenson, b Biddulph 0
Padgett, c Stephenson, b Palmer 30
Close, c Keith, b Whitehead 0
Bolus, lbw, b Langford 18
Wilson, J., b Biddulph 0
Birkenshaw, run out 1
Trueman, c Whitehead, b Biddulph 0
Wilson, D., not out 0
Binks, c Stephenson, b Langford 0
Extras 10
Total 237
Fall of wickets: 1-27, 2-145, 3-145, 4-176, 5-237, 6-247, 7-278, 8-283, 9-376.
Scoring rate: 2.69 per over.
Bowling: Biddulph F.T. 22-6-51-; Greetham 29-10-23-0; Langford 36 5-17-84-2; Whitehead 30-13-80-2.
SOMERSET.—First Innings: 10 for 1.
Today: 11-7.

Surrey v Sussex
THE OVAL.—With first innings 377 for the loss of 4 wickets.
SUSSEX—First Innings
Sheppard, c Fletcher, b Loader 4
Oakman, c Stewart, b Gibson 2
Dexter, b Bedser, A. ......
Parks, c Stewart, b Lock 6
Suttle, not out 8
Cooper, not out ......
Extras ......
Total (4 wkts) 377

Gloucs v Leics
STROUD.—With first innings wickets standing, Gloucester lead by 16.
GLOUCESTER—First Innings
Young, c Boshier ......
Milton, b Van Geloven ......
Pugh, b Van Geloven ......
Graveney, c Revill, b Boshier ......
Nicholls, b Spencer ......
Mortimore, lbw, b Boshier ......
Allen, c sub, b Boshier ......
Brown, b Spencer ......
Bashier, c Boshier ......
Meyer, b Boshier ......
Cook, not out ......
Extras ......
Total ......
Scoring rate: 1.86 per over.
Bowling: Boshier 20-2-60-3; Van 15.1-4-31-1-2

MCC v Essex
LORD'S.—M C C have 192 in their first innings.
Hill, c Taylor, b Bailey ......
Russell, lbw, b Bailey ......
Springall, lbw, b ......
Simpson, c Knight, b Insole ......
Watts, D., c Savill, b Knight ......
Titmus, lbw, b Bailey ......
Manning, not out ......
Watts, P. D., c Knight, b Bear ......
Tilly, c Savill, b Preston ......
Andrew, b Preston ......
Cotton, lbw, b Bailey ......
Extras ......
Bowling: Knight 30-2-; Preston ......
Greensmith 16-2-36-1; Bear 15-1-61-; Insole 9-2-18-0.

Daily Mirror

5d.   Tuesday, August 27, 1963   No. 18,564

Peter Wilson on the Calypso triumph

CHARGE OF THE DARK BRIGADE

It's the Charge of the DARK BRIGADE after West Indies' victory in the Oval Test yesterday. England skipper Ted Dexter grabs a stump and watches the invaders. Batsman Basil Butcher races for the pavilion after completing the winning run—the run that made West Indies 3—1 winners of the rubber.—Picture by Mirror Cameraman MONTE FRESCO.

By PETER WILSON

PLEASE, oh please, let's have the West Indian cricketers here EVERY year!

They have played cricket as it should be played—as it must have been played years before we were born.

As long as I live. I shall never forget the last two or three minutes at the Oval yesterday.

I'VE SEEN men win the world heavyweight title.

Cricket? Man, this was the greatest!

I'VE SEEN the beginning and the end of five Olympic Games.

I'VE SEEN an Englishman win Wimbledon.

I'VE SEEN countless Cup Finals.

Patrolling

But NEVER have I witnessed a scene to rival the drama and emotion of this.

For hours, we had known the West Indians were going to win—and how

deservedly! The police had been patrolling the boundary, waving back the kinky-haired, jinking youngsters, the man in the green-and-yellow Jamaican robe, the scores waving the West Indies flag, the lovely chocolate girls teetering on their stiletto heels or bounding on their flat soles.

And then, with six runs to go, like chain lightning running through this supercharged, cartwheeling, bugle-blowing, cheering crowd there was the

sudden surging forward of perhaps 5,000 happy-crazy people from the Islands in the Sun to the boundary ropes.

Hurling

I don't know how to describe it. It was like pouring hot chocolate sauce over green pistachio ice as they seethed over the grass and stood five, ten, fifteen deep, waiting for the winning hit.

England played it seriously right up to the end. No comic gesture. No batsman going on to bowl. Not this time.

Test veteran Brian Statham, who had taken the new ball only a few overs before, was still hurling them down.

As the total went up one by one, the West Indian fans rushed on to the field and then back like children

Continued on Page Four

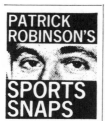

PATRICK ROBINSON'S SPORTS SNAPS

Jap yap tires Tulloh

EUROPEAN track champion Bruce Tulloh yesterday flew wearily into London with the British team—day-dreaming about his double-sprung bed at home in the Thames-side village of Wargrave.

"I couldn't sleep during the Tokyo International Games," he said. "The noise those 10,000,000 yapping Japs make in that city is something awful!"

Tulloh who stayed wide awake enough to land a great gold medal triumph in the 5,000 metres, spotlights this as the big problem facing the Olympic stars in Tokyo next year.

"Most things like presents for home, are cheap," added Tulloh. "But night clubs are expensive."

Which is sad news for a friend of mine from Essex, who runs 200 metres rather well.

WEALTHY England cricket skipper Ted Dexter has invited the top people from Lord's to a luncheon deep in the City of London on November 14. "Ted, branded the world's most conservative captain after the West Indies series, says the lunch is "to pay penance for my captaincy this year."

BOOKMAKERS are angry about talk of a Tote monopoly A spokesman at a London firm said yesterday : " Racing is richer for the industrious bookies who are often unreasonably maligned. We would be unfairly in the cart if the Tote plan comes off to plough the punters' cash back into racing.

And I would on behalf of all indignant bookies, some might even have to go out to work !

WHY DON'T the Football League and the Professional Footballers' Association get together to work out a contract suitable to all of them. Then we could be spared these long months of boring wrangling and talks of strike.

I know a lot of players are fed up to the teeth with this constant bickering because, as one put it : " It slowly leaves an impression that we are only in this game for the money."

How unfair !

PAT SAGE, British athletics team manager, pops about Tokyo: "Had a bit of trouble with the language. The team kept getting different instructions from different people, all at the same time— and all in Japanese."

Many happy returns:

ENGLAND 2   REST OF THE WORLD 1

THE DAY THE F.A. CELEBRATED ITS 100th BIRTHDAY, THIS WAS THE PROUD SIGHT ON THE SCOREBOARD. 'BUILD IT INTO WEMBLEY AS A REMINDER' SAYS HACKETT

GREAVES—KING of THEM ALL

By DESMOND HACKETT

England 2   Rest of World 1
Paine, Greaves   Law

Attendance 100,000   Receipts £90,000

WEMBLEY Stadium, the traditional stately home of English football, became alive with the noble noise of mighty cheering when 11 men of England kept their pledge and destroyed 16 of the greatest men in world Soccer yesterday.

Did I say 11 men? There were only 10 Englishmen on the field when Jimmy Greaves, the hero of an heroic afternoon, scored the winning goal three minutes from the end.

England captain Jimmy Armfield lay stricken with cramp behind his own goal, striving to lift himself to follow the furious, proud battle by his team.

But that goal by Greaves, who has written his own history into the Wembley arena, loosed off the greatest surge of pride in an England win that I have ever heard.

SUCH POISE, SUCH SKILL

Every one of the 100,000 who framed the green grass of Wembley rose to acknowledge the Soccer men of England.

And how England deserved this tremendous salute ! I have never seen an England team play with such poise, with such determination, or with such skill.

It was so splendidly fitting on the Football Association's 100th birthday that England should win playing the English way.

For when this absorbing game, so rich in the tapestry of so many styles, was through, it was names like Greaves of England, George Eastham of England, and Gordon Banks of England, which were spoken with admiration.

The destruction might well have been complete if England could only have got that goal that unluckily escaped them in the first 50 seconds.

Bobby Charlton sent a well-planned corner kick to Ray Wilson. The England left back aimed it hard into goal and Greaves whipped in a shot which Russian goalkeeper Yashin blocked with his body.

Eastham, the supreme planner of the game, then gracefully swept a pass down to the racing boots of Greaves and Yashin had to dive frantically to check a score.

IMPUDENT PAINE

There were long spells of quiet as the crowd watched, absorbed by this chess style Soccer. They were aroused again, though, when Charlton split open the World defence and Yashin made an astounding save from Bobby Smith.

As the game moved to half time England looked most likely to succeed.

The Rest of the World, according to plan, took off four players. Among the replacements was Puskas, for Eusebio, the most dangerous intruder into England's defence. But, much as the crowd welcomed back to Wembley the old galloping major, England treated the newcomers with no more respect than the departing battalion.

Young Terry Paine, almost impudently started a move which ended in Greaves having his shot kicked off the line. Greaves had a goal worth waiting 100 years for disallowed and the World side brought on Seeler, of Germany, as replacement for French right-winger Raymond Kopa.

Then, just as I had said to a colleague, "England will win now," Bobby Moore sent Smith away.

JOYOUS

Smith's long pass was chested down to Greaves, and worked round to Paine, who joyously slashed in an historic goal.

The noise was stilled as Puskas, the wise man of the World's forwards, threaded a pass through the England defence for Denis Law, who had been the greatest menace to England, to draw Banks and flick the ball impudently into goal, with only eight minutes left.

Yet this was the challenge which produced the glowing spirit of England.

Charlton's shot hit a post with a crash. Greaves hit the inside of a post and the ball came out. And the three-lion badge of England finally became roaring and alive when Greaves scored.

REMINDER

As I left the stadium late in the evening there still rose high on the edge of the new roof the glorious signal: England 2 Rest of the World 1.

I suggest this should be built into the pattern of the stadium, as the historical reminder of the day the Football Association became 100 years old.

WEMBLEY 1963

MUCH MALIGNED ENGLAND OUTSHONE "THE REST OF THE WORLD"

AND FOR ONE DON'T BLAME TEAM MANAGER ALF RAMSEY IF HE'S LAUGHING HIS ANIMATED HEAD OFF.

WHAT AMAZING SCENES WHEN TERRY PAINE SCORED FIRST FOR ENGLAND

SPLENDID OLD ENGLISH GENTS WHO'D SAT SILENT AT MATCHES SINCE 1863—BURST INTO LIFE.

JOLLY BRAVO and all that

AND WHEN THE RUSSIAN REFEREE DISALLOWED A GREAVES GOAL

THEY GAVE A FAIR IMITATION OF A HIGHLAND PIPE BAND WARMING UP.

THEY LET THEIR HAIR DOWN AS IF THEY'D JOINED THE BEATLES.

BUT IT WAS JIMMY GREAVES WHO LOOKED THE BEST IN ALL THE WORLD

THEY'LL BE TALKING OF JIMMY IN 2063!

WHEN ENGLAND TAKE ON A TEAM FROM MARS WITH FIVE SUBSTITUTES FROM THE MOON ALLOWED TO PLAY IN THE SECOND HALF.

Roy ULLYETT.

Greaves 1 Charlton 2 Law 3
—That's Riera's rating

By CLIVE TOYE

FERNANDO RIERA, of Chile, coach to the Rest of the World team, chose Jimmy Greaves as "The English player I would most like to have in any future world team."

Riera picked Bobby Charlton as the second best, and made it a winning trio for British football by naming Scotland's Denis Law of the third team as the third best.

Fourth and fifth in the rating of greatness were Spain's centre-forward Alfredo di Stefano and Russia's goalkeeper Lev Yashin Djalma Santos, the great Brazilian back, who has faced England four times, said : "This is by far the best England team I have played against."

And Riera said : " Win the World Cup with this team ? Of course it is possible for England. And not only in English conditions —I mean anywhere."

Apology

England manager Alf Ramsey said : " No one would doubt it was a serious test for the England players if they saw how exhausted they were. They played their hearts out.

" Of course they did a lot more running around because of the inaccuracy of their passing.

" But I was pleased at the effort the team showed, and pleased with the excellent reactions from the crowd.

Referee Bobby Davidson, of Scotland, apologised for the decision which angered the crowd and robbed Greaves of a goal, before Terry Paine scored England's first.

Greaves got the ball in the net after being fouled outside the penalty area.

Davidson pulled the play back for a free kick to England. And he admitted " That's the sort of decision every referee hates to make. But I blew up the second Greaves was tripped. It was certainly a foul and I couldn't know that Greaves would score."

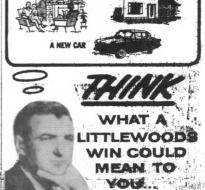

AN ASSURED FUTURE FOR YOUR FAMILY — A NEW HOUSE — A NEW CAR

THINK WHAT A LITTLEWOODS WIN COULD MEAN TO YOU AND SEND YOUR

LITTLEWOODS THIS WEEK

This is it—the goal that beat the World. Time: the 87th minute. Scorer: Jimmy Greaves, the inimitable cockney

---

Last night's Soccer
FOR THE REPORTS, TURN TO PAGE 22

F.A. CENTENARY MATCH

ENGLAND (0) 2   REST OF WORLD (0) 1
Paine, Greaves   Law

DIVISION III

CREWE (0) 0   C PALACE (2) 2.
5,885   Button, Allen
LUTON — (1) 1   BRISTOL C (1) 4
Walden—5,207   Morton 4/2, Ayres, Derrick, Clark

DIVISION IV

ALDRSHT (1) 2   BRAD CITY (0) 2
Burton, Towers   Hellawell, Thorpe 2—5,597
BRADFRD (2) 2   ROCHDALE (1) 2
Burns, Fryatt   Richardson, Morton—5,484
CHESTER (0) 0   BRIGHTON (0) 0
8,766
EXETER (2) 2   TRANMERE (0) 0
Phoenix, Mitchell, 5,701
Curtis, Henderson
Rees
GILLNGHM (1) 2   TORQUAY (0) 0
Yeo, Gibbs

ENGLAND.—Banks ; Armfield, Wilson ; Milne, Norman, Moore ; Paine, Greaves, Smith, Eastham.

REST OF THE WORLD.—Yashin (Soskic) ; Di Santos (Eyzaguirre), Schnellinger ; Pluskat, Popluhar, Masopust (Baxter) ; Kopa (Seeler), Law, Di Stefano, Eusebio (Puskas), Gento.

OLDHAM —(1) 1   MILLWALL (1) 2
Sievwright   Obeney 2
9,758
READING (0) 1   PRT VALE (0) 0
Allen   8,553
WREXHAM (3) 3   BRNMTH (2) 2
Phythian,   Coughlin 2,
Metcalf, Griffiths   Crickmore, Singer
9,236

FOOTBALL COMBINATION.—Div I : Southampton 1 Chelsea 0. Div II : Brentford 2 Southend 1.

SOUTHERN LEAGUE.— Crawley 3 Yieovil 2—Romford v Nuneaton, postponed to November 6.

GREYHOUND WINNERS AND TONIGHT'S SELECTIONS

CRAYFORD—7.38 Friendly Karan 3—1,
Nobody 4—1 (F 4-8 26-6). 7.44 Mena Rae
7—4 fav, Dandelin 5—1 (F 4-8 33-8).

HAWKEYE'S ONE-DOG SPECIAL
8.30. CATFORD
Honey Moon King

HAWKEYE'S FANCIES
CATFORD.—8.30, Honey Moon King (nap). 8.15, Jaunty Step. 8.30, Moonshine Scott. 9.30, Ocean Chief.

OTHER SELECTIONS
READING.—7.46, Duke of Fame. 8.15, Sea Percy. 9.8, Nulla Yo Young. 9.26, King's Daughter (nap).

CLAPTON.—8.51, Bir Percy. 9.8, Nulla Yo Young. 9.26, King's Daughter (nap).

SOUTHEND.—8.15, Blackenergy (nap). 8.43, Cheerio Princess. 9.5, Duntown Theme. 9.13, Olarda's Major.

THE GAMBOLS ..... *by Barry Appleby*

NO, NO, GEORGE / NOT THAT, PLEASE / PLEASE GEORGE / THERE MUST BE SOME WAY TO FREE THIS ZIP !

©1963 Daily Express

Printed and published by Beaverbrook Newspapers Ltd., Fleet-street, London, E.C.4; Great Ancoats-street, Manchester, 4; and Albion-street, Glasgow, C.1.

FABULOUS FRED MAKES IT 301

Oval goes wild as Trueman sets Test wickets record

BOYCOTT STILL THERE—BUT DEXTER IS OUT

by DENIS COMPTON

FABULOUS Freddie Trueman, written off by many as a Test has-been, yesterday became the first bowler in the world to take 300 Test wickets. He achieved his ambition at 13 minutes to 3 after one of the most electrifying spells of cricket ever seen at the Oval.

The Australian total stood at 367 for eight in this fifth and final Test—Trueman's total at 299.

He had taken two wickets—those of Ian Redpath and Graham McKenzie—with the last two balls before lunch and a hat-trick for the Yorkshireman was a lively possibility.

No one wanted to miss what could have been the most dramatic joint achievement—a hat-trick and a world record.

And the terraces and stands were packed, and police guarded the boundary after lunch as Dexter set an umbrella field for Neil Hawke.

IT MISSED . . .

Trueman tore up to the wicket to a crescendo of roars from the crowd, but the ball missed bat and stumps and the almost unbearable tension was relieved.

The crowd had to wait until a further 24 runs had been scored before Trueman finally reached his fantastic target.

He had Neil Hawke caught by Colin Cowdrey in the slips, and the entire Oval erupted in a thunder of applause.

They rose to acclaim the tremendous feat of England's great-hearted Freddie, and the cheers and claps rang across the ground.

He had suddenly and dramatically bowled England back into the game, and after some bright hitting by Tom Vievers, the Australians were eventually all out for 379—a lead of 197 on the first innings.

England, when they began their second innings, showed once more that they were intent on chasing the runs.

Geoff Boycott and Bob Barber put on 80 for the first wicket before Barber was out, and after Ted Dexter had added a bright and breezy 25 England finished the day 132 for two, needing 65 to wipe off the arrears.

HIS DAY

But the day belonged to Trueman, who in his 65th Test match has accomplished the seemingly impossible in the comparatively short span of 13 years.

Freddie's fantastic career has never progressed on an even keel—sometimes plumbing the depths or at times reaching heights that no other bowler could ever hope to reach.

And yet his timing has always been perfect. Throughout his turbulent and magnificent career, he has consistently proved both his critics and fans wrong with some remarkable bowling performances just when it was thought he was past his best.

Now the selectors will find it difficult to exclude him from the forthcoming tour to South Africa.

The Australians were intent on quick runs when they began the day. They put on 39 before Wally Grout was out to Cartwright.

Veivers, who joined Redpath, quickly dispelled any doubts about his injured thumb by hitting Titmus for a mighty 6 over mid-wicket.

AGGRESSION

The partnership realised 50 in the hour, with Veivers producing almost entirely all the aggression and dominance. But the crowd showed little reaction to Veivers's dashing display.

They followed the excitement of Trueman's spell which ended with him getting Grahame Corling—and the 301st Test wicket of his career.

But this did not alter the fact that Australia, all out at 379, were in a very nearly impregnable position with a lead of 197 runs. Only the most aggressive and daring approach by the English batsmen could give them any possible chance of squaring this series.

This, I sincerely hoped, was going to be Ted Dexter's instructions. What did it matter whether we lost this match providing we went down with all our guns firing and giving cricket a much-needed shot in the arm.

It was quite obvious at the start of our innings that England were not going to waste any time. Geoff Boycott was in splendid form.

He was particularly severe in anything short outside the off stump. His square-cut was played to perfection, and his driving off the back foot a delight to watch. Barber too played some lovely strokes off his legs.

But at 80 Barber played across and a fraction late to McKenzie and was out l.b.w.

Dexter began by pulling Veivers with great ferocity to the ropes. He then had two wild flashes at McKenzie without making contact, but then drove a half volley from the same bowler in the most thrilling fashion for four.

There was no doubt about Dexter's intentions. Another crashing drive from Dexter off Veivers was partially stopped by Lawry, yet such was the force behind it that it still raced to the ropes.

Dexter and Boycott played such exhilarating cricket that 40 runs came in 30 minutes. But it did not last much longer, and Dexter, slashing once too often at McKenzie, edged the ball into the safe hands of Bobby Simpson.

He had played as if he had a train to catch, and it gave us all a glimpse of how the game of cricket should be played.

SCOREBOARD

ENGLAND.—First Innings 182 (Hawke 6—47).

SECOND INNINGS

G. Boycott not out	74
R. Barber lbw McKenzie	29
E. Dexter c Simpson b McKenzie	25
F. Titmus not out	0
Lb 4	4
Total (2 wkts)	132

To bat: C. Cowdrey, K. Barrington, P. Parfitt, J. Parks, F. Trueman, T. Cartwright, J. Price.

Fall of wickets: 1—80, 2—120.

Bowling to date.—McKenzie 15-4-47-2, Corling 5-0-19-0, Hawke 18-6-32-0, Vievers 15-8-30-0.

AUSTRALIA

First Innings

R. Simpson c Dexter b Cartwright	24
W. Lawry c Trueman b Dexter	94
N. O'Neill c Parfitt b Cartwright	11
P. Burge lbw Titmus	25
B. Booth c Trueman b Price	74
I. Redpath b Trueman	45
W. Grout b Cartwright	20
T. Vievers not out	67
G. McKenzie c Cowdrey b Trueman	0
N. Hawke c Cowdrey b Trueman	14
G. Corling c Parfitt b Trueman	0
B 4, lb 1	5
Total	379

FALL OF WICKETS.—1—45, 2—57, 3—96, 4—202, 5—245, 6—279, 7—343, 8—343, 9—367, 10—379.

BOWLING.—Trueman 33.3-6-87-4, Price 21-2-67-1, Cartwright 62-23-110-3, Titmus 42-20-51-1, Barber 6-1-23-0, Dexter 13-1-36-1.

UMPIRES.—C. Elliott, J. Crapp.

● Jubilant Freddie Trueman hugs Colin Cowdrey, who caught two for the Test record-breaker

HOW THEY FELL

298 . . Redpath b Trueman 45

299 . . McKenzie c Cowdrey 0

300 . . . Hawke c Cowdrey 14

301 . . . . Corling c Parfitt 0

Soccer's Top Team is lining up for YOU

STAND by for the sports thrill of the year . . . the start of the new League football season next Saturday.

The fans will pack the terraces and stands . . the star players and the star teams will all be in action again.

And, as always, the Sunday Express Top Team of ace writers and reporters will be there to give you the best football service of any newspaper

ALAN HOBY

His Big Game Specials are unrivalled in Soccer reporting. His vivid style captures all the excitement, all the drama. His up-to-the-minute features spotlight the star names and big talking-points in football.

DANNY BLANCHFLOWER

There's a new field for this controversial character this season. In addition to his weekly column with its provocative approach to all sporting arguments, Danny will frequently join the match-reporting team to describe games in his own inimitable fashion.

STANLEY MATTHEWS

He will comment on the Soccer scene with all the authority of his lifetime as a top star

JAMES CONNOLLY

He knows everyone who matters in football. He travels round the clubs, big and small, gathering scoops for Soccer News.

DENIS COMPTON

A top-class outside left for Arsenal and England, Denis can "read" a football match with the same expert eye that makes him such a popular cricket commentator. He joins the reporting team when the cricket season ends.

KEN LAWRENCE

He will tour the clubs for headline stories—for the human stories that fascinate every football fan.

BIG GAME SPECIALS

A report of your home-town team's match is the first thing you expect to read on Sunday morning. You will find it in the Sunday Express big-game special editions, with a corps of Soccer experts bringing you all the highlights.

Don't miss this super Soccer service. Join the Sunday Express team

NEXT SUNDAY

TWIN TROUBLE AT THE TOP

WITH Worcestershire and Warwickshire wilting under pressure yesterday, the County Championship struggle becomes a much more open and fascinating affair.

Worcester, the leaders, crumpling before Gloucester's seam attack, were dismissed for 143 at Cheltenham. It must have made them happier when they heard that challenging Warwick were also having their troubles.

Bowlers Brian Brain and Norman Gifford, in a gallant eight-wicket stand, raised 55 in 70 minutes that averted a Worcester disaster. The first seven wickets had fallen for 84. Gloucester had put on 84 for three wickets when rain stopped play.

After losing early and cheap wickets, Derby, thanks to a solid 54 from Ian Buxton and a purposeful 72 from Derek Morgan, climbed to 183. Then Warwick cracked before Harold Rhodes (3—10) and Les Jackson (2—8) and lost five incredibly quick wickets for only 25.

Lancashire leg spinners Tom Greenhough (5—36) and Sonny Ramadhin (3—21) shot out Somerset for 97—their lowest total of the season—at Old Trafford. After losing Green, Pullar, Grieves, and Marner to the pace bowling of Palmer for only 17, Lancashire recovered well.

There was little to cheer the Leicester crowd as Hampshire plodded carefully through the day. That was until Brian Timms and Derek Shackleton opened up after tea. They smacked 105 in a 90-minute ninth-wicket stand and pushed Hampshire to 314.

After Ken Taylor and Phil Sharpe had given Yorkshire a solid start with 99 for the first wicket against Sussex, it was left to John Hampshire (71) to stave off a collapse and Yorkshire reached 232 for six.

Bedford 3 Watford 4

WATFORD tried 18 players at Bedford and manager Bill McGarry said after: "We still have one or two problems."

Emery put Bedford two up after 25 minutes but McAnearney, Owen, and Larkin saw Watford ahead.

A Crisp own goal levelled matters and Larkin won it in the 87th minute.

ARSENAL PROBLEM STILL WING-HALF

Portsmouth 1 Arsenal 5: by RAY COLLIER

ARSENAL had a fairly effortless win over Portsmouth in the friendly at Fratton Park without their forwards having to work too hard. They had better luck with their shooting than Portsmouth, who showed quite a bit of spirit.

The home team, however, lacked the necessary bite in front of goal.

The main lesson to be learned is that Portsmouth still have quite a way to go before they can fulfil their supporters' dreams of seeing the club back in the First Division again.

Arsenal's principal weakness still seems to be at wing half, where Peter Simpson was not too successful.

This meant more work for George Eastham and Geoff Strong in scheming the chances, although the inside forwards did penetrate Portsmouth's back-pedalling defensive plan on a number of occasions with success.

Portsmouth tried out their striker attacking plan with four forwards up and deep-lying Albert McCann acting as the linkman.

PUNCHY LEWIS

This produced some good efforts from John Gordon, who took over from the transfer-listed Ron Saunders at centre forward, and from their £7,000 newcomer Cliff Portwood, who was unlucky not to claim a couple of goals.

The other linkman was the right half, and in this respect Brian Lewis packed more punch in the second half when he took over from Bobby Campbell.

Don Howe, the new Arsenal right back, had a relatively quiet game, although Dodson gave him some trouble early on.

But in general the Arsenal defence was too powerful for Pompey, with Jim Furnell making several smart saves in goal.

He was beaten by John McClelland after eight minutes, but Eastham equalised after 20 minutes. Strong headed two more goals before the interval. George Armstrong flipped in the fourth after 65 minutes, and Joe Baker got the fifth from a solo effort two minutes from time.

Bobby Smith cheers fans

Brighton 3 Charlton 1

STYLISH Charlton, one up after four minutes when skipper Mike Bailey burst through for a splendid solo goal, later had the steam taken out of them by Brighton—and Bobby Smith.

Six thousand Brighton fans went to the Goldstone ground hoping to see Smith show some of his England touches, and they were not disappointed. Bobby blasted a 28th-minute equaliser, and was mobbed by a crowd of happy spectators at the finish.

In an all-action first half—more like a League match than a practice—Brighton matched their higher-class opponents and snatched the lead just before the interval when Jack Smith scored from six yards.

Impressive

Some of Charlton's approach work was highly impressive with Bailey the inspiration at right half. Later he went off with a cut nose, and Brighton skipper Jimmy Collins scored with a penalty seven minutes from the end after Brian Kinsey had handled a terrific Bobby Smith drive.

Kinsey had a good match, despite conceding that penalty when Smith's drive knocked him flat. He headed a goal-bound Collins shot off the line and gave clever winger Wally Gould few opportunities.

Big John Hewie was equally impressive.

Dour Bailey stops Sydenham gallop

by SYDNEY SPICER

A SEMI-FIT Trevor Bailey, cricket's rot-stopper-in-chief, put on the old familiar act again at Leyton, with Essex tottering against Surrey. Thanks to Bailey and to aggressive displays by Barry Knight and Brian Taylor, Essex recovered to reach 326 for nine.

Bailey decided only at the last minute that he was fit to play, and he does not expect to bowl in the match, because of a pulled muscle near the ribs.

Three Essex wickets were down for 21, and then they had another setback.

Gordon Barker, who always looks so good while he lasts, slashed at a ball from David Sydenham outside the off stump and was smartly caught at cover by Mike Willett.

Rash stroke

With a transfusion of Bailey blood, Barker would never have attempted such a rash stroke. Now it was 30 for four, and Sydenham had taken three for 11.

Knight, who has not been in the runs of late, joined his skipper and got his head down. Essex were spared further shocks, and at lunch the fifth wicket pair had raised the score to 91.

In the afternoon session Knight played a stimulating innings.

Knight reached his 50 out of 82 and, when Ron Tindall came on with off-spin, struck him for a full-blooded 6 which made the stand worth 100 in 125 minutes.

Knight scored 42 of his 76 in the hour before lunch. Then he mistimed a drive off Tindall and holed out at long-on. He had hit ten 4's and a 6.

Bailey plodded on, with Taylor at the other end. Taylor, hero of the previous day's run-chase, for a time found difficulty in getting the ball away.

Suddenly he opened out with a spate of fours at the expense of Tindall and Stuart Storey, mainly from lusty, old-fashioned pulls. He pulled Storey for six to reach 51 out of 79 for the sixth wicket, and had hit six 4's and a 6, and completed his thousand runs for the season, when he was bowled for 58.

When Bailey was adjudged l.b.w. on the shrieking appeal of Sydenham, using the new ball, he had been there four hours for 67 and given no chance. His was a restoration job thoroughly well done, as the score, 260 for six, confirmed.

Robin Hobbs straight-drove the third 6 of the day during a lively ninth-wicket stand which took the total gaily past 300.

UNDERWOOD TAKES 6-43

KENT left-arm bowler Derek Underwood exploited a receptive Dover wicket yesterday to take six wickets for 43 runs in 28 overs as Northants were skittled out for 144 by tea.

After an early reverse, when they lost Reynolds brilliantly caught by Jim Prodger off Dye for five, Northants were steered out of trouble by Colin Milburn (31) and Roger Prideaux (24) who put on 52 for the second wicket.

Then Underwood started his breakthrough with only Peter Watts (35) offering any real resistance. In the five minutes before tea Underwood whipped out the tail-enders.

Kent made a disastrous start. After opener Mike Denness had hit Dave Larter for 4 through the covers, he was caught by Reynolds off Larter. Worse was to follow when David Nichalls was bowled by Larter just after hooking a loose ball to the boundary.

Luckhurst and Bob Wilson contained the Northants bowling during the closing stages of the day. Wilson, using a number of strokes which demonstrated his versatility, forced the pace and he tamed both Crump and Scott. Even Larter was unable to penetrate the dogged but decisive partnership.

Then Milburn took a catch at short square leg off Scott to dismiss Wilson for 34. Prodger plodded to keep up his end for Luckhurst in a slow and uninspiring close.

SPORTING SAM . . . . by Reg. Wootton

Stand-in Wallace dazzles West Ham

Liverpool 2 West Ham 2: by ALAN HOBY

THEY swayed there, a multitude of heads moving hypnotically in alternate directions just as they had done last season—the great Anfield choir spraying and spilling in their thousands down the steeps of Spion Kop.

They chanted their familiar rallying cry "Liverpool . . . Liverpool. . . ." But in the seventh minute of this stirring and dramatic Charity Shield match which Liverpool should have won, the Kop roar was cut off as if an enormous gag had been stuffed into their mouths.

Liverpool's centre forward, Alf Arrowsmith, lunging into an awkward tackle on West Ham right-winger Peter Brabrook, fell to the ground his face contorted with pain.

Arrowsmith had torn ligaments in his left knee.

FANATICS

And in that moment of misery for those fanatical "Scouses" you could almost read the thought drumming through their minds: Would Arrowsmith be fit for Liverpool's first-leg European Cup match with Reykjavik in Iceland tomorrow night?

For a moment their spirits soared as Arrowsmith hobbled back, only to collapse again as he turned on the ball. This time Liverpool's leader was helped off for good—Phil Chisnall came on as substitute—and is out of the Cup match.

Already of course Liverpool had to field another reserve—20-year-old Scot, Gordon Wallace from Garrowhill, at inside left in place of Ian St. John, still not in training.

But in a first half crammed with glorious incident and marred only by the finicky finishing of West Ham it was Wallace who dazzled and delighted.

Indeed, in the 29th minute after centre forward Johnny Byrne of all people shot wide at an open goal, Wallace flashed Liverpool ahead.

An uncharacteristic mistake by an off-form Bobby Moore—the West Ham skipper tried to trap the ball far too nonchalantly and failed to connect—let in the quick-silver Wallace whose crashing shot hit the post and ricocheted in.

But in the 42nd minute cultured West Ham levelled when a Bovington chip—close-tackling Eddie had a good game—caught the tall Liverpool defenders flat-footed. And there, running clear, was Byrne, pulling the ball down for it to slide off his boot just inside the post.

In the second half, however, the Kop choral society was in better voice. Four minutes after half-time Liverpool showed how to beat the modern defence in depth.

STATUES

With Moore, Burkett, Brown, Bovington, and Bond standing off like statues Liverpool's doughty right back Jerry Byrne steamed up and pounced on a short pass from the splendid and tireless Ian Callaghan—surely he must play for England soon?—and amid an exultant roar Byrne thumped a diagonal 40-yard fireball which hit the net while goalkeeper Jim Standen was still diving.

Now Liverpool were in full flow. Tiring West Ham, with Moore faulty in his control and too often pulled out of position, were over-run.

It looked Liverpool's match but six minutes from the end centre-half Ron Yeats and his defence were for once beaten by a Brabrook cross. Goalkeeper Tommy Lawrence could only push out the ball to Geoff Hurst who slammed the equaliser.

Left-winger Johnny Sissons, inside-left Hurst, centre-half Ken Brown, and left back Jack Burkett joined Bovington as West Ham's men of the day.

Liverpool? They were robbed.

ATHLETICS SPECIAL
Great Britain v Poland match report—Page 23

PUNCHLESS BRENTFORD

Brentford 0 Nottm. Forest 3

FIRST DIVISION Nottingham Forest coasted to victory against a punchless Brentford side that can hardly view the Third Division rigours ahead with too much confidence after this performance.

A hat-trick by Colin Addison clinched the game for Forest. Addison, in fact, might have had four goals, but Chick Brodie made a fine one-handed save to tip a powerful drive over the bar.

Some measure of excuse for Brentford was that schemer Jimmy Bloomfield, their £10,000 signing from Birmingham, had to sit the game out through injury, and his craft was sadly missed in the middle of the side's 4-2-4 formation.

Only Mark Lazarus, who set the game alight with a series of runs, proved a threat to the Forest defence. Newcomer Joe Bonson had few chances to shine.

Alan Hinton, who gave Allan Jones a trying afternoon, set up Addison's opening goal after five minutes.

An unnecessary handling offence by George Thomson gave Addison a 70th minute penalty and his shot blasted into the net and back into play.

Four minutes later Addison clinched his hat-trick at the second attempt.

A GREAT DISPLAY BY GEORGE COHEN

WILL Spurs step up the pressure for Fulham's brilliant defender George Cohen? That was the question intriguing onlookers at Craven Cottage after the England full-back's great display in the club's trial which Whites won 3—1.

Spurs other "wanted" man Johnny Haynes was out with an ankle injury.

Scottish international Graham Leggat at centre forward, Dave Metchick and Bobby Howfield scored for the Whites. Centre-forward Reg Stratton replied for the Blues.

Terry Price, 17-year-old England youth international led the taming of Leyton Orient's first team by the reserves at Brisbane Road.

Right-winger Price teed up the first goal for Tommy Dunne before weighing in with two himself.

Dave Dunmore and Ted Phillips pulled two goals back before the interval and Phillips saved the first team with a second half equaliser.

Millwall player-manager Billy Gray has got together a nice blend of youth and experience at the Den.

But what is badly wanted is somebody who can take the chances laid on by Len Julians, Roy Dwight, Roy Senior and Jimmy Whitehouse.

Julians and Dwight scored for the Blue and Whites and Clarke and Curran for the Red and Whites.

Hope's winner for West Brom

West Bromwich Albion beat Ajax of Amsterdam 1—0 in Amsterdam last night. Inside-left Bobby Hope scored in the 50th minute.

The Sunday Express incorporating the Sunday Dispatch is printed and published by Beaverbrook Newspapers Ltd., Fleet Street, London, E.C.4; Great Ancoats Street, Manchester 4; and Albion Street, Glasgow, C.1. No. 2377.

Courage was the word for great Olympics climax

REBEL ABEBE'S KILLER DOUBLE . .

Tokio, Wednesday

THE athletics programme in the XVIII Olympic Games came to an end today in a magnificent climax, the keynote of which was one word—COURAGE.

The courage of all the men who ran in the 26 miles 385 yards marathon, for courage is what you need even to compete in this "killer" . . . no matter whether you finish first or fifty-first.

The courage of Robbie Brightwell who in his last serious track appearance ran himself down to his knees.

And I mean those last six words literally, for that was how he ended on the track after winning us yet another silver medal in the 4 x 400 metres relay.

The courage of Alan Simpson running the race of his life behind "Man of the Games" Peter Snell in the 1,500 metres.

He ended fourth—but he finished flat on his face like a knocked out boxer, having given his all. And no man can give more than that.

The courage of Dorothy Hyman—another running the last race of her career —who after an injury-crippled season "found" that extra yard or so which separates the champion from the commoner.

And so she "anchored" our girls into third place in the women's 4 x 100

metres relay, gaining the British team the bronze medal which has so far eluded us in these medal-happy Games.

Some performances transcend nationality and that of the Ethiopian Abebe Bikila was one of those performances.

Heroes

Until today, fourteen marathons had been run in the Olympics since they were revived in 1896.

But no one man born of woman has been able to triumph more than once in this excruciating experience which does not separate the men from the boys but the heroes from the men.

Today Abebe Bikila, a sergeant in the Ethiopian Imperial Guards, did it just five weeks after an appendicitis operation!

His time of 2h. 12m. 11.2s. was the fastest ever for the marathon and was 3m. 5s. faster than the one he returned to win the title in Rome four years ago.

What it means is that he averaged nearly 12 m.p.h., or almost a mile every five minutes. FOR OVER TWENTY - SIX MILES.

At 1 p.m. the field of sixty-eight wound its way like the gaily-coloured tail of the longest kite you've ever seen out of the stadium and into each man's individual loneliness.

Cavalcade

It was a sopping, spongy grey Tokio day with the thermometer registering over 68 degrees, high humidity and a lack of air which left the flags circling the stadium limp as washing on the line.

Ben Boubaker, of Tunisia, led out of the stadium—give him his one moment of joy — and of our three runners, Ron Hill was in third place.

Brian Kilby was last but one and Basil Heatley was roughly in the middle of the field.

As soon as they got out on to the road the cavalcade of 136 legs, knotted hairy, sweating legs—black, brown, olive, yellow, ivory legs — was picked up by their escort.

I refer, of course, to three white-helmeted and goggled motorcycle outriders who, at a little over 12 m.p.h., were to accompany them for the next twenty-five miles.

Out In Front

After 5 km. big Ron Clarke of Australia—third in the 10,000 metres, unplaced in the 5,000 — was leading from Ireland's Jim Hogan and Tunisia's Haddeb Hannachi.

It took just 28m. 17s. for Abebe to wrest the lead from Clarke . . . and thereafter the Ethiopian was never headed.

At 15 km. (45m. 35s.) the incredible consistent pace of Abebe had him out in front of Hogan and Clarke.

Now they've been running for an hour, pounding along to the continuous roar of a crowd a million strong, thronging the roadside, jamming the balconies perched on every vantage point, a swarming anthill of people.

At the turning point,

Tobis Takyumachi, just outside the village of Kanto Mura, Abebe starts the return haul six yards up on Hogan, with Clarke 200 yards farther back.

Heatley was the first British runner to reach the turning point, half a mile behind Abebe.

Hill was forty yards behind him and Kilby yet another forty yards further back.

Frantic

Twenty-five kilometres. The Abebe-Hogan gap is ten seconds.

Clarke is 1½ minutes behind Hogan; Heatley has moved into ninth place, Kilby is tenth, three seconds behind.

Thirty kilometres. Abebe frame spare with spindly chicken's legs, impassive face moustached and topped with black crinkly hair, and one finger be-ringed, is running through the inner suburban streets lined with cherry trees.

The crowd is going even more frantic as a Japanese. Kokichi Tsuburaya, with Jozsef Suetoe, of Hungary, moves up on Hogan.

Clarke has dropped back to fifth place.

Heatley is now fourth, with Kilby just behind him and Suetoe is beginning to flag.

Hogan had had it. He is being passed by runner after runner.

Now Abebe, relentless, remorseless Abebe, is acknowledging the cheers of the huge crowd gathered round Shimjuku railway station.

Then, at 3.10 p.m. precisely, a fanfare of

To think he might have been shot!

trumpets — the marathon champion's accolade—and the cheers from the crowd heralded the entry of the gladiator into the arena.

Never varying that crocodile-gobbling stride of his, Abebe circled the red shale track to thunderous applause.

Then came an incident unique in my experience of a dozen or more marathons. After mopping his face with a small hand towel, Abebe went into a new act.

In the centre of the field he touched his toes half a dozen times; lay on his back doing cycling exercises; kicked his legs so that his feet touched the ground behind his head.

He speaks only Ethiopian, but in the universal language of sport he was telling 75,000 people how much he still had in him !

Then he held his hands aloft and turned to the four sides of the stadium to acknowledge the homage of the crowd

Explosion

And no sooner had he finished this than the biggest explosion of applause in the whole eight days of athletics broke out as Japanese champion Tsuburaya treacled his way into the stadium . . . only to be followed seconds later by our own Heatley.

As Tsuburaya plodded his way tensely along the back straight, the frantic cries from the Japanese thousands stilled when, 220 yards from home, Heatley ground past him.

For eight long days, the crowd had sat praying for a Japanese success and

now their silver man was being turned into bronze before their very almond eyes.

As Heatley was crossing the finishing line Tsuburaya, twenty yards to the rear, began to waver and when he crossed the line he was reeling rubber legged.

He was, in fact, the only one of the leading runners to show any signs of distress. Kilby, who was fourth, was quite composed, as was Hill in nineteenth place

Revolt

Two years ago, Abebe Bikila was on the "wrong side" when the Ethiopian Guard rebelled against Emperor Haile Selassie—a revolt ruthlessly put down.

But Abebe was not punished because, as a sergeant, he was held only to have carried out his officers' orders.

He said: "I shall train on for the next Olympic Games in 1968, and I expect to win easily in Mexico."

Abebe's courage had lasted for almost two and a quarter hours.

Robbie Brightwell's was compressed into under three-quarters of a minute. But what a performance!

Tim Graham just about held his own in the first leg, but Adrian Metcalfe was in third place when he handed over the baton to John Cooper.

When Cooper, in turn, passed it on to Robbie, we were fourth.

Coming into the final bend Robbie was still fourth. He was still there fifty yards from home.

And then it happened.

The fuse was lit. The detonator ignited. The bomb exploded.

Past Jamaica's George Kerr he clawed his way, past Wendell Mottley he raged.

And although he could not catch flying Henry Carr, of the USA, he anchored us into a new world and Olympic record of 3m. 1.6s., just 0.9s. behind the American.

As he crossed the line Brightwell crumpled on to the track.

He had to go on his knees after Cooper helped him up, and then his fiancee, Ann Packer, got to him.

After kissing him and kissing him again, the 5ft. 6in. girl was supporting the 6ft. 2in., 13st. man towards the dressing room.

Afterwards Robbie said: "This is undoubtedly the finest athletics team Britain has ever sent abroad, and I'm proud to have been its captain.

"This relay success was a wonderful team effort with no man deserving more credit than another.

"We all gave all we had. Maybe what clinched it was my anger when about sixty yards from home Wendell Mottley elbowed me in the ribs as I tried to go past him

Hopping Mad

"In a race as hard as that you aren't even feeling in the best of health at such a moment and made me hopping mad to get past him."

Talking of not being in the best of health, Metcalfe said frankly:

"All I know is that after, when we were lying in the room where we keep the medals, I was all over their p—i flowers !"

All I can add is that this relay finished off about the most satisfactory day I can ever remember in British world athletics . . . or indeed one in any sport.

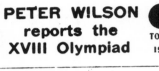
PETER WILSON reports the XVIII Olympiad   TOKIO 1964

He has just achieved the "impossible"—by becoming the first man in history to win two Olympic marathons. Now Ethiopia's Abebe Bikila exercises the ache out of his whipcord legs while he waits for his nearest rival—Britain's Basil Heatley—to cross the finishing line . . . over four minutes behind him.

The Evening News
and STAR

No. 25,754   LONDON MONDAY OCTOBER 26 1964   PRICE 4d.

THE GOLDEN DAYS TOKIO, 1964

BRITAIN'S OLYMPIC TRIUMPHS

SOUVENIR PICTURE EDITION

THIS is a Special Souvenir Edition to commemorate the great achievements of Britain's Olympic team in the Tokio Games, 1964.

Our athletes excelled themselves with four gold and seven silver medals.

Mary Rand won a gold, silver and bronze; Ann Packer won a gold and a silver.

Here are our medal winners:

GOLD

Mary Rand
Long Jump (22ft 2in) World Record

Lynn Davies
Long Jump (26ft 5⅜in) UK National, Empire & Commonwealth Record

Ken Matthews
20 Km Walk (1hr 29min 34sec) Olympic Record

Ann Packer
800 Metres (2min 01.1sec) World Record

SILVER

Mary Rand
Pentathlon (5,035 pts), UK National, Empire and Commonwealth Record

Ann Packer
400 Metres (52.2sec.) European and UK National Record

Robbie Brightwell
4 x 400 Metres Relay (3min 01.6sec.) European, UK National, Empire and Commonwealth Record

Tim Graham
4 x 400 Metres Relay

Adrian Metcalfe
4 x 400 Metres Relay

John Cooper
4 x 400 Metres Relay

Paul Nihill
50km. Walk (4hr. 11min. 31.2sec.)

Maurice Herriott
3,000m. Steeplechase (8min 32.4sec.) UK National, Empire & Commonwealth Record

Basil Heatley
Marathon (2hr 16min 19.2sec).

John Cooper
400 Metres Hurdles (50.1 sec.) UK National Record

Bobby McGregor
100 Metres Freestyle Swimming (52.5sec.)

John Russell
Coxless Fours (6min 47.04 sec.)

Hugh Wardell-Yerburgh
Coxless Fours.

Bill Barry
Coxless Fours.

Jesse James
Coxless Fours.

Keith Musto
Flying Dutchman, Yachting (5,556pts).

Tony Morgan
Flying Dutchman, Yachting.

Louis Martin
Middle-Heavy Weight lifting (475 Kilograms).

Bill Hoskyns
Individual Epee.

BRONZE

Mary Rand
4 x 100 Metres Relay (44.0sec.), U.K. National Record.

Janet Simpson
4 x 100 Metres Relay.

Daphne Arden
4 x 100 Metres Relay.

Dorothy Hyman
4 x 100 Metres Relay.

Peter Robeson
Grand Prix Equestrian (Riding Firecrest)

The race that shook the world and thrilled Britain. . . . Ann Packer (55) wins the gold medal and cracks the 800 metres world record.

FINAL MEDAL TABLE

	Gold	Silver	Bronze		Gold	Silver	Bronze
United States	36	26	28	France	1	8	6
Soviet Union	30	31	35	Canada	1	2	1
Japan	16	5	8	Switzerland	1	2	1
Germany	10	22	18	Ethiopia	1	0	0
Italy	10	10	7	Bahamas	1	0	0
Hungary	10	7	5	India	1	0	0
Poland	7	6	10	South Korea	0	2	1
Australia	6	2	10	Trinidad	0	1	2
Czechoslovakia	5	6	3	Tunisia	0	1	1
Britain	4	12	2	Cuba	0	1	0
Bulgaria	3	5	2	Argentina	0	1	0
Finland	3	0	2	Pakistan	0	1	0
New Zealand	3	0	2	Philippines	0	1	0
Rumania	2	4	6	Iran	0	0	1
Holland	2	4	4	Brazil	0	0	1
Turkey	2	3	1	Ghana	0	0	1
Sweden	2	2	4	Ireland	0	0	1
Denmark	2	1	3	Mexico	0	0	1
Yugoslavia	2	1	0	Nigeria	0	0	1
Belgium	2	0	1	Uruguay	0	0	1

Mary Rand, the girl who gave Britain a sparkling start with her sensational long-jump series that ended with a world record and complete annihilation for her American and Russian rivals.

The hug that millions saw on television after a proud wife had watched her husband Ken Matthews walk his way to the 20,000 metres title.

Mary Rand and Lynn Davies, travelled 7,000 miles and proved that they were the greatest.

Pain-wracked Robbie Brightwell sprawls after his fantastic last lap burst that brought us the 400 metres relay silver medal.

STAFFORDSHIRE
WEEKLY SENTINEL

POTTERIES EDITION

COUNTY, AGRICULTURAL, AND PICTORIAL NEWSPAPER

No. 5,798—Est. 1854.　Registered at the General Post Office.　P　N　FRIDAY, APRIL 30, 1965　Telephone: Stoke-on-Trent 29511　THREEPENCE

Unforgettable farewell tribute to the greatest footballer of all time

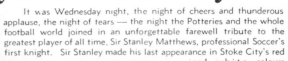

"Wonderful night," says Sir Stanley

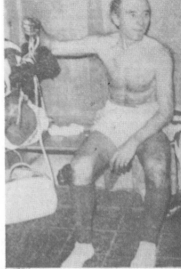

It was Wednesday night, the night of cheers and thunderous applause, the night of tears — the night the Potteries and the whole football world joined in an unforgettable farewell tribute to the greatest player of all time, Sir Stanley Matthews, professional Soccer's first knight. Sir Stanley made his last appearance in Stoke City's red and white colours before a crowd of 35,000 inside the ground and a vast audience of 112 million television viewers.

RIGHT: The moment for tears. Off came the boots and, for the last time, the renowned No. 7 shirt. BELOW: The stars applaud. Nearest the camera is Puskas.

A piper leads Sir Stanley on to the field for his last appearance at the Victoria Ground in Stoke City colours. LEFT: Shaking hands with Sir Stanley Rous, President of F.I.F.A. Said Sir Stanley at the end of the match: "It was a wonderful night and the crowd gave me an ovation that I shall remember to the end of my days."

Di Stefano leads

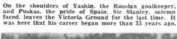

On the shoulders of Yashin, the Russian goalkeeper, and Puskas, the pride of Spain, Sir Stanley, solemn faced, leaves the Victoria Ground for the last time. It was here that his career began more than 33 years ago.

Taking the field for the International XI. v. Stan's XI.— in the lead Di Stefano. LEFT: Smiles and cheers. BELOW: A section of the crowd at the Stoke End. The International XI. won 6-4.

Applause for their leader—Sir Stanley's team welcome him on to the field. BELOW: Another section of the crowd at the Stoke end. At the end of the game, the crowd broke into a chorus of "For he's a jolly good fellow."

News at a glance

All Stoke City's professional staff, apart from two junior players, have been retained by the club for next season.

Among 12 Port Vale players given a free transfer is Irish international outside-right Billy Bingham, signed from Everton two seasons ago.

Approval has been given by the Minister of Education and Science to Stoke-on-Trent Education Committee's proposal for a sixth-form junior college—keystone in the plan for revision of the city's secondary education system.

Hanley's big redevelopment scheme, incorporating the central bus station and multi-deck car park, combined with the £1 million shopping precinct scheme in Old Hall-street, has been given the go-ahead by the Ministry of Housing and Local Government.

Mr. J. H. C. Peters, Commercial Manager of the Stafford and Kidsgrove works, is among three new directors elected to the board of the English Electric Export and Trading Co., Ltd.

Chesterton - born singer Jackie Trent won a place in the Top Twenty this week, her record "Where Are You Now?" moving up from number 30 to number 17 on Monday.

Sunday Mirror

6d.   May 22, 1966   No. 163

Heads clash in the sixth, then a terrible cut opens

GALLANT HENRY

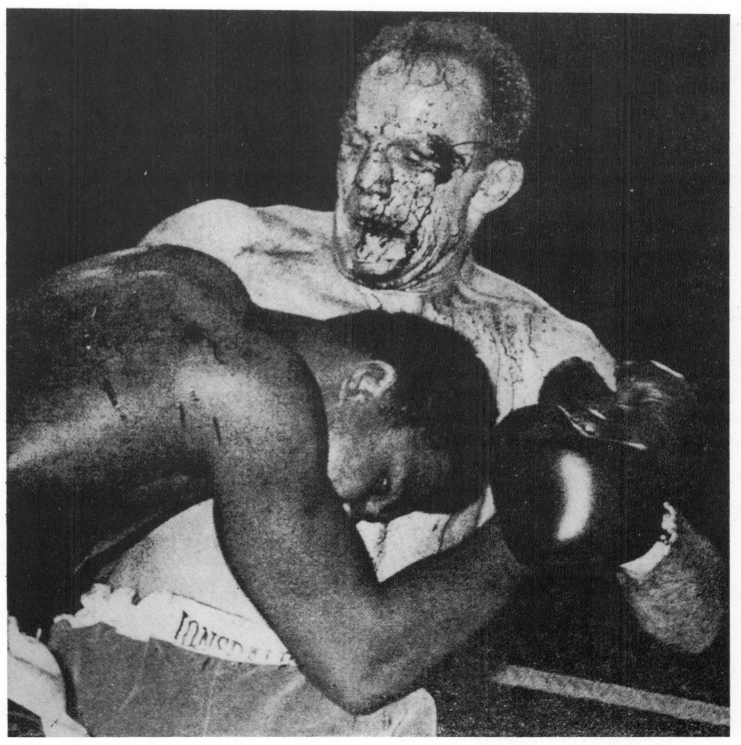

Cooper, blood-drenched from that gashed left eye, battles on. But his brave bid is almost over.

This was the moment that ended his dream

THIS was the moment when Henry Cooper's golden dream died last night.

The moment when he knew that he had failed to wrest the world heavyweight championship from Cassius Clay.

The gallant Englishman is still full of determination.

But defeat is only seconds away.

The end of his dream is written in blood that courses down his face from a cut eye.

'Sorry'

The cut, a terrible cut, opened in the sixth round of the fight at Highbury.

After the fight, in an exclusive interview with Lionel Crane of the Sunday Mirror, Cooper said:

"I don't know whether he hit me, but people around the ring say the cut over my eye was opened by his head."

Clay, too, talked about the cut.

He said of the flow of blood: "You could hear it come.

"It hurt me too much. I just did not like hitting him . . .

"I am really sorry for such an ending. I'm not celebrating."

Evening Standard

44,201   MONDAY, AUGUST 1, 1966   4d.

CHAMPIONS of the WORLD

Moment of triumph

A dream come true! England have won the World Cup, the match is over . . . and captain Bobby Moore holds aloft the Jules Rimet trophy.

He is being chaired round Wembley by three-goal Geoff Hurst (left) and Ray Wilson. Others in the picture are (left to right) Martin Peters, Roger Hunt, George Cohen and Bobby Charlton.

The full England team was: Gordon Banks; Cohen, Wilson; Nobby Stiles, Jackie Charlton, Moore; Alan Ball, Hurst, Charlton, Hunt and Peters.

More pictures

—Pages 12, 13, 24

The Jamaican Weekly Gleaner

Price: SIXPENCE

WEDNESDAY, AUGUST 17, 784, KINGSTON W.I.

In Jamaica and the United Kingdom—6d per copy; in North America—25 cents per copy; by surface mail anywhere except U K and Europe—10d per copy; other rates on Application Newspaper Post Registered at the G. P. O. London

- **Kenyan thrills**
- **Games crowd**
- **England leads with**
- **27 gold medals**

KEINO RUNS MILE IN RECORD 3:57.4

KEINO WINNING

THE oldest track mark of the British Empire and Commonwealth Games — Roger Bannister's one-mile record set in 1954 — went at the National Stadium in Kingston on Thursday night. And the man who erased it was Kenya's magnificent Kipchoge Keino, the Games three-mile champion.

Jamaica was seeing her first sub-four minute mile as the Kenyan policeman hit the tape in 3 minutes 57.4 seconds in the first heat. Bannister, the first man to break the four-minute mile barrier had set his 3 minutes 58.8 seconds at the Vancouver Games in 1954.

Way ahead of the field the sensational Kenyan set his own pace, finishing 50 yards ahead of England's Walter Wilkinson and Australia's Keith Wheeler. And His Royal Highness, Prince Philip, Duke of Edinburgh who had declared the Games opened on Thursday was on hand to see this remarkable run.

A fine performance was also turned in by Trinidad's amazing Wendell Mottley who scorched the Stadium track in 45.2 seconds 440 yards—a Games record.

● Wins marathon

Scotland's stout-hearted Jim Alder weathered the fiery early morning sunshine to take the gruelling marathon (26 miles 385 yards) run in two hours 22 minutes 7.6 secs. The silver medal went to Bill Adcocks of England and the bronze to New Zealand's Mike Ryan.

Una Morris, Jamaica's brightest hope for a medal in the 220 yards final, weakened after hitting the home-stretch. Another Jamaican, Vilma Charlton also failed to come among the medals.

England has maintined her lead in the Gold medals tally picking up six on Thursday to bring her count to 27. Australia was second with 16, Canada next with 9 and Trinidad and Tobago fifth with six gold medals. The Games ended on Saturday.

DAILY EXPRESS

No. 20,711　　THURSDAY JANUARY 5 1967　　Weather: Wintry showers, bright spells later.　　Price 4d.

● Moment by moment — camera shots to study as Bluebird takes off, somersaults, and finally plunges into Coniston Water

Bluebird's death leap

PICTURE BY EXPRESS CAMERAMAN PETER JACKSON

At 310 m.p.h. on the smooth water of Coniston, Campbell's Bluebird, nose almost vertical and engine screaming, somersaults to disaster

THIS IS WHY

The path to disaster: Photonews, Pages 4, 5

300 m.p.h. WAS TOO MUCH FOR A 13-YEAR-OLD BOAT

Express Staff Reporters

DONALD CAMPBELL died on Coniston Water yesterday because he was too brave to admit that he was trying to do the impossible with too little.

He had too little money. In the frustration of waiting, perhaps he showed too little patience. And in his bravery he cared too little for the vital margin of safety.

In the picture above he is pinned in the cockpit of somersaulting Bluebird, a moment from death. But his voice on the radio is calm: "She's tramping—I'm going—I'm on my back—I'm gone."

A deep sigh was heard. Then the "G" of this fearsome somersault at over 300 miles an hour would have blacked out the final impact.

The money

As darkness fell over the steel-grey strip of the Lancashire lake last night, and divers and salvage men put off their work until the morning, Donald Campbell's friends asked and answered the question of WHY?

TOO LITTLE MONEY: The fact is that Campbell badly needed a new boat. It would have cost £100,000, and he just did not have that kind of money.

As it was he put a new engine into the 13-year-old hull of Bluebird for £10,000—"and he had a difficulty in financing that," said Mr. Eric Norris, one of three brothers who helped design the boat.

TOO LITTLE PATIENCE: Campbell had been waiting at Coniston for nine frustrating weeks for the right conditions for a record run.

When he did look like breaking the record at Christmas his observers were absent. Yesterday, when dawn showed the lake like glass, he could hardly wait.

Mr. Andrew Brown, a Kendal business man who was an official observer, said: "Many times in the past he missed his chance because of the time it took to get the picket boats in position and establish that everything was set to go."

The target

On yesterday's first run Campbell topped the record. He turned straight round for the second run.

If he had waited just a few minutes the turbulence he had set up on the first run would have subsided completely. But he pressed on.

Another observer, Mr. Norman Buckley, said: "He could have come back slower and still beaten the record with perfect safety—but the 300 miles an hour target drove him on."

TOO LITTLE SAFETY: Eric Norris said: "My brother designed Bluebird for 250 miles an hour. You fit it with a more powerful engine and ask it to do 300. . . ."

The new Bristol Siddeley Orpheus jet airplane

➤ PAGE TWO, COL. FOUR

PRINCE PHILIP sent a personal message of sympathy to Mrs. Tonia Campbell from Sandringham last night.

He gave me a last wave

EXPRESS MAN BENSON: A GAME OF CARDS

By DAVID BENSON

DONALD CAMPBELL, a desperately superstitious man, felt he was going to die. At his cottage in Coniston on Tuesday night he told me: "I have the most awful premonition that I'm going to get the chop this time. I've had the feeling for days."

To ease his mind we played cards. That started badly, because the pack produced was green-backed. Unlucky green.

We persuaded Campbell to go on. Finally, in his blue sweater—lucky blue—he sat down to a Russian form of patience—and at once he turned up the ace and queen of spades.

"That's it," he said, looking up. "Mary Queen of Scots drew the same two cards the night before she was beheaded."

Switching

There was silence. Then we laughed it off. We got down to a game of pontoon. It was no ordinary game. Before Donald Campbell would make a call he had to consult his latest lucky mascot, Charlie, a rubber monkey that played the drums when a bulb on its tail was pressed.

"Stick" or "buy" or "twist"? Charlie answered by a roll on the drums.

In fact the little monkey was in good form. Campbell finished £2 up on the night.

But as I left he was depressed, and talked about "the chop." He looked up at the calm night sky. "Tomorrow looks like being the day," he said. "I only hope it is not my last."

Laughing

The fateful morning began at 6.30 for Campbell, with Coniston reported "like a mirror."

In the quiet of the boathouse he laughed about the night before and said: "That's the first time in my life I have won at cards."

I said it was a good omen. Then, as he had an ache in his neck, a constant reminder of his 280 - mile - an - hour crash in the Bluebird car in

➤ PAGE TWO, COL. THREE

TONIA FLIES TO LAKE

TONIA CAMPBELL went to Coniston last night by plane and car.

A friend had phoned to her London flat to tell her that her husband was dead.

In fur coat and black silk trouser suit she was met by officials outside Coniston village.

She told them: "I want to go to the cottage. Where is Donald? We've got to get him out tonight."

Mrs. Campbell—she is a cabaret star — was taken to the cottage overlooking the lake.

Later Lady Campbell, mother of Donald Campbell, arrived at Coniston. Her husband, speed king Sir Malcolm Campbell, died in 1948.

IN THE KNOW

WITH THE EXPRESS

400,000 motorists insured with the cut-rate London and Cheshire Insurance Company had their policies cancelled last night:
　　　　Page 10
Lord Helicopter: Hickey, Page 3
Why is nobody checking on Nato?: Page 6
Strike blacks out TV shows: Page 7
Workers get share loans: City, Page 9

DON'T MISS THE BOAT SHOW
Yesterday's opening—Page 7.
WIN a £5,000 yacht—Page 10

Sir Alf Ramsey talks to the Express: Page 12

LONDON POLICE OPEN FIRE IN CAR CHASE

By GEOFFREY DOWLING

A DETECTIVE fired two shots from a revolver into the air during a gun battle in a London street last night. It is believed to be the first time a Metropolitan police officer has ever opened fire when making an arrest.

It happened in Frithville Gardens, Shepherd's Bush —close to where three policemen were murdered last year and near the B.B.C. Television Centre.

Two men leaped from a car after a chase and blasts from two shotguns were aimed at four officers closing in.

Revolvers had been issued to the police, who were lying in ambush after a tip-off that the two men might be armed.

A violent struggle followed. One man was overpowered but the second broke free.

A B.B.C. employee, 25-year-old Brian Read, of Shinfield Street, Shepherd's Bush, said: "The cars came roaring down the road.

"The police appeared to be shooting as they chased the two men.

"Two policemen pinned one of the men against the car and wrested the gun from his hand."

Later a man was taken to Shepherd's Bush police station.

Art raid charge

Early today, 32-year-old Michael Hall, unemployed, of Knight's Hill, Norwood, was charged at Southwark police station with breaking and entering Dulwich College art gallery and stealing eight pictures.

Emigration boom

The number of emigrants to Canada from Britain and Eire last year is estimated at about 60,000—the largest number for decades.

Wall Street climbs

NEW YORK, Wednesday.—The industrial share prices index rose 4.73 points on Wall Street today, closing at 791.14.

Thump! Peter floors the Alp

ROME, Thursday. - England's Peter Boddington thrashed Austrian Kurt Koschauer into second round defeat in the European amateur boxing championships tonight.

The Austrian 16st. boxer tottered slowly as the Turkish referee counted him out on his feet.

An easy, heavy-weight champion-ship Boddington winning in the 6th 4th frame of Koschauer afterwards confirmed. He was among the thickest of it as they stayed tough.

"He told was getting on top after a spell of minutes.

COLLISION

In the four most damaging how-a blow proved a contestant's nose of pains.

T.e away Boddington came away to switch he was given a solid landed ten.

The Austrian A.b very bad in his second round. He worked on his legs as he moved to a as Boddington moved in and tough a solid chin, jaw and side.

Moves outside the court was a way to with a final ringed power of deliver.a solid landing shot Boddington in.

B.y Boddington was out or very very tough Western.went Dennis Avodhi g.c.r.b in the round so I w.t as the away against Peter D.wand. The r.t he end of the second found the end of the second.

OUTSCORED

Dan McMinden from Newry Co. Down via Coventry was classed a dog compliance M.r.r with Swiss Rieben.

Eric Alan Edwards A.r.t worked in W over a solid to Aust.n outpoint.d .n fi.ed.sn.d e.s.w.ns over A. g.r A.r Monican A.n.r over e .t.n Belfast's D.v Falkand Paddy Graham b.y Begin the bout b y w.sh. b.w.s.d.

FIRST SERIES Fly weight F Y.t.n

SERGEI'S STAMINA SINKS STILWELL

PARIS, Thursday. - Graham Stilwell of Leytonstone, No 1 British Boy and Davis Cup reserve was knocked out of the hard-ten.ed French championship in t.he e.v.n.ng, by Russ., No 1 Sergei Likachev in a match full of controversy.

were so badded in endu h.d.t because of the disput.ion and important w h the weather.

In the Russian b.m.o ask the rin a t.w.h s.w.w. verse and losing and depend.ng on t.b.d by which were pass k.r.d by t.he power of the fa.improov.ng Russian.

a.ws. despite 10 minutes set and look barly.n.ng from a w.n g.r.t the .o.th.bike power of the fa.w.r.d a s w.s D.n.v

a.d.t s.r.w. a. s.r.th s. Likachev h.l.ct.v.s.n.ed b by th w.n .t P.r.t.an a b of a.e and the last k.d.w up and w.cked at manager Herrera.

MEN'S SINGLES First Rd P Cornejo
Second Rd S Likachev
K Plichar s

Billy McNeill, captain of Celtic, parades in pride with the European Cup.

HELENIO HERRERA, boss of Inter, said :—

We did not have enough strength to resist the physical power and moral courage shown by Celtic. Right from the first minute they showed their stamina and heart.

They won and they deserved to win. We lost, but the match was a victory for sport.

JOCK STEIN, Celtic manager:

We won because we played great football. We were the only team in it that deserved to win the championship. We were constant on the attack, and I knew that in the long run we would win.

TINY CHALMERS, who scored the winning goal

I knew we could do it. But like everyone else I cannot believe it. I cannot remember how the ball went in.

SARTI, Inter goalkeeper: "We were beaten but I think I did my best."

REFEREE Tschenker (West Germany) wonderful game and Celtic fully deserved to win. Gemmell was the outstanding player.

TOMMY GEMMELL : When I started moving up and shooting I realised Inter had no answer. It seemed to throw them right out of their defensive pattern.

CELTIC SUPERMEN!

From DESMOND HACKETT
Celtic 2 Inter-Milan 1
European Cup Final
Lisbon, Thursday

☆ **G**LASGOW CELTIC, super, superb Celtic, marched proudly into Soccer history tonight when they became the first British team to win the European Cup.

Won is a tame word. They shattered Inter-Milan and the score was an affront to the magnificence of Celtic.

They were DEMANDING the Cup from the first moments of the final in the golden mould of the National Stadium.

And when they won it, their fans took over. They kissed the turf. They embraced the goalposts.

They danced, laughed, cried and waved their hundreds of banners a.t.is a . in defiance of it defenders of Bannockourn.

An impressive array of armed police and militars took one look at the invasion-minded and shrugged, and diploma.cary left the field to the victors rejoicing fans.

The Portuguese audience watched with amazement this ecstatic demonstration before finally rising to cheer the Scots as heartily as if their own team had won the Cup.

Celtic presented 11 stout-hearted men. But the player who won the admiration of the neutrals and the respect of the judges was left-back Tommy Gemmell.

Incredible

Stockings down and sleeves high he tore into the Italians with a fury that would have scared an Army battalion let alone 11 uncertain men from Milan.

First into action and last off the field, that was the bold Gemmell. At the end he fought his way through hysterical fans his Inter shirt a final token of a match that was nearly all Gemmell.

Celtic were a goal down after seven minutes when German referee Kurt Tschencher gave a penalty to Inter. It was an incredible decision because he was 40 yards away at the time.

Sandro Mazzola scored from the spot with a shot that sent goalkeeper Ronnie Simpson diving the wrong way. It was the only time Simpson was in real trouble.

Celtic stormed in with such command that Inter threw nine men into defence. Manager Helenio Herrera was tearing his hair and roaring commands from his touchline seat.

Great

Billy McNeill headed just wide. Bertie Auld hit the bar. And Gemmell commanded the greatest save of the game from goalkeeper Sarti.

Gemmell, battling with fury had his name taken for a foul on Bedin. The Italian, after deserting an Oscar for the manner in which he writhed in pain, got up and winked at manager Herrera.

After 61 minutes Gemmell scored the equaliser. Celtic were attacking with such command that the goal was made by right half Bobby Murdoch and right back Jim Craig.

Joyful

Ten minutes from the end Gemmell made the glory goal when Auld passed to Dave Chalmers who, without regard for the feelings of the tormented Celtic fans casually took his time before stroking the ball in.

Celtic will get £1,000 a man by way of bonus and they were worth every penny of it.

I shall never forget this night of Scottish joy.

The fans chorused "We are the greatest." I join them.

RIGHT : We're almost there! Celtic arms soar. Inter shoulders slump after Steve Chalmers (No. 9) had scored the second for the Scots.

BELOW : We're on the way! Celtic race back towards the centre circle as goalkeeper Sarti still fumbles after Tommy Gemmell's equaliser.

CATFORD

NORWICH

POOLE

HARRINGAY

READING

NEW CROSS

CLAPTON

STAMFORD BRIDGE

WHITE CITY

BRIGHTON

SOUTHEND

Ferguson signs

WEST HAM yesterday completed the signing of Aberdeen's Bobby Ferguson, Scotland's international goalkeeper for a fee which sets a new record for a British goalkeeper. It is thought to be in the region of £65,000, beating the £55,000 Liverpool paid for Tommy Lawrence.

Speedway details

CHALLENGE MATCH Oxford
BRITISH LEAGUE Sheffield

Soccer results

TOUR MATCHES
U.S NATIONAL LEAGUE
MITHRAS CUP FINAL Second leg
ESSEX THAMES SIDE CUP FINAL
LONDON YOUTH FA
SHIELD FINAL

DAZZLER BOOBYER FORGETS BAN

FRED BOOBYER last night set his records straight by the £2500 Blaxnit professional golf tournament at Malone, Belfast.

H—57 Maconi t.t.m.n.h.d.nd.d off a his b.rd

B.t.h w.as. in draught and h.r after a s.p.r.g. the swelling bustin and nd

B.b. ins b.v.t B.b.s.s.g.ys a g.nd how g.r.d tb.d. n.w.t.M.n.at. r.t r.w.nd

F.b. th.s. h.w.b.r.t.s.w.t T.s.r. h.r.n.t B.t.w. br.d.n.g .nd.d to th.nd.d a.nd th.d

N.s.b.w. Boob Br.wke w.t a.ws g.ven D.n br.nd.s A.n.r A.r.m.r D.r.on .nd B.r .n B.rn .n.d th.s.k R.by.t b.n.d

B.b.w.r F.r.d.nd a.b.w.s. a.s.w. g.b B.w.r.s.nd.d R.H.C.n.r h.ws. R.H.C

Women's and seniors' titles—Page 13.

TOIL TO TRIUMPH

GLASGOW CELTIC became the first British club to reach the European Cup Final, let alone win it. British teams have been beaten in eight semi-finals since the competition began in 1955-6. Here is the record (aggregate scores) :—

1955-56	Rheims	3 Hibernian	6 Semi-final
1956-57	Real Madrid	5 Man. Utd.	3 Semi-final
1957-58	Milan	5 Man. Utd.	4 Semi-final
1958-59	Schalke	1 Wolves	3 Qtr.-final
1959-60	Eintracht	12 Rangers	4 Semi-final
1960-61	Hamburg	5 Burnley	4 Qtr.-final
1961-62	Benfica	1 Tottenham	3 Semi-final
1962-63	Milan	5 Dundee	2 Semi-final
1963-64	Real Madrid	7 Rangers	0 Qual Rds.
	Inter-Milan	1 Everton	0 Qual Rd.
1964-65	Inter-Milan	4 Liverpool	3 Semi-final
1965-66	Partizan	2 Man Utd.	1 Semi-final
1966-67	Celtic	2 Inter-Milan	1 Final

Ramsey leads England song of praise

ENGLAND saluted Scotland's success last night.

Sir Alf Ramsey, manager of the England team now in Vienna, said :—

"For one short spell in the second half I wondered whether Inter's defensive pattern had stopped Celtic from making positions. But I thought it was a tremendous performance."

Bobby Moore said : "I was so one-sided it was odd to me."

Jimmy Greaves : What happened to Inter Milan? There was no one team in it.

And England's cup managers joined the swelling song of praise.

MAGNIFICENT

Don Revie (Leeds) : This was the finest performance I've ever seen from a British club. They were magnificent. The status Europe has the idea logging n in full-back. They could n othing above to the speed of Celtic particularly in th. B.u.k.

"Now I hope we win the Fairs Cup and Rangers the Cup Winners Cup to have a great sweep for British football.

Joe Mercer (Man. City) : I'm still getting my breath back. This was a fantastic performance Scotland's answer to England and we must all celebrate with them.

"I was carried away with the speed of it.

"When Inter scored from a penalty and Celtic despite everything pressure couldn't seem to come to grips I thought we'd take a Europe to break through.

INEVITABLE

"Then Gemmell scored his goal and I was amazed that Celtic would win. We saw a superbly trained team turn to glory.

Alan Brown (Sheff. Wed.) : A superb wonderful show.

"This together with a World Cup should emphasise the same of the next footba.t

"Europe's nothing to fear. The teamwork and confidence of Celtic was a great tribute to their manager Jock Stein.

MENNEN PUSHBUTTON deodorant

World's hardest-working deodorant suits hard-working Englishmen

MENNEN FOR MEN

Daily Mirror

4d. Monday, May 29, 1967 ◆ No. 19,727

Guns, sirens, bonfires, cheers for the Old Man of the Sea

HOME—TO A TRAFFIC JAM!

WELCOME TO THEIR HERO

It's a great moment for the little ships as they sail out to welcome their hero, Gipsy Moth IV, the greatest little ship of them all.
—Picture by Mirror Cameraman ALISDAIR MACDONALD.

An armada welcomes Sir Francis

Home . . . to a kiss from Lady Chichester.

By DOUGLAS SLIGHT, PAUL HUGHES and KENELM JENOUR

LONE voyager Sir Francis Chichester sailed home last night to a tremendous welcome—and a traffic jam of small boats.

A shore battery boomed a salute as the Old Man of the Sea crossed the breakwater into Plymouth Sound in the weather-beaten yacht Gipsy Moth IV at exactly 8.56 p.m.

His gallant and lonely round-the-world voyage—to Australia and back round the dreaded Cape Horn—ended in a storm of cheering and salutes from ships' sirens.

Fountains

There was also the spurting welcome of fountains of water from fire boats, and beacons on the hillsides.

The biggest armada of small boats seen since Dunkirk crowded near Gipsy Moth to escort 65-year-old Sir Francis in triumph over the breakwater "finishing line."

Later, at a Press conference at Plymouth Guildhall, Sir Francis gave graphic details of his great voyage.

Speaking about his ordeal as he rounded Cape Horn, he said: "I must admit I was frightened down there in those southern waters. Sailing up the Atlantic

CONTINUED ON BACK PAGE

Daily Mirror

5d. Tuesday, February 13, 1968 No. 19,948

Angry West Indians hurl bottles at players

TEST MATCH RIOT—POLICE SHOOT TEAR GAS AT CROWD

Battleground *Riot police patrol the pitch as the England skipper Colin Cowdrey calmly collects some of the bottles thrown by the angry West Indies crowd.*

WEST INDIES 204 FOR FIVE — RIOT HALTED PLAY.

The news agency message about the riots, flashed from Kingston.

From BRIAN CHAPMAN in Kingston, Jamaica

THE Second Test match came to a violent halt in clouds of billowing tear gas yesterday after a savage bottle riot by West Indies' spectators.

England's captain Colin Cowdrey was hit on the legs by flying bottles as he courageously approached the fencing to appeal for order.

Then armed police sprinted on to the pitch and fired tear-gas bombs into the angry crowd while players dashed to safety.

The ugly scenes came as England sent the West Indies crashing towards apparent defeat.

Umpire Douglas Sang Hue gave out local hero Basil Butcher, brilliantly caught at the wicket by Jim Parks.

Insults

The score was 204 for 5. West Indies needed 29 to avoid an innings defeat, and the crowd did not like it.

Insults flew over the wire barrier from the cheap enclosure.

Then came the bottles. At first, just a shower of them. Then a positive deluge.

Play stopped. More than sixty riot-police wearing helmets and carrying plastic shields ran on to the pitch as Cowdrey and West Indian skipper Garfield Sobers desperately tried to calm the rioters.

Suddenly the bottle-throwing subsided. Cowdrey even began helping the ground staff to pick up the bottles.

He spoke to a police superintendent and seemed to suggest that the police should leave the pitch so as not to antagonise the 12,000 crowd.

"I hoped to calm the crowd, but it was hopeless," he said. "About two or three bottles hit me on the legs."

Just as it seemed the match might restart, pandemonium broke out again. This time, the flood of bottles came from near the scoreboard.

The players sprinted off the field for safety, and the ugly situation really erupted.

Riot police in steel helmets and gas masks dashed towards the trouble spots with shields and batons.

Tear-gas bombs popped in the crowd. There were screams, shouts and panic

Cowdrey hit as he makes an appeal for order

as the spectators scrambled for the gates.

About twelve people were treated for bruises and cuts as ticket holders fled the pavilion when gas drifted across the field.

One hour after the riot, the popular side of the ground was almost cleared. Eighty minutes after the riot began, play started again.

Police mingled with the slowly returning crowds.

Batted

Basil D'Oliveira bowled three balls to finish his over interrupted by the rioting

A few more bottles were flung on to the pitch.

But the game went on. Holford and Sobers batted out the rest of the day when West Indies were 258 for five.

If necessary, the eighty minutes play lost yesterday will be made up today or tomorrow.

Cecil Marley, president of the Jamaican Cricket Association, said afterwards: "This day will go down in Jamaican history of sportsmanship and cricket as the blackest in its history.

"All right-thinking Jamaicans will forever be ashamed."

England thrown out of stride —See Page 23.

BOY, 14, TRIES TO JOIN THE LEGION

By MIRROR REPORTER

SCHOOLBOY Colin Smith, 14, wanted to be a man too soon. Adventure. Romance. That, he decided, was the life for him.

He packed a few things, told his mother he was going camping — and went off to join the French Foreign Legion. Although

Colin had only a few pounds, he travelled from his home near Newcastle upon Tyne to Paris by bus, ferry and lorry.

Then yesterday he marched boldly into the Legion's recruiting centre.

Motto

Unfortunately, the Legion —Motto: "Death Before Defeat"—said he was too young.

And the French police—alerted after Colin's mother had said that he might try to join the Legion — were already on his trail.

Colin was put into a taxi and taken to the British Embassy.

Last night, before being put on a train home, Colin said: "I don't know whether to be happy or sad. I think the Foreign Legion would have been

quite interesting, really. At the recruiting centre, I saw an officer, who asked me how old I was, and I said I was nearly nineteen.

Date

"But when they looked at my credentials, they found me out because I had altered a date."

Colin went on: "I had only £9 on me when I left

home. I've always wanted to join the Foreign Legion. Newcastle is a dump and so is my school. I wanted to get away."

He added: "Even though I didn't get into the Legion, it was a good adventure."

His mother, Mrs. Nora Smith, 51, said at the family's home in Weardale-road, Walker, Newcastle: "The trouble is that Colin wants to be a man before he's a boy."

Daily Mail
News Chronicle

NO. 22,374 | FOR QUEEN AND COMMONWEALTH | 4 | MONDAY, APRIL 8, 1968 | PRICE 5d.

Minutes after this.. death at 150 mph

A fault in Jim Clark's car?

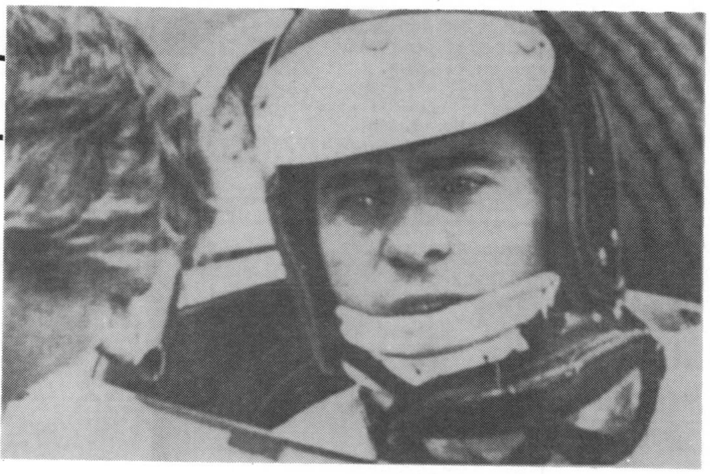

JIM CLARK TALKS TO A MECHANIC JUST BEFORE THE RACE

From BRIAN GROVES
Hockenheim, Sunday

JIM CLARK, Britain's greatest racing driver and twice world champion, died in a 150 m.p.h. mystery crash today.

On an almost straight stretch he suddenly zig-zagged across the Hockenheim circuit and crashed broadside into trees beside the track.

Tonight a commission of inquiry is trying to discover what made 32-year-old Clark's Lotus Ford Cosworth crash.

An official statement by the organisers, the West German Automobile Club, said the accident was caused 'apparently' by damage to the suspension.

Clark's team-mate, ex-world champion Graham Hill, said: 'The course there as a fairly gentle right-hand bend and Jimmy went off in a big slide.

No chance

'At the speed we were doing there, about 150 miles an hour, he had no chance. I believe it was a steering defect.

'The track there precludes the possibility of a driver mistake, because the driver doesn't have to do much other than put his foot on the floor.

'There was no other car involved so it looks very much as though something happened to the car. The engine could have seized or anything. We can only guess.

'It is a fairly new circuit and neither of us had raced here before.

Clark had already had trouble with the car. At breakfast this morning he told the hotel manager in Hockenheim, 25-year-old Georg Feitz: 'There is something not quite in order with my car.

'It looks as if I won't be able to start. The mechanics worked through the night till 5 o'clock this morning.'

But as he was finishing breakfast one of Clark's mechanics told him: 'Jim, your car is OK again. You'll be able to start.'

British driver Chris Irwin, who was some 200 yards behind Clark, said: 'The accident is completely incomprehensible to me.

'Clark wasn't obstructed by any other drivers. Suddenly his car seemed to sway.

'I took my foot off the accelerator to see what was happening and to make sure I didn't drive into Clark.

'Suddenly, as if it had been struck by an invisible fist, his car was swept off the track into the woods.'

Curve

Mr Graham White, competitions manager of the British Automobile Racing Club, said: 'I had breakfast with Jimmy.

'He seemed perfectly happy and normal, though he didn't like this circuit, but I don't think many of the drivers did.

'This was the most ridiculous accident. I have seen many accidents, but this one you cannot explain.

'It is a long, long right-hand curve which any driver will tell you can be taken absolutely flat out. The track was wet, but that shouldn't have mattered.

'It must have been a tremendous crash. The main part of the car was twisted and the engine and rear wheels went on.

'They bounced three times, taking big chunks of earth out of the bank.'

A German race marshal said the end of the car started swaying from side to side before the crash.

The chief Lotus mechanic, Jim Endruweit, said: 'There is no indication what happened. It may have been driver-error, but we just don't know. You cannot rule out that something went wrong with the car.'

Last night Clark appeared on German television and was asked if it was possible for a car to start with a defect. He said cars were tested so often that it could almost be discounted.

A late change of plans switched Clark—generally voted the greatest driver in world racing today—to Hockenheim.

He was to have driven a new 200 m.p.h. Ford in the six-hour BOAC race at Brands Hatch in Kent. But Mr Colin Chapman, the Lotus chief, wanted him to race in Germany.

Death came as Clark, bachelor Scots farmer who became world champion in 1963 and 1965, had been rated favourite to win again this year.

Clark's parents, Mr James Clark, 73, and his wife Helen, 71, of Kerchesters, near Kelso, Roxburghshire, were told of his death when they arrived at the home of friends.

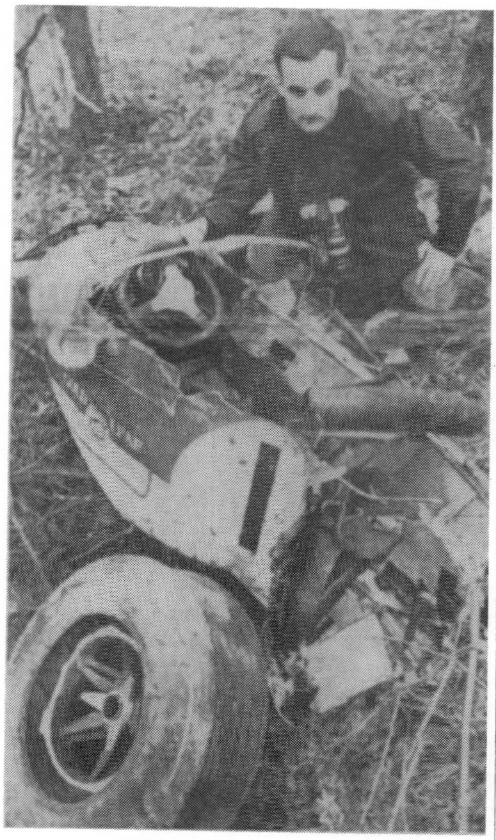

FRONT HALF OF THE WRECKED CAR. ANOTHER PICTURE, PAGE 5

THE MAN WHO WALKED FROM EVERY CRASH BUT THE LAST —PAGE FIVE

Comment

The two battles

A GREAT and good man is assassinated. Another man of great stature tries to calm a nation aroused to fear and violence.

From the murder of President Kennedy to the murder of Dr Martin Luther King LYNDON JOHNSON has been fighting two battles. He has been rocked on a tragic see-saw.

For just as he made real progress in providing rights and opportunities for the American Negro the conflict in Vietnam deepened. Now when hopeful word comes from Hanoi for the first time the race conflict in America breaks out with renewed bitterness.

As more funds and more troops have had to be diverted from the war on poverty to Vietnam, many poor Negroes have felt that their only chance of taking part in the Great Society was to be its cannon-fodder.

Martin Luther King stood for the hope that despite all this black and white Americans could live peaceably together, that it would never come to a full-scale fight.

Candle

YET Dr King was a realist. He understood the human legacy of suspicion and hatred. He knew he lived under the threat of death. But his calm recalled the words of Bishop Latimer, the Protestant martyr of Tudor times, as he was being burnt at the stake for his beliefs: 'We shall this day light such a candle by God's grace as I trust shall never be put out.'

Will this latest candle light the way to justice, or will it spark off a still more horrifying fire?

In the world outside—in the new Czech regime for example—the cause of freedom shines a little more brightly. But in America, so often the rescuer of freedom this century, the future is overcast.

Courage

IN Britain we can offer only our sympathy and our attention. As MR WILSON's reshuffled Cabinet shows, there is little prospect of startling or sudden change here. MR JENKINS describes the way ahead as 'two years of hard slog.'

But we can learn from the American experience just how racial problems fester if neglected. It is vital for Britain both to control immigration and to make sure that all who do settle here have the fullest rights and opportunities.

MR CALLAGHAN'S Race Relations Bill this week must be closely scrutinised to see whether it will help and not make friction worse.

This problem of race now bedevils the whole world. We shall need charity, caution and courage to solve it. That will not be easy. But we have seen how terrible is the price of failure.

WIN A VAUXHALL VENTORA—Page 4

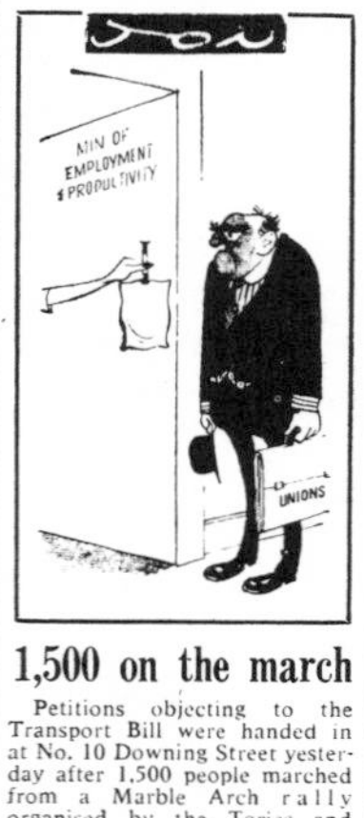

1,500 on the march

Petitions objecting to the Transport Bill were handed in at No. 10 Downing Street yesterday after 1,500 people marched from a Marble Arch rally organised by the Tories and motor agents.

Pilgrims drowned

KUWAIT: At least 74 pilgrims were drowned and more than 50 are missing after a launch with 400 aboard capsized off Dubay in the Persian Gulf.

Trouble trawlers

Five Grimsby trawlers were unable to sail at the weekend because of absenteeism.

Callaghan acts on race

Notices worded 'Europeans only' or 'No coloureds' will be illegal and employers and landlords will face prosecution for colour discrimination under the Race Relations Bill to be outlined in the Commons tomorrow by Mr James Callaghan, Home Secretary.

A Community Relations Board to help integration will replace the Government-sponsored Commonwealth Immigrants Committee.

Cattle plague again

Cases of foot-and-mouth disease were confirmed yesterday on two farms 25 miles apart. One, at Eccleston, near Chester, had an outbreak four months ago. The other, at Edstaton, near Wem, Shropshire, had not been affected.

Sailor on trial

MADRID: U.S. sailor Donald Cowles, 21, will face a court-martial at Rota, Southern Spain, today, accused of murdering British nurse Susan Taylor, 21, of New Eltham, London, S.E., last July.

Thing strikes a[illegible]n

STOCKHOLM: An 'incredibly powerful thing' has smashed a gaping hole through 3ft. thick ice in a second lake in central Sweden, not far from last week's landing. Scientists are baffled.

MOTHER AND TWIN SON DIE AFTER COCOA

By Daily Mail Reporter

SIX children lay ill in hospital last night as police investigated the death of their mother and three-year-old brother, a twin.

Mrs Eunice Shepherd, 38, collapsed into a chair after the family drank cocoa on Saturday night.

Her eldest boy, William, 13, ran from the house in Madam Banks Road, Dalston, Carlisle, Cumberland, to tell neighbours.

Mrs Shepherd was dead. The children, in their pyjamas, were ushered into the house next door. A doctor gave them salt water to make them sick. Mark, three, died in hospital.

Mrs Shepherd's husband, William, a 40-year-old handyman, was out at the time.

Cups and saucers taken from the house were sent to Preston forensic laboratory for tests.

An inquest will be opened today. Last night the children were out of danger. They are Mark's twin sister Barbara, Tina, six, Anne, seven, Pauline, eight, Lorraine, 14, and William.

SIX out of SEVEN winners for ROBIN GOODFELLOW at Kelso on Saturday PLUS a 100-30 nap at Ascot —See Page 11

Moon-and-back spaceship

MOSCOW: Russia launched an instrument-packed spaceship on what is thought to be the first Moon-and-back flight.

The unmanned spaceship, Luna 14, was reported to be on course and working well. Friday is its rumoured return date.

40,000 troops out as new riot flares

From STANLEY BURCH
NEW YORK, Sunday

FORTY THOUSAND troops held half a dozen riot-torn American cities today to save them from further racial violence.

The troops—both Regular Army and National Guard—ranged the scarred streets and set up strongpoints at the most vulnerable Negro ghetto landmarks.

They succeeded in making Palm Sunday start as a day of general if fragile peace.

First sign of renewed trouble came in Pittsburgh, where 700 police and National Guardsmen quelled a three-hour outbreak of looting and burning. The Pennsylvania Governor declared a state of emergency

Three nights of black violence, set off by the assassination of Civil Rights leader Dr Martin Luther King, had left at least 26 dead, more than 1,100 wounded, nearly 7,000 under arrest—and property damage impossible to assess yet.

In Washington *BORIS KIDEL reports:* More than 12,000 troops were deployed across the city today after three days of race riots which caused a casualty toll of seven dead and 894 injured.

Police reported 4,233 arrests —including 919 charged with looting—after the wild rampage of Negro gangs which left about 200 buildings destroyed or gutted by fire.

For the second day running a 4 p.m. to 6.30 a.m. curfew was ordered.

President Johnson, who decreed that it should be a day of national mourning, went to a memorial service for Dr King at a Roman Catholic church in a Washington slum area.

In Memphis *DONALD McLACHLAN reports:* The car park of a downtown motel, surrounded by the sorry homes of poor Negroes, became the centre of this mourning city.

Hundreds of black men and women and their children gathered and stared wordless towards the first-floor Room 306, where Dr King was carried after an assassin shot him.

Room 306, its single window blanked by orange curtains, is already a shrine.

Attorney-General Mr Ramsey Clark said on TV that 'a man on the run' was a suspect in Dr King's assassination. He added: 'We have a name we are working on. Whether it is the right name we'll have to see.'

Dr King's widow, Coletta, intends to take his place tomorrow in a march of 50,000 through Memphis. Her husband planned the march in support of the city's striking dustmen.

In London it was announced that Chancellor Mr Roy Jenkins will represent the Government at Dr King's funeral in Atlanta, Georgia, on Tuesday.

Where did America go wrong?—Page SIX.

DAILY MAIL
NORTHCLIFFE HOUSE, E.C.4
01-353 6000

LATE NEWS

TROOPS SENT TO BALTIMORE

Washington, Sunday.—President Johnson ordered federal troops into Baltimore area of Maryland to help put down race riots in which three people have died.

● WEATHER: Mainly dry. Details: Page SEVEN.

LATE WIRE.—Best from Edinburgh: FUTURE FAME (3.30) and PRINTER (4.0, nap).

Kings of Europe

Law (in hospital) sees extra time goal-burst crown the Busby/United story

KIDD celebrates his birthday goal

By BRIAN JAMES : Manchester Utd. 4, Benfica 1

After extra time. Score at 90 mins. : 1—1.

MANCHESTER United, for a decade and more the best-loved losers in the European Cup, finally won the trophy last night in a match that had begun full of hate.

After fighting for 12 years to reach their first final they found 90 minutes not time enough to grab the trophy and conceded a late goal to Benfica to stagger into extra time.

There in one great upsurge of skill and belief that brought Wembley to its feet, they destroyed the Portuguese with three goals in eight minutes. It was a superb effort and absolutely the right ending for absolutely the wrong sort of match.

Then, in the glare from the pitch, the team cavorted hugging the trophy to themselves with the delight that only the long-denied can ever know. And their manager, Matt Busby, stood rubbing that golden symbol of success, the reward for which he had planned with humanity and patience. United are the first English, the second British club ever to possess the cup.

Merciless

The evil of this night came in the first half when two teams, overcome perhaps by the value of that which they sought, fell upon each other in a cruel, graceless frenzy.

Not 30 seconds elapsed before the first free kick, but 30 more were to be recorded before half-time. The football these teams can play, the spectacle this match promised they crushed beneath feet seeking only to stop and destroy.

I make no excuse for United, they were as guilty as Benfica the Portuguese who had chosen to show the watching world the dark side of their nature. This was the Portugal who crushed Brazil mercilessly from the World Cup, not the Portugal who so gracefully lost to England.

Little of merit stands to be recorded of the first half, save perhaps three great chances that fell to Sadler and were wasted, or the run and shot from Eusebio that left the crossbar and Stepney both quaking.

Let it be said that referee Lo Bello's handling of the situation was futile: that he missed the malicious and saw and punished only the petty. But unlike Cruz, unlike Humberto he kicked no one, unlike Stiles, unlike Foulkes, he stood deliberately in no man's path.

Appalling

I felt the match lay in ruins at half-time, but the sense of the players somehow prevailed. Benfica again started the second half in militant mood, but United's decision to let the matter be settled by skill brought the game finally to heel.

And as soon as United began seeking their finest touch so Benfica's fate was seen to be sealed. Shots by Aston, for an hour United's most menacing forward, frightened Henrique though it was Charlton who was first to beat him.

A clever pass by Sadler found Charlton racing through. The pass was high—indeed, it looked too high—but Charlton rose to get the merest touch that was enough to edge the ball easily into the far corner.

Manchester could have sewn up this match with Best and Sadler missing from moves that delighted. And Benfica had settled into a posture that looked like surrender. Eusebio, the great threat, now looked a common enough player. His handshakes and gestures of good will meant nothing to those who remembered his appalling foul on Crerand.

But somehow Benfica aroused themselves to score with 11 minutes to go. The tall Torres reached to a long centre and headed the ball back across goal to where Graca lurked unmarked, Stepney's dive was formal, hopeless.

So extra time loomed with players of both teams lying like men dead having cramp massaged from their legs, and hope dinned into their ears.

Clearly, just as England had once needed to win a game they had seemed to concede, it was going to need a very great side to recover from this blow to morale.

But United somehow reached down to tap that streak of courage and skill that will now become famous.

Two minutes into the last half-hour and Best broke through. Adolfo had the ball, but the challenge of the Irishman left him motionless.

In an astonishing atmosphere Best still found the composure to delay his shot until the goalkeeper advanced and then dribble round to score.

Roar

Almost from the kick-off came United's third. A corner was swung in by Charlton, Kidd met it with his head, saw the ball rebound and nodded again to beat Henrique.

Then five minutes on into a famous period in this famous club's history Charlton found energy to make and take the final goal.

He put Kidd down the right and raced through to connect with the centre.

The rest was all delirium: the delight of the players, the jubilant roar of their vast swaying crowd, the bemused exit of Busby, trailing off wiping his face as though hiding tears.

He deserved this moment just as his team, because of their defiance, deserved their trophy.

If only the memory of an evening of quite astonishing drama could have been given a more generous, more fitting first hour.

Manchester United: Stepney, Brennan, Dunne, Crerand, Foulkes, Stiles, Best, Kidd, Charlton, Sadler, Aston. Benfica: Henrique, Adolfo, Humberto, Jacinto, Cruz, Graca, Coluna, Augusto, Torres, Eusebio, Simoes.

CHARLTON celebrates his second, clinching goal
PICTURES BY PATRICK LARKIN

BUSBY: I'm so proud

THIS is what the Wembley personalities were saying after Manchester United's great European Cup victory last night :

MATT BUSBY: 'The boys have done me proud. They came back into this match, just as they did against Real Madrid in the semi-finals, with a huge display of heart. I'm proud of them all. It's wonderful. I am delighted. I am proud.'

BOBBY CHARLTON joked about his first goal: 'That must have been my first header for about ten years. Maybe if I hadn't been going bald it wouldn't have gone in.

'I didn't notice that the goalkeeper had come off his line. In fact I thought the ball had gone wide. I thought late on in the game that we had missed our best chance, and I didn't think I could pick myself up because I was so tired. But we managed it for Matt Busby.'

JOHNNY ASTON : 'Blue shirts are lucky for our family. My father won a cup-winners medal for Manchester United 20 years ago wearing a blue shirt, and now I've a European Cup-Winners medal.

NOBBY STILES : 'We were shattered by the late Benfica goal. I felt exactly the same as I did in the World Cup final when Germany did the same thing to us.

'If Benfica had got another I believe they would have beaten us, but once we got into extra time we found more strength and began to play a bit.'

ALEX STEPNEY said : 'I had come out too far and was trying to get back when he hit it, but he shot straight at me and I made the save.'

EUSEBIO, in tears : 'We are pleased for United and Matt Busby. We are very disappointed, but we have won it before. They were too strong for us in the end.'

OTTO GLORIA, Benfica manager : 'The title is in very good hands. Manchester United played very well indeed. They are a strong club but playing at home was a big advantage.

'Some of our players like Adolfo, Torres and Coluna had knocks early on and couldn't produce their best form.'

JOE MERCER— manager of touring League champions Manchester City and fresh from Chicago : 'Absolutely wonderful. I am sending my heartiest congratulations to Matt Busby.'

Free inside the June issue of
GOLF WORLD magazine
—this 'SHOT MAKER' disc

* John Jacobs shows how to improve your game
* Great Readers Competition—Win a set of clubs
* Arnold Palmer on international golf
* How to score and win Instruction—Tips—World News
* The story behind the Masters
* Young Pro's revolt

GOLF WORLD
Britain's biggest-selling golf magazine
at your newsagent NOW — 3/-

JON'S SPORTING TYPES

'You mean with the hundred you won on Sir Ivor you bought a ticket for Wembley?'

Charlton misses England match

A BADLY bruised shin will keep Bobby Charlton out of England's game against West Germany in Hanover on Saturday. He hopes to be fit for the Nations Cup semi-final against Yugoslavia in Florence next Wednesday.

Everton full-back Tommy Wright, in Budapest with the Under-21 side, replaces injured clubmate Ray Wilson in the England squad, but is not expected to play in Hanover.

Other sport in brief

EUROPEAN CUP FINAL

Arsenal beat Japan

TOKIO : Arsenal beat the Japanese Olympic team, 4—0, with goals from Frank McLintock (2), David Jenkins and David Simmons. The game was watched by a record 70,000 crowd.

NEVER SAY DIE

NEVER SAY DIE was the spirit which won Matt Busby and Manchester United their Derby Day triumph. That and nothing else. But what more is there?

The European Cup rose to them from the débris of a final which began in the gutter of professional football but ended amid the exhaustion and ecstasy of braver and better themes.

Wembley, red with the banners of Old Trafford's Bastille, watched victory come in the most unexpected way. Unexpected, because after the ugliness of the opening contest, the poverty of its sportsmanship and the frustration of its hot-and-cold blowing refereeing, it was turned to senselessness and skill by the sheer need to strive for a settlement.

The turning point came as Busby calmed and encouraged his players sprawling wearily on the turf, waiting for extra time more as a crushed and defeated tug-of-war team than footballers about to seize a championship.

Arrogance

THEN IT WAS that the never-say-die spirit rose. But it was not only the spirit of Busby's determination. It rose from the Wembley pitch as it had for Alf Ramsey and England in extra time against Germany in the World Cup final.

It rose as it had for Jock Stein and Celtic when they were a penalty goal down against Inter-Milan in Benfica's home town a year ago.

What is it, this spirit? It is what lifts British football high above all its faults. It springs from the arrogance of bold physical strength and it expresses itself in a whirl of blind and deadly action.

Even so the opportunity might not have presented itself but for one individual contest which few had expected. This was between goal-scorer Eusebio and goalkeeper Stepney.

Stepney played to win this cup for Manchester United more courageously and skilfully than anyone else. There was nothing Eusebio could do to defeat him.

Challenge

THERE WAS another contest almost as decisive between Aston on the left wing and Adolfo at right back. No one at Wembley will forget the way Aston played his part. On the day, Best came out worse.

So, next winter Manchester United must try to master the students, Estudiantes of La Plata, whom they play for the Inter-Continental championship.

Neither Busby nor his team will shrink from another challenge in Argentina, but this time I believe FIFA's control will be strict and the teams will have a fairer chance of avoiding another Montevideo.

With this task ahead of Manchester United, and with Manchester City and Celtic also in the field next season when they defend this European Cup, Matt Busby faces the last and finest chapter of a stirring football story.

Rankmore signed for £10,000

Northampton have agreed to pay Peterborough a fee of about £10,000 for centre-half Frank Rankmore.

Preston are ready to take back former England Under-23 right winger Dave Wilson, with whom they were in dispute before he left for Liverpool last year.

Shrewsbury back Gordon Lee, 31, has been appointed team manager of Port Vale, second in command to Sir Stanley Matthews. Lee has been assisting Shrewsbury's manager, Arthur Rowley, for two years.

Halifax Town have appointed Miss Pauline Hicks, 30, as secretary.

MATCH FACTS

United		Benfica
22	Goal attempts	20
16	Inside pen. area	11
6	Outside pen. area	9
8	Saved	8
10	Off target	11
28	Fouls	24
8	Offside	1
5	Corners	2

As a result of Manchester United's triumph this is how the Football League clubs will line up in Europe next season.

EUROPEAN CUP: Manchester United and Manchester City.
CUP-WINNERS' CUP: West Bromwich and Cardiff.
FAIRS CUP: Liverpool, Leeds, Chelsea and (if a fourth entry is accepted) Newcastle.

CROSSWORK

No. 1102

HAVE FUN with this daily brainteaser. There are no clues : just fill in the missing numbers, working from left to right and top to bottom, taking each symbol as it comes. Single figures only. No noughts.

'Rod Laver overwhelmed Tony Roche... He is now indisputably the best player on earth'

YES—THE GREATEST

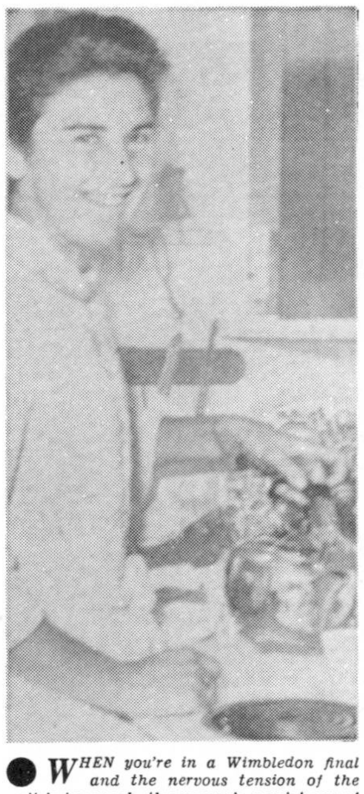

● *WHEN you're in a Wimbledon final and the nervous tension of the wait is too much, the answer's a quiet cup of tea. Judy Tegart of Australia, who meets Billie-Jean King in today's singles final, waits for the kettle—and today's dream of a Centre Court thriller.*

By FRANK ROSTRON

ROCKET ROD LAVER from Queensland yesterday treated 17,000 enthralled Centre Court spectators to a 61-minute blitz of tennis power and perfection.

He overwhelmed his five years younger Australian left-handed rival, Tony Roche, 6—3, 6—4, 6—2 to become Wimbledon's first Open champion.

I use the word overwhelm rather than outclass about so good an opponent as Roche, a likely world champion of the future.

But after battling nobly for a set and a half Tony's game disintegrated before the mercilessly sustained expertise of the magician of the world's courts.

Laver was the undisputed world's best amateur in his grand-slam year of 1962 when he won the Wimbledon title for the second time by thrashing another Australian, Martin Mulligan, just as ruthlessly in only 52 minutes. And yesterday, when Princess Marina presented him with the huge gold cup which goes with his winning £2,000 cheque, he had put the incontestable seal on a title that has been his for the last three or four years—"best player on earth."

That title is now indisputable. But—coming as this superb display did after his previous highest mark—the winning of the professional £5,000 championship against Ken Rosewall on the same court last August—I now side with those who more arguably rate him the greatest ever.

Newer have I seen past champions, present-day players, coldly analytical critics, and ordinary non-playing habitues of the Centre Court so thrilled. All were united in the tribute to one of the greatest displays of all-round tennis.

I confess that even a blase and reputedly cynical critic like myself, after years of watching the high and the low lights on the world circuits, was tempted to go overboard with them.

France's famous bounding Basque, Jean Borota, who is 70 next month, said: "Not Tilden. He couldn't volley like this. And that service. Who could have handled that? Not me or Henry Cochet, or Rene Lacoste."

Laver's manager, George McCall, said with dry humour: "After this I guess we'll persevere with this boy Laver and keep him on the pay roll."

Thrill

Laver's excited wife Mary, to whom Rod flashed one of his rare smiles as Roche ended the hopeless struggle by hitting a backhand return well wide of the sidelines, said: "He always turns it on when he has to and has made up his mind to play his greatest yet. It's not the money. It's hitting a peak like this that makes him happy."

Rod himself confessed that it was his greatest tennis thrill. It even exceeded his winning of the grand slam because he set his mind on becoming the first Open champion.

When asked whether he was going to turn amateur, Rod, who can earn twice this £2,000 singles prize in a couple of nights, said: "I turned amateur to win this one."

The play itself can be summarised simply. Roche was in the match with a chance for just 15 minutes.

This was the only time Roche's few backers had visions of collecting their 20—1 pre-championship odds.

Tony's only big chances were when he had a point for a break of Laver's service in the seventh game and another in the ninth. But each time Laver frustrated him.

A race

When Rod finally got the eighth game for a 5—3 lead it was as good as over. But the best was yet to come.

Roche hit deep drives and beautifully angled volleys that would have been winners against normal opponents.

But Rod not only rocketed back winners from the base line but picked up half-volleys in mid-court from his toes to whistles of amazement from the crowd.

In the third set Laver was in full cry, covering the court with astonishing speed. He went to a 4—0 lead and it was merely a race with the clock to see whether it would end within the hour.

Tough luck, Tony, to strike Rod at his hottest.

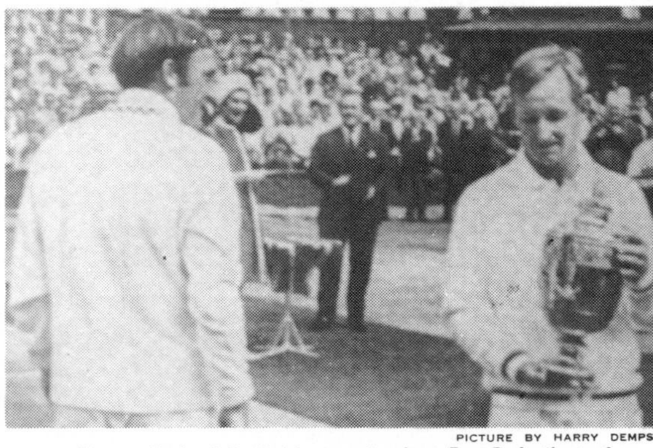

PICTURE BY HARRY DEMPSTER

Moment of triumph for Rod Laver as he shows Tony Roche the trophy

TODAY'S ORDER OF PLAY

CENTRE COURT

WOMEN'S SINGLES FINAL: Mrs King (US) v J Tegart (Aust)

MEN'S DOUBLES FINAL: J Newcombe, A Roche (Aust) v K Rosewall, F Stolle (Aust)

WOMEN'S DOUBLES FINAL: R Casals, Mrs King (US) v F Durr (Fr), Mrs Jones (GB).

MIXED DOUBLES FINAL: K Fletcher, Mrs Court (Aust) v A Metreveli, O Morozova (Russia).

IT'S TOUGH FOR BILLIE

By ALAN WILLIAMS

BILLIE-JEAN KING, 24-year-old Californian who today faces 30-year-old Australian No. 1 Judy Tegart in a bid to win the singles title for a third successive year, last night suffered her first Wimbledon defeat since 1966.

Billie-Jean, a triple champion last year, had survived a cliff-hanging women's doubles with Rosemary Casals against Judy Tegart and Lesley Bowrey. The score: 1—6, 6—1, 10—8.

It took the same tenacity and flair that characterised Billie-Jean's brilliant come-back against Ann Jones the previous day to pull the Americans through.

But the strain was too much and, although staving off three match points, Billie-Jean and Owen Davidson later lost their mixed doubles crown to three-times former holders Ken Fletcher and Margaret Court.

FAVOURITE

The Australians, showing much of the power and understanding that made them unbeatable in 1963, 1965, and 1966, won 6—4, 9—7.

Once they had pulled back from 0—2 in the second set they always had the edge.

Billie-Jean can still pick up £1,000 today by winning the singles and retaining the doubles title against Ann Jones and Francoise Durr.

The Russians have reached a Wimbledon final for the first time. In the last match of the day Alex Metreveli, 23-year-old Russian No. 1 and 18-year-old Olga Morozova surprisingly but worthily beat Fred Stolle and Ann Jones 6—3, 12—10.

The Russians plainly surprised their vastly more experienced opponents.

RESULTS

Winners in black, seeded players in CAPITALS. Results in draw order.

MEN'S SINGLES

1967 winner: J. Newcombe (Aust).

Final

R LAVER (Aust) bt A ROCHE (Aust) 6—3, 6—4, 6—2

MEN'S DOUBLES

1967 winners: R. Hewitt and F. McMillan (S Af).

Semi-finals

J NEWCOMBE, A ROCHE (Aust) bt R EMERSON, R LAVER (Aust) 6—3, 8—6, 2—6, 7—8; **K ROSEWALL, F STOLLE** (Aust) bt R HEWITT, F McMILLAN (S Af) 6—2, 6—3, 6—4

MIXED DOUBLES

1967 winners: O. Davidson (Aust) and Mrs. King (US).

Semi-finals

K FLETCHER, MRS COURT (Aust) bt O DAVIDSON (Aust), MRS KING (US) 6—4, 9—7; **A Metreveli, O Morozova** (Russia) bt F STOLLE (Aust) MRS JONES (GB) 6—3, 12—10.

WOMEN'S DOUBLES

1967 winners: R. Casals and Mrs King (US).

Semi-finals

R CASALS, MRS KING (US) bt MRS BOWREY, J TEGART (Aust) 1—6, 6—1, 10—8; **F DURR** (Fr), **MRS JONES** (GB) bt Mrs Lloyd, F MacLennan (GB) 6—1, 6—0.

The first Open Wimbledon

The Men's Singles Champion–Rod Laver and runner-up–Tony Roche

both used the famous Dunlop Maxply Fort–the world's master racket–and so did over 100 other competitors.

You'll play better with Dunlop

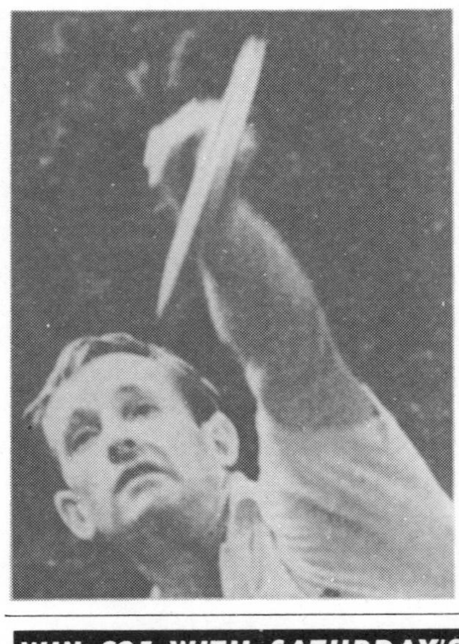

French 'dope' rider banned

From RONALD WHITE

ROYAN, Friday.

DANIEL VAN RYCKEGHAN, 24-year-old Belgian, landed a narrow victory in a mass finish on the road here to notch his first win in his second year of riding the Tour de France.

Then, as 91 finishers were given the same time of 5h. 25min. 26sec., race officials banned France's Jose Samyn after a dope test proved positive.

Britain's Arthur Metcalfe and Vin Denson both figured in fierce attacks during this 139-mile eighth stage.

But all attempts to escape failed—although in the hectic sprint finish several British white jerseys were tucked in the leading bunch.

Delighted Denson reported: "We had five in the first 20." Yes, the photo of the finish showed five of the six remaining Britons to be in the first 22.

★

And they won the third team award, thanks to Michael Wright, Metcalfe, and John Clarey.

Wright was ninth and the highest-placed Briton. He was tired at the finish and will welcome tomorrow's rest-day.

Jose Samyn is the only rider to be withdrawn from the Tour, although it was announced that more than one dope test had proved positive.

Samyn, who was also suspended for a month, did not appeal.

Dr. Pierre Dumas, in charge of Tour medical control, refused to comment on other tests taken.

EIGHTH STAGE (Nantes to Royan, 139 miles).—D Van Ryckeghem (Belgium), 5hr 25m 26s, 1; J Janssen (Holland), same time 2; F Bitossi (Italy), same time, 3.

BRITISH PLACINGS.—M Wright, 5hr 25m 26s, 9; A Metcalfe, 12; J Clarey, 18; R Addy, 21; B Hoban, 22; V Denson, 28 (all same time).

OVERALL PLACINGS.—G Vanden Berghe (Belgium), 43hr 45m 17s, 1; B Guyot (Fr), 43-47-46, 2; J Genet (Fr), 43-48-44, 3.

OVERALL BRITISH PLACINGS.—Hoban, 43hr 52m 44s, 46; Clarey, 43-52-56, 55; Wright, 43-53-1, 58; Denson, 43-53-12, 64; Metcalfe, 43-53-41, 72; Addy, 43-53-53, 74.

BATTLE HOTS UP FOR BRITISH OPEN PLACES

Casper sounds warning

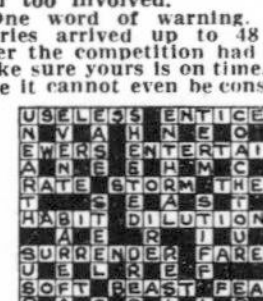

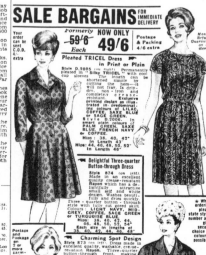

By RONALD HEAGER

CALIFORNIAN Billy Casper, world's top money winner of 1968, checked in at Carnoustie yesterday for his first British Open golf championship—and gave three good reasons for wanting to win.

They are the three babies he and his wife Shirley recently adopted. All are under six months old—a boy, Byron Randolph, and twin girls, Jennifer Laura and Judith Kathleen.

It brings the family of Mormon church preacher Casper up to six. He and Shirley have three grown-up children of their own.

Casper explained: "Shirley is not travelling the tournament with me so much and wanted something to occupy her time. I guess that is now taken care of."

But Shirley is on hand at Carnoustie to supervise the Casper diet which includes exotic dishes like buffalo meat and elk steaks.

They helped to cure Billy's allergies and trimmed him from a portly 15st. to a slim 12st. 7lb.

On the purely golfing side, there are three further reasons why Casper wants to follow fellow Americans Tommy Armour (1931) and Ben Hogan (1953) in winning the British title at Carnoustie.

Casper showed his ambition in saying: "Things have prevented my playing in the British Open in the past but I recognise this is a title every professional must have once in his career."

Billy, twice a Ryder Cup visitor to Britain (1961, 1965) also revealed how, at 37, he is pacing himself into the rank of world golf No 1 of 1968.

The money

His winnings this year of 130,000 dollars places him 40,000 dollars clear of his closest rival. And he has won four major events this year in 15 starts.

Each victory has followed a lay off varying from two to seven weeks.

Says Casper: "When I keep on playing too long, it's not my swing that goes wrong. I become mentally stale. Then I am my own worst enemy. I make too many wrong decisions."

Significantly, he adds: "I have come fresh to this one. I missed the Cleveland Open last week. I have heard Carnoustie is a great course and I'm here early to weigh up its problems."

Kel Nagle, the Centenary Open champion of 1960, was my companion on the plane to Edinburgh and he puts Casper among his Big Five for next week's Blue Riband.

Other four are American Jack Nicklaus, South African Gary Player, title-holder Roberto de Vicenzo, of the Argentine, and Kel's Aussie cobber Peter Thomson, five-times British title holder.

The V.I.P. arrival yesterday also included 1963 champion Bob Charles, the world's No. 1 left-hander from New Zealand and another Australian ace Bruce Devlin one-time plumber from Sydney who won the £12,500 Carling prize in 1966.

Overseas men dominated top places in the first day scores in the two qualifying tournaments yesterday.

At the par-71 Monifieth links, two Australians set the pace on 67. Frank Phillips, twice Australian Open champion from Sydney, and little Randall Vines, twice winner in the Far East this year.

Only one shot behind comes brilliant 20-year-old Springbok Bobby Cole, back at the scene of his 1966 British Amateur championship win as an 18-year-old. Also on 68 is experienced American circuit man Jerry Pitman.

The same tale is told of the other qualifying course, Panmure, where Sydney's 22-year-old Tim Woolbank is the pacemaker with a two-under-par 68.

Most spectacular shot of the qualifying round was by amateur giant from Dulwich, Peter Oosterhuis, who holed a wedge shot for an eagle 2 at the 404-yard 18th for his 70 at Panmure.

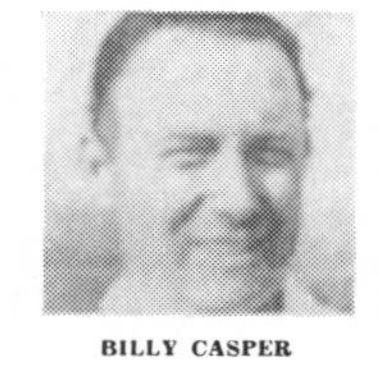

BILLY CASPER

LEADERS

MONIFIETH

67—F Phillips (Aust); R Vines (Aust). 68—R Cole (S Africa); J Pitmann (US). 69—G Cunningham. 70—*R Sweeney; L Ruiz (Argentine); J Martin, D Huish. 71—T Westbrook (Zambia); R Rennie; J Kinsella; H Lewis; P Green. 72—*C Cummings; I Wright; W Paterson; B Gallacher; A Gillies; E Brown; R Shaw (Aust); M Burgess. 73—*A Saddler; J Sharkey; M Gunn; M Ingham; I Macdonald; D Nash; E T Jones; M Plumbridge; D Gammon (S Africa); D Snowdon J McArthur (US); P Matkovich (S Africa); W Evans; D Talbot.

PANMURE

68—T Woolbank (Aust). 69—R Clegg, D Smart. 70—I Richardson, D Webster, *A Forrester, P Mills, C Greene, D Woodman, G Caygill, S Hunt, R Livingston, *P Oosterhuis, C Pennington, C Defoy, N V Drew.

71—K A Macdonald, R Bernardini (Italy), *R Shade, C Sayed (U.A.R.), L Fox, M Moussa (U.A.R.), L Ayton, G Gray, M Hall (S Afr), D Small, J Burns, R Walker. 72—W McCoudichie, N Sutton, *A O'Connor, M Roesink (Holl), H Habian (U.S.), J Sirman (U.S.), H Inggs (S Afr), P Townsend, A Halim (U.A.R.), A Skerritt (Waterford)

* Amateur.

GAB GOES OFF TO HOSPITAL

RUSSIAN speedway rider Gab Kadirov was taken to hospital with a suspected left-arm fracture after a spill in the 12th heat of the second speedway international between England and Russia at Newport last night.

The England team won 68—40 and so have a winning 2—0 lead in the three match series.

Exeter rider Martin Ashby was top scorer for England with a maximum of 17 points. And in his first heat he broke the track record with a time of 66.6sec.

His captain, Eric Boocock, scored 15 points, Norman Hunter 11, and Terry Betts 10.

The Russians' top scorer was Vladimir Smirnov with 13 points. Only two other Russians scored more than three points—their captain Igor Plechanov (11) and Gennady Kurilenko (9).

Lloyd the winner

Clive Lloyd, the West Indian batsman who is qualifying by residence, won Lancashire's single wicket competition at Old Trafford yesterday. He beat Barry Wood in the final.

REST OF SPORT IN SHORT

BOWLS

HOME INTERNATIONAL TOURNAMENT (at Belfast).—Wales 98 Scotland 95—England 103 Ireland 99. Scotland won on aggregate

CRICKET

AT EASTBOURNE.—Col Stevens's XI 369 for 5 dec (Brearley 181, Wainwright 70) and 241 for 3 dec (Bidwell 55, Brearley 53 not) bt **Camb Univ** 382 for 7 dec (Carling 118, Maywood 55 not) and 216 (Knight 68) by 12 runs.

AT OXFORD.—MCC 341 for 7 dec (Saeed 73, Leary 69) and 191 bt **Oxford Univ** 308 (Garofall 136) and 162 (Watson 58; Saeed 5—44) by 62 runs

TWO-DAY MATCH (at Utrecht).—**First day**: International Cavaliers 246 (B Davis 112, J Robertson 50). Holland 148 for 9 (H Rickse 44, N Murch 4—30)

GOLF

BRITISH UNIVERSITIES CHAMPIONSHIP (at Gullane).—**Semi-finals**: R Gray (Edinburgh) bt D Nelson (Queen's Belfast) 5 and 3; W Raymond (Strathclyde) bt J Noble (Dundee) at 19th. **Final**: Raymond bt Gray one hole

SPEEDWAY

INTERNATIONAL (at Newport).—**England** 68 (M Ashby 17, E Boocock 15, N Hunter 11, T Betts 10) **Russia** 40 (V Smirnov 13, I Plechanov 11, G Kurilenko 9)

BRITISH LEAGUE.—**Glasgow** 46 (J McMillan 10, O Berg 9, B Josefsson 7) **Poole** 32 (B Andrews 13, G Mudge 6)—**Wolverhampton** 43 (J Airey 12, J Bond 11) **Swindon** 35 (R Genz 8)—**Hackney** 48 (B Jansson 12, C Pratt 11, D Lukehurst 9) **Belle Vue** 30 (S Sjosten 10, T Roper 8, S Levai 6)

WIN £25 WITH SATURDAY'S CROSSWORD

TOO many anagrams on "Fears" and "Safer." Too many jokes about being taken for a ride. But a high quality entry nevertheless.

That was the judges' verdict on last week's £25 Saturday Crossword entry. Some entries failed by being too long and too involved.

One word of warning. Many entries arrived up to 48 hours after the competition had closed. Make sure yours is on time, otherwise it cannot even be considered.

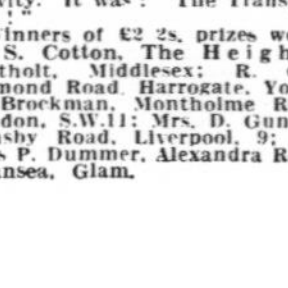

The winner, by a hair's breadth of emphasis in the way he phrased his clue, was Mr. Stuart Morton, of Mill Lane, Greenfield, Bedford. His puzzle is shown here and his cryptic clue to "Fares" had three of the looked-for ingredients: topicality, wit, and brevity. It was: "The Transport Bill!"

Winners of £2 2s. prizes were: H. S. Cotton, The Heights, Northolt, Middlesex; R. Gill, Jesmond Road, Harrogate, Yorks; H. Brockman, Montholme Road, London, S.W.11; Mrs. D. Gunson, Donsby Road, Liverpool, 9; and Miss P. Dummer, Alexandra Road, Swansea, Glam.

CUT HERE

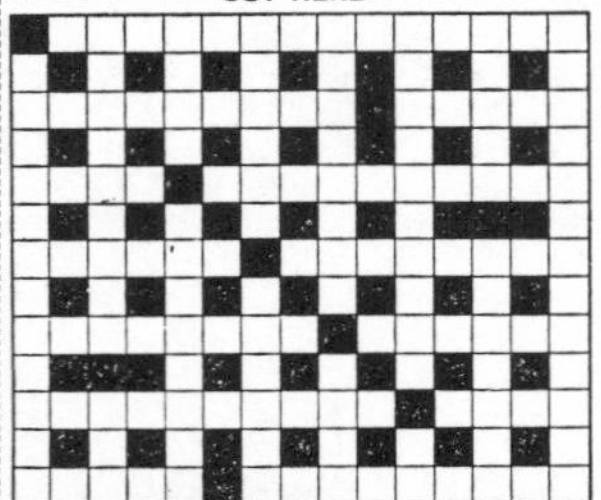

NAME ....

ADDRESS ....

....

Cryptic clue to "Beach" ....

.... 3,011

MAKE up your own puzzle in this square and add a cryptic clue to the word given. The Editor of the Daily Express together with the Crossword Editor, will judge each puzzle for quality and they will look for topicality, aptness or wit in the cryptic clue. One clue only, please. (Do not use obscure words and avoid hackneyed ones.)

Address your completed square to Crossword 3,011, Daily Express, 4, Racquet Court, Fleet Street, London, E.C.4 (Comp.), and send it to reach there by Tuesday first post. No entrance fee.

No letters, please, to underline the quality of any entry. Each competitor's work will be judged on its own merits.

GREYHOUND WINNERS AND HINTS

CHARLTON.—7.45 **Ahoy Honey** 7—4 fav (F 1-2 46/3). 8.1 **Radar Beam** 4—1 (F 3-2 83/-). 8.18 **Carmen Star** 6—1 (F 3-5 63/3). 8.35 **Light Fork** 3—1 jt-fav (F 1-2 40/3). 8.53 **Aviator** 7—4 fav (F 3-2 17/6). N.R. Stillanstar Toby. 9.11 **Breach's Bill** 2—1 fav (F 2-1 44/3). N.R. Fly Winch. 9.27 **Jammy Sammy** 11—2 (F 6-2 77/6). N.R. Proud Admiral. 9.45 **Andraid Harp** 5—2 (F 5-6 21/3).

HARRINGAY.—7.45 **Buff's Duke** 3—1 fav (F 2-4 31/9). 8.1 **Gothammist** 100—8 [illegible]

HAWKEYE'S ONE-DOG SPECIAL

7.30, NEW CROSS

On the Prowl

4—5 fav (F 4-3 10/3). 8.51 **Matten** 9—2 [illegible]

[illegible] 3—1 (F 5-6 166/-). N.R. Loughmore Lisa. 9.30 **Hi Tanza** 9—4 fav (F 2-1 80/3). 9.45 **Stirling Paula** 5—2 (F 1-3 39/-).

HAWKEYE'S FANCIES

CATFORD.—8.35, Movealong Helen. 8.52, Gordo's Prince. 9.27, Temple Jim. 9.45, Newgrove Teddy (nap).

CLAPTON.—8.15, Ambiguous. 8.30, Our Joe's Son (nap). 8.46, Geddy's Runner. [illegible]

SHREWSBURY TOWN F.C.

Applications are invited for the post of Manager of Shrewsbury Town F.C. [illegible] is a [illegible] man [illegible] giving details of experience and qualifications [illegible]

The Chairman, SHREWSBURY TOWN F.C., GAY MEADOW, SHREWSBURY.

SALE BARGAINS FOR IMMEDIATE DELIVERY

Your order can be sent C.O.D. 4/- extra

Formerly ~~59/6~~ *Each* NOW ONLY **49/6**

Postage & Packing 4/6 extra

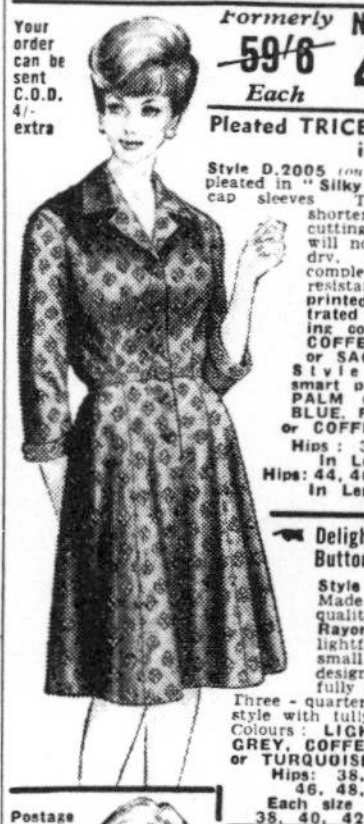

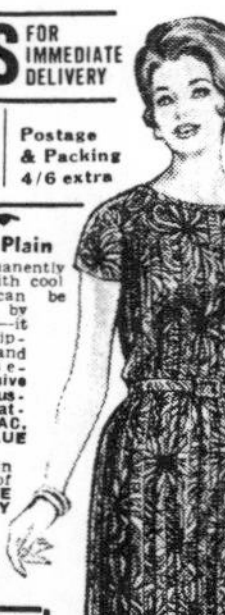

Pleated TRICEL Dress in Print or Plain

Style D.2005 *(on right)*. Permanently pleated in "**Silky TRICEL**" with cool cap sleeves. The length can be shortened simply by cutting the hem—it will not fray. Is drip-dry, non-iron and completely crease-resistant. **Exclusive printed design as illustrated in predominating colours of LILAC, COFFEE, SAXE BLUE or SAGE GREEN. Style D.2006.** In smart plain colours of **PALM GREEN, SAXE BLUE, FRENCH NAVY or COFFEE.**

Hips: 38, 40, 42" In Length 43"
Hips: 44, 46, 48, 50, 52" In Length 46"

Delightful Three-quarter Button-through Dress

Style 874 *(on left)*. Made in an excellent quality crease-resistant **Rayon** which has a delightfully attractive small self and white design. Washes beautifully and dries quickly. Three-quarter button-through style with fully cut gored skirt. Colours: **LIGHT NAVY, MID-GREY, COFFEE, SAGE GREEN or TURQUOISE BLUE.**

Hips: 38, 40, 42, 44, 46, 48, 50, 52, 54"
Each size in lengths of 38, 40, 42, 44, 46, 48"

Postage and Package on 2 or more garments 5/6 extra

★ When ordering please state style number and give second choice of colour if possible.

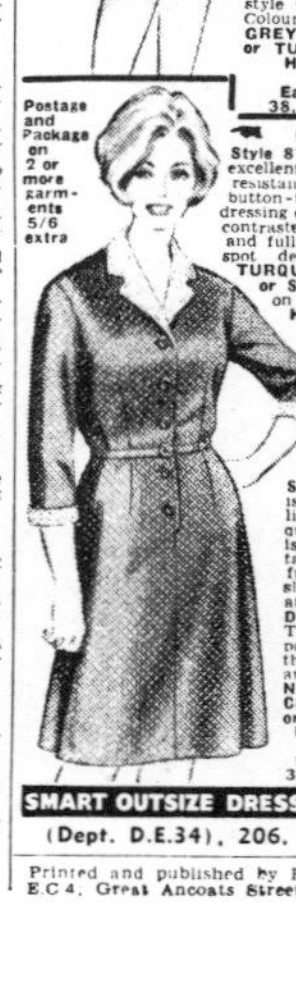

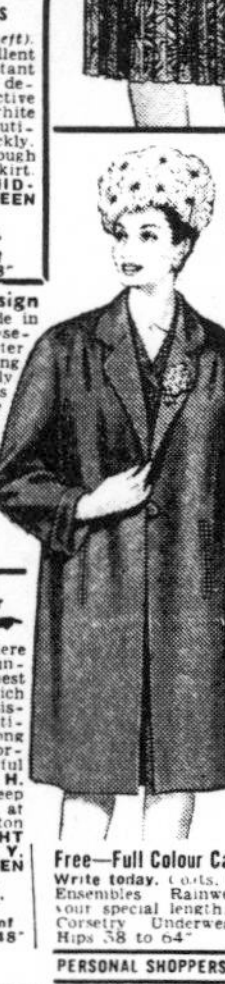

Charming Spot Design

Style 873 *(on left)*. Dress made in excellent quality, washable, crease-resistant **Rayon.** Three-quarter button-through front, making dressing easy and quick. Elegantly contrasted rever collar and cuffs and fully cut skirt. Small white spot design on grounds of **TURQUOISE BLUE, COFFEE or SAGE GREEN** reversed on collar and cuffs.

Hips: 38, 40, 42, 44, 46, 48, 50, 52, 54"
In Lengths of: 38, 40, 42, 44, 46, 48"

Smart Duster Coat

Style 875 *(on right)*. Here is an extremely smart unlined coat made in the best quality **Rayon Rep** which is completely crease-resistant and will wash beautifully. Collar has long slenderising revers decorated with a beautiful **DIAMANTE BROOCH.** There are two useful deep pockets. Coat fastens at the waist with a button and loop. Colours: **LIGHT NAVY, MID-GREY, COFFEE, SAGE GREEN or TURQUOISE BLUE.**

Hips: 38, 40, 42, 44, 46, 48, 50, 52, 54"
Each size in lengths of 38, 40, 42, 44, 46, 48"

Free—Full Colour Catalogue Write today. Coats, Dresses, Ensembles, Rainwear, in your special length. Skirts, Corsetry, Underwear, etc. Hips 38 to 64"

PERSONAL SHOPPERS WELCOME

SMART OUTSIZE DRESS Co Ltd

(Dept. D.E.34), 206, KILBURN HIGH ROAD, LONDON, N.W.6.

Printed and published by Beaverbrook Newspapers Ltd., Fleet Street, London, E.C.4, Great Ancoats Street, Manchester, 4, and Albion Street, Glasgow, C.1.

Daily Mirror

5d. Wednesday, September 18, 1968 ✦ No. 20,134

❛We are not prepared to receive a team thrust upon us by.. political foes❜

VORSTER PUTS BAN ON DOLLY

Before the ban—happiness. D'Oliveira pictured yesterday with his sons . . . Shaun, 3, on the left and Damian, 7.

By MIRROR REPORTERS

THE MCC tour of South Africa is almost certainly off.

South Africa's Premier John Vorster last night uncompromisingly banned any team that includes Cape Coloured cricketer Basil D'Oliveira.

And MCC secretary Billy Griffith declared: '' If the chosen team is not acceptable to South Africa, the whole thing will be called off.''

Mr. Vorster, in a blunt and blistering speech, had said that the team now selected was no longer that of the MCC, but the team '' of South Africa's political foes.''

But Mr. Griffith said the team had been chosen '' only on cricketing ability and with no political considerations involved.''

Mr. Griffith said the MCC would wait for the South African Cricket Association's reaction to '' Dolly's '' selection before making a final decision.

Dismay

The MCC, he said, could not decide '' just on what we have heard of Mr. Vorster's speech.''

But in Kimberley, South Africa, the president of the South African association, Mr. Wally Hammond, said the situation was now beyond their control.

The cricketing world reacted with dismay to Mr. Vorster's ban.

Doug Insole, chairman of the selectors, said: '' If the tour is off

Now it looks as though the tour is off

it is a tragedy. It would have been a wonderful series between what I believe to be the two best teams in the world.''

D'Oliveira himself said in Plymouth: '' This is a tragedy for cricket. . . . Nobody in the world of cricket can feel unhappier than I do tonight.

'' The last thing I wanted was that two great cricketing countries should stop playing each other.

'' I know it has happened because of me and that makes it a great personal tragedy.''

Only Colin Cowdrey, captain of the touring side, appeared optimistic.

He said: '' Mr. Vorster has talked about the non-acceptance of a team chosen for political reasons, but he has not actually said that he will not have MCC in South Africa.''

Open

'' It is my belief that he has left the door open . . . I am, therefore, optimistic that the tour will still take place.''

MR. VORSTER, who was speaking at a political rally in Bloemfontein, said South Africa is not prepared to have a team that has been forced on her by people

■ Continued on Back Page
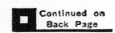

EXPORTS SMASH RECORDS

By ROBERT HEAD

Hopes of cut in Bank Rate as the £ gets a boost

BRITAIN'S trade with the world surged ahead last month.

Exports broke all records and there was a welcome drop in imports.

The trade gap—between what Britain bought and sold abroad — was the smallest this year.

It was slashed back to £30,000,000 in August compared with £81,000,000 in July. These good figures put new heart into the pound. There was a rush on the Continent to buy sterling.

The boost may encourage the Government to bring Bank Rate down tomorrow —or very soon.

This would save Britain millions of pounds of interest a year on our huge overseas debts.

It might also stave off the threat of another rise in the building societies' mortgage rates.

EXPORTS last month reached a highest-ever figure of £556,000,000—a rise of £27,000,000 over the July figure.

The Treasury warned last night that the August figure '' may be to some extent erratic.''

But the Government confidently believes that exports are now on '' a strongly rising trend.''

IMPORTS seem to show signs of flattening out.

Excluding imports of American warplanes, they fell by £13,000,000 last month to £652,000,000.

So when certain shipping, banking and insurance earnings are taken into account, the trade deficit totalled £30,000,000.

It is still too big for comfort and Britain will need a dramatic swing into the black if she is to repay her massive overseas debts.

Figures released by the Treasury yesterday showed that in the first half of this year the balance of payments deficit totalled £494,000,000.

That total is more than we lost in the whole of 1967.

This is what the Treasury had to say in its latest monthly report on the economy, issued last night:

PRICES in the shops have soared by 4½ per cent. since the pound was devalued in November.

The Treasury warns that the new increase in Selective Employment Tax will push up prices further.

WAGES have risen rather less than prices. If the increase in wages remains moderate, prices should show '' a much steadier trend.''

UNEMPLOYMENT has been rising, but this increase '' may be losing impetus.''

What the Mirror Says—See Page 2.

Evening Standard

44,888   THURSDAY, OCTOBER 17, 1968   ● ● 5d.   5

BLACK POWER GAMES UPROAR

MEXICO CITY, Thursday.

There was uproar in the Olympic stadium last night after a Black Power protest by two American Negro sprinters.

Tommie Smith and John Carlos stood on the victory rostrum and gave a Black Power salute as the American National Anthem was played.

Smith had just won the 200 metres final in a world record time of 19.8sec. Carlos came third.

At the medal presentation ceremony, conducted by Britain's Lord Burghley, Smith wore a black glove on his right hand and Carlos a black glove on his left.

BLACK SCARF

Smith had a black scarf around his neck. Carlos wore beads. Both wore civil rights badges—and so did the silver medallist, Australian lay preacher Peter Norman.

As the band played the Star Spangled Banner, Smith thrust his gloved right hand and Carlos his black-sheathed left towards the sky in a Nazi-like salute.

They glued their eyes on the ground and refused to look at the American flag as it was being hoisted to the top of the mast.

The stadium exploded with cat-calls and some of the spectators made thumbs down gestures as they would to a Mexican matador preparing for the kill.

Over in the stands, the wives of the two athletes laughed heartily with friends.

'HE'LL DIE'

"Wait until Avery sees this," said Mrs. Smith. "He'll die."

Moments later, in the Press interview room, packed with reporters from many nations, Carlos cut loose a bitter tirade at the white social structure and the many Mexican fans who had jeered at him.

"They look upon us as nothing but animals," he said. "Low animals, roaches and ants. I want you to print this and print it right. If white people don't care to see black men perform,

Contd. Back Page, Col. 5

Those Black Power salutes from Gold medallist Tommie Smith and Bronze medallist John Carlos, both of the USA.

Fists clenched in black gloves, they gave the salute and looked at the ground as the American flag was raised and their national anthem played.

Olympic reports—Pages 25, 46, 47

Jennie Lee robbed in party raid

GEOFFREY HOBBS

Miss Jennie Lee, the Arts Minister, had to leave a dinner party with a blanket wrapped round her shoulders last night after a thief walked off with her fur coat.

It was one of several belongings to guests stolen from the Georgian home of violinist Yehudi Menuhin, in The Grove, Highgate Village.

The thief is believed to have made his haul as nearly 30 well-known personalities listened to music after having dinner. The coats were in an upstairs bedroom.

Mr. Menuhin had arranged the dinner party to help raise funds for his School of Music.

The guest list included leading personalities from the entertainment, political and business world.

Rather cold

There were Lord Harlech, impresario Bernard Delfont and his wife, Lord Goodman, chairman of the Arts Council, millionaire MP Mr. Robert Maxwell, Sir Jules Thorn, chairman of Thorn Electrical Industries, and Mr. Max Rayne.

Those who lost furs besides Miss Lee were Mrs. Carole Delfont, Lady Strafford, Mrs. D. Samuelson, Mr. J. Norfolk and Mrs. Irene Kreitman, wife of Tesco's managing director.

"My reaction when I heard my mink coat had been stolen was that it would be rather cold going home," said Mrs. Delfont today. "And it was jolly cold. Luckily our car was not very far away."

After dinner, the guests had assembled in the Menuhins' drawing-room to hear recitals from the school's pupils. "The furs could quite easily have been taken then," said Mrs. Delfont.

The guests were in the middle of discussing fund-raising activities when the news of the theft was broken to them.

Mrs. Delfont said the thief's victims took their loss rather philosophically. "There just wasn't much we could do about it except admire the terrific nerve of the thief."

IN YOUR 48-PAGE STANDARD

Amusements Guide
Pages 20-21

MRS. JACQUELINE KENNEDY   **MR. ONASSIS**

'JACKIE KENNEDY TO WED ONASSIS'

BOSTON, Thursday. — The Boston Herald-Traveller reported today that Mrs. Jacqueline Kennedy, widow of the late President, will marry Greek ship-owner Aristotle Onassis before Christmas.

The newspaper said the marriage "could take place before the end of October." It added: "At all events it will take place before Christmas."

Mrs. Kennedy is 39. Mr. Onassis, 62, is a long-time friend of the Kennedy family and has visited them on many occasions. Last weekend he was a guest at the Kennedy home at Hyannis Port, Massachusetts.

Mrs. Kennedy and other members of the Kennedy family have frequently been guests of Mr. Onassis aboard his yacht Christina.

He has often taken Mrs. Kennedy sailing in the Mediterranean.

The newspaper said it learned of the impending marriage from "a completely knowledgeable source" which it did not identify further.

The paper added that the locale for the wedding remained a closely-guarded secret, but it was learned that New York, Maryland, and "a European city" had been under consideration by the couple.

No immediate comment was available from either Mrs. Kennedy or Mr. Onassis.
—News agency reporters.

News of the World reject bid

The News of the World Organisation today rejected the £26 million take-over bid from Pergamon Press.

News of the World directors, headed by Sir William Carr, have given preliminary consideration to the proposed bid and say that they are unanimous in considering the offer "completely unacceptable."

SEE PAGE THREE.

WEATHER:
Dry.
Lighting-up time:
9.21 p.m.
Details—Back Page.
45,377

Evening Standard

London: Tuesday May 19 1970

It looks like 'No' to the South Africans

CRICKET TOUR OFF TONIGHT?

Labour climbs down on the puppets

By ARTHUR HAWKEY

THE LABOUR PARTY has had second thoughts about its knocking campaign against the Tories and is cutting it short—as from now.

The controversial campaign opened last Wednesday and it had been planned to run the puppet posters and advertisements for about a fortnight.

But a few hours before yesterday's election announcement—when it was regarded as certain to come—Labour decided to stop the knocking immediately and

PUPPET HEATH
Second thoughts

go over to the positive side of the campaign; publicising their own men.

New blocks, featuring Chancellor of the Exchequer Roy Jenkins were rushed to Newspaper offices, but were too late to appear today.

Misgivings

The official line on the change of emphasis so soon is that the puppet campaign received so much publicity that to continue it over the originally proposed fortnight might bore the public.

But it is common knowledge that some Labour men have had misgivings about the wisdom of the knocking campaign. Once it became certain that the election date was to be announced last night, Labour's publicity committee decided not to risk a possible backlash of public opinion against the personalised campaign.

There has been a spate of calls to Labour Party headquarters "from Tory supporters, of course," complaining about the campaign.

The story of the Tory lady who rang the other day is Continued Back Page Col. 1

BARBER'S TIP: BACK PAGE.

By RICHARD LYNTON

IT NOW seems likely that the South African cricket tour of England this summer will be called off by the Cricket Council this evening. Events have, I believe, overtaken them—and their decision as to whether the tour should or should not take place.

The outcome of their final critical meeting will be given at a Press conference later today, and, said an MCC spokesman, there will be a "firm statement."

But the verdict may well have been given, in effect, by the Prime Minister yesterday when he announced that the election would be held on June 18.

Explosive situation

As things stand, June 18 is the first day of the first Test of the tour at Lord's.

Quite apart from the distraction of 30,000 people with their minds on anything but political problems, none of the parties would welcome a race riot on polling day or in polling week or, come to that, at any time in the run-up to the election.

Certainly, if the tour is not cancelled the election campaign will be held in the most explosive civil situation since the General Strike of 1926.

Meeting off

Meanwhile the meeting scheduled by members of the Cricket Council at Lord's this afternoon with Lord Hunt, the Bishop of London and Lord Gore-Booth, former head of the Foreign Office, has been cancelled.

They were to have made yet another "change your mind" plea, but in the latest circumstances this would appear unnecessary.

One member of the council who will not be at Lord's today is Kent captain, Colin Cowdrey. Before he led his team out to field on the third day of their current match against Warwickshire at Gravesend, he said:

"I am the only member of the council currently playing cricket and it was always part of the arrangements that if they could meet without interfering with a Kent game they would do so. They know my views, so my presence is not vital."

'£25,000 lost'

If the tour is called off today, or indeed at any time before June 6—the date of the first match of the tour against the Southern Counties at Lord's—the council will lose their premium, estimated at £25,000, which they have paid to insure the tour for a sum of around £200,000.

Meanwhile the pressure grows.

Another delegation which had a date at Lord's today comprised four Labour MPs and one Liberal, who were to have pressed for assurances that MCC-appointed stewards would have specific instructions in dealing with demonstrators and that dogs would not be used.

This meeting has also been called off.

Mr. Arthur Latham, Labour MP for North Paddington, said he had received a telephone call from Mr. Billy Griffith,

secretary of the MCC and of the Cricket Council, saying that it would now be "quite impossible" to meet the deputation.

Said Mr. Latham: "I hope and believe that this means that the South Africa tour is going to be cancelled. This in fact is the only explanation that could possibly excuse Mr. Griffith's last-minute message.

'Annoyance'

"Sudden change in the arrangements for our meeting will undoubtedly cause the MPs involved considerable inconvenience, annoyance and waste of valuable time.

"However, if the Cricket Council are able to announce later today or tomorrow that the tour is off, our feelings will be tempered by relief that wiser counsels have prevailed.

"If this should prove not to be the case, we shall have one hell of a lot more to say."

The deputation of seven represented 90 MPs who signed Mr. Latham's Commons motion calling for the cancellation of the tour.

Arrangements for today's meeting, made two weeks ago, had been twice confirmed.

Mr. Latham asked Mr. Griffith for an explanation for the cancellation "but Mr. Griffith said he was unable to offer one."

'Untold harm'

From Bridgetown (Barbados) the West Indies Cricket Board of Control said in a statement today that there never has been, and never will be, any cricket contact between the cricket authorities of South Africa and the West Indies while the South Africans maintain their apartheid policy.

The WIBC said irreparable harm would result from a South African cricket tour to England and the Board fervently hoped that the direct representations which have been made will result in cancellation.

Bishop Speaks out.—Page Nine

Police swoop on passport ring

By JOHN PONDER and KENNETH TEW

POLICE in India and Pakistan, alerted through Interpol, are trying to break up an organisation smuggling illegal immigrants into Britain with near-perfect fake British passports.

Regional Crime Squad detectives in Britain have recovered more than a score of the passports, printing machinery, rubber stamps, paper and other materials used in their manufacture.

The materials were recovered in a raid on a private house in a Home Counties town last week.

Colin Cowdrey—the man who will not be there.

Suspicious

Detectives from No. 5 Regional Crime Squad, with headquarters at Welwyn Garden City and London's No. 9 Regional Crime Squad have been working for several weeks to trace the source of fake passports.

They are believed to have been used by a number of Indians and Pakistanis who got into Britain with them — some through Heathrow Airport.

It is believed that the suspicions of one immigration officer who spotted a forged passport at Heathrow began the investigation.

EVENING STANDARD BRIEFING IN COLOUR

Get the

best out of Chelsea
PAGES 22-23

London housing warning
PAGE NINE

Foetus ban sparks new row
BACK PAGE

Fleet St. blaze inquiry
PAGE NINE

DAILY EXPRESS

No. 21,781 MONDAY JUNE 22 1970 Weather: Sunny spells; may be stormy later Price 6d.

SLIM LINE FOR WHITEHALL

By WILFRID SENDALL

PLANNING has already begun in Whitehall to revolutionise the machine of government.

This reconstruction will be Mr. Edward Heath's over-riding aim as Prime Minister.

He intends, in his first term of office, to provide Britain with a compact, efficient system, which will last into the 21st century.

Major moves can be expected in the autumn.

An early victim of the axe will be Mr. Wilson's cumbersome "overlord" system which governs the Ministries of Technology, Employment and Productivity, and Local Government and Regional Planning.

COMPACT

For the whole of Whitehall, the final pattern will consist of about a dozen compact Ministries.

Many functions of a strictly managerial and technical nature now carried out by civil servants will be hived off to public agencies, independent in their day-to-day operation and run on the lines of industrial concerns.

To carry out this basic structural change, Mr. Heath plans to recruit outside experts from industry, commerce, and, in some cases, the academic world.

These will not be "prestige names." They will be from the second flight of rising young managers or executives, trained in the most modern methods.

Their tasks will be temporary—to create new organisations in government which, after their departure, will run under their own steam.

One example of the kind of function which could be "hived off" is re-training in industry, a subject to which great importance is attached.

Other fields could be the hospital service, National Savings, Government purchasing and procurement of materials, and building.

Gradually the unwieldy departments will be pruned down, with a strict line being drawn between administration and management.

At the centre will be a new unit for "costing" the activities of government.

CONTROL

Control will be exercised by relating expenditure to the *value* which the community derives from a project, not simply by doling out the cash in little packets.

This evaluation is expected to show that some governmental functions are not worth doing at all, or could be better left to private organisations.

TOMORROW the new Cabinet will meet for the first time. Its first big decision will be whether a Queen's Speech should be prepared for a brief parliamentary session, with a new programme in the autumn, or whether a major programme for a full year's session should be brought in straight away.

The Queen will open the new Parliament on July 2.

A "GOLDEN BOWLER" scheme is being planned for civil servants affected by Mr. Heath's Whitehall streaming *(writes Chapman Pincher)*.

Surplus personnel recruited by the Wilson régime will be encouraged to leave for other jobs by the offer of lump sum gratuities comparable to those offered to axed Servicemen.

Along with the Ministry of Technology, the Ministry of Defence is expected to face some rigorous autumn pruning.

While increasing the proportion spent on "teeth" defences, the Government intends to cut the numbers of civilians employed, who now almost equal the number of Servicemen.

Unions like the Institution of Professional Civil Servants will oppose cuts but the Government hopes to overcome this with productivity deals.

The only Civil Service

PAGE TWO, COL. THREE

Determination: Tony Jacklin on way to victory

Jack-lin! He wins U.S. Open for Britain

PHILIP FINN: Chaska, Minnesota Sunday

TONY JACKLIN, 25-year-old lorry driver's son from Scunthorpe, Lincolnshire, tonight became the first Briton in 50 years to win the U.S Open Golf Championship.

It was a tremendous performance by the man who is already British Open champion. And he becomes the first Briton to hold both titles at the same time.

His £12,500 first prize is considered peanuts to the bonanza that now awaits the one-time, £3 9s.-a-week steelworks fitter—an estimated million dollars or more than £416,000.

He finished with a seven-under-par total of 281—birdieing the last hole with a superb 20ft. putt.

Jacklin, who will be 26 on July 7, is now almost certain to become a full-blown millionaire by the time he is 30.

Cramp

Despite pain from cramp in both legs, he battled with a bulldog spirit that had the crowd of 22,000 mobbing him at the end of the tournament on Hazeltine National course.

"*I feel numb. It was murder out there,*" he said afterwards.

None of the ecstatic fans knew about the fierce attack of cramp—that came on during his Saturday round. All last evening he spent with his legs wrapped in liniment.

Before he even went on to the course today he was grimacing. But he said, chuckling: "When I could see victory in sight, I would have gone round on crutches."

He said after the last hole today: "This is a tremendous moment for me. My legs feel like jelly. I don't think I've ever played under such strain and pressure, and I'm glad it's all over.

"There will be no wild celebration. I just want a quiet night, a chance to collect my thoughts."

After leading all the way he finished with a clear seven stroke lead over his nearest rival, 33-year-old Dave Hill from Evergreen, Colorado.

Jostled

The crowd jostled around him and cheered. It was some time before he could receive the personal congratulations on behalf of everyone in Britain from Mr. Allen K. Rothnie, the British Consul - General in Chicago.

Said Mr. Rothnie: "Young man, you have won the hearts of everyone back home."

Jacklin was hugged by his attractive wife, Vivienne, aged 27, a former Belfast telephone operator.

She had followed him every inch of the 7,151-yard course, mingling with the gallery so as not to distract his attention.

Afterwards, she could not hide the tears of joy as she told me: "I am the happiest woman in the world. I know Tony's parents will be as proud as I am tonight. This is the moment he has lived, dreamed and fought for."

LONDON: At Potter's Bar golf club, Hertfordshire, where Jacklin is tournament professional, club captin Mr. Wallie Dubabney said: "It's fantastic. What a party is going on here.

"The champagne came out when Tony reached the 17th hole. We knew then that he was certain to win."

Match report: Back Page

IN THE KNOW with the Express

Brazil's World Cup: 4-1

Express Staff Reporter

MEXICO CITY, Sunday.

BRAZIL are again world football champions. They won the crown by beating Italy 4—1 today, with goals from Pele, Gerson, Jairsinho, and Carlos Alberto.

Now Brazil have won three times and earn the Jules Rimet trophy for keeps. A new cup will be played for in Munich in 1974.

Brazil became the first country to score 100 goals in World Cup football. Jairsinho became the first player to score in every round including the final. And the team became the first to beat the post-war hoodoo that the side opening the scoring loses the final.

Desmond Hackett—Back Page

And inside:

WIFE WAS TIMING HIM AS CAR OVERTURNED AT 150 MPH

PIERS COURAGE

Piers Courage dies in race blaze

BASIL CARDEW

ZANDVOORT, Sunday.

WEALTHY race driver Piers Courage, heir to one of Britain's biggest brewery fortunes, died in his blazing car today after crashing in the Dutch Grand Prix at Zandvoort.

Only seconds earlier he had flashed past his wife, 25-year-old Lady Sarah Courage, timing him in the pits.

It was the 23rd lap of the 80-lap race and Courage, aged 28, and an old Etonian, was lying seventh in an Italian-built De Tomaso car entered by his friend Frank Williams.

Then as Courage took a bend at more than 150 miles an hour the car left the track, turned completely over and exploded almost at the same time.

A fireman in an asbestos suit tried to drag him out of the blazing wreck. But he was wedged too tight in the cockpit, and after a few seconds the fireman was beaten back by the flames.

FIERCE

They were so fierce that they set surrounding woodland on fire.

At first false hopes were raised in the pits where Lady Sarah, a fashion model and a daughter of old-time race driver Earl Howe, waited anxiously.

A broadcast message said Courage had escaped. But a marshal had mistakenly thought that a man he saw running from the car was the driver. It was the fireman who tried the rescue bid.

A little later the news that her husband was dead was taken to Lady Sarah, mother of two boys, Jasen, three, and Amos, born last February.

Said a spectator who was near the crash:—

"He was going through a fast right-hand bend with no other cars in sight at the time. His car seemed to swerve wide to the left."

Courage, son of Mr. Richard Hubert Courage, chairman of the brewery firm, took up race driving eight years ago.

His ambition, he said, was "to go as fast as I can and go on racing for as long as I can."

Immediately after the crash an inquiry began and although the Grand Prix went on—Jochen Rindt won in a Lotus 72 Ford at 112.95 miles an hour—the rest of the events were cancelled.

Photonews: Page 9

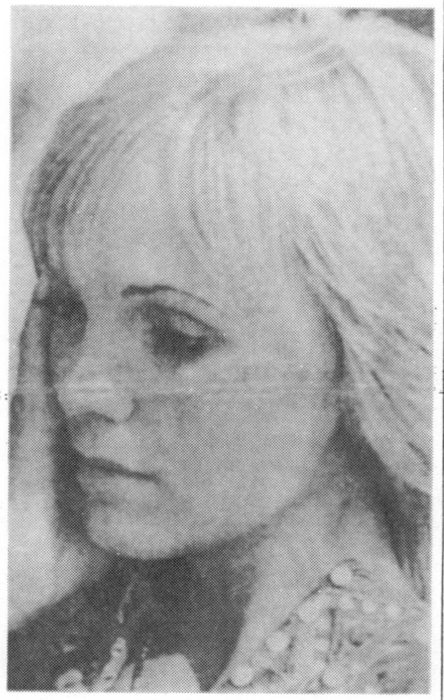

Lady Sarah before yesterday's race

Russians in hijack bid

MOSCOW, Sunday. — Twelve Russians, including three women, tried to hijack a plane at Leningrad Airport, it was reported today.

The 12, posing as holiday-makers, were seized by security men as they crossed the tarmac. Pistols and knives were found in their baggage.

Air stowaway frozen to death

PARIS, Sunday.—The body of a 13-year-old boy was found frozen on the runway at Abidjan airport, Ivory Coast on Saturday.

Jean-Pierre Viers, of Lyons, hid himself in the wheel-base of an airliner at Lyons airport and died from extreme cold about half an hour after the plane took off for Abidjan.

Train spotters home today

WARSAW, Sunday.—The two British train spotters held in a Polish jail for almost a month for alleged spying fly home today.

Jeffrey Flutcher, aged 28, of Surbiton, Surrey, and Ian Turnbull, 30, of Reading, Berkshire, were cleared of suspicion of gathering information about Polish transport installations.

Air-sea hunt

Three lifeboats — two from Southend and one from Margate — and a helicopter searched the Thames Estuary yesterday after a "Mayday" call from a launch with engine trouble. Later the vessel and her five-man crew were escorted to Southend.

Boeing alert

JERUSALEM, Sunday.—An El Al Boeing 720 on a flight to London made an emergency landing soon after take-off today when the pilot discovered the cabin air pressure was faulty. Passengers were switched to another plane.

First visit

BONN, Sunday. — Rumanian Prime Minister Ion Maurer arrives here tomorrow as the first Communist head of government to make an official visit to Bonn.

Britain's man at UNO loses job

NEW YORK, Sunday.—Britain's man at UNO, Lord Caradon, is quietly clearing up his personal and diplomatic business before returning home.

As a Minister of State he automatically lost his job with the change of Government last week. It is not known in New York who will take over.

Copter rescue bid fails

Mr. David John Beckerton, aged 28, of Springfield Road, Taverham, Norwich, was drowned in the sea at Winterton, nine miles from Great Yarmouth, yesterday.

An R.A.F. helicopter plucked him from the sea, but he was dead on arrival at hospital.

Israeli attack

CAIRO, Sunday. — Thirty-six Israeli Phantom and Skyhawk jets raided Egyptian positions for five hours along the entire length of the Suez Canal today, the military command announced.

Police move in

TOKYO, Sunday. — Police reported more than 150 arrests today as about 150,000 people throughout Japan demonstrated against the renewal of the U.S. Japan Security Treaty.

RIDDLE OF TOWPATH MURDER VICTIM

Express Staff Reporter

POLICE last night hunted a towpath killer who clubbed a 70-year-old man to death and dumped him in the River Thames.

Murder Squad men were called in after two schoolboys—out preparing for a Sunday boating trip—saw the body of retired commercial artist Thomas Cubitt Dhonau floating near Petersham Ait, near Twickenham, Middlesex.

Later an appeal went out to courting couples, fishermen, and strollers who used Warren Footpath at Marble Hill Park, Twickenham, on Saturday night or yesterday morning.

Mr. Dhonau — 5ft. 6in. tall with a moustache and small goatee beard—is thought to have been attacked there while on a walk from his home in nearby Marble Hill Close.

A police spokesman said: "Somebody must have seen what happened or something unusual.

"We would like anyone who was in the vicinity to get in touch with us."

A police launch recovered the body. A post mortem revealed head injuries from a blunt instrument.

Detectives kept Sunday strollers from the popular riverside area while they searched for clues.

Mr. Dhonau was wearing a green-grey check suit and a green shirt.

Judge Maria

MOSCOW, Sunday. — Opera singer Maria Callas arrived in Moscow today to join judges at the finals of the Tchaikovsky Musical competition. It is her first visit to Russia.

Doctors call a truce

Britain's junior hospital doctors last night called for a truce with the Government over their pay dispute.

Dr. Catherine Bradley, chairman of the 4,000-strong Junior Hospital Doctors' Association, said: "We now have a new Government. We feel that sanctions applied against the previous one should be temporarily stopped until we know the intentions of the new."

Arab protest to Spain

MADRID, Sunday. — Morocco has protested to Spain over a reported killing of 12 Arabs by security forces in the phosphates-rich colony of Spanish Sahara last week.

The desert colony is the first target of a new anti-Spanish alliance of Morocco, Algeria, and Mauretania, sworn to end Spanish colonialism in North Africa.

Army search for watch

An Army expert with a mine detector yesterday searched the back garden of a bungalow in Rathmena Gardens, Ballyclare, Co. Antrim—for the mechanism of a bride-to-be's gold watch.

Rosemary Logan, aged 28, lost the watch mechanism when she was working in the garden with her fiancé. But yesterday's search was unsuccessful.

Professor Roth dies

JERUSALEM, Sunday.—Professor Cecil Roth, a world-renowned authority on the history of the Jewish people, died in Jerusalem last night, aged 71.

Rush to save 'bends' diver

Skin diver John Boylett was rushed to a decompression chamber on board the ship Topmast, anchored in the Menai Strait yesterday.

John, 23, of Aston Hill, Queens Ferry, Flintshire, was diving at Anglesey when he surfaced too quickly and showed symptoms of "the bends."

Children in tablets alert

Three small children were taken to hospital in Birmingham yesterday after eating tablets found in a derelict house in Devon Street, Nechells. They were detained for observation.

The tablets were used in the treatment of tuberculosis.

Ward's crisis

Only emergency cases were being accepted last night at St. Helier Hospital, Carshalton,—Surrey's largest hospital—because of a shortage of clean linen caused by lack of staff.

Reunion for Heath

Express Staff Reporter

THE cheering went on into the night when Dumpton Gap Road welcomed home the new Prime Minister.

Five hundred waving, clapping wellwishers greeted Mr. Heath as he arrived at his father's house in Broadstairs, Kent.

The crush got so bad that at one point police closed the road on orders from security chiefs worried about the Premier's safety.

On the garden lawn, Mr. Heath said: "It is nice to be home. It is the ambition of every politician to come home like this."

He led his white-haired father, 81-year-old Mr. William Heath, and stepmother, Mary, down to the crowds pressing over the garden hedge chanting: "We want Ted. . . . We want Ted."

He clutched, grasped and shook hands with happy, laughing people to cries of "Good old Ted," "Wonderful," "We voted for you, Ted."

Later, dressed in pale-blue shirt, white slacks, and blue sneakers, he jumped into his official car and drove a mile down to his local sailing club to see old friends.

Then, a stroll on the promenade, stopping to sign autographs every few yards. He stuck his head into the cafés, shops, and candy floss and whelk stands to say "Hello." Bikini-clad girls blew kisses from the beach.

Security for Mr. Heath is to be stepped up after incidents in which a cigarette was stubbed out on his neck on Thursday and a pot of red paint thrown at him outside No. 10 Downing Street on Saturday.

Police chiefs feel that both attacks could have been more serious.

MR. WILSON, still at Chequers, is expected to start house-hunting today. His wife Mary supervised the final stages of the removal from No. 10 yesterday.

LATEST

TV-Radio programmes Page 10

SUEZ FLARE-UP

Twenty Israeli Skyhawks raiding Egyptian positions in the central sector of the Suez Canal, and a heavy artillery duel being fought across the waterway. Second raid in 12 hours.

PHONE (STD CODE 01) 353 8000

TELEX 21841

CHAMPION, ANNE!

By CHRIS LANDER and FRANK PALMER

Picture by KENT GAVIN

PRINCESS ANNE, cheered on by a 20,000 crowd, became Europe's Number One rider yesterday.

She beat the cream of Continental and home riders with a clear round in the show jumping section at the European three-day championships—one of the world's big three events

And the crowd at the Burghley horse trials in Lincolnshire went wild with delight.

It was a fine achievement by the 21-year-old Princess—pictured after her victory—who has done little riding this season because of an operation two months ago

Beer

What makes the win even more remarkable is the fact that Anne was entered as an individual, not as a member of the Great Britain team.

The British team filled the next seven places after Princess Anne.

In the sponsors' marquee afterwards, the Princess seemed surprised to find reporters waiting.

" Don't blame me," said Prince Philip, beaming. " I'm only here for the beer."

When he heard that, the Daily Mirror was present, he said : " I didn't know the Mirror reported show jumping." Back came the reply : " It

And a memo to the Duke: She's made the Mirror report show jumping again

will tomorrow." Princess Anne added amid laughter : " You only reckon to give us a little piece."

Anne declined a glass of champagne and said : " I feel I'm never really fit.

" But in the last three weeks I have been playing a lot of deck tennis on Britannia and running up a mountain every day."

Anne said of her horse Doublet, a gift from the Queen : " As far as I'm concerned there is no other one."

She has no plans to ride him again this year.

But provided she has a good performance at Badminton in the Spring, she and the horse seem certain to be chosen for the British team in next year's Olympic Games in Munich.

Anne received her prizes yesterday—the Raleigh Trophy, £250 and the European Championship gold medal—from the Queen.

FROM PHILIP, A FOOT-IN-IT FOOTNOTE

LIFE as a member of the Royal Family has one big hazard, according to Prince Philip.

The danger. Whenever he opens his mouth he might put his foot in it.

But in an interview in today's Industrial Management magazine, the Prince makes it clear that the hazard doesn't worry him.

He says: "There are hazards particularly, I suppose, in saying anything in public.

" If you get off the kind of bromide and the cliches and the rather flatulent statements which one can so easily make, you are immediately setting out across rather thin ice.

" And occasionally I go through—this is one of the hazards and it is just too bad." Most of the interview is on the Prince's views on environment, which he describes as " the only vital moral problem of today." He forecasts strict anti - pollution laws. " I foresee the time when there will have to be a code of practice accepted by everybody, by Government and by industry and by the conservation bodies."

The Prince adds: " It will have to be backed by legislation. It will have to be given some sort of sanction because everybody's hands need to be tied, not just industry's."

THE Sun

FORWARD WITH THE PEOPLE   3p.   Thursday, May 25, 1972

POLICE BATTER FANS IN SOCCER RIOT

Before the riot . . . jubilant fans rushed onto the field to congratulate Rangers' goal-scorer Stein.

100 hurt as Rangers take Europe title

THOUSANDS of British football fans rioted last night as they were charged by club-wielding Spanish police.

At least 100 supporters were injured, some seriously. Others were arrested.

Several police were taken away with their faces and heads bleeding, as Glasgow Rangers fans ran wild in Barcelona.

About 200 policemen were beaten back by a storm of broken chairs and bottles.

But at one point a dozen rioters—all Glasgow fans—lay unconscious on the pitch of the Camp Nou stadium.

Trouble began as the supporters celebrated their club's 3-2 European Cup Winners' Cup victory over Moscow Dynamo.

They ran on to the pitch waving flags and banners.

HAIL

Immediately, armed police moved in . . . clubbing anyone in their path with their wooden batons.

Some fans ran back to their seats under a hail of blows.

But others retaliated. Several shouted "Fascist police" and "Popery."

Ambulancemen ran in among the mob picking up the injured.

The fans still refused to be shunted off and re-formed in bigger groups to charge back at the police.

It was several minutes before the stadium could be cleared—and the fans streamed into Barcelona streets to continue the celebration.

Last night delegates from the Russian team protested to European football President Hanz Widecker, who had been watching the match.

They complained that two of their star players had been injured by bottles thrown by Rangers supporters.

But they did not ask for a replay.

Dynamo coach, Konstantine Beskov, said: "My players had to dive flat on their faces and were **very** frightened."

MATCH REPORT —BACK PAGE

STAR GOLFERS QUIT AFTER 'IRA' DEATH THREAT

By ANTHONY DORAN

NINE British golf stars are withdrawing from a tournament in Dublin following death threats purporting to come from Sinn Fein, the IRA's political wing.

The nine include Neil Coles, Brian Huggett, Bernard Hunt and Peter Oosterhuis.

A letter headed "Sinn Fein" and bearing a Dublin address has been sent to several British players.

It "strongly advises" them not to take part in the tournament organised by Carrolls, the cigarette firm, which starts on June 20. "Our country is at war with your country," the letter says.

"Some of our extremist elements have vowed to take action against public figures from Britain and we cannot guarantee your safety."

Oosterhuis, who is playing at Bognor Regis, said last night: "Go over there? Not bloody likely."

The Official and Provisional wings of Sinn Fein last night denied sending the letters.

The names of Mairin de Burca and Tony Heffernan appear as signatures.

But Miss de Burca, a Sinn Fein official, said she did not sign the letter.

The most popular liqueur in the world.
Drambuie

London
Tuesday
August 29, 1972
No. 28,171 3p

Evening News

Night Special

PAGE ONE
WHOLE FOOD
VEGETARIAN RESTAURANT
10 a.m. to Midnight. 7 days
293 FINCHLEY ROAD, N.W.3.
Close to Finchley Rd. Tube.
01-435 9967

HH

The film Britain must ban — SEE PAGE SIX

CHEATS! British chief accuses Iron Curtain countries

OLYMPICS STARS ON 'NERVE DRUG'

From DOUG IBBOTSON
Munich, Tuesday

BRITAIN'S Pentathlon team manager Major Monty Mortimer today accused the East European countries of "beating the system" in Olympic competition.

He was referring to dopes which, he said, could be detected only by taking a pint of blood from an athlete.

He made these charges to me as Sergeant Jim Fox, Britain's overnight leader in the Pentathlon, scored a disappointing 188 out of a possible 200 in the shooting event and slumped in the overall position.

Major Mortimer said: "You saw the Russian shooting in the next stand to Jim. He looked as if

SERGEANT JIM FOX—"The tension was terrible."

he was taking a morning stroll not in the least interested in the electronic scoreboard.

"I simply do not believe that any young athlete can shoot like that unless he has had a needle of some sort.

"The Hungarians are ahead of the world in pharmaceutical development and the rest of Eastern European countries are not far behind.

"The International Olympic Committee have rules concerning the use of drugs, depressants and stimulants. They have a list of banned drugs. But it doesn't take long for scientists to produce drugs that are not on the list and administer them in such minute quantities that it would take a pint of blood to detect them.

"Nerves play a hell of a part in shooting. Even a couple of sherries or a glass of white wine is enough to improve a competitor's score by five shots. It would make a tremendous difference to anyone competing here. But you simply dare not risk it.

"I am not saying we should try to compete with the big nations in the use of subtle drugs. We stand by the tradition of the British Olympic Association, who are very good to us.

TRADITION

"But I do say we should officially explore every legitimate means of catching up or having the system regularised.

"Some of the cheating has to be seen to be believed. In Mexico I know of one pentathlete who concealed a breathalyser bag full of urine in his underpants and produced a sample from it—at the required body temperature—for the dope test. Needless to say he had a fantastic score."

The appearance of Fox after his disappointing performance fully endorsed Major

Contd on Back Page

It's a golden dive for Micki King. Micki, a captain in the U.S. Air Force won the women's Olympic springboard gold medal in Munich. For today's Olympics report, see Pages 12 and 14.

Munich 1972

IN PAGE 12
Jesse Owens' little black book
Spitz . . the greatest of them all
Britain's swimmers flop again

BRITONS LOST IN JET CRASH

A PRIVATE jet crashed in the Alps with two British Caledonian Airways crew on board.

Police in Munich said that although the plane carried only the two crew members, the possibility could not be ruled out that there were two passengers aboard.

The two crew members were named as Capt. Leonard Levene and First Officer John Kourdoulos.

The plane, a twin-engined American-built Lear jet, took

off yesterday from Gatwick for Innsbruck, said a British Airports Authority spokesman.

It was believed to be owned by banker Mr. Loel Guinness, a former Tory MP for Bath.

The plane was Swiss-registered under the company of Vodavia of Lausanne.

A British Caledonian spokesman said the crash happened on the 10,200ft. Zugspitte mountain, the highest peak in the Bavarian Alps.

"We supply crew under an arrangement with Vodavia," he added.

THE WEATHER

The Meteorological Office forecast:

THIS EVENING: Fine with sunny spells.

TOMORROW UNTIL MIDNIGHT: Cloudy at first then long sunny spells; wind east to north-east, light or moderate; warm, maximum temperature 22 deg. C 72 deg. F. OUTLOOK: Little change. IRISH SEA: Slight. NORTH SEA: and CHANNEL: Slight to moderate. BAROMETER: 1020.0 mbs. (30.12 inches), falling.

Lighting-up time 8.24 p.m. until 5.50 a.m. tomorrow. Sun sets 7.54 p.m., rises tomorrow 6.10 a.m. Moon rises 9.18 p.m., sets tomorrow 1.58 p.m. Last Quarter Thursday. High water London Bridge 5.21 a.m., 5.35 p.m. Tomorrow 6.11 a.m., 6.18 p.m.

Anne flies to Games

Princess Anne will fly from Dyce, Aberdeenshire, this afternoon to join the Duke of Edinburgh in Munich.

The Queen is to remain at Balmoral.

Mayfair blaze

Firemen from three stations put out a fire which damaged the Orlando Sauna Beauty Coiffeur in Dover Street, Mayfair.

GOING TO BLAZES

My son has become a fireman.—Essex father.

£10 a week Ford claim

A PAY demand of up to £10 a week for 50,000 Ford workers in Britain could face the company when the present wage agreement runs out in February.

Leaders of the Ford shop stewards are recommending that there should be a new minimum rate of £1 an hour.

The claim seeks pay rises of up to 30 per cent for some men and could cost the company more than £30 million.

Holy deadlock

Asking to be excused from giving evidence in a shoplifting case, PC Stephen Poile told Croydon magistrates today: "I will be on my honeymoon."

"Can't the other officer in the case attend?" asked the magistrates. "She is the one I am marrying," added PC Poile.

£100,000 raid

Evening News Reporter

A GHOST gang netted more than £100,000, it was revealed this afternoon, after they hid away in a London post office after closing time.

Police believe the gang calmly walked into the post office in Great Portland Street, Marylebone, just before closing on Friday.

They hid in different parts of the building without being noticed and when the building was locked up they set to work on the strong room.

CZECH MATE

He met his wife when he went to Prague on business. —Finchley woman.

GALLOPING INFLATION

The money he wasted on horses has doubled in the past five years. — Kent woman.

Judge bans love poems to woman doctor

By T. H. JOHNSTON

A HIGH Court judge this afternoon banned 65-year-old Mr. Robin Castle from sending love poems to a 35-year-old woman doctor.

An application by Dr. Sally Elizabeth Flew, senior medical officer for the Borough of Richmond, for an injunction against Mr. Castle was granted by Mr. Justice Boreham, the Vacation Judge sitting in chambers.

In her writ, Dr. Flew claims damages against Mr. Castle for trespass to her home at Pepys Road, West Wimbledon, and her car.

RESTRAINT

She also sought an injunction, which the judge granted, restraining Mr. Castle, who lives in Caxton Road, Wimbledon, from fixing documents to her wall, fence or gate or communicating with her either orally or by writing.

After the short hearing Mr. Castle said he fell in love with Dr. Flew about two years ago.

He had written hundreds of poems about her. "She inspires me and I would marry her if I could," he said.

Dr Flew, who qualified in 1960, is an obstretician, gynaecologist and surgeon, and is a member of the Royal College of Surgeons. Mr. Castle, balding and bespectacled, lives only a mile from her.

I saw frantic waving from Prince's plane

By GARRY MAY
Evening News Air Correspondent

WHY DID Prince William make such a tight turn in his Piper Cherokee seconds before it crashed?

That was the question confronting the Government's accident investigation team at Halfpenny Green airfield this afternoon.

Eye-witness Mrs. Jessie Bishop reported that the Prince's co-pilot Mr. Vyrell Mitchell seemed to be "waving frantically" at the second plane, which took off simultaneously, apparently because it was TOO CLOSE.

But air race organiser Mr. Michael Hennessy countered that the tight turn was "OVER-ENTHUSIASM" in an all-out attempt to win and this caused the tragedy.

The only other explanation appears to be a sudden LOSS OF POWER which forced the Prince to try to turn back and land again.

Mrs. Bishop, of Gospel Ash Road, Halfpenny Green, near Wolverhampton, was standing in her garden close to the end of the runway watching the planes take off.

Personal friend

She said she thought co-pilot Mr. Vyrell Mitchell was trying to attract the attention of the second aircraft which took off simultaneously with Prince William's plane.

Mrs. Bishop said: "The two planes were very close together and as they came over I could see the co-pilot waving frantically.

"You could see the pilot and co-pilot in the plane they were so low. You couldn't see their faces as they were both wearing goggles.

"I don't know whether the co-pilot was trying to warn people on the ground or the pilot of the other aircraft.

"I think he must have been trying to signal to the other pilot because the planes were very close together."

Mr. Mitchell would have been in the right-hand seat on the side of the Cherokee nearest to the second plane being flown by Mr. Timothy Phillips.

Mr. Phillips, managing director of Bally Free Aviation of Dublin, was a personal friend of Prince William and is reported to have stayed at the 30-year-old Prince's home at Barnwell Manor on the night before the crash.

He was being interviewed today by Government air accident investigators Mr.

MRS. JESSIE BISHOP
"Planes were very close"

George Casley and Mr. Arnold Broomfield.

The crash experts have set up an HQ at the Royal Oak Inn near the airfield. They expect to produce a preliminary report on the death crash in two weeks.

Investigator Mr. Casley commented: "We have been looking at film of the Prince's take-off."

All the planes at yesterday's Goodyear Air Race took off in pairs and banked to the left soon afterwards to join the racing circuit.

The Prince's plane was slightly behind and below Mr. Phillips's aircraft and banked steeply over on its port wing.

Mr. Phillips's plane was seen making a similar manoeuvre at a slightly more shallow angle above the Prince's Cherokee G-AYPW.

The steep bank by the Prince's plane was unusual and the Royal pilot may have been trying to tighten his turn to avoid a collision with the second plane.

BBC Television viewers last night saw film of the whole sequence from take-off to the crash.

Mr. Casley went on: "There may be other people who took pictures of the aircraft shortly before it crashed. "We are appealing to anyone who has film of this kind to come forward as it may be useful in determining how the crash happened."

Sqn. Ldr. J. L. "Jock" Malt-

Continued on Page 7

INVALID DUKE TOLD OF CRASH

THE NEWS of Prince William's death was being broken to his father, the 72-year-old Duke of Gloucester, at the family's country home at Barnwell Manor near Oundle, Northamptonshire.

The Duke has been an invalid for two years with a circulatory illness. But his equerry said today: "There is no reason to suppose that he will not be strong enough to take the news."

The safest course..

a Rover from Henlys

And the easiest

Henlys for the Rover 2000, with its 30 award-winning safety features. Henlys for the Rover 3500 automatic or 3500S manual – both combining safety with exceptional power. And Henlys for a realistic part-exchange offer – to make it easier to buy the Rover of your choice. Today.

HENLYS
first for Rover

Devonshire House, Piccadilly, London W1X 6HB (01-493 9151).
Henly House, Euston Road, London NW1 3AX (01-387 4444).
Finchley (01-349 1221). Hendon (01-205 4031).
Catford (01-698 1144). Parkway (01-485 5721).
Croydon (01-684 4283). Hounslow (01-570 5442).
Watford (Garston 73281). Chingford (01-524 1411). Aylesbury (4727)

Britain freezes Amin's £10m. aid

By JOHN DICKINSON
Evening News Political Editor

THE new £10 million loan to General Amin's Uganda Government has been "frozen" because of the expulsion of the Asians, the Foreign Office said this afternoon.

The British Government is not going so far as to say the loan will not finally be handed over. Ministers are continuing to watch events.

But they are obviously uneasy about public opinion in Britain.

A Foreign Office spokesman, referring to criticism of the loan being kept open, said this was not the position.

Two years

He said: "A £10 million loan was agreed in principle last year. [*It was signed in August.*]

"At the time when the present trouble developed, it had not been agreed how the money should be spent.

"Action on the matter was then suspended, and that is still the position."

In fact, aid has been going from Britain to Uganda at the rate of about £4·5 million a year for many years.

Amin says: I'll solve Ulster problem—PAGE FIVE.

Closing Prices Edition

'JAIL STRIKE SPREADS

(See Page Three)

Parkhurst "roof top" strike spread to nearby Camp Hill prison where more than 50 inmates squatting on high roof.

WALL STREET opened slightly lower in moderately active trading.

OLYMPIC RESULTS
SHOOTING

Trap (Olympic Trench): 1 A Scalzone (Itl) 199 (W and OR), 2 M Carregh (Fra) 198, 3 S Basagni (Itl) 195.

VOLLEYBALL

Men Group A: Poland bt Tunisia 3-0 (15-6 15-11 15-1).

CYCLING

100 kmetres Team Road Race: 1 USSR 2hr 11min 17.8 sec; 2 Poland 2:11:47.5; 3 Holland 2:12:27.1; 4 Belgium 2:12:36.7; 5 Norway 2:13 27.7; 6 Sweden 2:13:36.9; 7 Hungary 2:14:15.5; 8 Switzerland 2:14:33.6.

Other placings: 14 Britain 2:16:18.0; 27 Ireland 2:21 37.8.

K.O WIN FOR ALAN MINTER

Crawley light middleweight Alan Minter knocked out Guyana's Reggie Ford in the second round of his first Olympic fight in Munich this afternoon.

THE NEWS

SWING INTO SPRING WITH THE NEWS

Phone (Editorial and other business) 51 0351
Classified 51 0191

Adelaide: Saturday, September 2, 1972   7c*

LAST EXTRA

Crosswords 5, 8
Mitchell 4
Strips 6
Television 5
Weather 13

WEATHER   Fine. MAX. TEMP. (to 3 p.m.) 24.5 C. Sunset 5.58.

Kerry falls, calf 'cut'

MUNICH, Fri. (AAP): Australia suffered a shock today when steeplechase champion Kerry O'Brien fell in his 3,000 metre steeplechase heat and was injured.

O'Brien, world record holder for 3,000 m., smashed into a hurdle 250 metres from the finish and lay motionless on the track for some, seconds.

He was near to tears after the race as he told of the fall.

This is his story:

"I was going so well at the time. You don't know how thrilled I was.

"I've had weeks of pain from injuries and today everything was going right. I know I would have filled a place to qualify for the finals.

"As we turned for the final lap I thought to myself 'at last the sun is shining.'

"I was about to make a run when a runner behind clipped my heel. I didn't falter because I had to keep running. So I decided to kick off the shoe.

Rolled over the hurdle

"When I did this, I started my approach to the hurdle, but my left heel and ankle, which were taped, slid. I couldn't get up.

"I more or less slid into it and struck the bar with my right shin. Then someone spiked me in the left calf and I rolled over the hurdle.

"I was getting a little tired in the last lap, but I know I would have made it."

O'Brien said he would make a decision tomorrow on whether he would start in the Olympic 5,000 metres next week.

In the 400 m hurdles semi-final, Gary Knoke was beaten by a false start that wasn't. He drew the outside lane, right beside a loudspeaker through which he heard a "second" bang from the starter's gun and thought it signalled a false start by one of the runners behind him.

Knoke finished last, then unsuccessfully protested at an "unfair start."

WITH that golden glow again, Shane Gould (right) congratulates United States placegetters Shirley Babashoff (left) and Keena Rothhammer after the 200 metres freestyle.—Today's AAP-AP radio picture.

Her third gold medal

MUNICH, Friday: Shane Gould again blitzed her rivals to capture her third and Australia's fifth gold medal at the Olympic Games tonight and became our greatest individual gold medal winner at one Games.

The sensational Sydney schoolgirl turned in a scorching 200 metres freestyle in the world record time of 2 min 03.56 sec.

Her three gold medals for the 200 and 400 freestyle and the 200 metres individual medley equals the record of America's Debbie Meyer at the last Olympics in Mexico City in 1968.

Shane has now set herself for her fourth gold medal and another world record in the 800 metres on Sunday.

"Things are going well for me now," she said. "I know what's going on and I feel pretty confident."

She intends to play more of a waiting game in the 800 metres.

"But really I'll play it by ear," she said.

Tonight it was almost a

From News man Dick Tucker

super - confident Shane who strolled towards the starting blocks.

Gone was the tension and determination in her walk before the 400 metres on Wednesday night when she was out to atone for her 100 metres defeat.

As planned

She even allowed herself the luxury of a wave to friends and a smile before she tensed herself for the race.

Once she hit the water there was no stopping her. She surged to the front, setting such a blistering pace that she burnt off her rivals.

"I intended to go ahead as quickly as possible, run my race, and let the others follow," she said.

"And it worked out perfectly."

Shane, who is now ooz-

The Americans Shirley Babashoff, the world record holder, and Keena Rothhammer made courageous challenges, but they were futile against the flying Shane.

But Shane admitted afterwards she had to pull out all the stops.

"My legs were killing me over the last lap, but I just kept on kicking harder and harder because I knew the Americans were catching up," she said.

She said she swam the race exactly as she had planned.

ing with confidence, had an extra special reason for turning in such a sizzler tonight.

She was determined to grab back the world record. Babashoff had claimed from her in the American trials early last month.

Tonight she clocked a

magnificent 2 min 03.20 sec to slice 1.64 sec off Babashoff's mark.

South Australia's exciting swim prospect Debbie Palmer swam well, though unsuccessfully, here today.

She got through the first two heats of the 110 yards backstroke in her fastest ever times before going out in the semi-final with a seventh placed 1 08.29, again her best for the distance.

Earlier she had swum an outstanding second to Shane Gould in a heat of the 200 metres freestyle, but her time of 2 10.29 did not qualify her for the final.

The News on Cocos

The News Group team has arrived on Cocos Island and the first exclusive story to come out of the controversial Indian Ocean island will appear in the Sunday Mail tonight.

Mr. John Clunies Ross.

"king" of Cocos Island, talks about allegations that conditions there are "close to slavery."

The News on Monday will publish further stories and pictures.

No. 15,286—Registered for posting as a newspaper—Category B.

Daily Mirror

BRITAIN'S BIGGEST DAILY SALE

3p   Wednesday, September 6, 1972   No. 21,351

15 DIE IN MUNICH MASSACRE

Minister baits the fatal trap

THIS was the moment when the bait was cast, when the trap was sprung. West German Interior Minister Hans-Dietrich Genscher, on the extreme left, listens with his officials to the demands so pointedly put forward by one of the guerillas in the Munich Village drama. Genscher negotiates politely enough, along with his aides. But in the end the deal he arranged was destined to have only one result . . . the ruin of the Arab terrorist plot. And the terrible cost: many innocent lives.

From DENIS MARTIN in Munich

FIFTEEN people died yesterday in the Massacre of the Munich Olympic Games.

Eight were Israeli hostages snatched by a five-strong gang of Arab terrorists.

They died in a shoot-out between police and the guerillas at Munich airport.

The terrorists had shot dead two Israelis in a dawn raid at the Olympic village.

Earlier it was reported that three of the guerillas were shot dead in the battle at Fuerstenfeldbrueck military air base — and a fourth man blew himself up with a grenade rather than face capture.

A policeman was also killed.

Attack

A massive hunt was launched for the fifth Arab, who fled from the base during the shooting.

The bloody climax to the guerilla raid — which led to the suspension of the Olympic Games — came after hours of tense negotiations at Israel's headquarters in the village.

It was there that two Israelis were murdered by the gunmen in a dawn attack aimed at forcing the Israeli Government to free 200 jailed Arab terrorists.

It seemed that the terrorists had won a major part of their grim battle when West German Government officials

Hostages killed at airport

agreed to let them take their eight hostages to Cairo, using an airliner waiting at the military base.

The Arabs herded their captives aboard two helicopters which took off immediately for the base.

Three senior politicians went to the air base with them — Federal Interior Minister Hans-Dietrich Genscher, Bavarian Interior Minister Bruno Merck, and former Federal Minister Franz-Josef Strauss.

The 16-strong party travelled in three helicopters.

The fierce gun battle broke out when the helicopters landed and the terrorists got out with the hostages.

Instead of being on the verge of victory the Arabs had manoeuvred themselves into a trap.

German Government spokesman Conrad Ahlers said later: "It was never intended to let them go."

OLYMPIC NIGHTMARE Pages Two and Three

THE DYING FLAME Centre Pages

GOLDEN IDOL

Undimmed by tragedy, the Olympic glories of Mark Spitz

From JOHN SMITH
Sacramento, California,
Saturday

OLYMPIC swimming champ Mark Spitz relaxes . . . ready for the souped-up campaign that will turn the seven-medal winner into a million-dollar superstar.

Behind him are the tensions and tragedy of Munich.

THE TENSION of winning seven gold medals and proving himself the world's best swimmer.

THE TRAGEDY that resulted in seventeen deaths after the Arab guerilla raid on Israel's Olympic headquarters.

Before Spitz lies a future which looks as golden as those Munich medals the 22-year-old Californian scooped up.

And in the best US tradition America's latest superstar is being wrapped up, packaged and marketed like a new wonder detergent.

Hysteria

Millionaire Sherm Chavoor, who coaches Mark, has a sign on his desk at the Arden Hills Swimming Club, near Sacramento, which he owns.

It says "Ulcer Dept." And the hysteria surrounding Spitz is certainly ulcer material.

"Look, I'm too busy to talk to you now," grey-haired Chavoor barked into the telephone.

"Everything's going crazy here. The White House has been on. They want Mark to fly to Washington to meet the President.

"The Bob Hope TV Show called — they want Mark on their programme. Oh, and yeah, Universal Pictures rang from Hollywood to talk about a film deal.

"An interview? How much are you willing to pay? And you'd better start talking in thousands. From now on this boy isn't talking to anybody for free."

Spitz, who gleefully renounced his amateur status in a welter of rewarding financial deals, slumped in a chair nearby, looking slightly dazed.

Privacy

"I cherish privacy," he explains. "It's scary, all of a sudden being in the public eye.

"I can't believe it. I'm a hero in the US. You can go all your life, and then suddenly you strike something and everybody goes bananas."

He smiles at the suggestion he might become the new film Tarzan, just as champion swimmer Johnny Weissmuller did. "Weissmuller wore a skimpy suit," said Mark. "I don't think I want to expose myself that much. But I could learn to yodel."

A rare grin flashed beneath the dark moustache that gives him the dashing good looks of Omar Sharif. "Maybe I'll do some nudie movies."

It's a joke.

But if the manly Mr. Spitz ever stars in a skin flick, he'll have plenty of volunteers to play the leading lady. Mail from adoring girl fans is pouring in.

Wonder swimmer Mark Spitz . . . and the magnificent seven Olympic golds.

Picture: Terry O'Neill   © Stern Magazine, 1972

BIGGEST EVENING SALE IN THE WORLD

Evening News

London Wednesday June 20, 1973 No. 28,419 3p

Night Special HH

Ex-champion slams boycott of Wimbledon, source of the riches

STUPID! MONEY-MAD STARS OF TENNIS

By Fred Perry

THE WORLD'S top tennis stars' boycott of next week's Wimbledon championships was attacked today by Fred Perry.

He said: "To kick Wimbledon and the public in the pants on the eve of a great tournament is just not my cup of tea."

Mr. Perry. three times winner of the Wimbledon singles title and now a world-famous tennis commentator said that instead of playing the game for the love of it, "the stars play for what they can get out of it."

There is a power struggle going on. It has been simmering for a long time and it is just very unfortunate it should come out at Wimbledon.

But if it wasn't there it would have been somewhere else.

All the players involved have made a lot of money out of the game and they nearly all made their reputations at Wimbledon.

Bigger than any player

The game is bigger than any player. Tennis players are like buses, there's always another one along in a minute.

The walk-out is the most terrible thing for the game—it's stupid, no matter what the reasons.

It's about time that someone understood that the game is more important than any individual or group of individuals. It's the game that counts.

The players will suffer for the next two weeks, because here they are in London and there is no-one paying the bills. All the tennis players I have ever known are always interested in who is going to pay the bill.

As far as Wimbledon is concerned it is not going to hurt it one little bit. It will be interesting to see the reaction of tennis playing public and tennis watching public.

Money is the God

We shall have to see what happens from there. One thing puzzles me is that if this power struggle continues, and officers are stripped of some of their powers, which seems to point on the surface, who is going to take care of the game in the various countries of the world?

It seems to me that the main God of this game is money . . . M-O-N-E-Y. I know these boys love to play tennis, it's their life. But more and more there is a nasty thought creeping into this thing—that instead of playing because they love it, they play for what they can get out of it.

I am sorry to see that this thing has come up during Wimbledon. Why Wimbledon was chosen, goodness only knows. It is the greatest tournament in the world.

● Nikki Pilic, the Yugoslav at the centre of the row, said tonight both the professionals and the international federation had used Wimbledon. "We could have saved Wimbledon if we could have talked about it."

He was speaking at Heathrow before flying home. "I am willing to fly back at a moment's notice. Wimbledon IS tennis and I love the English crowd. But I must leave. The endless phone calls and the pressures were getting me down."

Both sides say 'no surrender'

By JOHN OAKLEY

WIMBLEDON'S row with the world's top tennis stars was in deadlock tonight with both sides saying: "The ball is in YOUR court."

FOR the 70 professionals who are boycotting the world's greatest tournament their leader Cliff Drysdale said: "It could now be an all or nothing fight which, in the end, the players will win."

FOR Wimbledon, the championships chairman Herman David declared: "We shall not be offering any compromise. It is up to the players whether to compete or not."

'Still time to talk'

He added: "There is still time for talks between the international federation and the professionals, although it is getting a little late."

He discounted suggestions that Wimbledon could break the deadlock by accepting the entry of Yugoslav star Nikki Pilic, although he is banned by the international body.

"The simple answer is No," he said. "We are backing the body which represents the whole world of tennis. The professionals are working for the professionals."

Cliff Drysdale, president of the Association of Tennis Pro-

Continued on Page 13

I WILL PLAY SAYS ILIE

ILIE NASTASE, tennis glamour boy, said today: "It is 98 per cent certain that I shall be playing at Wimbledon, although I have pledged to boycott the event.

Nastase the No. 2 seed who was beaten in last year's classic final, is under orders to play by the Rumanian Tennis Federation.

"They pay my fare and hotel bills in the Davis Cup. I am feeling awful. I want to support my fellow professionals."

He had tried to contact the Federation offices in Bucharest but, so far, without success.

Then he added: "I still feel that things will be all right and everyone will play. But move will have to come m the ILTF."

ACK PAGE: "Miserable" ylor pulls out and what le row is about.

GUMBOOTS FOR ASCOT

It was a Royal Ascot wash-out for fashion today, but Mrs. Sylvan Mason, 27, beat the weather—and saved her hat — with gumboots and umbrella. The traditional Royal procession down the course was called off because of the torrential rain and the Queen went straight to the Royal Box. See News Talk—Page Three.

Philip to visit Moscow

Prince Philip is to spend two days in Moscow before attending the European three-day equestrian championship in Kiev in September.

He may pay courtesy calls on some of the Soviet leaders.

It will be the first visit to Russia by a member of the Royal Family since the 1917 revolution.

£90,000 gem

A 26-carat emerald was sold at Christies today to a Swiss dealer for £90,000—the most expensive stone ever sold by Christies in London.

Car men go back

Eighty plant attendants at the Austin-Morris works at Cowley voted today to end their three-week-old strike.

AWAY BANKER

I am saving for a holiday in Spain.—Hillingdon man.

CENTRE POINT TO BE LET—FLOOR BY FLOOR

CENTRE POINT, the 34-storey office block owned by multi-millionaire Mr. Harry Hyams, is to be let floor by floor.

Mr. Hyams has abandoned his condition that the block in Charing Cross Road, could be let only to one client. It has been empty for 10 years.

It is now likely that a number of firms will move in and major alterations will have to be made to cope with this.

Britain's oil bonanza—Walker

Britain's balance of payments will improve in the 1980s by at least £1,000 million a year through the discovery of North Sea oil, Trade and Industry Secretary Mr. Peter Walker said today.

Don't talk to Heath, Scanlon ordered

By JOHN DICKINSON
Evening News Political Editor

THE GIANT engineers' union this afternoon banned their leader, Mr. Hugh Scanlon from attending future Downing Street talks on Britain's economic problems.

The union's policy-making national conference at Eastbourne ordered him to withdraw from the TUC team after a bitter two-day debate.

The move was seen as a setback to Mr Heath's efforts to do a deal with the TUC.

CRUCIAL

The Prime Minister, though aware that some union leaders resent the attempted domination of their affairs by the big guns of Mr. Scanlon and Mr. Jack Jones of the Transport Workers, knows that any Government success with the TUC must depend upon the effectiveness of the unions' negotiating team.

The participation of Mr. Scanlon and Mr. Jones is crucial to any worthwhile understanding—and Mr. Heath believes such an understanding is crucial for the Government's economic policy.

The deal between Government and TUC could now be crippled before it had even started.

Boy's death fall

A four-year-old boy, Gregory Bailey, died this afternoon after falling from an 11th floor flat in Stockwell Road, Stockwell.

Lambton: 'Why my wife was so calm'

NEW YORK, Wednesday.

LORD LAMBTON, who resigned from the Government following the disclosure of his association with call girls, said today there was one lesson he had learned: Don't get caught.

The 50-year-old former Minister for the RAF, was asked in an interview on American TV whether he had learned any lesson from the sex scandal.

"Well, I suppose there are always lessons to be learned from everything," replied Lord Lambton. "I mean, people want to be more careful and above all, people don't want to be found out."

Lord Lambton said his wife had accepted the situation with calmness and sympathy. This showed the difference between American and English women.

Lord Lambton: People don't want to be found out.

Attractive aristocrat

"English women realise that their husbands are not ideal, and that it is male characteristic to wander and stray upon occasion," he said. "But the American woman thinks her husband must always be faithful.

"The social result is, of course. that many marriages which break up in America, would not do so in England, because the incidental infidelities would simply not be thought important."

The interviewer reminded Lord Lambton that he was an attractive aristocrat and asked him: "Why did you have to pay?"

"A person in my position always likes going outside the confines in which he lives," replied Lord Lambton.

Lord Lambton emphasised that no security problem was involved in his relationship with call girls.

Asked if getting him mixed up with prostitutes could be the work of an international spy ring, he replied:

"I think that is nonsense really. Casual relationships are almost the last occasion when you discuss secrets. They are occasions for physical activity. They are not occasions for mental conversation.

A strong urge

"The danger of people giving away security is not to casual call girls or the equivalents, whatever they are, but to mistresses, and to clever friends. And when people drink too much."

Lord Lambton said it was not possible to set up moral standards for public, as opposed to private individuals because "men with great ambition very often have with it a strong sexual urge that isn't satisfied easily."

But, he said: "If you are put into a position where you make a fool of yourself and consequently the government of which you are a member, there is no alternative but resignation."

Meanwhile in an article today in the West German magazine Stern, Norma Levy—the call girl with whom Lord Lambton had a relationship—made some outspoken comments.

She said she voted for the Conservatives in the last

Continued on Page 3

CLOSING PRICES Page 15

IN THE NEWS TOMORROW

Thursday Cinema

Will life the day after tomorrow be any better than it is today?

FELIX BARKER examines the questions in reviews this week of three films with a common theme.

Thursday Interview

FRANKIE McGOWAN talks to THE VIRGIN SOLDIER

Thursday Fashion

You may not get to Bermuda. Getting into long shorts is another matter.

MIA SCAMMELL Young fashion expert is in holiday mood this week. Report with picture.

'SMEAR' ROW OVER BIG BANKS

By MAURICE ROMILLY

LABOUR demands for a Government inquiry into the cancelled banking merger between Hill Samuel and Slater, Walker were rejected by Sir Geoffrey Howe, Minister for Trade and Counsumer Affairs in the Commons tonight.

An angry scene erupted with cries of "smear" from Tory MPs after Mr. Wedgwood Benn from the Opposition Front Bench had pressed for an investigation.

Sir Geoffrey Howe, said the proposed merger did not raise issues which required investigation by the monopolies commission.

But Mr. Benn asserted that what had happened had graver implications. The proposed merger was promoted by two men well known to the Minister and supported by the Governor of the Bank of England.

He suggested there had been "efforts by Ministers" to cover up the unacceptable face of capitalism in respect of the deal.

In training

New 90 mph trains each seating 322 passengers will be used on the Eastern Region between Essex and London next year.

WEATHER

CLOUDY AND RAINY

TONIGHT: Cloudy, rain at times. Tomorrow: Cloudy but dry, becoming brighter with sunny periods, fine in evening, max. temp. 19C (66F), wind moderate north westerly. Outlook: Becoming warmer and staying dry. Barometer: Rising.

Irish Sea: Moderate, becoming slight. Channel: Moderate. North Sea: Slight, becoming moderate.

Sun sets 9.21 p.m. rises 4.43 a.m. Moon rises 11.39 p.m., sets 10.32 a.m. High water London Bridge 5.21 p.m. Tomorrow 5.54 a.m., 5.55 p.m.

Pollen count in London: 23 (low). Forecast: Similar.

The Great Monsoon — Page THREE.

Fosby

Drawn by Roy Nixon

One man's fight to save victim of Grand Prix

RACE AGAINST TIME

David Purley . . . vain rescue bid.

ONE MAN'S desperate bid to save a fellow racing driver from a fiery death is captured in a dramatic sequence of three pictures.

David Purley abandoned his car during the Dutch Grand Prix yesterday and rushed to the wreckage of fellow-Briton Roger Williamson's Formula One March.

It was to be a tremendously courageous—but hopeless—battle.

Purley knew that each second counted in his frantic race against time. First he tried to lift Williamson's car, but failed.

Then he grabbed a nearby fire extinguisher and played the foam over the blaze.

But the flames were too fierce to be beaten by one man with such limited equipment.

With a look of despair and anger on his smoke-blackened face, Purley walked away, head bowed, from the funeral pyre of 25 - year - old Williamson.

Driver David Purley sprints along the trackside to Roger Williamson's overturned car . . .

. . . he makes a superhuman effort to right the car and save the trapped driver . . .

. . . finally, in desperation, he plays a fire extinguisher on to the blazing machine.

Jackie, the sad victor
Grim-faced British ace Jackie Stewart with his prize after winning the tragic race.

THE GAMES

OUR MAN IN NEW ZEALAND —Charlie Stuart

Gold again for marvellous Mary

WHAT A GREAT GIRL

CHRISTCHURCH, NEW ZEALAND.

MARVELLOUS, MAGNIFICENT MARY PETERS . . . . Northern Ireland's golden girl again. The bubbling blonde from Belfast stood on the victory rostrum here this afternoon, a Gold medal round her neck and the strains of the Londonderry Air echoing round this beautiful Queen Elizabeth II Stadium.

A golden finish to a golden era for Ulster.

At 34, the Olympic champion waved a glorious goodbye to the gruelling five event penthathlon, a competition she has made her own in the past four years, with a hairsbreadth victory to remain champion of the British Commonwealth as well.

"I told the people of Northern Ireland I would win for them and I've done it," she laughed as the happy crowd of well wishers jostled round her minutes later.

The tension of the tiny victory margin — just three tenths of a second separated Gold from silver —was washed away as the thunderous cheers of the New Zealanders, who have come to love this remarkable girl, reverberated round the stadium and carried all the way to the Games village 10 miles away.

NEVER HAS THERE BEEN A MORE POPULAR VICTOR.

The atmosphere in the stadium was electric in those final hectic minutes before the result was announced. No one was quite sure who had won at the end of the 200 metres—the last event of the day. Mary had come second in 25.00 seconds just behind the girl who had pushed her hard all day, Modupe Oshikoya, an unknown and unrated Nigerian.

Despite the tension, Mary spotted six of Ulster's paraplegic team, who called at the stadium to see the last stages of the pentathlon, and ran over to congratulate them on their feats in Dunedin.

Still we waited as the mathematicians calculated furiously. Then what seemed like hours later came the announcement . . . Peters 1st, 4.455 pts., Oshikoya 2nd, 4.423 and Ann Wilson (England) 3rd, 4.236 pts.

The crowd roared to life and Mary leapt for joy. Among the first to congratulate her were two old friends of the late Buster McShane, Belfast dentist Derek Monteith, just recovered from an appendix operation, and Bill Cook, now a businessman in Bermuda but is originally from the Ormeau Road.

Next to see her was her father, Arthur, and little niece, Vanessa, who lives in Sydney and had travelled all the way to see Mary compete for the first time. Then came the medal presentation by Sir Alexander Ross, chairman of the Commonwealth Games Federation. He was only one of many who Mary kissed to-day.

Then the stadium stood to attention and the band played the "Londonderry Air" as the Ulster flag was hoisted above, the giant scoreboard, fluttering proudly between those of Nigeria and England.

Despite her eight hours of exertions Mary looked marvellous on the victor's rostrum. She blew kisses to the near 20,000 crowd who had waited behind to watch the medal presentation and dealt admirably with 80 journalists at a post-victory Press conference.

And she told them that her main aim in life was to see that synthetic track built at Upper Malone. What a booster her exploits to-day should give that venture.

Her trip to Los Angeles before Christmas and her early arrival in Christchurch have certainly paid off. It was only a 32 point or less than half a second victory at the finish—but it was a victory and that's what counts.

Now let's take a look at each of the five events of the pentathlon.

100 M HURDLES

With a 10 am start there were barely 5,000 people in the stadium. A cold, windy day had put a dampner on the atmosphere. In the first heat of the hurdles Mary got off to a great start and led all the way to win in 13.94

Not Mary's fastest time for this event but good enough to give her second place overall, because in another heat Oshikoya recorded 13.72

SHOT

This was when Peters came into her own. Each throw she took improved upon the last one. Her first was 13.51 metres, the second 15.00 and the third 15.05. Beforehand she had looked tense and nervous. After her last effort there was a big smile. She had won the event by 13 centimetres from Kiwi Barbara Poulsen (best throw 14.82 metres).

So the golden girl went for a lunchtime rest 70 points ahead of her nearest challenger Poulsen. But could she keep it up during the afternoon?

HIGH JUMP

There was deadlock in this event with Mary locked in a grim battle with Wilson, who had moved into a challenging position, and Oshikoya. The girls started at 1.55 metres and all went clear until they reached 1.74 metres. All three failed at 1.77.

So each took 974 points and Mary was now over 200 points ahead of her nearest challenger, Jones. Poulsen dropped to third when she could only manage 1.58 metres.

Mary, was obviously confident at this state, giving me the thumbs up sign to the Press box as she waited for the long jump to start. The sun was out and the crowd had grown to over 20,000 and they were in a happy mood after that great win by local favourite Dick Tayler in the 10,000 metres.

LONG JUMP

After her first jump of 5.81 metres, there was an agonising wait while the victory ceremony for the 10,000 metres took place. Mary sat quietly behind the rostrum knowing that she could be mounting it in less than two hours' time.

She messed up the second and could not improve on the third. However, the first jump was good enough even though several girls bettered it. Mary stayed in front overall.

200 METRES

So it all depended on the 200 metres—it was just like Munich all over again. Could the 34-year-old Belfast heroine bow out with a gold medal round her neck. Mary was 109 points ahead of the talented Nigerian Oshikoya, with Wilson third.

Oshikoya had come right back into the reckoning with a fantastic long jump of 6.50 metres and had shown her undoubted speed over the hurdles earlier in the day.

Peters started well, but there was no stopping the Nigerian. She rounded the bend as if her life depended on it. But Mary held on firmly, gritting her teeth and taking second place about three yards behind the Nigerian.

She had done it again, a third gold medal in Commonwealth competition. Oshikoya finished in 24.15 secs, Mary 25 secs dead. So after eight hours gruelling competition only 0.35 of a second separated gold and silver. The Nigerian had needed to win by 1.2 of a second.

Mary consoled the shy little Nigerian girl and there was a hug for British team colleague Ann Wilson. A great pentathlon career had come to an end. WILL THERE EVER BE ANOTHER LIKE HER?

Golden girl Mary Peters waves after her victory in the Pentathlon event. With her is England's Ann Wilson, who came third.

England's David Bedford appears to hit Kenya's Paul Mose during the 10,000 metres. Throughout the race Bedford and the three Kenyan runners appeared to be locked in a duel.

Dave flops again in 10,000 crawl

DAVID BEDFORD flopped again today. England's world record-holder could only finish fourth in a brawling 10,000 metres in the Games.

Bedford who admitted afterwards that he had tried to punch Kenyan Paul Mose during the race, explained: "I lost my cool with all the shoving going on and that was it."

Bedford said: "The three Kenyans were up to every antic in the book. One grabbed my shorts. All I saw was this hand come out and I thought 'Crickey, he's a queer.' It turned out to be Juma and I shouted at him, 'Hey, cut it out'."

Juma, who took the bronze medal, commented, "It was a very tough race. All the way I knew I had to stick to Mr. Bedford. Then I went with Mr. Black."

The race was won by New Zealand farmer, Dick Taylor, in 27 minutes 46.4 seconds with England's David Black taking the silver medal in 27-48.6. Juma's time was 27-57.

Bedford, who was spiked, said he was pushed unto the grass by another Kenyan, Patrick Kiingi. He lost his temper when the jostling and elbowing continued.

"I turned to have a swing at one of the Kenyans," said Dave. "Then I remembered I was in a major race and stopped myself in time. But I had lost my cool — AND IT LOST ME THE RACE."

Black, who lost the final dash for the line against Taylor, said: "Five or six of us kept getting in each other's way and I got spiked."

Dough Goodman, England's team manager, said he would not protest about the Kenyan tactics. "This is something you must accept in top world races," he said.

Taylor (25), followed the advice of coach Arthur Lydiard to the letter.

"I told Dick to stay out of the way and let the Englishman and Kenyans battle it out with each other — and leave the race for him. I knew the Kenyans would try to kick Bedford to death."

Taylor will decide on Saturday whether to run in the Games' 5,000 metres.

Bedford pondered over whether to run in the 5,000, officials called him away for a second attempt at a dope test. "What do they want from me," said Dave sadly—"Blood."

Now a real cloud hangs over Bedford's head. Will he decide to change tack and go for either the marathon or steeplechase, or give up completely the sport to which he has been totally committed? This was a question in everybody's mind today.

Coach Lydiard didn't think big Dave should be written off because of this failure. "But until he has a more intelligent approach to training, he will have a series of disappointments," said the New Zealander.

One win and medal is theirs!

LADY LUCK smiled on two Ulster boxers in the draw for the Games boxing starting to-morrow.

Both John Rodgers and Gordon Ferris received byes into the quarter-finals, which means they must win only once to figure among the medals.

Welterweight Rodgers faces Robert Daver (Australia) or Patrick Cakantini (Fiji) and cruiserweight Ferris moves in against Salusala Viva (Fiji) for a semi-final place plus a bronze medal at least.

Davy Campbell meets Reading's Tommy Deane in his first fight and Ray Heaney, of Lurgan, faces Tommy Williams (Birmingham) at lightweight.

Williams is the least experienced of the English team and Heaney is in with a splendid chance.

Featherweight Gerry Hamill looks to have a simple task against Steve Meta (Gambia) while Dave Larmour clashes with a Zambian opponent, Tiketh Fecua. This could be a tough one

MY DAY—BY MARY

IT WAS A LONG hard day for Mary with the five events stretching over eight hours. Afterwards she described it to me writes Charlie Stuart.

"I didn't sleep at all last night, but then I never do before a big competition. I eventually got out of bed at 7-30 and had some tea and toast. We left the games village an hour later.

"When I reached the stadium the tension was tremendous. I have never known anything like it. The girls weren't speaking to each other at all. But when we got on the track for the hurdles it eased a little."

After the medal presentation, she said: "I am going to miss athletics terribly. But I hope my performance will inspire young people in Northern Ireland to do even better.

"The Gold Medal means everything to me. I once said I wanted to win it for Buster. I know he would have been proud of me today. I first competed back in the Cardiff Games of -958 and it's a great feeling to bow out with a gold medal.

"Now I am looking forward to competing in the shot, high jump and 110 hurdles next week. I'll keep trying hard for my country," she said.

Later I helped her speak direct to her friends in the Telegraph sport's department. Just as she did after her Olympic triumph. "It was just like Munich all over again. Fantastic. There is no way of describing just how I feel," she said.

Then Mary inquired: "How is my track fund going? I have been collecting dollars out here and I hope my win today will give it another boost.

"To see that track completed and the young people of Northern Ireland competing on it is now my main ambition."

'CJ' battles into final

THE determined little Jim "C.J." Kirkpatran courageously into a final place in the 110 110 metres hurdles.

He was first off his blocks and was clearly ahead after 50 metres but faded in the closing stages to finish behind the winner Berwyn Price (Wales) 13.97 seconds, with Aussie Vincent Plant second in 14.21 and the Nigerian Cole-Adeola third in 14.32.

But there was disappointment for our other athletes. Joe Chivers finished fourth in his heat of the 400 metres in 47.8 seconds, the winner being European champion David Jenkins (Scotland), in 47.0. Chivers started poorly, gathered speed at 200 and looked as though he might sneak a place in the final but was pushed out of third place by England's John Wilson. In fact he missed out by just a 100th of a second.

Our two young girl sprinters Linda McCurry and Averil McClelland were both eliminated in their heats of the 100 metres—but they faced world class opposition.

Linda was fifth in 12.37 seconds while Averil was sixth in her heat in 12.33 seconds.

The badminton players were not so fortunate at the Cowles stadium and they do not get the opportunity of a second chance, Colin Bell being the only winner in the singles which opened today.

Bell, the Irish Open champion, had a comfortable first round win over Satokh Singh of Malawi 15-2, 15-2. But David Doherty was no match for Asif Parpia of India going down 15-8, 15-2.

Although both girls were beaten in their opening matches neither was disgraced. Barbara Beckett the 22-year-old former Lisburn girl who now lives and plays in Brimingham put up a great fight against Nancy McKinley of Canada, the No. 3 seed. She won the first 11-6 but she missed her chance of clinching victory when she allowed the Canadian to take the second 12-11 after having a match point. The Canadian had regained her poise in the third and ran out a comfortable winner 11-4 for the match.

Dorothy Cunningham, who only returned to the game six months ago after a break did remarkably well against the English internationalist Nora Gardner from Essex. Mrs. Cunningham made the English girl fight all the way for the points and forced her to ten-all in the second set. But the St. Jude's player just could not sustain her effort and lost the set and the match. The final score in favour of Miss Gardner was 11-6, 12-10.

In the mixed doubles, Miss Beckett and Bell were eliminated in the first round by the Canadians Harris and Rollick 15-12, 15-6, while Mrs. Cunningham and Doherty lost 15-1, 15-2 to Gunalan and Ng of Malaysia.

Straining every sinew Mary Peters streaks ahead in the 100 metres hurdles one of the events which she won in the pentathlon.

Fast green does not worry Roy

NORTHERN IRELAND'S bowlers got off to a promising start at the Woolston Workingmen's Club. Coleraine's Roy Fulton, a bronze medallist in Edinburgh in 1970, and the oldest man in the Northern Ireland team won both his opening singles matches. So, too, did Billy Pimley and Billy Tate in the pairs.

However, the rink — Gerry Sloan, Jimmy Craig, Jimmy Donnelly and Jimmy Dennison — lost their opening match in the afternoon to Western Samoa.

Fulton, unperturbed by the fast green, scored a 22-13 win over Guernsey's Roy Du Feu, a 41-year-old landscape gardener, and in the afternoon session proved much too good for Harry Lakin of Malawi.

Pimley and Tate were in dynamic form, beating Gurnsey's Don Ingrouille and Cyril Smith 36-12 in their opening game and then turning in a five-star performance against Malawi.

They started off well with Pimley building perfect heads for Tate to play into and after being down early on, levelled the score on the fifth end, Tate taking out a Malawi wood for three shots.

They both continued to turn it on in style and finished up 21-14 winners.

In the fours Dennison surprisingly dropped two points against Western Samoa. This is one match the Ulster boys should have won, but in the early exchanges it was clear that the going would be tough.

Four exciting pages of Telegraph sport

NOW MARY LOOKS TO THAT TRACK

MARY PETERS has one ambition left now — to see that synthetic track established at Malone Playing Fields.

Already the Government have agreed to give up to £30,000 on a pound for pound basis but the remainder must be raised from public subscription.

Various fund-raising efforts are now in the pipeline with an appeal to industry and the public due to be made within the next two weeks.

SUBSCRIPTIONS CAN BE FORWARDED TO ANY BRANCH OF ANY BANK IN NORTHERN IRELAND OR TO THE MARY PETERS TRACK FUND, PO BOX 25, BELFAST. INQUIRIES ON THE FUND SHOULD BE MADE TO MALCOLM BRODIE (BELFAST TELEGRAPH) CONVENER of THE FUND-RAISING COMMITTEE.

A wine and dine boxing tournament involving Ulster and Rumania is being organised on behalf of the fund. Tickets at £10 each can be obtained from Eddie Simpson (Lashbrook Advertising-Belfast 32343).

Telegrams flood in

HUNDREDS of telegrams flooded into the Games Village as Mary's friends from all over the world cabled the congratulations.

Among them was one from the Secretary of State, Mr. Francis Pym.

It said, "Congratulations on yet another well-earned Gold. Ulster is proud of your splendid performance."

Chief Minister, Mr. Brian Faulkner on behalf of the NI Administration, cabled: "Well done, Mary. To become the first gold medal winner in the Games is a tremendous boost to the NI team. Itis a fitting climax to a glittering career. Ulster is justifiably proud of your achievement. All the best to all the team."

The Lord Mayor, Alderman William Christie extended the city's "warmest congratulations" and adding, "Well done, Mary."

The Belfast Telegraph Newspapers also cabled their congratulations.

Games Results in detail — Page 25

MALCOLM BRODIE'S IRISH LEAGUE SOCCER PREVIEW — PAGE 24.

FOUR JAILED

Charles Freel, of Creevy Ave., and Kenneth Owens, of Warren Grove, jailed for 8 years on blast charge. Samuel Ferguson, of Glenview Ave., and Edmund McKay, of Clare Way, jailed for five years for part in blast.

LETTER BOMB.

Security man injured by letter bomb at Pilkington Brothers, St. Helen's, Lancs.

FOOTBALL.

Intermediate Cup, second round replay—Star of the Sea 5, Omagh Town 0.

1-0. DONCASTER—Master Blarney (12-1) 1; Castle Pride (3-1) 2; Straight Lane (8-1) 3. Seven ran.

Printed and published by BELFAST TELEGRAPH NEWSPAPERS LTD., at Royal Avenue, Belfast, BT1 1EB, NORTHERN IRELAND (Tel. No. 21242. Classified Ads. 21299). Also publishing at LONDONDERRY.

Registered at the Post Office as a Newspaper.

BRITISH LIONS RULE THE WORLD

CHRIS LANDER salutes Rugby's master skipper WILLIE JOHN McBRIDE

WILLIE JOHN McBRIDE, carried off in triumph as his British Lions made themselves masters of the Rugby world, said: "We've finished the job we came to do. This is the day I've been waiting for."

The giant Irishman, who celebrated his 34th birthday last month, had led his side to a crushing 26—9 victory over the Springboks in the third Test at Port Elizabeth, clinching the series 3—0 and ending a seventy-eight year run of South African domination on their own territory.

Yet it was typical of Willie John's character that he should stop in the players' tunnel to salute his reserves, the men not lucky enough to have appeared in the Tests.

McBride said: "Nobody knows the loyalty everyone ever has given me on the tour.

"Our unbeaten record has to be put down to thirty-two players, not just the sixteen who have played in the Tests. I shall always remember their dedication."

No wonder his players adore him.

Even the South Africans worship him.

Wonderful

Children run up to him wherever his familiar figure appears. Women of all ages want to be able to say "He spoke to me, looked at me with those wonderful blue eyes and gave me a lovely warm smile."

Men want to boast that they shook hands with Willie John. They all wish he was a Springbok.

Everywhere the tour party have gone in South Africa, I have heard people saying: "If only Willie John was on our side !"

One of the most moving tributes to the man who must now rank as the greatest player in the world came in the Afrikaans stronghold of Pretoria.

There, in the prison officers' club, after the Springboks had suffered humiliating defeat in the second Test last month they applauded him on to

THE GOOD GODFATHER . .

The pride of the Lions Willie John McBride is chaired off in triumph

the stage. And spontaneously they broke into singing the song they reserve for their special heroes, "Long may he live."

Willie John found it hard not to show how moved he was by the reception.

I recall, too, his own moving voice. At Windhoek, he brought a dance to a standstill with softly sung Irish ballads.

The Lions left their tables to clap and cheer the man who has become their Rugby godfather.

One of his sayings is:

"The show goes on ... another town, another match, there's no turning back, and nobody knows the pain."

It must have run through Phil Bennett's head when a South African's studs raked and slashed his ankle at Pretoria.

Bennett went down in agony after scoring a brilliant try, and blood was seeping through his sock.

In any other circumstances a player would have gone off for treatment but Willie John

went up to him and said in his firm but quiet way: "Benny, we need you."

Bennett stayed on for a pain-racked final half-hour to help the Lions through and kicked an important goal with blood running through his right boot.

That's the measure of the esteem in which McBride is held.

At Bloemfontein, as the Lions went down into the final scrum losing 9-7 to Orange Free State, he said: "We mustn't lose now, we've come too far. Gentlemen, one last

shove please." The Lions produced it, and scored the winning try.

Irish centre Dick Milliken recalls the night before the first Test in Cape Town, Milliken's Test debut.

The captain, who was appearing in his 71st Test, said to the young man from Bangor: "This is the most important game of my life."

Milliken told me later: "I just couldn't let him down after he'd said that."

Players almost fell

over themselves to oblige when I asked for their opinions about the captain.

Ian "Mighty Mouse" McLauchlan, Scotland's skipper, said: "It's the man's sincerity and undying enthusiasm that impresses me.

"He's such a big man in every way. He says he can't stand little men, and he doesn't mean midgets like me—he means small-minded, petty men. He ignores them."

Gareth Edwards, the most capped Rugby

player in the world, said: "He leads by example. His attitude in matches and training is sufficient for everybody to get the message.

"He doesn't have to say anything. I cannot remember another Rugby player respected so universally."

Fellow-Irishman Fergus Slattery knows Willie John as well as anybody, having played alongside him in 21 internationals.

"He doesn't ask anyone to do anything he's not prepared to tackle himself," said Slattery.

"He's the complete player's man. He must be the only current player in the world who has become a Rugby legend.

"I have never played under a greater leader of men."

And the world's greatest full back, John Williams, says: "I'd feel ashamed if I let him down. That's the hallmark of his greatness."

Springboks hail the Kings

SOUTH AFRICA 9 pts., BRITISH LIONS 26

SPRINGBOK skipper Hannes Marais generously led the tributes after the Lions had sealed the series with their Third test win in succession, writes Chris Lander.

Marais, hailing Willie John McBride's side as Rugby kings told me:

TOUR OVER FOR INJURED BROWN

GORDON BROWN one of the Lions' Test heroes, will not play again on the tour.

The big Scottish lock had his right hand put in a metal splint after breaking two finger bones on Saturday.

"Your Lions have devoured us from start to finish. They are the greatest side I've played against

"They won in New Zealand and now they have become the first team to take a series here in seventy-eight years.

"Nobody can deny them the title of world champions. It's difficult to see how we can stop them making it a grand slam in the last Test."

For the Springbok camp it is

'LIONS DEVOURED US FROM START TO FINISH'—MARAIS

a picture of unrelieved gloom after three defeats in which the Lions have run up 66pts to 21 and scored eight tries to none.

The Springboks were seen off not only as footballers but as fighters.

Hatchet-man Moaner van Heerden became the latest South African forward to find it doesn't pay to mix it with these Lions.

John P. R. Williams's back bears the marks of one vicious assault by van Heerden, but the ill-tempered Northern Transvaal lock must have regretted his attempts to intimidate the Lions

Fifteen minutes from the end he was forced to retire with suspected fractured ribs.

The South Africans were more competitive than in the previous Tests. But after being penalised four times for dirty play, they seemed to despair of getting anywhere.

Gordon Brown demoralised them by plunging through a line-out for a try from their throw-in—and a hopeful scoreline of 3—3 suddenly became a 7—3 deficit.

Then Andy Irvine landed an incredible 63-yard penalty — surely the kick of the tour—

after pulling an easier shot from forty yards.

Next Phil Bennett dropped a goal from thirty yards, despite an ankle which needed pain-killing injections before the kick-off.

The final quarter of an hour brought the try of the tour. Dick Milliken worked the ball to Llanelli wing John J Williams, who threatened to go outside his opposite number but heard J. P. R. Williams screaming for the ball on the inside.

The Welsh full back was checked short of the line, but by now John J. was accelerating on a diagonal run behind J. P. R. for a try that broke the Springboks' hearts.

SOUTH AFRICA.—Snyman (three pens.) LIONS.—J. J. Williams (two tries) Brown (try), Irvine (two pen., and con.) Bennett (two drop goals).

Britain's injuries pile up

From JOE HUMPHREYS in Sydney

BRITAIN'S Rugby League squad preparing for the deciding third Test against Australia on Saturday, are still battling desperately against a crippling run of injuries.

Bill Ramsey, flown out as replacement only ten days ago, and David Eckersley both received shoulder injuries in the 24-12 victory over Newcastle on Saturday.

In addition Jim Mills, who did so much in Britain's second Test victory, is doubtful with a bad thigh injury.

Australia's selectors have axed more than half their side.

AN IDOL SAYS 'THANK YOU' TO HIS FANS

Soccer loses a legend as Pele retires on a night of emotion

BY SPORTSMAIL REPORTER

IT was the end of a legend. Tears streaming down his face, the player in the number ten shirt dropped to his knees in midfield and, with outstretched arms, shouted 'Obrigado' to his fans.

From the 32,000 spectators in the Vila Belmiro Stadium, Santos, a thunderous ovation and chant of 'Pele ! Pele !' erupted.

The most idolised player in Soccer's history was saying 'Thank You' to his admirers at the end of a career which lifted him from poverty to the millionaire class.

'The world will live a thousand years before a new Pele appears,' said Santos trainer Sandor Kocsis.

These sentiments will echo around every footballing nation as the achievements of the 33-year-old hero of three World Cup-winning teams are recalled.

In his 18 year-career Pele scored more goals than any other professional footballer — a staggering 1,216 in 1,254 games. And with his incredible ball-control and peripheral vision he added an extra dimension to Soccer's traditional skills.

It was a night of intense emotion as Pele bowed out. The final moment came in the 21st minute of a league match between Santos and Ponte Preta.

Suddenly Pele dropped to his knees.

The other players stopped and approached, some of them touching the head of the idol. And the spectators were stunned into silence by the realisation that the final moment had at last come.

Slowly rising to his feet, King Pele, as the negro footballer has been known for most of his career, removed for the last time his black and white striped number ten Santos shirt—a number which may never be worn again by a Santos player for a move is under way to have it replaced by number 12 as a mark of homage.

Followed by the other players and a crowd of photographers he trotted round the pitch, tears still rolling down his cheeks.

Then, as the dark figure vanished into the tunnel leading to the Santos dressing-room, the era of Pele became part of football Arantes do Nascimento in

It had been known before the match began that Pele would play for only 20 or 25 minutes because of a thigh injury

Pele, his career over, does his final lap of honour.

World Cup winners to miss speedway tour

By DAVE LANG

E N G L A N D, undisputed world speedway champions, are sending only a shadow squad to Australia to defend the Ashes this winter.

Shock news when the riders were announced yesterday was that not one of the team that won the World Cup for England in Poland is in the party.

Top stars Peter Collins (Belle Vue, Manchester), John Louis (Ipswich), Dave Jessup and Ray Wilson (Leicester), Malcolm Simmons and Terry Betts (King's Lynn), are all unavailable.

All but Collins are married, and are reluctant to be away from their families at Christmas.

The Lions to travel are:

Nigel Boocock (Coventry captain), Reg Wilson an Doug Wyer (both Sheffield), Eric Broadbelt (Poole), Jim McMillan (Hull), and, making their first trip to Australia, youngsters Kevin Holden (Exeter) and Chris Morton (Belle Vue).

Exeter chief Wally Maudsley will manage the squad for the first time.

England have completely conquered Europe this summer, with wins against Poland, Sweden and the Soviet Union They rounded off a tremendous year with a World Cup win in Katowice three weeks ago.

Undoubtedly, it was the World Cup-winning squad that Australian fans wanted to see—and complaints are expected

British Speedway Promoters' Association secretary Ron Botts commented: 'They are the best riders available, and certainly won't let England down. They are all triers.

Big match in the British Speedway League this weekend is the clash of the top two in the Second Division, Birmingham and Eastbourne, in Sussex on Sunday.

Birmingham seem to have the League title wrapped up but the two clubs must meet again before the end of the season in the Division Two Knockout Cup final.

Aitken is cleared of booking

FORMER Manchester City managers Joe Mercer and Ron Saunders teamed up yesterday to help Aston Villa defender Charlie Aitken.

Manager Saunders took Aitken to an FA disciplinary meeting in Manchester to appeal against a caution in the Football League Cup-tie at Everton on September 18.

And Mercer, a spectator at the match, gave evidence on Aitken's behalf.

Final verdict of the Comission was that they were not completely satisfied that he was guilty of ungentlemanly conduct and the caution was not recorded.

Birmingham City striker Ken Burns failed in his appeal against a booking.

Angling mammoth

THE BIGGEST single fishing contest in the world is being held this Sunday on the Warwickshire River Avon, the River Severn, Worcestershire, and the Birmingham - Worcester Canal.

There will be five thousand competitors, and the Birmingham Anglers Association have the mammoth task of organising the four-hour event.

Each competitor will be hoping for a good draw, enabling him to fish the middle reaches of the Severn in search of one of the huge barbel shoals which frequent the Stourport, Hampton Loade Ferry areas.

But with over 70 miles of bankside being fished on the Severn alone, lady luck will be the deciding factor.

Leeds bid £225,000 for Currie

By BILL MALLINSON

LEEDS have made a £225,000 straight cash offer for Tony Currie, Sheffield United's 26-year-old England man.

Sheffield had hoped to get £350,000 to ease their financial problems. But those problems may soon develop into a crisis as they slide towards the Second Division.

The fact that Sheffield have ruled out a player-exchange deal, illustrates the pressure.

And last night it seemed that the Leeds offer may be the best as other clubs hesitate over investing this kind of money in one player.

That must have been obvious to United's board, who yesterday discussed Currie's third transfer request in four months.

Arsenal out

Arsenal could raise £300,000 but they want two players for that sum, and manager Bertie Mee made it clear they had dropped out of the hunt for London-born Currie.

He said: 'We were interested 18 months ago but now we are not in the market.'

I expect Currie will be told today that he will still not be allowed to move. But that situation could change overnight.

Winger Alan Woodward's transfer request was also discussed yesterday. He, too, is likely to be told he must stay . . . at least until a suitable offer comes in.

LATE WIRE. — Sedgefield: KERTOSSEL (nap, 1.15) and PHILMONT (3.45).

JON on the man who made a million by going downhill

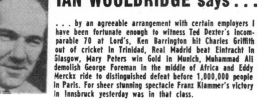

KLAMMER (left) takes the Olympic title from Russi (right) . . . and a kiss from Russi's friend Michele Rubli.

IAN WOOLDRIDGE says . . .

. . . by an agreeable arrangement with certain employers I have been fortunate enough to witness Ted Dexter's incomparable 70 at Lord's, Ken Barrington hit Charles Griffith out of cricket in Trinidad, Real Madrid beat Eintracht in Glasgow, Mary Peters win Gold in Munich, Muhammad Ali demolish George Foreman in the middle of Africa and Eddy Merckx ride to distinguished defeat before 1,000,000 people in Paris. For sheer stunning spectacle Franz Klammer's victory in Innsbruck yesterday was in that class.

KLAMMER . . . in 80 m.p.h. action

The Immortal
Klammer's 80 mph gold

CHAMPIONS are men who deliver on the day. Great champions are men who face crushing odds and still deliver on the day.

And then there are immortal champions. They are men who face crushing odds and conquer with such brilliance and style that unconsciously you hold your breath till your ears sing merely watching it.

Such a champion is Franz Klammer, who yesterday hurled himself down 3,000 yards of solid ice on the upper flanks of Austria's Mount Patscherkofel in 1min. 45·73sec. to win what Alpine aficionados proclaim the greatest Olympic downhill ever.

One measure of his achievement was that not one of his 74 rivals begrudged his triumph by so much as a covetous glance. They wrung his hand and conceded that only one skier in the world could have done it . . . Klammer.

The crushing odds against him were threefold.

Overnight, to a corporate groan across his native Austria, Klammer was drawn to come 15th out of the starting gate : the last and worst possible position for the seeded fast men.

Then, with the Blue Riband event of the Winter Games less than six minutes old, it became clear that the Swiss were prepared to fling their bodies down the Patscherkofel with the doomed philosophy of Kamikaze men in a bid to stop him.

Their Bernhard Russi, defending champion and third man down on the fastest ice, flashed over the finish line in a time which caused experts to believe the computers had blown. His 1min. 46·6sec. had slashed nine seconds off Klammer's official course record. It was the Alpine equivalent of the three - and - a - half - minute mile.

Airborne

Klammer's half-hour wait at the summit must have seemed like the Stone Age. Eventually the digital clock began to spin hundredths of seconds against his number and he was on his way, bouncing, twisting, lifting one ski, then the other, at times totally airborne.

The third crushing blow was to come. At the halfway mark with the swiftest runs of the piste behind him, he was only third fastest. Even loyal Austria, whose idolised son he is, gave him not a chance.

Their Anton Steiner had already crashed, losing a ski which drove into a hut like a spear, in frenetic pursuit of Russi.

From the halfway mark you could plot Klammer's descent by the sound. The roars grew and grew as he leaned into turn after turn — until suddenly there he was, a tiny, double-bent figure in vivid yellow streaking wide from the left-hander which takes them into the last 300 yards to the finish.

He came on, crouching, at more than 80 miles an hour, until he suddenly threw his hand up. It was over. The clock had stopped at 1min. 45·73sec.

It is hard to say how long it was before Klammer knew he was champion: that he had just raced the race of five lifetimes ; that he had come as close as the human can to achieving the impossible and that in less than two minutes with the commercial contracts now open to him, he had won himself £1 million as well as an Olympic gold.

Two seconds, perhaps.

Again he threw up his arms in ecstasy, skied gently down to his colleagues and was lost to sight.

The 17-year quest of the 22-year-old farmer's son who first took to skis to slide down a hillside to his infants' school was over.

With brilliance and style, against massive odds, in the face of supreme, courageous and at times reckless opposition, he had confirmed a coveted definition of sport. Immortality is when those who watched you win will never forget it.

Worth it

He did not, incidentally, wear those revolutionary new skis with the holes in the front. That, it may now be revealed, was a publicity stunt. He did not wear the gold-and-black gear of the Austrian team. His vivid yellow outfit, not at any great financial loss to Klammer himself one presumes, will now be publicly marketed wherever two or more skiers are gathered together.

It would be wrong, though to carp at the commercialisation of it all. Klammer was worth every penny he didn't officially earn.

'Several time I nearly lost it and fell,' he said. 'It was terrible on the corners. I don't mind confessing now that I never thought I could do it, just as I'm sure Bernhard Russi was convinced he could never lose.'

Austria stopped for the race. It was just as well—they may never see another like it.

WINTER OLYMPICS EXTRA—Page 31

QUICK CROSSWORD

ACROSS
1 Foolish (7)
7 Rubbed out (6)
8 Story (7)
9 Blow (4)
10 Dislike (4)
12 Retainer (7)
14 Spring back (7)
16 Contest (4)
18 Smile (4)
20 Meaning (7)
21 Vessel (6)
22 Foot-lever (7)

DOWN
1 Plume (7)
2 Unspoken (5)
3 Responsibility (4)
4 Paid (7)
5 After-effects (8)
6 Individual (6)
11 Iniquity (8)
12 Cutting (7)
13 Supporter (7)
15 Team (6)
17 Audibly (5)
19 Liberated (4)

THURSDAY'S SOLUTION.—ACROSS: 1 Expeditious. 7 Halo. 8 Silence. 9 Pie. 10 Noble. 11 Cement. 13 Samson. 16 Diner. 18 Awl. 19 Intends. 20 Away. 21 Merchandise DOWN: 1 Enable. 2 People. 3 Desert. 4 Talon. 5 Omnibus. 6 Shebeen. 11 Cadmium. 12 Monster. 13 Season. 14 Malawi. 15 Ornate. 17 Ranch.

PEANUTS
by Schulz

© 1975 by United Feature Syndicate, Inc.

No. 24,784

Daily Mail, Printed and Published by Associated Newspapers Group Ltd., Carmelite House, London, EC4Y 0JA (Tel. 01-353 6000), and Northcliffe House, Deansgate, Manchester, M60 3BA (Tel. 061-834 8600). Registered as a newspaper at the Post Office. Second-class postage paid at New York, N.Y., Friday, February 6, 1976 © Associated Newspapers Group Ltd., 1976.

Mirror Sport

Tuesday, March 8, 1977   No. 22,737
Telephone: (STD code 01)—353 0246
CHANNEL ISLANDS 7p

LILLEE'S LASH!

Aussie whips up Test hate with angry outburst

From MIRROR CRICKET REPORTER in Perth

DENNIS LILLEE scarred another day of success in his personal bid to destroy Dennis Amiss with a passable imitation of a bad-tempered schoolboy.

Lillee, whose sole purpose here seems to have been to demoralise further the sagging confidence of England opener Amiss, exploded petulantly in a mid-afternoon incident on the final day of the drawn match with Western Australia.

It was sparked off when Amiss halted Lillee as he ran in to bowl to Geoff Miller, because Western Australia captain Rod Marsh was still moving his leg-side field.

Lillee galloped on and angrily hurled the ball into the ground, then gave Amiss a stream of verbal obscenities.

Hostile circle

When Amiss got to the striker's end, Lillee brought all ten fieldsmen into a hostile circle around the bat. Then, to hysterical chants of "Kill, kill" from one section of the crowd, he delivered a rearing bouncer that ricocheted off Amiss's shoulder.

The rest was predictable. After another mid-pitch exchange of words, more bouncers and a round of ironic clapping from Lillee as Amiss fished vainly for a short ball, the fast bowler got his man.

Amiss, by now a sadly hypnotised figure who hopped and flashed in desperation, departed to a catch by Marsh, although he later insisted that he had not even played a shot, let alone got a nick.

It was the ninth time in 11 attempts that Lillee has dismissed him and it tags on the end of a run of scores that reads: 0, 0, 0, 2, 4, 5, 0, 10 and 0

Lillee, unquestionably, has done his job—and it bodes badly for England's chances in the Melbourne Centenary Test starting on Saturday.

He has also done his bit for the psychological war by going on record in an Australian paper as calling this MCC side "a pretty unimpressive

team." MCC's management refused to break their dignified silence last night despite obvious anger over Lillee's behaviour.

Team manager Ken Barrington and selector Charlie Elliott were both incensed by his attitude, but Barrington said: "Everyone on the ground saw what happened and it is not my job to comment on it."

Captain Tony Greig sensibly avoided comment and he has enough worries with an aching back.

"But I shall be okay for Melbourne," he said.

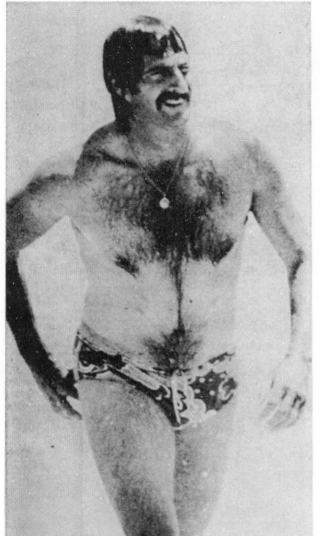

Rising from the waves . . . the demonic Dennis Lillee in all his glory and raring to get at England's batsmen.

DENNIS AMISS

SCOREBOARD

WESTERN AUSTRALIA.—First
Innings: 326-8 dec
Second Innings: 218-4 dec

M C C.—First Innings: 244-8
dec (Brearley 61, Barlow 60,
Miller 56).

Second Innings

Amiss, c Marsh, b Lillee	29
Miller, c Serjeant, b Malone	22
Randall, c Clark, b Malone	31
Woolmer, c Brayshaw, b Malone	51
Barlow, c Lillee, b Mann	10
Greig, c Marsh, b Mann	6
Knott, run out	0
Brearley, not out	58
Old, c Marsh, b Lillee	5
Selvey, not out	23
Extras (lb 1)	1
Total (8 wkts)	**239**

Bowling: Clark 11-1-59-0;
Malone 19-2-83-3; Lillee 9-4-25-2; Mann 13-0-71-2.

Match drawn.

Just capital! The Rebels are tuned in

By GRAHAM BAKER

WHITE CITY have struck on a capital idea to secure their future in British League speedway.

A deal has been signed for them to be sponsored by Capital Radio, and they will race this season as the Capital Rebels.

The Rebels, whose gates were disappointing last season, are sure to be given a significant boost by the London commercial station.

"This could mean the salvation of the sport in the area," said Rebels boss Bob Dugard.

LAST NIGHT'S FOOTBALL

THIRD DIVISION
Port Vale ..... 1 Peterboro' 1
Cullerton   Lee (pen)
H.T.: 0—1   4,417
Wrexham. ...g. 2 Tranmere 0
Whittle,
Shinton
H.T.: 1—0   7,473

FOURTH DIVISION
Darlington .... 5 Scunthorpe ... 2
Seal, Ferguson   Kilmore
Rowles,   Keeley
Maitland,
Craig
H.T.: 0—0   2,134
Stockport ....g. 1 Hartlepool 0
McBeth
H.T.: 1—0   2,649

SCOTTISH LEAGUE.—Div. I:
Clydebank 2, Hamilton 0. H-T:
1—0

CENTRAL LEAGUE.—A. Villa
V 1, West Brom. 2; Hudders-
field 0, Leeds 1.

**F A YOUTH CUP.—Fourth
Round:** Charlton 1 (Goodah),
Derby 3 (Cork, Falconer 2).

**FA TROPHY — Third Round.
Second Replays:** Slough 2, Crook
1 (Slough home to Morecambe).
Chorley 2 Wimbledon 0 (at
Walsall) (Chorley home to
Dagenham)

Wimbledon out as double trouble hits Donaldson

Chorley 2, Wimbledon 0
WIMBLEDON had all the class but Chorley punished them for two mistakes in last night's FA Trophy third round second replay at Walsall.

The Southern League club were woefully weak in front of goal whereas Chorley went ahead after 56 minutes when a mistake by Donaldson enabled Barrow to send Pearson through.

Donaldson bundled Pearson off the ball in the 86th minute and Dickinson scored from the spot.

NEWS OF THE WORLD

APRIL 3, 1977 THE LARGEST SUNDAY SALE No. 6,955

STILL ONLY 10p Sunday's top value

Selwyn likes a bit of magic on the side PAGE 15

The Misery of the Moor Rosalie Shann exclusive PAGE 9

Why the factory Romeo lost his job PAGE 9

TRIPLE RUM!

And let's raise a glass to Charlotte

■ HE'S done it again! Red Rum, the Aintree wonder horse, made history yesterday — winning the News of the World Grand National for the third time. And excited fans rushed on to the course in delight as he romped home 25 lengths clear of Churchtown Boy (20-1), Eyecatcher (18-1) and The Pilgarlic (40-1)

■ It was Rummy's fifth National. In addition to his 1973 and 1974 victories he was runner-up in 1975 and 1976. Jockey Tommy Stack said after yesterday's triumph: "No joking—Red Rum will be heading for the winning post again next year." And last night bookies were already quoting him at 20-1.

■ HATS OFF to Charlotte Brew, the 21-year-old girl jockey who made it the first Petticoat National. Odds against her mount, Barony Fort, winning were 200-1.

■ She was determined to finish the 30-fence course. But Barony Fort refused at the 27th, just four from home, and Charlotte had reluctantly to give up.

FANTASTIC, I'LL BE BACK TO TRY AGAIN

EXCLUSIVE

CHARLOTTE BREW talking to Maureen Lawless

WHAT a fantastic race the Grand National is! Talk about thrills. I'm going to keep coming back. You won't be able to keep me away.

The atmosphere on the course is electric. You get caught up in it. I know it sounds crazy, but I had no nerves at all when I came up to the start.

It was far more nerve-racking in the paddock before the race.

It's such a small area and there were so many horses. And everybody is looking at you.

The parade past the stands was an ordeal too, because Barony Fort doesn't like being led and he was raring to go. He could sense the excitement.

Although I've come in for a lot of criticism, nearly all of the jockeys turned to me at the starting gate to wish me luck.

And the crowd kept shouting: "Come on, Charlotte." It just made everything more exciting.

I didn't have time to be nervous. Before I knew it, we were away.

They went off at a fantastic pace. And Baron, who is fairly slow, was already in the rear. But that's where I wanted him to be.

I was able to keep him on the outside, out of the way.

Before you know it, the first fence is in front of you. You don't have time to think about it. I saw a lot of horses go down in front of me at the first fence.

Then we were over the second and we settled down into our stride.

The third is the one I was most worried about. It's far more difficult than it looks.

As we approached it, I could see horses and riders all over the place.

But being at the back on the outside I was able to keep out of the way.

SHOUT

Coming into Valentine's for the first time, Baron jumped it straight as a die. It was passed in a flash.

We came into the Canal turn and I could see Baron looking at loose horses running past. I had to shout to him to concentrate on the fence, because I don't think he was looking at it properly.

The Chair was my worst moment. There were three horses milling around. One almost came across in front of me and I was nearly pushed out.

But every time we jumped a fence there was a cheer from the crowd and I really felt I was doing it for them.

All the way round, Baron jumped superbly. I let him pick his stride. He just flew Becher's and Valentine's the second time round.

But I was beginning to really have to ride him. It was quite hard, but he loved it.

If he'd had horses in front of him, he'd have gone on more.

It's hard pushing a horse on over those kind of fences, especially when he's tiring.

Even so, I thought we would finish.

But then, coming into the fourth from home, he was travelling too slowly and approached the fence slightly wrong. Suddenly we were both in the ditch together.

For a second, we were squashed up against the fence.

I didn't fall off and he was up in a flash. But it was too much to ask him to carry on.

So I pulled him up and trotted back with one of the jockeys who had caught a loose horse.

By this time, I knew that Red Rum had won the race and I was tremendously thrilled about it.

I'm really disappointed that I didn't finish, but after this experience, there's no doubt about it—I'll be back again.

My only real worry was Baron getting hurt.

To me he's my one and only.

If anything had happened to him, I don't know what I'd have done or how I'd have felt.

But he loves the course and he loves the race. So I'll definitely be back next year.

My parents bought Baron for me as a Christmas present four years ago. He has been the only horse for me ever since.

What I'd really like is a faster Baron.

I proved all my critics wrong. I've proved that I'm fit enough and experienced to ride the course. I've proved that I'm no trouble to other riders.

Now my one ambition is to win the National.

DIET

AFTER the race Charlotte celebrated with chocolate cake and champagne — a change from her diet for the last week.

To shed weight she has been eating only bread for breakfast, skipping lunch and dining on three pieces of cheese in the evening.

She needed to weigh in at 9st 10lb to make her handicap weight 10st. And she just made it.

Since she qualified for the National last year by coming fourth in the Greenall Whitley Foxhunter Chase over the Aintree course, she has been in strict training.

People who doubted her toughness—like some of her fellow - jockeys — didn't know that at that time she was riding with a broken nose and cracked ribs.

Charlotte and her mother drove from their home in Coggleshall, Essex, with Barony Fort on Wednesday to prepare for yesterday's race.

While many other jockeys

Continued on Page 2

PAGE ONE OPINION

WHAT A HORSE!

Red Rum ran home a clear and confident winner of the News of the World Grand National. And even punters whose money went elsewhere cheered this storybook ending.

WHAT A HORSE!

Of course Rummy was confident. Hadn't he done it twice before, as well as running up twice? Now he takes his unrepeatable place in the history books as the winner of all time.

WHAT A HORSE!

What more is there to say?

Two brutes and a little girl

By BARRY POWELL

THE mother of a four-year-old girl wept tears of rage as she talked of two men who molested her child.

One was jailed for three years for raping and indecently assaulting the girl. The other got two years for indecent assault.

"Ten years should have been the minimum for that monster and his friend," the young mother told me.

"My child still wakes up screaming nine months after it all happened.

"When I or my husband try to comfort her she doesn't know who we are for quite a time.

"Her mind is scarred by those attacks.

"I'd like to kill those two men, I'd like to see them dead for what they did to my baby."

Admitted

The 22-year-old rapist, Raymond Donner, was sentenced by Mr Justice Kilner Brown at Nottingham Crown Court in February.

Donner, of Chance Drive, St Giles, Lincoln, admitted the rape and indecent assault.

John Chapman, 21, of Snowberry Gardens, Birchwood, Lincoln, was sentenced at the same court last week

CHAPMAN: He risks violence in jail

by Mr Justice Hutchinson for indecent assault. He denied the charge.

Lincoln police have been shaken by the leniency of the men's sentences.

One senior officer told me: "It's very difficult to explain to junior officers how their diligence and hard work has shown such poor results.

"There is already within police forces up and down the country great frustration about light sentences of this kind.

"This is one of the reasons why more police are leaving the force than are being recruited each year."

Mr James Jardine, chairman of the Police Federation, told me: "For a long time we've been advocating much more severe sentences for assaults of this kind.

Lynch

"Police officers who investigate these crimes see the results.

"In this case, when you bear in mind the age of the girl, it amazes me that the men got only three and two years."

Mr Kenneth Kavanagh, a senior probation officer, and chairman of the Parents' Advisory Group on sex education, said: "There is a real feeling among parents that their children are just not protected.

"There's growing talk of resorting to lynch law to get justice."

At last week's trial, Chapman's counsel pleaded with the judge to give him a light sentence. Mr Stephen Coward said: "He will run the daily risk of violence from other prison inmates."

WEATHER

BRIGHT at first, rain or snow later. Max temp 9C (48 deg F). OUTLOOK: Cold.

Your pay rise limit—a fiver

EXCLUSIVE by Gordon Leak

CHANCELLOR Denis Healey is to stand firm on a £5 pay plan. He will take a tough stance in negotiations with the TUC in the next few weeks.

Any flexibility or restoration of differentials will have to be within that limit. And the hard line must lead to a head-on clash with union chiefs like Jack Jones, Joe Gormley and Clive Jenkins.

They are looking for a deal to at least keep pace with the 16 per cent cost of living increase in the past year.

But the Chancellor is determined that the total pay boost under the Stage 3 policy will be under 10 per cent.

He reckons he has already raised take-home pay four per cent by raising tax allowances and promising to slash two per cent off the 35 per cent standard rate of income tax if the unions play ball.

So actual pay rises must be kept below six per cent when the new deal comes into force in August.

Mr Healey plans to inject flexibility into the new deal. It will include pay bargaining at factory level, with management and unions deciding how the kitty should be shared.

Differentials

In that way, some differentials could be restored.

He is sceptical about giving the go-ahead for productivity deals, although he has not ruled out such deals, he believes they are open to abuse and phoney claims.

Another blow to union hopes will be Mr Healey's refusal of a general prices freeze.

Social Services Secretary David Ennals underlined the Government's tough mood on pay in a speech at Durham yesterday.

He said: "We want a bit of room to manoeuvre the wages cake within the baking tin while it is cooking.

"But we have no intention of cooking the mixture in a kitchen colander.

"It is no good having a pay policy so full of holes that anything can get through it."

Shadow Chancellor Sir Geoffrey Howe slammed Transport Worker leader Jack Jones's demand for an all-round price freeze.

Militants

He told Tories in Gloucester: "It would clobber profits and destroy jobs."

Militant unionists today launch a campaign against Stage 3.

More than 1,500 delegates will attend a conference in Birmingham called by British Leyland shop stewards.

Car workers, miners, railwaymen, dockers, engineers and white collar workers will be represented.

They aim to organise support through industry to kill off the Social Contract when Stage 2 ends on July 31.

● The Labour Party treasurer, left-winger Norman Atkinson, last night called for the sacking of Mr Healey and his Treasury team, and urged the Prime Minister to appoint a new "economic overlord."

He said the Budget—and particularly the 5½p on petrol duty—was "either crass stupidity or political sabotage."

EXCLUSIVE

I'll do it my way

The Chancellor writes for the News of the World on Page 12

The new face in the romance riddle of Charles

By WENDY HENRY

YET another beauty entered the royal romance stakes this weekend when she flew to her family's holiday home, where Prince Charles is guest of honour.

Amanda Knatchbull, 19-year-old granddaughter of Earl Mountbatten and daughter of Lord and Lady Brabourne, arrived at the island of Eleuthera, in the Bahamas, just ahead of the Prince.

Amanda is better known for her connections with another royal Prince. She started at Gordonstoun School the same day as Prince Andrew, and the two were friendly.

Buckingham Palace say that Amanda and Charles are old family friends and that, most firmly, is that.

A spokesman said: "Amanda has met Prince Charles on several occasions at Earl Mountbatten's home in Hampshire. The families are closely related."

Lately, Charles was not on such friendly terms with Amanda's brother, 28-year-old Norton Knatchbull.

He was reported to have broken with his girlfriend, Penelope Eastwood, because of her dates with the Prince, his cousin.

Last month Charles took 22-year-old Penelope to see Terence Rattigan's West End play, Separate Tables. Norton was said to be furious.

But he and Charles appear to have buried the hatchet. For Norton, with his other brothers, also joined their parents at the island villa.

Amanda and brother Norton of a family gathering

Smoking Special Report: Page 7

DAILY EXPRESS

No. 23,927   Thursday June 2 1977   Weather: Dry, sunny   8p

THE JUBILEE KING!

Lester's crown as he rides into history

By James Lawton

LESTER PIGGOTT, of the iron hands and parchment face, celebrated his 25th Derby yesterday with a win fit for the king of the Turf — and fit for the Queen in her Jubilee year.

He permitted himself a small smile and made, for him, a big speech. "It was," he said, "a good race."

Afterwards at Epsom they were talking in millions about the value of his horse, The Minstrel. But no one put a price on the genius of Piggott.

Of course, he is a millionaire already. For his two and a half minutes' work in the Derby he will collect 10 per cent of the £82,000 prize money plus bonuses— making around £20,000 — and maybe a share in the horse from the owner, Mr Robert Sangster. And at 5—1 he made a packet for thousands of punters.

That two and a half minutes' work was made possible by a lifetime of dedication and sacrifice. His only food before the race was a cup of coffee and a slice of toast, with a cigar. And his celebration dinner with his wife Susan consisted of a steak and salad with a sip of champagne.

Winning trainer Vincent O'Brien, a small, grey-haired man from Tipperary, said: "Lester believed in The Minstrel. He talked me into bringing it to Epsom.

"There were some doubts, but when a man like Lester speaks you listen. I admire him so much as a rider and a man—his judgement is just marvellous".

So marvellous that he chose to ride The Minstrel instead of Hot Grove, which finished second with Willie Carson.

Lester was an 18-year-old in the second year of the Queen's reign when he brought home Never Say Die for his first Derby win with a panache that stunned the old-timers. And 23 years later Epsom saw the full flowering of his talents with his eighth win—another record, of course.

Even after such a victory the man remains uncannily aloof. But as the Royal Family looked on in delight Piggott said: "It was lovely to win in the Queen's Jubilee year."

The Queen herself excitedly applauded him past the post.

But let the final accolade come from another great jockey, Henry Samani, the Frenchman beaten into third place on favourite Blushing Groom.

"Piggott rode a beautiful race," he said. "He is so *professional*."

● In the 4.50 race Piggott's mount Marinsky was provisionally disqualified from third place for "savaging" Relkino and almost sending Willie Carson flying.

'Stop the invasion'

BRITAIN was mobilising the Western world last night for a diplomatic offensive aimed at forcing Premier Ian Smith to withdraw his troops from Mozambique.

As the official news agency there said Rhodesian planes were bombing "railway stations, farms, schools and the population," Dr David Owen Britain's Foreign Secretary, sent a strongly worded Note to Mr Smith and had talks in Paris with the French and German Foreign Ministers and the U.S. Secretary of State, Mr Cyrus Vance.

In London, the Foreign Office said Britain and the U.S. were considering an appeal to the United Nations Security Council to compel Rhodesia to withdraw its troops.

In Washington, a State Department spokesman said of Mr Smith: "Only a madman would think he can stem the events of history and inevitable majority rule for Rhodesia."

Smith's last stand: Page 4.

EXPRESS PICTURE BY PHOTOGRAPHER OF THE YEAR DAVID CAIRNS

A smile from a great winner...Lester Piggott after yesterday's triumph

William Hickey (HE'S ALWAYS RIGHT!) **tips the Derby winner: Centre Pages**

SCOTLAND'S HORDES RIP UP WEMBLEY

JUBILEE THUGS

THEIR team came and conquered. They just came and destroyed. Practically everything in sight.

Scotland's fans, fired by victory among other things, tore up the Wembley pitch with a crazed viciousness that made appalled bystanders wonder what the rioters would have done if their "fitba" heroes had lost.

The spoils of the invaders include chunks of turf, remains of the broken goals.

It isn't the first time Scotland's hordes have gone over the top at Wembley. They did it ten years ago when their team beat the then world champions England. They won't do it any more. Wembley are to fence off the pitch. It's cheaper. And safer.

LAST STAND—A policeman makes his point

WEMBLEY BELONGS TO SCOTLAND—And how! This is what the fans did after their team had ripped England to pieces

LAST POST—Still upright, but only just

JUBILEE MUGS

Channon Europe move is on

By TERRY McNEILL

SPECULATION increased last night that Mick Channon is about to follow his best pal Kevin Keegan into European football.

Channon, 28, is now the most wanted player in England and I'm convinced he will be playing abroad next season.

A German club and two from Belgium, Anderlecht and Bruges, have watched Channon repeatedly for the past month and a deal that would cost one of them around £300,000 will not be delayed much longer.

Channon, who unlike Keegan, has two young children, is one of the highest-paid players in this country, but a move into Europe would triple his wages.

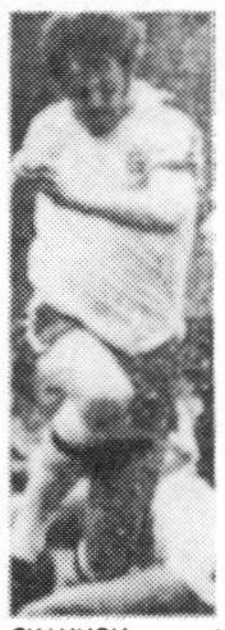

CHANNON — next to go?

GEORGE 'NO' TO ZURICH

CHARLIE GEORGE'S £230,000 transfer to Swiss club FC Zurich is off. Derby's former Arsenal striker met Zurich officials in London yesterday—then decided against the move.

Derby chairman George Hardy said: "I think it was more a reluctance to uproot his home and family and move to a foreign country than any problem over cash or conditions. We are by no means disappointed. We were not trying to get rid of him."

£90,000 NEEDHAM FOR QPR

QUEEN'S Park Rangers have lined up a successor to Frank McLintock.

They expect to sign Notts County centre-half Dave Needham this week for £90,000.

Six-footer Needham is 28—and rated one of the outstanding defenders in the Second Division.

Boost

He hopes that a move to QPR will boost his career, just as it did for his former County teammate Don Masson.

Masson has gained Scottish international recognition since joining QPR two years ago.

But, ironically, he has now asked for a transfer — though manager Dave Sexton is reluctant to part.

REG DRURY

Scots take England and Wembley apart

By FRANK BUTLER

England (0) 1 — Channon pen (87 min)
Scotland (1) 2 — McQueen (43), Dalglish (61)

Attendance 100,000. Receipts £309,000

TABLE TOPPERS

	P	W	D	L	F	A	Pts
Scotland	3	2	1	0	5	1	...5
Wales	3	1	2	0	2	1	...4
England	3	1	0	2	3	4	...2
N Irel'd	3	0	1	2	2	6	...1

WEMBLEY belonged to Glasgow this Saturday night as the bewildered England team was left going round and round.

And it seemed large chunks of Wembley's famous turf also belonged to Glasgow as wild Scots tore up patches to take home as souvenirs of the day their heroes trounced England.

Damage costing thousands of pounds was done as Scots fans knocked down fences in a mass invasion of the pitch and destroyed both goals.

Not since the first Cup Final at Wembley in 1923 have so many spectators swarmed on to the playing surface.

BATTLE

In that original overflow, one policeman on the famous white horse was able to control the crowd.

This time hundreds of police were hopelessly outnumbered, and valiantly as they strived they had no chance in the battle against the Scots invaders.

It took well over 40 minutes for the police, aided by officers on horseback, to persuade the Scots to clear the pitch.

By November, when Italy come to play England in the World Cup, fences will almost certainly have been erected at Wembley. There must never be a repeat of this shambles.

It was estimated there were 45,000 Scots at Wembley. It looked more like Hampden Park as they dominated the scene with thousands of flags, tartan scarves and tam o'shanters.

The English fans were just invisible faces in the 100,000 crowd.

This Wembley takeover by Scotland inspired the team. The Scottish fans had drowned the National Anthem before the game when they set up a shrill whistle as Prince Philip stood to attention.

And then the Scots team swamped England, making Don Revie's problems as the party leave for Brazil today really difficult.

There's no doubt Scotland deserved to win, but what a tense game it was. There was too much needle for good football and I feared at one time that the tempers of certain players who tackled so hard might erupt and the match become a blood-bath.

Scotland were much superior in midfield and at least set a pattern that eventually brought their first victory at Wembley for ten years and kept for them the British Championship.

England played with more drive than against Wales last Tuesday, but still lacked purpose. But the lack of strength in midfield meant they were always struggling.

When Gordon McQueen got his head to Asa Hartford's free kick, following handball by Phil Beal in the 43rd minute, I felt some sympathy for Revie.

Against Wales, Don had been frustr ated by one of his old Leeds players, Terry Yorath. Now it was another of his Elland Road boys, McQueen, who was helping to bring about yet another embarrassing moment for him.

Scotland's second goal, after 61 minutes, caught England's defence on the wrong foot. Hartford had picked up a ball on the halfway line and sent Willie Johnston away. He centred for Bruce Rioch to pass back to Lou Macari and then Kenny Dalglish pushed the ball into the corner of the net through a crowd of players.

DESPERATE

The England goal three minutes from time was too late to give them the inspiration to fight back. McQueen tripped Trevor Francis and Mick Channon scored from the penalty spot.

Revie must be a worried man. He called on two substitutes. In the first half he brought on Trevor Cherry for Brian Greenhoff and later Dennis Tueart for Ray Kennedy, but they seemed desperate changes for the sake of change.

What concerned me most was that England seldom set up a move that looked like producing a goal. Where can Revie now turn. Which skilful player has he not tried? Brian Talbot solved none of his problems, and man for man Scotland were superior.

In Danny McGrain, the Scots had the one player of world class. He displayed true skill and judgment for 90 minutes and stole the game.

I wasn't too happy with Hungarian referee Palotai. He seemed at times shaken by th burning intensity of both sides and the roaring Scottish crowd.

He showed the yellow card to Dave Watson and also to Willie Donachie and Cherry for a spot of bad temper, but at times seemed to lose grip on the game and made one or two odd decisions. I don't envy Revie his task in South America, having had such a bad British championship, I can't understand how he seemed to think this was not such a bad result or a poor display.

I would be a very worried team manager after such impotent displays against Wales and Scotland.

HOW THEY RATE

ENGLAND. — Clemence 7; Neal 7; Mills 7; Greenhoff 7; Watson 7; Hughes 8; Francis 7; CHANNON 8; Pearson 7; Talbot 7; Kennedy 7.

SUBS.—Cherry 7; Tueart 7.

SCOTLAND.—Rough 7. McGRAIN 9; Donachie 7. Forsyth 8; McQueen 7. Rioch 8. Masson 8; Dalglish 8; Jordan 7; Hartford 8; Johnston 7.

SUBS.—Macari 7; Gemmill 6.

GAY GORDON—McQueen races back after netting Scotland's opening goal with a great header

MILLS DOUBT FOR BRAZIL

ENGLAND left-back Mick Mills is doubtful for the opening match of the South American tour against Brazil in Rio on Wednesday, and could face a fitness battle for the other two games in Argentina and Uruguay.

Mills damaged a knee in the early stages against Scotland but disguised his handicap by battling through the 90 minutes.

Last night, he needed intensive treatment at England's hotel and a lot may depend on whether there is any reaction this morning. If Mills is ruled out, Emlyn Hughes could revert to left-back.

JUBILEE KINGS

Verdict on the one-day Test

By RICHIE BENAUD

LAMBS to the slaughter. That summed up the England and Australian batsmen at Edgbaston yesterday.

But pace bowlers John Lever and Bob Willis turned up Jubilee kings for England as the Aussies were swept out for 70 in a 101-run defeat to go two down in the mini-Test series.

Lever played the leading role with four for 20 in 11 overs. Willis backed up with a vital two for 14 in his six-over stint.

England weren't blasted out by Jeff's Thomson's pace, though he bowled well in his nine overs. It was the extremely unlikely combination of Greg Chappell and Gary Cosier that won the honours as the home batting disintegrated.

But Australia succumbed to pace, losing six for 8 by tea and the game was all but over.

Chappell and Cosier must have been surprised at their success.

Swinging

Within the confines of their abilities as change bowlers, they bowled very well, using the conditions and swinging the ball prodigiously.

But the phrase nominating statistics as "lies, all lies," was never more underlined as the pair took all ten wickets.

Thomson, a surprise last-minute inclusion by the Australians, could be excused a disbelieving look at the scoreboard. He bowled fast and well despite his nil return.

The Australians must have been pleased with Cosier and Chappell. They should have been delighted with Thomson's rhythm and pace and the fact that he showed not the slightest effect from his efforts.

Greg Chappell would cheerfully forgo the prize money from these one-day matches if he thought he could run "Thommo" into fitness and form for the Jubilee Test at Lord's.

I watched Thomson very closely, even on the slow-motion BBC replay, and there was nothing in his run-up and action to produce any disquiet to the Australian management.

When they can field an attack of Thomson, Malone, Walker and O'Keeffe with Greg Chappell and perhaps Cosier in reserve, they will give a good account of themselves with the ball.

They will need to do that if one takes into full details their batting yesterday.

The ball swung and moved a little off the seam, but the batting was pathetic.

They will need to improve enormously in the next two weeks if they are to withstand the England pace bowlers.

● LEVER'S OUR MAN OF THE PRU—
Peter Smith reports, Pages 22, 23

PETER SMITH ON TWO CRICKET SHOCKS

BOYCOTT BLOWS HIS BIG CHANCE

GEOFF BOYCOTT, the only player to turn down the chance of joining the Kerry Packer cricket circus, has missed out on his first chance of making a come-back with England this summer.

The 36-year-old Yorkshire captain and opening batsman, has recently had talks with Alec Bedser, chairman of England's selectors, about his future.

But I understand that not once did Boycott take the step which could lead to his recall after a three-year absence. That of telling Bedser he wanted to play for England again.

This Boycott must do after turning his back on Test cricket in 1974 before the wider implications of a possible recall can be taken into consideration.

He asked not to be considere dagain that summer after being dismissed cheaply in both innings of the opening Test against India at Old Trafford.

Later that year he withdrew from the MCC party which went down 4-1 in Australia.

Even if Boycott had made himself available it is not certain he would be selected, despite being the best batsman in the country.

There is still strong feeling in some quarters that he should not play again after turning down needed.

BOYCOTT—missed chance

SUSSEX FACING IMRAN REVOLT

COUNTY championship cricket faces the threat of being disrupted during the next few weeks over Sussex's signing of Pakistan Test all-rounder Imran Khan.

Players from at least two county sides are still determined not to play against Sussex following the Cricket Council's decision to allow Khan to play in competitive matches after July 30th.

And those from three other counties are planning some form of protest action during their games against Sussex.

This became clear during the last few days following a snap poll taken by Cricketers Association secretary Jack Bannister among regular first team players throughout England.

He will not reveal names but it is known that Somerset, Essev and Glamorgan players are strongly opposed to Khan's special registration. And I understand Yorkshire and Warwickshire players are also deeply concerned.

The result of the poll shows that players from nine counties — including some of Khan's Test colleagues — are unanimously opposed to his being allowed to play without serving a year's residential qualification.

In view of the strong feeling at all levels, Sussex should consider not playing Khan.

TREBLE CHANCE CHECK

	1	2	3	4	5	6	7	8	9	10	11	12	13	14
	1½	1½	3	1	1	1	1½	1½	1	1½	1	1	1	1

	15	16	17	18	19	20	21	22	23	24	25	26	27	28
	1	3	1½	2	1	1	1½	1	1½	1½	1	1½	1	3

	29	30	31	32	33	34	35	36	37	38	39	40	41	42
	1	1	1	1½	1½	1	1½	1½	1½	1½	1	1½	3	1½

	43	44	45	46	47	48	49	50	51	52	53	54	55
	3	1½	3	3	1	1	1½	3	1½	1	1	1	1

Claim by telegram for 22½, 23 or 24 points. It could be a jackpot. Only eight score-draws on all coupons.

LO

Printed and Published in England by News Group Newspapers Ltd., 30 Bouverie Street, London EC4Y 8EX. Tel: 01-353 3030 Registered at the Post Office as a newspaper.

4-6, 6-3, 6-1 and she's the champ

BY GINNY, IT'S MINE!

I'LL MAKE IT MINE!

Sixteen nail-biting years: See Page 3

THURSDAY'S EXPRESS

How she did it and the people who helped: Page 3

The moment Virginia Wade won the Wimbledon women's crown for Britain in front of the Queen yesterday. Anguish turns to ecstasy and the Centre Court crowd joins in the jubilation.

PICTURE BY HARRY DEMPSTER

YOUNG ENGINEER FOR BRITAIN—AN EXPRESS CHALLENGE: PAGE 10

Mirror Sport

Wednesday, July 27, 1977   No. 22,857
Telephone: (STD code 01)—353 0246

TEST BAN ON ..

CRICKET rulers gave the 51 superstars who have defected to Australian television magnate Kerry Packer's pirate circus an ultimatum at Lord's yesterday: Toe the line with us—or you're OUT!

If the players opt for Packer, they will be banned as official Test performers from October 1.

And the hard line was completed by the International Cricket Conference with a strong recommendation to member countries to expel the rebels from domestic competitions as well.

To implement the international ban, the I C C introduced a new sub-rule which sets out Test match qualifications.

Tense

All decisions were unanimous at a tense four-and-a-half-hour meeting, chaired by MCC president Tadge Webster and involving two delegates from each of the six Test-playing countries.

Theoretically, players could appear for the Packer pirates, quit and then apply for Test re-instatement.

But, in fact, it would be wrong for the pirates to set too much store by the I C C "re-entry clause."

I C C secretary Jack

Cricket's bosses scuttle pirates

By PETER LAKER

Bailey declared: "It will be fairly tough for them to get back once they have committed themselves elsewhere.

"A player's country must first agree that he is wanted, despite his past. Then it will take an I C C majority to approve his official application."

This is the end of the road for all who cross the October deadline.

And cricket authority's final answer to Packer's cynical attack on the world, based as it was on a squabble with the Australian Board over exclusive T V rights, will come when the member

countries meet individually.

The Test and County Cricket Board (England), who have so far made all the running, with the recommendations relating to domestic cricket, meet on August 5.

Extended

The Australian board meeting follows the return of their team in September.

In each case — and West Indies, India, Pakistan and New Zealand have pledged support— the Test ban on the

pirates will be extended automatically to the respective domestic scenes.

England bowler Derek Underwood said: "I have given the matter plenty of thought and I shall be sticking to my decision to play in the international series in Australia this winter."

Kent skipper Asif Iqbal, who plays for Pakistan, said: "I have enjoyed playing my test cricket but I don't think any Test cricketer has ever earned proper financial rewards."

England wicketkeeper Alan Knott added: "I'm under contract to Mr. Packer and there is no way I will be changing my mind about my decision to take part in his series in Australia this winter."

Secretary Jack Bailey announces the penalty for being a pirate. Picture: ALISDAIR MACDONALD.

FAN BAN OFF!

But United fear trouble on League opening day

MANCHESTER UNITED and Chelsea supporters, banned from away games during last season because of hooliganism, face a head-on clash on League kick-off day.

Soccer's two most notorious travelling armies are on a direct collision course for August 20 after yesterday's decision to lift the ban on season ticket-holders and official supporters club members.

On that date Chelsea return to the First Division at West Bromwich and United open their programme at Birmingham City

And last night David

By BOB RUSSELL

Smith, chairman of United's 40,000-strong Supporters' Club, called for a rapid re-arrangement — 'in case the worst happened."

While welcoming yesterday's decision of the Department of the Environment's working party on crowd behaviour Smith warned:

'Difficult'

"The confrontation of United and Chelsea fans at Birmingham's New Street Station couldn't have come at a more difficult time.

"It's going to put a tremendous immediate strain on the people who have been made responsible for the behaviour of the fans and on this

particular occasion I think there should be a re-think.

"We can't afford a repetition of last season's troubles otherwise it's the end of away games for all of us.

"But to make our efforts effective we need time and this unfortunate clash with Chelsea fans who will also be travelling on the same trains as some of our London supporters is the last thing we wanted.

Smith recommends that either Chelsea or United should switch their opening fixture.

One way out of the dilemma would be for British Rail to push ahead with their plans to utilise smaller, more localised stations for

football fans— in this case Hawthorn Halt, near West Brom's ground.

Another consideration is a package deal ticket covering admission, rail fare and special buses from station to ground.

Meanwhile, Chelsea were delighted the ban has been lifted.

A club spokesman said: "It was with this

decision in mind we formed the official Chelsea Supporters Club recently. We've had a big application for membership and identity cards will be issued and anyone who steps out of line will not be eligible for away trips.

"This way we hope to channel supporters and control their actions."

'WE'RE NOT BAD BOYS'

Hudson, Supermac speak out

Pages 26, 27

Daily Mail

FRIDAY, AUGUST 12, 1977   8p (CHANNEL ISLANDS 9p)

After his exile ... Boycott's crowning triumph

SALUTE THE MAN OF THE CENTURY!

By PETER JOHNSON

GEOFF BOYCOTT became the hero of a sporting fairy tale that even he didn't think was possible in the Test match against Australia yesterday.

He became only the 18th cricketer in history to score 100 centuries and the first to achieve it in a Test match.

Just for good measure, he did it— with 110 not out—in front of his home Yorkshire crowd at the Headingley ground in Leeds.

Singing

It was only his second game for England since his comeback after a three-year self-imposed exile. And in that first match he had scored 107 and 80 not out.

All this was such Boys' Own Paper stuff that even Lancashiremen — and people who profess not to be interested in cricket—had to cheer.

As for those in the ground, hundreds invaded the pitch to congratulate him as he reached his hundred and thousands gathered in front of the pavilion after the match, chanting, singing, and drawing their hero out to the balcony for seven or eight curtain calls.

One youngster even made off with his cap as a souvenir,

Turn to Back Page

Cricket's newest legend : Delighted Geoff Boycott celebrates his triumph.

Riddle of the missing Red yacht

AN Iron Curtain team in the Fastnet yacht race have disappeared.

Last night there was growing speculation that the four-man crew of the Polish boat Spaniel were sailing to America to seek political asylum.

The yacht started the race —from Cowes, round the Fastnet rock off Southern Ireland —and back to Plymouth with 290 other competitors last Saturday.

On Sunday it reported that it had withdrawn because of damage caused during Cowes week.

It was assumed the vessel would return to Cowes.

Since then the yacht—one of Poland's three-boat Admiral's Cup team in the 600-mile race —has not been sighted. There have been no distress calls from the vessel.

The Spaniel — worth £60,000 to £70,000 — is skippered by Polish yachting hero Kazimierz Jaworski, who is the team captain.

Last night, the Polish team's mother ship, Krzystof, was berthed in Millbay dock, Plymouth where the only English-speaking member of the crew said he was as mystified as everyone else-

Mr Jaworski is well known in Plymouth. He was there last year as a competitor in the singlehanded Transatlantic race — aboard the same boat.

Weather conditions—a fair wind from the South—would be right for the dash across the Atlantic. And the yacht was fully provisioned for a long ocean race.

Race details—Page THIRTY.

Jones forced into pay revolt

By ROBERT PORTER
Industrial Correspondent

JACK JONES, architect of the social contract, was forced last night to sabotage the last plank of pay policy—the 12-month rule.

By order of his giant transport union he signed a letter opposing the policy of a year between pay settlements.

The decision is a massive blow to Mr Callaghan's hopes of limiting pay awards well into next year.

It is growing more unlikely by the hour that the Government will be able to hold on to its fragile special relationship with the Trades Union Congress.

Personal

In an act which must have run counter to his deepest personal feelings Mr Jones was obliged by his finance and general purposes committee to put his name to a letter which will go to all regional secretaries of the Transport and General Workers Union.

The letter assures them that at next month's Congress at Blackpool Britain's biggest union will cast its 1·9 million block vote against any pay restraint — including the 12-month rule.

The union voted last month to oppose further wage restraint. But TUC leaders had hoped that the decision would not include positive action to sabotage the 12-month rule.

But today is happy Friday

By PATRICK SERGEANT

TODAY is happy Friday on the economic front.

We should see another sharp fall in interest rates to their lowest since the present system began in 1972.

Interest rates are tumbling faster than ever, and the Government is not moving to stop them. The banks, building societies and others will follow the Government lead.

Chancellor Healey went on holiday smiling broadly at the good news about July's overseas trade and British prices that we shall also have today.

Money is pouring into London — too much for our comfort — and bankers expect an early beginning of the task of dismantling our foreign exchange controls.

City : Page 25.

END OF THE WORLD

IT LOOKS like demob day for Ally's Army . . . the end of the world ! Last night millions of broken-hearted Scots accepted the harsh reality that we are on the way out of the World Cup—ridiculed failures of Argentina '78.

The dream of golden glory seemed last night no more than a nightmare . . . with 1974 finalists, Holland, still to face on Sunday.

Scotland's abysmal failure to destroy little Iran painfully slammed home the bitter truth that despite all the pre-World Cup euphoria . . . WE ARE JUST NOT GOOD ENOUGH.

Ian Archer reports : Page 40.

SCOTLAND SHOCKER AGAINST IRAN

The Express flies home with Johnston

'I feel like a leper'

Johnston with West Brom manager at Heathrow

By Michael Brown

SCOTLAND'S Willie Johnston arrived home yesterday "feeling like a leper" and close to tears.

Looking pale and drawn Willie told me as we flew from Paris : "All I need is a tinkling bell.

"I've been through hell since this bombshell broke . . . nothing could be worse than what I'm going through now."

As Willie sat back on the last lap of the long journey from Argentina, he said : "I'm going to take my punishment.

"The decision about my international future has been made. Whether I accept it is another matter, because really I did nothing more than take a couple of little yellow pills to get rid of a head cold."

The little yellow pills showed up in his dope test after Scotland's match with Peru.

"Some people have said I was trying to make up for being 31 and taking pills to pep me up. That's crazy. I just had a cold and I wanted to be sure of playing and doing my best.

"In fact, I played a lousy game." But the pills—stimulants containing Fencamfamin—were on the banned list issued by FIFA and that was why the tough, popular little winger was booted out.

He said : "There are over 400 drugs on the banned list. But nobody ever showed it to me. And I had no idea that the little yellow pills were on it. They're just the sort of thing you'd take from the Aspirin cupboard at home and quite harmless."

Were other members of the team taking them ?

"That's not a question I can answer, but they are taken commonly by athletes of all sorts. They don't make you a star. They just stop your nose running and clear your head.

"I'd had about a dozen of them altogether which I had brought out with me to beat off a cold. I wasn't 'on' them. I never thought of them as being drugs at all."

Now he was on his way back to face the music of sneers, jibes, hostile Press reporters and excited condemnations on radio and feeling like a leper ever since. All I needed was the little tinkling bell.

"Nobody can have any idea what it is to fall this far. I haven't been able to talk to a

Turn to Page 2

WELCOME HOME NAOMI

DAILY EXPRESS

THE VOICE OF BRITAIN

No. 24,240   Thursday June 8 1978   Weather : Becoming brighter   8p   ★★★

Sealed with a kiss—the sea epic of the decade

WORLD BEATER!

THE EXPRESS GIRL WHO WAS FASTER THAN THEM ALL: CENTRE PAGES

Picture by

Reg Lancaster

TENDERLY, triumphantly the boat comes in . . . to a lingering, unforgettable kiss.

The long-distance loneliness of Naomi James, sailor extraordinary, ends in the arms of her proud husband Rob.

And today the girl who beat the world single-handed, in her yacht Express Crusader, steps ashore to an astonishing welcome.

Dartmouth is all dressed up for the big moment when she sails into its tiny, picturesque harbour.

It's dazzling

The Devon holiday town is bursting at the seams to acclaim record-breaking Naomi after her nine-month, 30,000-mile epic journey, sponsored by the Daily Express.

It's a dazzling carnival. The flags are up, the shops closed and the hotels overflowing. Local boatmen are taking sightseers out to the finish line at the mouth of the River Dart when Naomi arrives this morning.

Last night the harbourside pubs were full as old men of the sea, who doubted she would ever make it, toasted her in Devon cider.

Naomi, 29, will be played ashore by a Royal Marine band beating out her favourite tune, Sailing. Then she goes on a tour of Dartmouth in an open-topped car before heading across the Dart once more to a welcoming reception

Page 2, Col. 4

● STORM AS CHARLES ATTACKER IS JAILED: PAGES 4 AND 5
● TRAGEDY OF SINGLE PARENT WHO COULDN'T COPE: PAGE 2

1976	beat Nastase 6-4, 6-2, 9-7	1977	beat Connors 3-6, 6-2, 6-1, 5-7, 6-4	1978	beat Connors 6-2, 6-2, 6-3

CHAMPAGNE PERRY— A BORG HAT-TRICK

FRANK BUTLER
reports Wimbledon '78

BJORN BORG, at 22, is not only the world's undisputed No. 1 tennis player, but is arguably the most perfect tennis machine to have played on Wimbledon's Centre Court.

In shattering America's Jimmy Connors 6—2, 6—2, 6—3, in this one-sided final lasting 108 minutes he played as near to perfection as is humanly possible.

He equalled our own Fred Perry's 42-year-old record of three successive titles and 69-year-old Fred was on the Centre Court at the finish to congratulate the silent Swede and to console Connors who still couldn't believe what had happened to him.

Borg not only raised his game, but saved his finest tennis of the tournament for this final.

I felt sorry for 26-year-old Connors. He tried by sheer muscle power to intimidate and pressurise the Swede who never lost his concentration for one second.

The champion did not allow himself the luxury of a smile or a scowl until the very end when a pressurised Connors hit the last ball out, Borg went on to his knees, joined his hands in prayer, and looked up to the heavens and smiled.

GUTS

At last we were convinced he was a mere mortal. Connors still looked on incredulously five minutes afterwards when the Duke and Duchess of Kent went on court to pass on the magnificent gold cup.

The American had shown tremendous sportsmanship and guts despite all his frustration but now he placed both hands on his hips and on his face was a scowl as black as the storm clouds above.

He finally forced himself to give three feeble handclaps for his conqueror.

I'll follow that son of a bitch to the ends of the earth —Connors

He couldn't understand how Borg whom he had beaten eight times out of 13 matches, demoralised him this time.

There were times when Connors stood as helpless as a baby as the Swede calmly aced him.

And not only did Borg outclass him with service, but he always went one better with volleys, lobs and extraordinary forehand passing shots.

It was as cold and nasty a winter's day as I've ever attended at Wimbledon. Yet the Swedish "iceberg" reduced the temperature of the hot-blooded American to below freezing point.

Every time Connors tried to pressure the Swede out of his natural game, Borg simply destroyed him with every stroke in the book.

Everyone was led to believe we would see a repeat of last year's classical final which went to five sets with Borg a narrow winner.

MAGIC

Connors had begun well enough taking the first two games, but then the Viking produced his magic with such unbelievable accuracy that even veterans on the Centre Court gasped at his remarkable shots.

Connors began to crack as early as the third game when he served the first of his four double faults in the match. It was the beginning of the end when Borg broke so early. The Swede took the next six games to win the first set 6—2.

To Connors' credit he fought right to the very end, even though he was outclassed.

The only threat from Connors came when he led 3—2 in the third set and it seemed that Borg was tiring just a little.

But the Swede came back to out-serve Connors with a love game and then won the vital seventh game to lead 4—3.

Borg, still so very young, has the world to conquer. His £19,000 prize means little to him for he is already a millionaire, but he is after the grand slam. He has the U.S. and Australian titles to go having won Wimbledon and the French crowns.

This has only been done by Don Budge in 1938 and twice by Rod Laver in 1962 and 1969.

PRAISE

Borg has many years ahead to achieve it more than once.

Connors was still wondering 30 minutes later how Borg had demolished him in three straight sets. Having praised the expertise of the Swede Jimbo still wouldn't accept Borg as his boss.

With a nervous laugh Connors said almost affectionately: "I'll follow that son of a bitch to the end of the earth. I'll follow that son of a bitch everywhere.

Maybe he will. But if Bjorn Borg can ever produce the perfection of Wimbledon '78, all that Jimmy Connors will be able to achieve will be to finish second to the finest tennis son of a bitch I've ever watched.

He'd be great even on ice, says ace Fred

FRED PERRY said that even on ice Bjorn Borg would be a great player.

"It was a brilliant performance. He is quite fantastic," went on Perry who first spotted Borg playing in Paris at the age of 16 and predicted then that he would be Wimbledon champion.

"No one will ever know what would have happened if we could turn back the clock so that Bjorn and I played each other.

"I have promised to buy him a meal for equalling my record, providing that he gets a razor and shaves off his beard."

Borg said: "I am very happy because before the match I knew this was the biggest game of my life. I was surprised by how well I played. I did not expect to do it so easily.

"He missed a lot of his first services and I forced him to make the errors."

Borg said he will go for his fourth successive title next year without fear.

"I will want to win," he said. "But it will not upset me so much if I lose as it would have done this time."

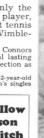

STRESS AND STRAIN—Connors goes full stretch for another cross-court rocket from Borg

TRIPLE CHAMPIONS—Fred Perry's smile of congratulations says it all : You were just great, B...

POWER AND GLORY—It's a prayer of thanks from hat-trick man Borg
Match pictures by BRIAN THOMAS

FINGER LICKIN' LUCK

Scare—then Brearley's OK for Pru

By PETER SMITH

ENGLAND captain Mike Brearley was involved in an injury scare for the third time this year at Lord's yesterday.

But last night he came back from hospital confident he'll be fit to lead England in the first Prudential Cup match against New Zealand at Scarborough next Saturday.

Earlier, in Middlesex's match against the tourists, he had walked angrily from the wicket, fearing the worst again in his benefit year of torment.

DISGUST AND PAIN

He had thrown down his bat in disgust and pain after being rapped on his right hand by New Zealand fast bowler Richard Hadlee.

The ball caught him on the third finger of his right hand—the finger he chipped earlier in the summer, forcing him to miss the two Prudential games against Pakistan. But this time the injury was merely bruising.

The ball that caused it flew straight to Bob Anderson, at short square leg, ending Brearley's bid to find form and build on his undefeated 70 against Essex on Friday. He had made 23.

Earlier this year, Brearley had to fly home from Pakistan, after a left-arm break. That injury put him out of the final Test and all three in New Zealand.

IN THE WARS— Brearley doubles up in agony

He has struggled since, but yesterday he looked confident for his first hour until Hadlee struck with a 3 for 3 burst in 21 deliveries.

Mike Smith fell leg-before, Brearley followed and Clive Radley—another England scalp—went two balls later.

It might have been four in 22 balls, but umpire Tom Spencer was unimpressed with the entire New Zealand side thought they had Keith Tomkins caught behind first ball. Middlesex ended at 80 for four in the 3-hour 3-minute possible between the showers and bad light.

Billie Jean misses a winning score

BILLIE JEAN KING, the greatest post-war woman tennis player, was denied her 20th title and Wimbledon record in the mixed doubles final yesterday.

Partnered by Australian Ray Ruffels, she was beaten 6—2, 6—2 by Frew McMillan and Betty Stove, the Dutch girl who lost in three finals last year.

Afterwards, Billie Jean said: "I would like to have won, not because it was the 20th time, but because I would like to have the feeling of winning again."

RECORD

The American, after 17 years of Wimbledon competition, shares the record of holding 19 titles with Elizabeth Ryan, another American now 86, and after failing this time she cannot possibly have many more chances left.

Whereas Miss Ryan won all her titles in doubles events—12 women's and seven mixed—Billie Jean has interspersed hers with six Wimbledon singles championships all won between 1966 and 1975. She has also won nine doubles and four mixed doubles titles.

McMillan was the only double winner of the championships. Earlier he teamed with Bob Hewitt to beat Peter Fleming and John McEnroe 6—1, 6—4, 6—2 in the men's doubles semi-final.

ILIE NASTASE was beaten 6—3, 6—4 by Austrian tennis coach Jan Kukal in the international Linz tournament yesterday.

Nastase, barred from Grand Prix tennis for three months, is hoping to keep in shape at the smaller venues.

MERCER SHOCK

MERCER—problems.

JOE MERCER won the £42,414 Joe Coral Eclipse Stakes at Sandown yesterday — and was then sensationally banned for the second time in a week.

Mercer picked up a seven-day suspension when he finished third in the Paddock Maiden Stakes on Buckland and was disqualified for " careless riding."

● Full story—Page 18

TURNER REJECTS NORWICH
BOND SLAMS LUTON DEAL

By TERRY McNEILL

NORWICH manager John Bond is furious after losing a trans-Atlantic tug-of-war for Chris Turner, 26-year-old Peterborough centre-half.

Turner, playing for Boston Teamen on loan for the summer, has gone to Second Division Luton for £100,000.

Bond told me last night: " I'm disgusted with Luton. I've given my chairman, Sir Arthur South, all the details.

" I'd played everything according to the rules, both with Peterborough and Turner, and I'm upset.

" I offered him £75 a week more than Luton and he told me he wanted to play for us.

" Then when I spoke to him on Friday, he said that Luton had upped their offer."

Turner's switch to Luton means that Peterborough will ask West Ham to name a price for Bill Green. West Ham will sell and the price is likely to be around £60,000.

Another West Ham man in demand is forward Pop Robson. Bond has made a written offer but Hammers boss John Lyall says it's too small.

Everton are favourites to get Micky Walsh, Blackpool's Irish international striker, valued at over £300,000.

Birmingham are Everton's rivals for Walsh and if they lose the race then they will go for another Irishman—QPR's Don Givens.

Givens has finished his contract and under the new freedom charter for players, Rangers have to transfer him.

Rangers themselves are still hopeful that Ipswich will sell midfield player Colin Viljoen on instalments.

Bobby Moore is going to America to play for Seattle for the rest of the summer. Moore, 36, leaves today.

Points win for the three-time ring king

YES ALI IS THE GREATEST!

IT'S ALL OVER . . . and Muhammad Ali walks into history.

More pictures Page 6.

MUHAMMAD ALI is back where he belongs — heavyweight champion of the world.

He won the title a record third time with a runaway 15-round points decision over the pretender Leon Spinks.

"I'm the greatest ever," Ali mouthed to the fans — an all-time record indoor crowd of 70,000 in the New Orleans Superdome.

But the tired man of last February, beaten over the

By REG GUTTERIDGE
in New Orleans

same distance by plodder Spinks, became the buoyant boy of 36 years, seven months and 29 days.

This was Ali dancing all over again and Spinks, a brave, honest trier, barely got a look in.

The decision, delayed ten minutes as the ring announcer waited for a mob of Ali wellwishers to get out of the ring, was unanimous, though, in my view, a little generous to Spinks.

Referee Lucien Joubert and judge Ernest Cojoe both scored ten rounds for Ali, four for Spinks and one even.

Judge Herman Duitreis had Ali the winner 11-4.

Spinks, looking depressed and weary, left the ring immediately after the announcement of Ali's victory.

Ali, strangely subdued, hugged Spinks before the ex-champion departed.

The punching prophet

geared himself perfectly for the final curtain though he told me in the ring, before the verdict became official, that he still wanted six months grace to consider his retirement.

I remain convinced that Ali will not subject himself to the drudgery of training again to fight the younger Larry Holmes, who is the World Boxing Council's heavyweight champion.

Energy

Holmes, a ringsider here, is a more competent boxer than Spinks.

Ali, rarely speaking above a whisper, was surrounded in his dressing room by his

entire entourage, except Angelo Dundee, who had exerted a lot of energy rowing with the referee after the sixth round.

The trainer could not accept that the referee had penalised Ali.

Bundini Brown, Ali's yelling aide, collapsed in the ring afterwards.

Veronica Ali was seated close by.

And Muhammad again confirmed that he wanted the recognised six months grace to decide his future.

"Thank God it's over," he said.

"That was some last fight but it's too good to give it away so soon. I don't think I'll ever fight again, but I

don't want to announce my retirement right away."

Then he went on:

"It was a beautiful fight. I did everything right.

"Using my legs is what did it.

"I don't want to take anything away from Spinks. He's no bum, he's a great fighter and he's gonna be better with experience.

Then Ali teased the interviewers. "I can't dance for 15 rounds can I? You said I couldn't. Just not possible.

"I trained three months and had you all set up and made suckers out of you."

Not guilty, champ.

We always believed it was

Contd. on Back Page

YOUR COMPLETE RACING PAPER STARTS IN PAGE 2.   GREYHOUND SPECIAL 4 & 5

London: Wednesday

May 30, 1979

Price: Ten pence

Evening

STANDARD

CITY PRICES

The gamble that cost him millions is over

PACKER STOPS THE CIRCUS

KERRY PACKER—he signed the world's big names for big money.

Standard Reporter

THE BITTER battle between Kerry Packer and official cricket ended today.

Packer's pirates hauled down the flag after the Australian millionaire signed a 10-year agreement with cricket chiefs.

Television magnate Packer appears to have achieved the aims which prompted him to start a two-year war with established cricket—but it is a victory which has cost him millions of pounds.

Packer's Channel Nine network is to televise Australian cricket for the next three years, and in return he will wind up World Series Cricket, the showbiz-style circus which snapped up the world's most talented players at enormous salaries.

Woolmer—'surprised'

Now Packer plans to pay off the 68 players who signed contracts with him. And with many on £13,000-a-year contracts for two years or longer, the basic cost of closure will be in the £2 million bracket.

Under the deal, one of Packer's companies will have exclusive rights to promote cricket. One surprise in the peace package was that the World Series logo will be worn by Australians in one-day internationals.

A joint statement by Australian Cricket Board chairman Bob Parish and WSC managing director

DEREK UNDERWOOD — one of 68 for the pay-off.

TONY GREIG—eligible for England again.

Lynton Taylor said: "World Series Cricket will cease to promote cricket matches in Australia or elsewhere during the term of the 10-year agreement."

Among the stars who joined Packer were England Test men Tony Greig, Derek Underwood, Bob Woolmer, Alan Knott, John Snow and Dennis Amiss, who all received vastly higher salaries than they could have hoped to earn in the official game.

Bob Woolmer, 29-year-old Kent opening batsman who was on 25,000 Australian dollars a year, said today: "I'm slightly surprised. I thought he'd continue. But I'm pleased that I'll be available to play for England again. Now I know where I'm going, perhaps it will clear up my mind to get some decent performances behind me. My top score in first-class cricket is 40 in five knocks by the end of May!

"WSC cricket lacked the camaraderie of the county circuit, and was probably the hardest type of cricket I have played. But I have my friends in it and it was something new. In a way, it's disappointing it ended so abruptly."

Worldwide, Packer signed Australia's Greg and Ian Chappell, Dennis Lillee, Jeff Thomson, Ian Redpath and Rodney Marsh, Pakistanis Asif Iqbal, Zaheer Abbas and Mushtaq Mohammed, West Indians Clive Lloyd, Viv Richards, Andy Roberts, Wayne Daniel and South Africans Mike Procter and Barry Richards.

Those names—and the money Packer was paying—convinced the cricket authorities that World Series Cricket meant business. Official cricket's response was to try to ban Packer's men from the English games.

To the courts

Packer's answer was a High Court action in the autumn of 1977. After a 31-day hearing, which cost around £250,000, Packer emerged as the victor, with Mr Justice Slade ruling that a ban on Packer players would be an unreasonable restraint of trade.

Packer brought in innovations which are likely to change the face of cricket permanently, with or without the World Series. This includes the introduction of floodlit matches, using a white ball and coloured cricket kit instead of the usual whites.

News of the Packer peace came 72 hours before England pick their 14 for the Prudential World Cup, which starts on Saturday week with England v Australia at Lord's.

Will they bring back any of the men who defected to Packer?

Chairman of selectors, Alec Bedser, said today: "We have always selected on merit on the proviso that the players were available full-time. Our record over the last two years under Mike Brearley has been very good. We have a very successful side, and a loyal bunch of cricketers with a wonderful team spirit.

"Underwood, Woolmer and the others will be considered along with the others on our shortlist. But no-one has a right to expect to play for England. The greatest honour in the game anyone can have must be earned."

Neave: Irishman ordered out

by Patrick McGowan

AN IRISH building worker has been served with an exclusion order after being questioned for a week by Anti-Terrorist Squad detectives investigating the bomb murder of Airey Neave.

James Scanlon was one of four people arrested at dawn on Tuesday last week in North London and for a week he was questioned at London's most secure police station, Paddington Green.

Now he has been served with the exclusion order he is being held at Brixton Prison until his appeal against the order has been heard.

At the prison last night Mr Scanlon's girl friend was allowed to see him.

Outside there was a picket protesting at his detention. The picket included members of the Irish Republican Socialist Party which Mr Scanlon helped to found in Ennis, County Clare, nearly five years ago.

TV and radio: 29 • Letters: 19 • Londoner's Diary: 20 • Entertainment Guide: 22 • Eating Out: 25 • City: 46 • Sport: 49

DAILY Mirror

Monday, December 10, 1979   9p

KENNEDY

The boy who would be President

—Centre Pages

The man who socked the Doc

—Page 3

CAUGHT BEHIND

SMACK! Australian cricket star Greg Chappell bats a streaker hard across the bottom.

He was furious when the naughty nude dashed on to the Melbourne pitch during yesterday's match against the West Indies.

The Aussie skipper landed the lad a hefty swipe — as he did three seasons ago when a Test match against New Zealand in Auckland was just as rudely interrupted.

Yesterday's streaker was sent running for cover into the boo-ing crowd—and the arms of the law.

But only a few moments later, Chappell was caught out too. Australia were stripped of victory.

And England's team Down Under were left contemplating their own winning streak.

● Peter Laker — See Page 27

Picture by ERIC PIPER

Robbo: I'll shut Leyland

By CHARLES LYTE

RED ROBBO threatened yesterday to bring British Leyland to a standstill unless he got his job back.

The sacked Leyland union leader claimed that Industry Secretary Sir Keith Joseph was behind his dismissal.

Robbo — Derek Robinson — told cheering students at their Blackpool conference that he would first have to go through the "charade" of the engineering union's inquiry into his sacking.

"Then we intend that Longbridge will come to a stop," he said.

"Nothing will move in or out of any of the Leyland works.

"We will seal the ports so that no Leyland products will leave the country."

Mr. Robinson was sacked for publishing a pamphlet attacking plans to close, totally or partially, thirteen Leyland plants.

He said: "I have no doubt at all that the

● Turn to Page Two

London : Tuesday
January 15, 1980
Price : Ten pence

Evening

STANDARD

CLOSING PRICES

MPs join in as pressure grows for new games site

'STOP THE MOSCOW OLYMPICS'

by Robert Carvel

POLITICAL pressure for not holding the 1980 Olympic Games in Moscow grew this afternoon as Mrs Thatcher ordered British diplomats to give fullest non-military backing to American plans for retaliation over the Soviet invasion of Afghanistan.

While the Western nations discussed concerted action at meetings in Brussels the Prime Minister was expected in the Commons to reiterate the Government's condemnation of Russia.

Earlier Tory and Labour MPs joined in a "hands off Afghanistan" protest meeting at Westminster.

Sixty MPs signed a Parliamentary motion urging the Olympic authorities to reconsider the Moscow venue "in view of Russian aggression." They said the Soviet Government must be denied the important propaganda weapon provided by the games.

An all-party group of 41 MPs also tabled a blunt demand that the Games should be held somewhere else. A number of Mps signed both motions.

In Brussels Deputy Foreign Secretary Sir Ian Gilmour urged other EEC countries to adopt an agreed programme of economic sanctions. This programme would include a ban on Common Market butter, wheat and advanced technology sales to the Soviet Union as well as curtailment of trade credit.

The Afghanistan crisis was also considered at a separate meeting under NATO auspices. For once the French Government took part.

No power

At this meeting Foreign Minister of State Douglas Hurd had instructions to back to the hilt the American call for a collective boycott of the Games if they cannot be moved away from Moscow.

There was some doubt in Whitehall about how far France, Germany and Denmark might go in supporting the tough Anglo-American line. There were some signs of a lukewarm response.

Mrs Thatcher believes that a substantial Western demonstration over the Olympics in which Russia has invested much money and prestige would be a severe psychological blow to the Kremlin.

However, the Prime Minister is recognising that all the Government can do is to create a climate of opinion and offer guidance to the British Olympic authorities.

There is no Government power to ban British athletes from competing wherever they like. But they would certainly have no financial backing from the Sports Council for going to Moscow.

One suggestion which would have Whitehall backing if

Contd. page 2, col. 6

Neil Allen—BACK PAGE

Evening Standard: Stuart Nicol
DR PRUDENCE TUNNADINE — "Sex is not something you approach as if you were qualifying for the Olympics."

Love and sex, by Doctor Prudence

by Keith Dovkants

COMFORT for anyone whose sex life does not include whips, leather, handcuffs or swinging from the chandeliers comes today fro mthe British Medical Association.

Far from being "gourmet sex," deviation can be downright dangerous, says Dr Prudence Tunnadine in a new BMA publication.

Dr Tunnadine, an attractive 50-year-old who describes herself as "happily divorced," urges in her booklet, Sex and Nonsense About Sex, that we reconsider the modern philosophy of whatever-happens-to-turn-you-on.

"There's no A-level in sex—it's not something you approach as if you were qualifying for the Olympics," she said today at her Harley Street surgery.

"Much of the recent material written about sex has suggested that we're just a collection of moving parts and that knowing the right tricks and the right buttons to press produces the right results.

"I believe that we've allowed the topic to become badly slanted—we have gone straight from the Victorian view that sex was purely physical and bad, to the idea that it is purely physical and good."

Dr Tunnadine says that many modern books give the impression that bondage, for example, is just a normal variation of ordinary loving.

Insight

But, she claims, this tendency to give respectable authority to outlandish love-making is wrong, and she advocates confidence in what she calls "straight" sex.

"In all this preoccupation with gourmet sex, as it is often presented, the emotional aspect is lost sight of." she said.

But Dr Tunnadine's idea of straight sex includes oral

Cont. on Page 2, Col. 1

Soccer killers : London hunt
PAGE THREE

Jury leak : No contempt
PAGE SEVEN

DAILY Mirror

Saturday, July 5, 1980   10p

WIMBLEDON 80
Evonne storms back

QUEEN MUM !

By JOHN JACKSON

IT WAS Mother's Day on the Centre Court yesterday as Evonne Cawley dazzled her way to her second Wimbledon title.

Before a 15,000-strong crowd she beat former champion Chris Lloyd 6—1, 7—6.

It made the Australian wondergirl the first mother to clinch the title in 65 years.

In floods of tears the new Queen of the Centre Court hugged her husband, Roger.

And then she revealed that her victory would mean delaying plans to increase her family.

Evonne, 29, who has a three-year-old daughter, Kelly, said: "I must be back next year to defend the title. So Kelly must wait for a brother or sister."

Evonne first won the women's singles title in 1971. The nine-year gap is the longest time any women's Wimbledon champion has had to wait for a second crown.

● See Back Page

Meanwhile

McEnroe turns on the old McEnrot again

● **THE HATE MATCH:** Back Page

● **PETER WILSON REPORTS:** Pages 26 and 27

PETROL DOWN

By ANTON ANTONOWICZ

BRITAIN'S oil giants declared a petrol pump price war last night.

Both Esso and Shell slashed 2p off a gallon from midnight.

Other companies are expected to join the forecourt battle soon.

The price cuts mean that motorists in the London area will now pay an average of £1·35 for a gallon of four-star.

Esso launched the price war by announcing a cut at lunchtime yesterday. After a hasty boardroom meeting, Shell bosses said they would follow suit.

BP, the country's third largest forecourt suppliers, are expected to come to the same decision this weekend. A spokesman for the firm said: "We are having to assess the situation in the light of Esso's announcement. It came as a complete surprise to us."

Esso and Shell say the reductions have been made in response to "competitive conditions" in the market.

Both firms have been under pressure from hypermarket garages where four-star petrol is being sold at around £1·31 a gallon.

The AA welcomed the reductions last night. A spokesman said: "This has to be good news for the motorist."

But the Motor Agents Association, which represents petrol station owners, said the price war could drive many independent garages out of business.

A spokesman warned: "Their profit margin has already been screwed down to less than 3p a gallon and the latest cut could push them over the brink."

DONE IT! Triumphant Evonne yesterday.   Picture: MIKE MALONEY

Daily Mail

SATURDAY, AUGUST 2, 1980

12p

8-page TV Mail

Magnificent Coe runs the race of a lifetime to win the Olympic Gold

ECSTASY!

Golden moment as Coe lunges to victory ahead of Straub and Ovett

Picture : Joe Marquette.

THIS is THE moment of Sebastian Coe's lifetime, the split-second of triumph in the Olympic 1,500 metres in Moscow yesterday.

But Coe did more than win the gold medal. He lifted the soul, he ennobled his art, he dignified his country, and he emerged a very great young man.

Watching him run home, invincible, over the

From IAN WOOLDRIDGE in Moscow

last 300 metres in Moscow, was unforgettable. Watching him afterwards made you even prouder, for his conduct in triumph matched his humility in disaster.

Some fool of a non-running poet once called triumph and disaster 'those two imposters,' but when you're down there justifying two years of austere living against hundredths of a second, that's a considerable misconception.

Sebastian Coe, 23, and from Sheffield, wasn't here to settle some parochial feud by incinerating Steve Ovett, 24 and from Brighton. For six days Coe had had to live with himself for running so far below his intellect in the 800 metres and losing to Ovett that his only challenger yesterday was himself.

He accepted that challenge in the Blue Riband of the Games, won, permitted himself the luxury of the huge beaming smile of the happiest man in the world on a single lap of honour, and then, I swear to God, was the calmest man in a room full of those who came to hear him talk of it . . .

He said : 'It was nice to climb that mountain. It was an absolute must to win. I felt very much more relaxed than just before the 800, possibly because that was the one I was expected to win. I just felt a different person today.

'It was a very smooth race. That was the key to it. I was able to do what I'm best at—running freely and uncluttered. I started relatively easily and latched on to second or third spot.'

Coe went on : 'I was surprised there wasn't more

Turn to Page 2, Col 1

INSIDE: James Wentworth Day 7, Gardening 21, Holiday Mail 22, 23, Prize Crossword 23, City 24, 25, Quick Crossword 24, Junior Letters, Strips and Stars 26, Sport 27-32

Beaumont, Faldo may be barred over S. Africa links

Lee Trevino

Stan Smith

G. Vilas

Floyd Patterson

Bob Lutz

Billy Beaumont

John Feaver

Nick Faldo

John Carleton

Lesley Charles

B. Thompson

Nick Job

Peter Thomas

W. Humphreys

David Russell

Gary Birch

Keith Waters

Harvey Becker

Nigel Burch

S. Bennett

BLACKED

British sport stars facing a ban

ALL the sports men and women pictured on this page are on a United Nations "apartheid" blacklist, it was revealed last night.

It is the latest move in a publicity war that hit England's cricket tour of the West Indies and could now wreck all sport world wide.

THE OFFENCE

Golfer Nick Faldo and England Rugby stars Bill Beaumont and John Carleton top the British section of 39.

Their offence : They have recently played or are planning to play in South Africa.

In all, the list prepared by a U.N. committee names 185 athletes in 10 sports from 21 countries, including 44 Americans, 33 French, and 15 West Germans—and some Africans.

Golfer Lee Trevino and tennis

By PHILIP FINN in New York and MICHAEL O'FLAHERTY in London

players Stan Smith, Bob Lutz, Dick Stockton, Cliff Richey, and Guillermo Vilas are in the American section.

So are two black boxing stars— former heavy-weight champion Floyd Patterson and the present holder Mike Weaver.

French names include the entire international Rugby team, captained by Jean-Pierre Rives.

Among Australians is tennis player Kim Warwick.

THE HEARINGS

The UN Committee Against Apartheid is holding three days of hearings in Conference Room 4 of the General Assembly building in New York. More names—perhaps including cricketers—are expected to be added to the list.

There will be another meeting in

Paris in May which will probably produce a hard resolution.

Committee chairman Mr Akropode Clark, U.N. Ambassador for Nigeria, said : "I think we are making perfectly clear what we feel about countries who go along with apartheid."

THAT MATCH

At home, England captain Bill Beaumont said : "I'm not particularly surprised or bothered. At the time I led the Lions in South Africa I made my views known—I don't support apartheid but I think South Africa has made advancements towards multiracial sport, especially in Rugby."

But Beaumont and John Carleton are due to play in a special match in South Africa next month. "I will have to reconsider that if it is going to jeopardise my career with England," said Beaumont.

John Carleton agreed : "I might have to reconsider."

Golf star Nick Faldo, recently

Page 3 Column 1

Ian Mosey

Brian Sharrock

Nigel Sears

Paul McGarry

Michael King

John O'Leary

John Whiteford

A. Chandler

Philip Morley

Glen Ralph

Dick Stockton

David Poole

Chris Moody

Cliff Richey

Mike Weaver

Kim Warwick

Peter Hedges

Peter Barber

Andrew Murray

BUDGET : MAGGIE IN WAR WITH THE WETS—PAGE 2

STAR WEEKENDER

Auckland, Saturday, March 28, 1981 ★   Phones: Editorial, general 797-626; advertising 794-666   Price 20c (Home delivery Auckland 15c)

Nothing bigger . . . and nothing better
70,000 hit fun run road

SCORES FEARED DEAD IN BUILDING COLLAPSE

Several people were killed
when a multi-storey residential
block under construction collapsed at Cocoa Beach, Florida.
Scores more were feared
buried under tonnes of steel
and concrete. — NZPA —
Reuter.

weekender briefing

Latest Polish talks fail

WARSAW, Friday— New
Government free union talks
today failed to end Poland's
crisis following a "warning"
strike by millions of Poles.
But further talks have been
set for tomorrow.
Solidarity leader Lech Wal-
esa, who ordered his 10 million
union members out on strike to
press the Government into accepting a list of stiff demands,
told newsmen nothing had been
settled during the latest talks.—
NZPA—Reuter.

● Millions stage strike — Page
4

Sunday sport

ATHLETICS.— Pakuranga club's open
handicap track meeting, Lloyd Elsmore
Park, noon.
BOWLS.— Auckland centre champion-
of-champions fours, Papatoetoe head-
quarters, 8.30 a.m.
SOCCER.— Rothmans league: Mt
Wellington v Takapuna City, McKinlay
Park, 2.30; Hanimex North Shore v
Rangers, Taharoto Park, 2.30.
YACHTING. — Marine Rule team
series, Orakei, 10 a.m.

Inside

● Who says cemeteries are
spooky places? Weekender
meets two men who have plenty
of evidence to the contrary.
Ronald Lockley visits a strange
volcanic island and Pulse looks
at a new dental theory.
     — Page 5
● Bromhead . . . and column
comment on social castaways,
gangs, and unfounded space
scare and marketing images.
Plus new books — and if you
think things are tough today a
New Zealand author will put
you wise with recollections of
farming in the Depression of
the 30s.
     — Page 6
● Complicated air fares, a club
for globetrotters and a country
pub with a "royal touch" — the
travel pages have the stories.
     — Pages 10 & 11

It was the biggest . . . and the
best yet.

The Auckland Star's Round the Bays
run today confirmed it is New Zealand's biggest mass social and sporting
event and the biggest fun run in the
world as at least 70,000 people made
the 10.5km run from Fanshawe St to
the St Heliers Reserve.

The ninth run got under way with the
man who dreamed up the idea in 1973
— Mayor Colin Kay — proclaiming the
event "not a run, but a happening."

After thanking the Star and the
Auckland Joggers Club for organizing
the run, Mayor Kay — who brought the
happening idea back from Sydney —
fired the starter's gun at 9.30 on the
dot.

But, for the first time, there were as
many thousands ahead of the starting
line as there were behind it.

Fanshawe St, usually a seething
mass of runners moments after the
"off," was already packed shoulder-to-
shoulder with people who could not get
down to the start.

Mayor Kay — himself one of the
city's keenest joggers — predicted
yesterday that this run was going to be
the biggest and he was right.

"I could tell by the number of people
jogging in the streets in the evenings,"
he said.

After the start and the thousands of
runners crowding Victoria Park had
moved off, Mayor Kay, who has taken
part in every fun run, joined in at the
tail of the field with children in
pushchairs surrounding him.

Fittingly, a long way ahead of him
one of his employees — Auckland City
Council recreation officer Paul Lee —
was out in front of the field.

Lee (25), who has raced, trained and
coached with crack British runner
David Moorcroft and is a graduate of
Loughborough College, "the" college
for physical education training, passed
through the finish gates in 28m 50s.

"I enjoyed it and I'll do it again next
year," said Lee, who runs 100 to 160km
a week in training.

Another early finisher was Rod
Ginn, who admitted afterwards he had
started from the Ferry Buildings.

"There were just too many people to
get down to the start line," he said.

A four-man team from the Laser
Breeze company took just on 30
minutes. One of them was New
Zealand road running titleholder Max
Cullum, who said: "We had a blooming
good tail wind but it was a bit warm."

The weather turned out fine for the
big event. Only an hour before the
start heavy rain fell over the course
but the sun was shining strongly when
9.30 came round.

The official entry was 34,392 but
once again this number was more than
doubled by the unofficial fun runners.

The biggest team in the run was
entered by L. D. Nathan, with 719
runners. Foodtown put up a 432-strong
contingent.

At the finish, there were 96 gates in
the 75 metre-long scaffolding structure, twice as many as last year, and
there was no congestion as the tidal
wave of finishers poured in.

A joggers' club official said most
participants felt this was the best-
organized fun run yet.

"People have recognized the importance of spreading the after-run activities around the area, rather than all
congregating here at St Heliers," he
said. "The change has been very well
accepted by all the business houses."

Onlookers joined in the spirit of the
event, as usual. Thousands of people
lined the run and many sprayed
runners with their garden hoses as
they went past.

Near Kohimarama Beach, a traditional jazz band was playing, which
brought cheers from runners.

One regular runner reported: "More
people were running longer this year,
they seemed to be fitter.

"The field was packed right up to the
finish and there were fewer strag-
glers. It was a very even run."

The usual post-run carnival had
moved over the hill to Madill's Farm
reserve where the traditional bar-
becues and cold drinks were waiting
for the entrants.

St John Ambulance and the Army's 1
Field Hospital (25 people headed by
Royal Army Medical Corps Major
Phillippa White) dealt with the usual
crop of minor injuries that occur
during the run.

An hour after the start, they had
treated 10 people for sprains, cuts and
blisters.

One of them was 70-year-old Bill
Rickard, who was knocked over twice
on the run and needed treatment for
cuts and grazes.

But he was full of smiles. "I'm as fit
as a fiddle and I love this run," he
laughed.

Ambulancemen on the route treated
one young man for a cut leg, another
for a suspected broken ankle and an
elderly runner who was feeling faint
from the heat.

A teenager was probably the most
unfortunate runner of the day.

He was struck by a swing at Victoria
Park before the start and was taken to
Auckland Hospital with minor injuries
to his spine.

● The full list of finishers will be
published in next Saturday's Auckland
Star.

● More pictures, Page 12. Back Page

Quay St is packed with some
of the 70,000 runners who took
part in the Star's fun run
today. In the biggest field yet,
the runners stretched for almost 5km long the waterfront
on their run to St Heliers.

Wimbledon's clean-up campaign flops on Day 1

THE SHAME OF JOHN McENROE

By JOHN PASSMORE and HARRY HARRIS

WIMBLEDON sizzled straight into controversy yesterday when John McEnroe came within two tantrums of being thrown out of the tournament on Day One.

It had been hoped that a new system of disciplinary penalties for misbehaviour, introduced by the professional tennis players' own governing body, would discourage the kind of antics for which the No. 2 seed has become notorious.

But it did not stop McEnroe losing his temper and abusing officials—or not until he had pushed the system close to its limit.

After being warned by the match umpire, he was twice penalised a point. The next sanction on the scale would have been the loss of a game—and after that, disqualification.

The Wimbledon tournament referee Fred Hoyles who became involved in the row with McEnroe said afterwards : 'Just two more abusive outbursts by him and he would have been disqualified, make no mistake about that. I don't like being sworn at.'

Disputing

McEnroe, who at 22 has still not curbed the temper that earned him the teenage nickname of SuperBrat, boiled over on Court Number One as the temperature went into the eighties.

He began disputing linesmen's calls in the first set of his match against fellow - American Tom Gullikson. In the second, in a rage, he repeatedly banged his racket on the ground, stood on it to break it and kicked it in the air. Then he smashed the replacement against a chair.

At this point, match umpire Edward James from Llanelli issued a public warning for 'abusing your racket Mr Mc-Enroe.' *This warning was Step One in the five-stage penalty*

CRASH ! McEnroe breaks a racket

Turn to Page 2, Col. 2

WALLOP ! A racket gets a kicking—and McEnroe gets a warning

McENROE TOPPLES KING BORG

Yankee Doodle Dandy

Yankee John Mac came to town,
A chip upon his shoulder;
But still he gunned down Great King Borg,
Now Mac's the title holder.

★ By KEN MONTGOMERY

■ Beaten Bjorn Borg congratulates the new champion—and now he can shave off that beard

JOHN McENROE, yankee-doodle angry, is the new king of Wimbledon.

With immaculate timing, the magnificent American chose to topple the invincible Bjorn Borg on the Fourth of July, Independence Day.

McEnroe, the angry young man, is a worthy champion. He defeated Borg, five times Wimbledon champion, 4-6, 7-6 (7-1), 7-6 (7-4), 6-4 in a fabulous heavyweight battle which see-sawed through 3 hours 22 mins, 310 points and what must have been a million near-heart attacks.

We have waited a year for an action replay of last year's unforgettable five-set thriller, which made Borg king for the fifth time.

The wait was well worthwhile, for although some of the tennis in this wonderful final was hardly out of the top drawer, the suspense was agonising. The drama dripped with almost every stroke that was played.

Borg, one of the great champions, refused to surrender his crown lightly. He fought tooth and nail to the bitter end—an end which came at 5.29 on a Wimble-

Bjorn loser at long last

don scoreboard which had recorded 41 straight victories for the superman Swede.

But Borg was Yesterday's Man at the finish. Yankee-doodle McEnroe deserved to stick a feather in his cap, for he showed bravery beyond any call of duty in winning a title he has coveted for so long.

Three times in those nail-biting 202 minutes, McEnroe was on his knees. Literally!

Chased

Both men chased shots which mere mortals like ourselves had already started to applaud as winners from the other end.

Both men served sketchily, Borg clocking-up 10 aces to McEnroe's 8. The Swede served only four double faults to the American's 10.

Throughout a match

which could not have been more exciting had it been played on a circus highwire, McEnroe behaved magnificently.

That fiery Irish temper was kept in check, although at times the young New Yorker must have been on the verge of erupting.

As early as the second set—Borg had taken the first by 6-4 in only 36 mins—McEnroe's short fuse could easily have been ignited.

A loudmouth in the noisiest Centre Court crowd I have heard interrupted his second service with an idiotic call of "Get the referee, John".

McEnroe glowered, then shouted "Thank you very much", before going on to take the game.

The second set saw the tide start to turn. It took an hour to complete, but it brought Mc Enroe level when he finally won the tie-break by a runaway seven points to one.

As if by divine intervention, the sun came out at that point. McEnroe must have firmly believed it was to shine on him.

In a thrilling third set, he saved four set points in the tenth game. Once again it went to a tie-break.

Once again, the ferocious, fiery Irish southpaw kept his cool, took the tie-break 7-4, and the miracle was now a possibility.

But as the match progressed Borg produced some of the greatest recovery shots even the Centre Court has seen.

He looked like dropping his service in the eighth game but from 15-40 down he produced the best winner of the tournament, after a McEnroe dink had hit the top of the net and bounced almost dead.

Disbelief

The entire McEnroe family — dad, mum, and two young brothers — all shook their heads in disbelief.

When Borg saved his service game, we felt that yet another memorable confrontation could continue for ever.

But McEnroe held service comfortably and in the final, fateful, game of a magnificent, memorable final, the king was finally dethroned.

Borg saved one championship point but there was nothing he could do about the second, when McEnroe drove a blistering forehand past him down the line, then jumped yards in the air to greet his victory.

MEN'S SINGLES FINAL — J McEnroe (US) bt B Borg (Sweden) 4-6, 7-6, 7-6, 6-4.

MIXED DOUBLES FINAL: F. D. Mcmillan (South Africa) and Miss B. F. Stove (Netherlands) bt J. R. Austin and Miss T. A. Austin (USA) 4-6, 7-6, 6-3.

■ Lady Diana Spencer won the fashion points again at Wimbledon yesterday. This time in a turquoise, red and white jacket and skirt.

THAT'S MY BOY

KEN JONES

IT was there. A winner. John McEnroe had done what Wimbledon's high priests feared he would.

The bad guy had finished first and there was much twitching around bloodless upper lips.

McEnroe had dared to suppose that his talent was bigger than the place, that he did not have to conform to Wimbledon's pathetic elitism.

He'd been accused of savaging the tournament's sophistication, but sophistication means worldly and Wimbledon can hardly claim to be that.

Not while it adopts postures moulded in the officers' mess, not while it expects millionaires to behave like other ranks.

It was this more than anything that provoked McEnroe into a mood of blatant sourness, that made even his most committed supporters cringe.

A self-appointed victim, a target for vicious interrogation, he spat invectives at his tormenters and bled like they wanted him to.

But there was always the suspicion that there was more to McEnroe than this and that he had reached the point in his game where he was capable of taking Bjorn Borg in the final.

He took him in four sets with barely a murmur of dissent, suffering the bad calls when they came, raising his arms when cheered for restraint.

It may be that only the splendid Borg and Jimmy Connors fully command his respect. That his interest so swindles against lesser men that he needs a flame of conflict.

The interest was at full pitch against Borg yesterday. McEnroe served magnificently against a magnificent player. He looked what he is, a tremendous athlete.

With the second of two match points in his favour, with what was to be the winning shot floating wide of Borg's right hand, McEnroe admitted that he offered up a brief prayer.

If God had nothing better to do than watch Wimbledon, then maybe he did nod John McEnroe's way. If so, he isn't a bad judge.

LOWE FLIES HIGH!

BRITAIN had three winners on the second day of the three-day swimming international against Russia in Kiev.

David Lowe won the 200-metres butterfly in 2 mins 03.65 secs, Janne Grayswark took the women's 100-metres butterfly in 1min 03.33 secs and Gaynor Stanley clinched the

woman's 400-metres individual medley with a time of 5 mins 03.07 secs.

Russia now lead the international by 137 points to 87.

Test cricket history...reported by PAT GIBSON

Willis sets Ashes ablaze

England war dance of delight by Taylor after his catch gave Willis another victim

ENGLAND yesterday completed the greatest Test comeback since the Ashes were still smouldering in their urn.

And suddenly cricket's most enduring contest is ablaze again, after what England's learned, literate captain Mike Brearley could only describe as "a fairytale."

Only once had a team won a Test match after being made to follow-on . . . in 1894, when A E Stoddart's England beat Australia by 10 runs in Sydney.

But that is what Brearley's England did at Headingley — to beat Australia by 18 runs in an unbelievable third Cornhill Test. Or should it still be Ian Botham's England, since it was his unforgettable 149 not out that inspired their sensational recovery?

Finest figures

No one was more inspired than Bob Willis, who shattered Australia with eight for 43 — the finest figures of his Test career and the best by an England bowler at Leeds.

He began his trail of destruction by taking three wickets for no runs in 11 balls just when Australia were looking like making their task of scoring 130 to win a formality.

Instead, they lost their last nine wickets for 55 in only 98 minutes and went off to Scotland—where they have a one-day tomorrow—to lick their wounds.

"We didn't do much wrong . . . apart from lose the game," said captain Kim Hughes accepting defeat with considerable grace for a man who had expected to have his hands on the Ashes the night before.

"It's terribly disappointing to blow a match when you've played so well throughout—apart from two sessions.

"But there was nothing we could do about Ian Botham's batting yesterday or Bob Willis's bowling today."

In fact, the day began disappointingly for Willis, who could help Botham to add no more than five to England's overnight 351 for 9 before becoming Terry Alderman's sixth victim of the innings.

Havoc

And there was no hint of the havoc he was to cause as Australia moved to 56 for the loss of Graeme Wood, caught behind in Botham's second over.

Then Willis changed ends—and immediately he was a different proposition.

Trevor Chappell, who had battled away for 70 minutes, was caught off the shoulder of the bat trying to fend off a flier . . . 56 for 2.

With two runs added, Botham was back in the action, diving to catch Hughes at second slip off Willis. And at the same score Graham Yallop was smartly taken at short leg off another Willis

8–43 and he levels the series for England

lifter in the crucial last over before lunch . . . 58—4.

For the first time in the match, England sensed they could win—and they knew it when Chris Old got into the act by hitting Allan Border's leg stump . . . 65—5.

John Dyson, who had made exactly half of Australia's 68 in two hours, was next to go, losing his concentration to hook at Willis and glove a catch to Bob Taylor . . . 68—6.

Australia's spirits sagged when Rodney Marsh was more successful in hooking Willis, but skied to deep fine leg, where Graham Dilley took the catch with commendable aplomb . . . 74—7.

Geoff Lawson's only contribution was to edge Willis to Taylor and become the veteran's wicketkeeper's 1,271st

victim, breaking John Murray's all-time record in first-class cricket . . . 75—8.

Ray Bright and Dennis Lillee kept Australia's hopes flickering — and, on his own admission had Brearley worried, with a ninth-wicket stand of 35 that took them within 20 of victory.

Triumph

But then Lillee was caught by Mike Gatting, running and tumbling in from deep-mid-on off Willis who finally yorked the gallant Bright to seal England's triumph.

Afterwards both captains condemned the Headingley pitch—but no one who witnessed one of the most amazing cricket matches was complaining.

HEADINGLEY.—England won by 18 runs.

AUSTRALIA.— First Innings 401 for 9 dec (Dyson 102, Hughes 89; Botham 6—95).

Second Innings
Dyson c Taylor b Willis 34
Wood c Taylor b Botham .. 10
Chappell c Taylor b Willis 8
Hughes c Botham b Willis .. 0
Yallop c Gatting b Willis .. 0
Border b Old 0
Marsh c Dilley b Willis .. 4
Bright b Willis 19
Lawson c Taylor b Willis .. 1
Lillee c Gatting b Willis .. 17
Alderman not out 0
Lb 3, w 1, nb 11 .. 18

TOTAL 111

Fall of wickets.— 13, 56, 58, 58, 65, 68, 74, 75, 110.

Bowling.—Botham 7-3-14-1; Dilley 2-0-11-0; Willis 15-1-13-8; Old 9-1-21-1; Willey 3-1-4-0.

ENGLAND.—First innings 174 (Botham 50; Lillee 1—49).

SECOND INNINGS
(Overnight : 351 for 9)
Botham not out 149
Willis c Border b Alderman 2
B 5, lb 3, w 3, nb5 16

Total 356

Fall of wickets.—0, 18, 37, 41, 105, 133, 135, 252, 319.

Bowling. — Lillee 25-6-94-3; Alderman 35-6-135-6, Lawson 23-4-96-1, Bright 4-0-15-0.

PREVIOUS TESTS
Trent Bridge : Australia won by 4 wickets. Lord's : Drawn.

● **WILLIS—The Man Who Thought He Was Finished —Pages 38 and 39**

BUT, OH, WHAT AN AWFUL PITCH!

ENGLAND'S fifth-day hero, Bob Willis, joined Test skippers Mike Brearley and Kim Hughes last night in condemnation of the Headingley pitch.

He said : "It was not a great wicket to bat on and thanks to Ian Botham's magnificent contribution we had something to bowl at."

He added: "I don't think Nottingham or Leeds were up to Test match standard."

Brearley agreed : "The pitch was not really satisfactory for Tests and batsmen needed a lot of luck to survive.

"Halfway through the Test I thought it was a mistake to leave off-spinner John Emburey out of our side, but he would have had a few overs today and how could we have guaranteed that he would take wickets as quickly as the seamers?"

Hughes said : "It was the sort of pitch on which you could always expect lots of wickets. You could play

another 10 games here and no side would make 175."

But he took no credit away from England : "We were very very disappointed but I thought they played very well and deserved their victory."

■ CRICKET authorities have seen the light after Saturday's crowd protest when play was abandoned at Headingley. Now umpires in this Ashes series can resume play any time during the extra hour if the weather improves after a stoppage.

IT'S ALL OVER . . . Bright's middle stump goes and England have won the Test

Shergar £2m ransom demand

DERBY WINNER STOLEN

DERBY winner Shergar is being held by gunmen today who are demanding a £2,000,000 ransom for the horse's return.

The gunmen struck at the Aga Khan's stud farm at Ballymany, Newbridge, Co Kildare, last night.

The head groom, Mr John Fitzgerald, and his family, were tied and locked in a room.

Mr Fitzgerald was then taken at gunpoint to the stables and ordered to point out the animal — reputed to have a stud value of between £12 and £30 million.

One of the gunmen drove a horse box into the stable yard and loaded the horse.

Mr Fitzgerald was then blindfolded, forced to

by Patrick Clancy and Christopher Poole

lie face down in the horse box and taken hostage.

Mr Fitzgerald was freed more than four hours later but was unable to make out his surroundings.

As the gunmen were leaving, one of them told Mr Fitzgerald that they would be looking for a £2,000,000 ransom for the safe return of the horse.

He was told not to contact police for three hours and to wait for further instructions this afternoon.

Police said they had set up road blocks throughout the country. They were waiting for the kidnappers to make the next move.

The Aga Khan was told of the ransom demand at his Paris headquarters. A spokesman there said he would probably make a statement later.

Shergar trained throughout his racing career at Newmarket by Michael Stoute, established his reputation as one of the world's greatest racehorses during the summer of 1981.

High summer

In early June he won the Derby at Epsom by a record 10-length distance to earn almost £150,000 in prize money.

The horse, a product of the stallion Great Nephew out of the French mare Sharmeen by Val de Loir, then went to Ireland to win the Irish Sweeps Derby at The Curragh with Lester Piggott up.

Swinburn was back in the saddle for the King George VI and Queen Elizabeth Diamond Stakes in July and Shergar, at 5-2 on, one of the shortest-priced big race candidates of the post-war era, completed the great high summer treble by winning once more.

By this stage of his career, Shergar was attracting keen interest from leading American stud farm owners and the Aga Khan was already under pressure to sell him across the Atlantic as a high-vlue stallion property.

Soon after came the announcement that Shergar would stand as a stallion at the Aga's stud in Co. Kildare where the great horse had been foaled in 1978.

CHAMPION . . . Shergar with jockey Walter Swinburn after his 10-length Derby triumph in 1981, with owner the Aga Khan.

TV: 21 • Entertainment Guide: 14 • Letters: 12 • Ad Lib 13 • Patric Walker: 23 • Delia Smith: 25 • City: 31

Champ's power-show just out of this world

SPACE-AGE MARTINA'S A KILLER QUEEN...

THERE'S MANY A SLIP . . . Not for Martina Navratilova, though. When her skirt went adrift in the first game, she smilingly adjusted her dress before smashing her way to victory.

WIMBLEDON RESULTS

WOMEN'S SINGLES
Final

M NAVRATILOVA (U.S.) bt A JAEGER (U.S.) 6—0, 6—3.

MEN'S DOUBLES
Final

P FLEMING, J McENROE (U.S.) bt T E and T R GULLIKSON (U.S.) 6—4, 6—3, 6—4.

WOMEN'S DOUBLES
Final

M NAVRATILOVA, P SHRIVER (U.S.) bt R CASALS (U.S.) W TURNBULL (Aust) 6—2, 6—2.

MIXED DOUBLES
Semi-finals

Holders: K Curren (S Af) Miss A E Smith (U.S.)

J LLOYD (GB), W TURNBULL (Aust) bt F STOLLE (Aust), P SHRIVER (U.S.) 6—7, 6—3, 6—4.

WOMEN'S PLATE
Final

A Brown (GB) bt A Tobin (Aust) 3—6, 6—3, 6—3.

MEN'S Over 35's Final

C Dibley (Aust) bt R Moore (S Af) 6—2, 6—2.

Men's Over 35's Doubles
Semi-finals

S STEWART (U.S.), F STOLLE (Aust) bt C Dibley (Aust), J Filoll (Chile) 6—4, 7—6.

BOYS' SINGLES
Semi-finals

S Egberg (Swe) bt P McEnroe (U.S.) 6—6, 7—6, 6—2.

GIRLS' SINGLES
Semi-finals

P Paradis (Fr) bt N Herreman (Fr) 6—3, 6—2—B Hy (Hongkong) bt B Randall (Aust) 0—6, 7—5, 6—4.

BOYS' DOUBLES
Final

M Kratzmann, S Youl (Aust) bt M Nastase, O Rahnasto (Rum) 6—4, 6—4.

GIRLS' DOUBLES
Final

P Fendick (U.S.), P Hy (Hong Kong) bt C Anderholm, H Olsson (Swe) 6—1 7—5.

TODAY'S PLAY

CENTRE COURT — Men's singles final: C Lewis (NZ) v ★J McEnroe (U.S.). Mixed doubles final: ★S Denton (U.S.), Mrs Billie Jean King (U.S.) v ★J Lloyd (GB), Miss W Turnbull (Aust).

COURT ONE.—Boy's Singles final: S Edberg (Swe) v J Frawley (Aust). Girl's singles final: Miss P Paradis (Fr) v Miss P Hy (Hongkong). Over 35s men's doubles final: S Stewart (U.S.), F Stolle (Aust) v O Davidson (Aust), E Drysdale (S Af).

★ Seeded players

MARTINA NAVRATILOVA, the "bionic woman" of world tennis, destroyed 18-year-old Andrea Jaeger 6—0, 6—3 on Wimbledon's Centre Court to capture the women's singles crown for a fourth time.

Watched closely by her coach, Mike Estep, and her friend Nancy Lieberman, the former basketball star who motivates her to "hate" opponents, Martina produced power-packed space-age tennis to erase poor Andrea in 54 one-sided minutes.

by ALAN HOBY

This brings the 26-year-old champion's record for the past year to a staggering 139 wins, with only four defeats.

Apart from a few valiant flourishes in the second set, the blonde American looked like a little girl lost.

Andrea claimed afterwards that she "was not nervous" in that one-sided 16-minute opening set. But she certainly looked it.

"The reason she trounced me in the first set," said Andrea, "is that I didn't start well and she did."

Martina, who has dropped only 25 singles games in 5hrs 30min work this Wimbledon, said with pride: "It is very satisfying, as always, to win Wimbledon. I have been in four finals and won them all, and that is pretty special. It has not been done many times.

"It all seemed too easy at first, but then Andrea started to produce some great passing shots and I had no answer. But even then I knew she had a huge mountain to climb.

"I try to win every match, because if I don't people believe I am coming apart at the seams. But I don't let it get to me.

"Many players think that perhaps I'm too good, but they would give their eye-teeth to be in my position. I have to put my reputation on the line every time I go out there."

Of the incident in that opening game when the belt round her white dreses worked loose and she had to hold up the game while she smilingly re-tied it, Martina said: "Before the match I put my skirt on early and tied it rather loosely for comfort.

"I forgot to re-tie the skirt and felt it going. It was on its way down, and I was holding it with one hand while hitting a forehand with the other.

"Fortunately I did not have to play another stroke in that rally, which I won."

After breaking her opponent's service in the second, fourth and sixth games, when Jaeger twice double-faulted, Martina, one set up, had her majesty temporarily disturbed by a low-flying plane droning across the sky.

With the score at 2-1 in the second set, Czech-born Martina shrugged her shoulders, stopped playing and glanced up to spot the message on the plane's trailer, which said: "Please use the Post Code."

Said the champion later: "It went through my mind that I had received a letter from a man who wanted an answer, but I didn't know the post code."

Well, merciless Martina may not have known the code but she certainly knew how to dominate her opponent.

She was aided, too, by a cruel decision in the fifth game which robbed her opponent of a crucial point just when she was forcing Martina back from the net with some fine cross-court passes.

With the score at 3—2, the heavens fell in on poor Andrea when, at break point, a blazing Navratilova forehand, which looked clearly out, was given in.

The complaining Andrea deliberately pointed to the spot, but the decision stood and, instead of levelling at 3—3, split seconds later she had lost the game. Cruel luck.

'Real pain'

Said Andrea: "That bad line-call was a real pain because at that point I was getting my game together."

Yet with the crowd crying, "Come on, Andrea," she battled back and even won another game. But you cannot halt an irresistible force.

Though Andrea saved three match points she finally — and desperately — hit her forehand out under the sort of pressure few players could withstand.

Ranked No. 3 in the world, Miss Jaeger is obviously a sport. She even giggled when she hit one piercing winner in this somewhat embarrassing final.

She may have had a point, too, when she said: "I don't think you can say Martina is the greatest player of all, just on this Wimbledon. I feel she needs to win a few more Grand Slam titles."

Maybe . . . but even though Navratilova was not quite at her imperious best, she is certainly the best I have seen since the days of 'Mo' Connolly.

And she certainly deserved the feast she enjoyed last night. "I am going to eat everything I have not been allowed in training, especially Czech dumplings with sugar, butter and cheese in them," she said.

Martina had every reason to be happy. Partnered by American Pam Shriver, she had later returned to the Centre Court to beat Rosie Casals and Wendy Turnbull 6—2, 6—2 in the women's doubles final.

STILL FIGHTING . . . But Andrea Jaeger's on the way out.

Easy for Mac

by ROY McKELVIE

JOHN McENROE and Peter Fleming remain the outstanding doubles pair in the world.

They took the doubles title with ease beating the Gullikson twins, Tom and Tim, 6—4, 6—3, 6—4 in an hour and 48 minutes.

This was a leisurely performance lacking the sparkle usually associated with men's doubles at this level. There were only ripples of applause from the Centre Court crowd.

Never once did McEnroe and Fleming look like losing their service. Never once was it threatened. It was left to the unfortunate Tom Gullikson, the left hander of the pair, to lose his service three times—once in each set.

Dropped

He dropped it at 4—5 in the first set, at 3—5 in the second and in the third game of the third set.

It was enough to allow the winners freedom to play as they wished.

Fleming once said that the best player on court, showing the same wonderful touch in doubles that he has in singles.

Fleming osce said that the best doubles pair in the world was McEnroe and anybody else, and, indeed, that was how it looked on this occasion.

Just right

The, 6ft 5in Fleming ambled about the court, sometimes appearing sluggish, but usually doing the right thing at the right moment.

The twins found his service particularly difficult to take. Feming consistently served down the middle of the court to the right-handed Tim, and varied his direction to the left handed Tom. It didn't matter which way McEnroe served, the twins found it almost impossible to do much with the ball.

There were a few deft touches, the occasional drop shot from McEnroe, some lobs and angled volleys. Service aces from anyone were few.

I'M not following in my brother's footsteps. I'm just doing my own thing. I never give him any advice about his behaviour and never would. I have learned from his experiences that it is not worth getting excited on court. So I try to be very calm, and I think I have done a decent job of it.

PATRICK McENROE, just 17.

When the right-handed Tim was serving against McEnroe, the twins tried the Australian formation—both men on the same side of the court—but earned nothing from it.

The only real excitement came in the last game of all when Fleming, serving for the match, reached 40-love.

On the first match point, McEnroe tried a spectacular cut across court and volleyed out. On the second, Tim cut into the middle of the net and brought off a winning volley. The third match point was Fleming's.

Since McEnroe and Fleming first came together in 1978 they have won 39 doubles titles and been finalists on 10 other occasions. They have now won Wimbledon three times, the U.S. Open twice and the Masters championship five times.

The first

The Gulliksons, who put out the second seeds Kevin Curren and Steve Denton in the semi-final, are the first twins to reach Wimbledon doubles finals this century.

They have quite a good record on grass, beating McEnroe and Fleming at Queen's Club in 1980. Most of their wins have been in ordinary grand prix tournaments.

JOHN'S JOY

JOHN LLOYD gave Britain's battered Wimbledon image a final-day boost by reaching the mixed doubles final for the second successive year in partnership with Australian Wendy Turnbull.

They beat Australian veteran Fred Stolle and American Pam Shriver 6—7, 6—3, 6—4 and now face Steve Denton and Billie Jean King in today's final.

The match hung on the seventh game of the final set when the Anglo-Australian pair captured Shriver's service after a game of four deuces.

That gave Lloyd and Turnbull a 4—3 lead which she immediately increased to 5—4 with a love game. Lloyd held his serve for the match in a frantic finale.

Another boost for Britain was provided by 18-year-old Amanda Brown, daughter of Norwich City boss Ken. She won the Ladies Plate at the expense of Australia's Amanda Tobin 3—6, 6—3, 6—3.

Geoff's warning

by HENRY BLOFELD

NEW ZEALAND handed England a warning that they will not be a push-over in the coming four-match Test series.

Geoff Howarth hit 88, while John Wright cracked 85 to give the tourists a tremendous start, before unbeaten Evan Gray (67) and Richard Hadlee (76) pushed the score to 388—5 at the close.

Howarth, Wright and Hadlee are players who have benefited enormously from their experience in county cricket and is one of the reasons New Zealand are such an improved side.

Somerset were without Ian Botham (groin strain), Viv Richards, who has a cold, and Peter Roebuck was rested.

SPORTING SAM . . . . . . by Reg Wootton

FLACK IN A FIX

by MIKE BRETTELL

THE Edgbaston pitch was the centre of controversy for the second time in a week as 22 wickets tumbled for only 208 runs in the top-of-the-table clash between Warwickshire and Middlesex.

Bernard Flack, the Warwickshire groundsman, who is also the TCCB Inspector of Pitches, admitted that he expected to be "on the carpet."

The dubious wicket produced 28 wickets in two days in the game against Yorkshire last Monday and Tuesday.

"I am surprised and disappointed with this pitch," said Flack.

"This is our Test match wicket and normally I wouldn't expect it to turn until the fifth day.

"But I wasn't able to give it sufficient water and that is the problem."

Leaders Middlesex thought they were sitting pretty after dismissing Bob Willis's men for only 113 in 49·3 overs.

105 wickets

Spinners Phil Edmonds (5 for 26) and John Emburey (3 for 15) had done their job and took their season's tally to 105 wickets.

The wicket had the batsmen in trouble all day as the ball turned appreciably for the spinners and produced variable bounce for the fast bowlers.

Dennis Amiss was the top scorer with 25 and the others to reach double figures, all under 20, were Andy Lloyd, David Smith, Asif Din and Willis.

There was one miraculous catch from Middlesex skipper Mike Gatting who flew to his left to take a third slip catch to dismiss Lloyd.

But Middlesex, in reply, soon ran into trouble as Willis produced a devastating spell.

He had three principal batsmen trapped lbw as the ball kept low, and finished with figures of 10-5-8-3.

With Paul Downton, Clive Radley and Keith Tomlins all out, veteran spinner Norman Gifford added to their discomfort by bowling Roland Butcher.

Middlesex's difficulties con- without scoring, Gatting went tinued. Richard Ellis departed lbw to Gifford and, incredibly, they were down to 41 for 6.

Further misery awaited them and they were soon sent crashing all out for a wretched 78 off 50·1 overs.

Emburey (23) and Gatting (15) were their chief run-getters.

At the close Warwicks were 17 for 2 in their second innings after 11 overs.

Gillespie goes

by RAY BRADLEY

TROUBLE-TORN Coventry could become the centre of more transfer activity this week, even though new manager Bobby Gould is taking a short holiday in Tenerife.

Scottish defender Gary Gillespie (22) became the latest to join the Highfield Road exodus when he signed for Liverpool in a £325,000 deal. He was also a target for Arsenal.

"With no disrespects to Arsenal, I don't think any young player with ambition could do better than join the champions," says Gillespie.

Three more

At least three more pay rebels are likely to leave Coventry after refusing contracts.

Defender Paul Dyson is set to move to Stoke, who want him as replacement for centre-half Dave Watson, who joined Vancouver Whitecaps at the end of the season.

Top scorer Steve Whitton is wanted by West Ham as successor to Francois van der Elst, who has returned to Belgium and hopes to sign for Lokeren. Only snag is the £350,000 fee Hammers are demanding.

Midfielder Steve Hunt could be yet another departure from Coventry. West Brom have renewed persistent interest and may offer a player-exchange deal.

Two of Bobby Gould's targets are Chelsea midfielder Mike Fillery and Palace winger Vince Hilaire, transfer-listed at his own request.

But Hilaire was last night having second thoughts over a move after hearing that Palace had joined the hunt for Middlesbrough midfielder Stan Cummins and Scottish striker Joe Jordan, who is returning to Britain after two years with A.C. Milan.

Jordan is also being chased by Chelsea and Manchester City.

Midfielder Paul Davis has withdrawn his transfer request and will stay with Arsenal.

Brian Clough last night blocked Mark Proctor's proposed transfer from Forest to Sunderland.

The Forest boss was angered by Sunderland's delay in completing a £100,000 deal for the England Under-21 midfielder, who was on loan to the Roker Park club last season.

RAY'S STING IN TAIL

by SIMON SMITH

TAILENDER Ray East produced a swashbuckling knock to rescue high-riding Essex from a disastrous position at Trent Bridge.

Not for the first time in a distinguished career, the slow left-arm bowler put a sting in the tail, slamming 45 in a 50 partnership with anchor-man John Lever to rock rampant Notts.

The pair lifted the Essex total from 124 for eight to 178 before hero Ray was run out.

Lever (18) and young Neil Foster (25 not) added valuable runs as the visitors, who had slumped from 63—3 to 124—8, were finally all out for 211.

Earlier, Graham Gooch took 110 minutes over his 21. Ken McEwan contributed a patient 31 and Keith Pont and Derek Pringle (36) added 49 for the fifth-wicket before three wickets crashed at 112.

In reply Notts were rocked when opener Tim Robinson was caught at second slip by Gooch without a run on the board from Foster's first ball. And with Derek Randall going for 16, Notts were struggling themselves at 39 for two by the close.

THE WEEK-END GAMBOLS . . . . . by Barry Appleby

The Sunday Express, incorporating the Sunday Dispatch, is printed and published by Express Newspapers p.l.c., Fleet Street, London EC4P 4JT, and Great Ancoats Street, Manchester M60 4HB. Registered as a newspaper at the Post Office. No. 3,356

Australia wins America's Cup—after 132 years

MAGIC MATILDA!

Australia II—she stunned America.

From IAN WOOLDRIDGE in Newport, Rhode Island

IT HAPPENED, and it happened in the manner of lurid fiction.

Australia II sailed back from the Dead Sea here last night, to beat Liberty, win the America's Cup, and leave this nation speechless.

Two-thirds of the way through the accurately billed Race of the Century, you would not have risked tenpence on Australia's chances, at 100 to 1.

Outsteered by the brilliant Dennis Conner, outpaced by an American boat that had shed 1,000-lb. of ballast to defend 132 years of unthreatened high-seas supremacy, Australia looked irrevocably doomed, as the unluckiest also-rans in sport and Waltzing Matilda looked set to become a lament.

Helpless

And then they won. They won a 4¼-hour race by precisely 41 seconds.

As America watched in helpless agony —and there is no greater frustration than urging a yacht to speed up in God's own good time—John Bertrand, Australia's self-effacing skipper, sailed right out of nowhere, straight past Liberty and unerringly into the pages of sporting history.

So the seemingly impossible was accomplished. The trophy won by America off the Isle of Wight in the presence of Queen Victoria in 1851 and never endangered in 24 challenges, finally fell.

It is due to be handed over by the New York Yacht Club — in whose premises it has been symbolically fastened to a plinth by bolts—within the next 48 hours.

To its autocratic members and to millions of Americans, it will be akin to surrendering the Crown Jewels, for it was the symbol of American human and technological superiority. How they lost it

Continued on Back Page

Appalling truth behind Maze breakout

BRENDAN McFARLANE, aged 31, from Ardoyne, Belfast; jailed for life for his part in the bar bomb murder of five Protestants seven years ago; leader of the Provos in the Maze during the 1981 hunger strike campaign.

KEVIN ARTT, aged 24, from Belfast; jailed for life this summer on the word of super-grass Christopher Black for murdering Mr Albert Miles, assistant governor of the Maze, shot in front of his wife.

HUGH COREY, aged 27, from Moneymoore, County Derry; jailed for life in 1977 for the murder of a UDR soldier. Corey, said to be the Provos' Londonderry commander, was to serve at least 20 years.

Freed—to kill again

By EDWARD SCALLAN

THE IRA planned the mass breakout from the Maze Prison to free a specific group of top terrorists.

The others involved were decoys ordered to divert the pursuing security forces so that the leaders could get away.

And, with 21 out of the 38 prisoners who escaped still on the run last night—nine of them convicted murderers—the plan seemed to have worked.

The most dangerous trio, all still free, were: Brendan McFarlane, killer of five Protestants in a bar bombing and the commander who led the Provisionals in the Maze during the 1981 hunger strike campaign; Kevin Barry Artt, gunman who killed a Maze assistant governor: Hugh Joseph Corey, killer of a UDR man and formerly the Provisionals' Londonderry commander.

It emerged that they were on a list of ten to 15 senior men serving long sentences in the Maze who, the Provisional IRA decided, were now needed outside to restore the terrorist command structure shat-tered by the recent activities of the Ulster supergrasses.

The list was smuggled into the prison and Republicans serving shorter sentences—from five to ten years—were ordered to sacrifice themselves if necessary for the sake of their leaders.

Ulster Secretary Jim Prior admitted yesterday that it looked as though *all* the inmates in the Maze's H-Block 7 were involved in the breakout, although 89 were left behind.

Some created diversions inside the jail. Others actually got out and then distracted the pursuing troops

Turn to Page 2, Col. 1

Elsie Tanner to quit The Street

ELSIE FOR 23 YEARS

PAT PHOENIX, star of TV's Coronation Street for 23 years, is to quit the series.

The 58-year-old actress who has become a national institution in the role of Elsie Tanner has decided not to renew her Granada contract when it expires on November 19.

Her decision comes in the wake of the sacking of her long-time friend and colleague Peter Adamson, who played Len Fairclough.

Last night Miss Phoenix said: 'I have resigned. But I am going to honour my contract and I will go on as usual until November 19.

Headache

'I could say a lot but I am going to comply with the terms of my contract and I will not say anything about why I am leaving until I have completed it.'

Her bombshell decision leaves the show's script writers with a second major headache —how to write out one of the show's best-loved characters shortly after devising the killing off of Len Fairclough.

It is understood that Miss Phoenix, who has been in the show since the first episode in December 1960, told executive producer Bill Podmore of her decision after rehearsals in Manchester yesterday.

Denied

Granada's chief Press officer Norman Frisby said: 'There is a chance of her staying on a little to get written out.

'She could be written out in a way which would allow her to return from time to time.'

The actress had been back in the studios for only one week after spending three months starring in the play Verdict in Bournemouth with her boyfriend, actor Anthony Booth.

Earlier this year she was quoted as saying that she wanted to quit the show because she didn't have good enough story lines and was fed up with Granada.

But later she denied some of the reported comments.

Killed off together? — Page NINE

DAILY Mirror

Wednesday, February 15, 1984   16p   ★

Torvill and Dean .. they're just perfect

1	2	3	4	5	6	7	8	9
6.0	6.0	6.0	6.0	6.0	6.0	6.0	6.0	6.0

PERFECTION: Torvill and Dean get maximun marks for artistic interpretation from the Olympic judges. They scored three more sixes for technical merit.

PURE GOLD

British pair skate to Olympic glory

BRITAIN'S Jayne Torvill and Christopher Dean skated to Olympic gold last night in the greatest exhibition of ice dancing seen anywhere in the world.

Flag-waving fans showered them with flowers after their stunning interpretation of Ravel's Bolero took the gold medal in style. The nine judges gave the couple 12 perfect scores of six, including a string of nine sixes for artistry and three more for technical merit.

It was the first time any skaters have got twelve sixes in the competition. After their triumph Christopher said: "We have reached the pinnacle tonight. It was the hardest competition we have ever had but worth it. I can't remember skating. It just came and went. There were so many people out there rooting for us. It was great support."

Jayne added: "I can't believe it. I felt I wanted to go out there and perform and I was happy there were so many people from England—and Nottingham especially"

Asked if they might be getting married soon they both laughed

From FRANK TAYLOR and JOHN JACKSON in Sarajevo

and Christopher replied: "No not this week."

The couple's coach, Betty Calloway, said: "They skated as well as they can. Absolutely magnificent.

"It was one of the best I have seen and I was more than proud of them."

Jane and Christopher's victory fulfilled a promise they made after coming fifth at the Lake Placid Olympics four years ago.

They said then: "We will be back next time to win."

Last night they did just that.

Now the couple, who have not been beaten since 1980, hold all the major ice dance titles—World, European and Olympic.

And they are set to become millionaires when they turn professional after defending their world title in Canada next month.

● MPs cheered when news of the gold medal was announced in the Commons last night.

SIZZLING: Torvill and Dean during their dazzling performance last night.

ELTON WEDS IN WHITE

See Centre Pages

DAILY Mirror

Thursday, March 1, 1984   16p

Bow tie Di!

By JAMES WHITAKER

PRINCESS Diana turns on another stunning performance as she arrives for a concert of one of Britain's top rock bands. There were wolf whistles as Diana walked in wearing a white dinner jacket, satin black trousers, a white full-necked blouse . . . and a black satin bow tie.

Twelve thousand rock fans rose to greet her at the concert, given by the chart-topping group Genesis. At Diana's side was Prince Charles, dressed in a double-breasted grey suit. The lights at Birmingham's National Exhibition Centre faded as they stood on the steps to the concert hall. Then a spotlight picked them out as they made their way to a raised seat for the two-hour concert.

BATTERED: Blood streams down the face of an England fan after a punch-up in Paris.   Picture: MONTE FRESCO

AN ENGLISH soccer fan was near death in Paris last night after a day of violence before, during and after a game with France.

He was in intensive care in a Paris hospital with three stab wounds in the back. Fourteen other Britons had head injuries after baton charges by French police.

BLOODY DISGRACE

Soccer's night of madness—Back Page

Los Angeles Times

Circulation: 1,064,392 Daily / 1,331,666 Sunday · Wednesday, May 9, 1984 · CC† / 120 pages / Copyright 1984, Los Angeles Times / Daily 25¢

Soviets Pull Out of L.A. Olympics

Anti-Russian 'Hysteria,' Danger to Athletes Claimed

Games Officials Pledge to Work to Reverse Decision

By EVAN MAXWELL and KENNETH REICH, *Times Staff Writers*

The Soviet Union, claiming its athletes would be endangered by "anti-Soviet hysteria," said Tuesday that it would not participate in the Los Angeles Olympic Games.

Los Angeles Olympic organizers and local leaders said they will "do everything in our power" to reverse the decision, which was announced in a sharply worded statement from the Soviet Olympic committee. The decision was released by Tass, the official Soviet news agency, within three hours of the beginning of the Olympic flame's trip across country from New York to the Coliseum in Los Angeles, where the Games are to begin July 28.

"Extremist organizations and groupings of all sorts, openly aiming to create 'unbearable conditions' for the stay of the Soviet delegation and performance by Soviet athletes, have sharply stepped up their activities," the Soviet statement, issued in Moscow, said.

'Impossible' Situation

"Heads of anti-Soviet, anti-Socialist organizations are received by U.S. Administration officials. Their activity is widely publicized by the mass media.

"In these conditions, the national Olympic committee of the U.S.S.R. is compelled to declare that participation by Soviet sportsmen is impossible," Tass said.

Although the statement was similar in tone to others issued by the Soviets in the last several months, the official withdrawal from the Los Angeles Games seemed to catch both organizers and Reagan Administration officials by surprise and caused consternation in Los Angeles and Washington.

Officials including Peter Ueberroth, president of the Los Angeles Olympic Organizing Committee; Los Angeles Police Chief Daryl F. Gates and White House spokesman Larry Speakes said that the Soviet fears were "groundless" and that Soviet Olympic visitors would be well protected.

The immediate effect of the Soviet withdrawal was unclear, but a number of officials expressed fears that many Eastern European countries and some Third World nations might join the boycott, which some observers believe is in direct retaliation for the U.S. boycott of the 1980 Games in Moscow.

Olympic organizers in Los Angeles, however, said they do not believe the statement is the "final word" from the Soviets.

Harry L. Usher, LAOOC general manager, admitted in a press conference Tuesday afternoon that the Tass statement was "disturbing" but said that preparations are continuing "for the participation of all athletes."

Usher said it was "unlike" the Soviets to announce such a decision in Tass without first notifying the

Please see BOYCOTT, Page 20

MORE STORIES ON BOYCOTT

- Diplomats believe East Bloc will join Soviet withdrawal. Page 21.
- U.S. boycott wasn't a rousing success, but Carter official still defends it. Page 21.
- Ban the Soviets Coalition exults in Moscow's decision. Page 21.
- Chief Daryl Gates invites Soviets to inspect Los Angeles security plans. Page 20.
- No refunds for buyers of Olympic tickets. Page 20.
- Soviet absence would tarnish most medals. Sports.

Hart Wins Close Races in Ohio, Indiana

Mondale Is Victor in Maryland, N. Carolina; Jackson 2nd in 1 State

By ROBERT SHOGAN, *Times Political Writer*

WASHINGTON—Battling successfully to keep his presidential candidacy alive, Gary Hart won narrow victories over Walter F. Mondale Tuesday night in the Ohio and Indiana Democratic primaries.

Mondale easily defeated Hart in the day's two other primaries, in Maryland and North Carolina, with Jesse Jackson edging Hart for second place in Maryland and running third in the other three states.

Returns from the four states:

Ohio, with 91% of precincts reporting: Hart 42%, Mondale 40% and Jackson 17%.

Indiana, with 85% reporting: Hart 43%, Mondale 40% and Jackson 13%.

North Carolina, with 90% reporting: Mondale 36%, Hart 31% and Jackson 24%.

Maryland, with 97% reporting: Mondale 44%, Jackson 26% and Hart 25%.

The overall results allowed Mondale to maintain his huge delegate lead over Hart. The former vice president has 1,528 delegates, only 439 short of the 1,967 needed to nominate, and Hart has only 887.

Cloud of Doubt

Nevertheless, the net impact of Hart's unexpectedly strong performances in the two Midwest industrial state contests, particularly in Ohio, raised a cloud of doubt over the expectation that Mondale would clinch the nomination before the convention begins July 16. And it served to heighten the significance of the June 5 primaries, particularly those in California and New Jersey, and of next week's Oregon and Nebraska primaries.

Perhaps more important, the returns in Ohio and Indiana also raised some potentially serious questions about Mondale's strength in the general election, should he become the party's standard bearer.

One sign of long-range trouble for Mondale emerged from an NBC News exit poll in Indiana. About half of the voters polled said labor unions, which have played a vital role in Mondale's campaign, have become too powerful. And these

Please see VOTE, Page 14

United Press International

Gina Hemphill, the granddaughter of Jesse Owens, and Bill Thorpe, grandson of Jim Thorpe, carry Olympic torch in New York City on the first leg of the long journey to Los Angeles.

Libya Reportedly Foils Raid on Kadafi's Home

Strongman Believed to Have Survived; Regime Accuses Britain, Sudan of Training Commandos

From Times Wire Services

ROME—Commandos attacked Libyan leader Moammar Kadafi's fortress home in Tripoli on Tuesday and seized a building before they were overpowered in fierce fighting, the Italian news agency and diplomats reported. Libya said all the attackers were killed.

A Western diplomat in Rome said that according to preliminary intelligence reports from Tripoli, the Libyan strongman survived the attack, as he has survived other coup attempts during his 15 years in power.

The official Libyan news agency Jana, without reporting an assault on the barracks where Kadafi normally lives, said terrorists took hostages in a residential building before all were killed by counterattacking Libyan forces.

Many Reported Dead

The Libyan agency said that the attackers, whose nationalities were not disclosed, were trained by Britain and Sudan.

No death toll was immediately announced, but a traveler reaching Athens from Tripoli quoted a Libyan militiaman as saying there were "many dead."

Egypt's Middle East News Agency quoted Damascus radio as saying that Syrian President Hafez Assad conferred by telephone with Kadafi after Tuesday's fighting.

Western diplomatic sources said about 20 rebels were still holding out in late afternoon, although they were surrounded and their resistance was fading.

There was no formal U.S. government reaction to the reports, but a State Department official said in Washington on Tuesday morning that he understood that the firing around Kadafi's barracks was diminishing.

Western news agencies in various capitals were contacted by callers claiming to represent the National Front for the Salvation of Libya,

Please see LIBYA, Page 27

'This Is So Great'

News Fails to Darken Spirit of Torch Relay

By PETER H. KING, *Times Staff Writer*

NEW YORK—Undeterred by heavy rain and reports of a Soviet withdrawal, a succession of uniformed torchbearers passed the Olympic flame through New York City on Tuesday, commencing a relay that will carry the traditional Grecian fire on a serpentine course across the country to Los Angeles for the July 28 opening of the Games.

The relay runners and their sizable entourage of police cars with screaming sirens and flashing lights elicited cheers, whistles and some first-class wisecracks from New Yorkers who leaned out office windows and lined streets for a better look at the slow-moving spectacle.

"Oh wow, this is so, so great," said Gina Hemphill, granddaughter of track great Jesse Owens, after running side by side with Bill Thorpe, grandson of the legendary Jim Thorpe, for the first of the relay's 15,000 kilometers. "I can't believe all these people came out in the rain."

Spanish Proverb

Word of the Soviet announcement had not reached Los Angeles Olympic President Peter V. Ueberroth, Mayor Tom Bradley and other dignitaries by 8:45 a.m., when they arrived at the United Nations Plaza for a ceremonial send-off, and International Olympic Committee President Juan Antonio Samaranch proved himself to be something less than a prophet as he told a small audience huddled under umbrellas of an old Spanish proverb "that rain brings good luck."

For the first three hours of the relay, however, it appeared as though Samaranch might have been on to something. Despite the rain-slicked streets and subsequently clogged traffic, the relay stayed on schedule over its meandering course, stopping sidewalk traffic, creating a commotion and generating expressions of good will—and in some cases befuddlement—almost everywhere it went and from most everyone it met.

Please see RELAY, Page 23

Carter Hawley Wins Victory

Judge Rejects SEC Move in Firm's Takeover Fight

By NANCY YOSHIHARA, *Times Staff Writer*

Carter Hawley Hale Stores Inc. scored a major victory on Tuesday when a federal judge rejected government arguments that the Los Angeles retailer had used illegal tactics to fight a takeover bid and preserve its independence.

U.S. District Judge A. Wallace Tashima vindicated Carter Hawley and rejected a contention by the Securities and Exchange Commission that the company had violated federal securities laws by making massive purchases of its own stock.

Tashima's ruling, if not overturned on appeal, would severely jeopardize a month-old attempt by The Limited Inc. to take over the parent of The Broadway and other major retail chains.

The ruling is also a setback for the SEC, which considered the case a significant test of how fast and under what conditions companies may buy up their own stock to fight off a hostile takeover attempt. The SEC charged that Carter Hawley had engaged in an "illegal tender

Please see CARTER, Page 17

Banks Increase Prime Rate Again, to 12.5%

The nation's major banks increased the prime lending rate for the third time in two months, to 12.5%, sparking renewed fears that rising interest rates may stifle economic growth and lead to a recession next year. Details in Business.

Ethics of $150,000 Payment to Reagan Official Studied

By RONALD J. OSTROW, *Times Staff Writer*

WASHINGTON—A Los Angeles law firm that represents savings and loan associations across the country gave an unusual $150,000 payment to Norman H. Raiden when he left the firm to become general counsel of the Federal Home Loan Bank Board—the chief federal regulator of the savings and loan industry.

And the payment by the firm of McKenna, Conner & Cuneo—made to Raiden on Jan. 2, a month after he had started his federal job—was designed in part to soften the impact of the sharp pay cut Raiden took when he accepted the new position, according to Daniel N. Belin, Raiden's successor as managing partner of the firm.

Raiden was paid as much as $275,000 a year at McKenna, Conner & Cuneo, while his Home Loan Bank Board salary is $66,000 a year

Belin said the special payment, which was more than three times the amount Raiden would have received under the severance formula spelled out in the firm's partnership agreement, also reflected Raiden's nearly 25 years of "extraordinary" service to the firm, which grew from four attorneys to 150 attorneys during his tenure.

The payment could raise ethics questions for Raiden because a section of the U.S. Code prohibits both the giving and receiving of a supplement to a federal salary. The payment is under review by the Office of Government Ethics.

The statute is designed to prevent federal officials from accepting financial support that might compromise their independence. The issue is particularly sensitive in Raiden's case because he is now involved in regulating the savings and loan industry, with which his old law

Please see PAYMENT, Page 13

But a Silver Lining Is Seen

Olympic Finances, Sports Quality Expected to Suffer

By KENNETH REICH, *Times Staff Writer*

If, as now appears likely, the Soviet Union and many of its allies in Eastern Europe and the Third World do not show up for the Los Angeles Olympics, the impact on the Games is bound to be profound.

Financially, the private Los Angeles Olympic Organizing Committee stands to lose up to $90 million from contracts that would be subject to "downward arbitration."

In sports quality, the Olympic leaders have to be aware that seven of the top 10 medal-winning countries at the Montreal Olympics in 1976 were from the Soviet Bloc and that a Soviet boycott of Los Angeles would probably have a greater negative effect on athletic quality than the American-led boycott of Moscow in 1980.

But some Los Angeles Olympic leaders were saying Tuesday that there may be a silver lining to an Eastern Bloc boycott.

Now, at long last, they were saying, the people of Los Angeles and the rest of the United States, who have been in their view all too blase about the Games, will rally to them out of national pride and a desire not to let the Soviets ruin the Games.

Paul Ziffren, the board chairman of the Olympic committee, said that Tuesday morning, shortly after the Soviet Olympic committee statement flashed on the news, he began receiving telephone calls from peo-

Please see IMPACT, Page 26

Views of U.S. Experts on Kremlin

Action Seen as Retaliation and Effort to Harm Reagan

By ROBERT C. TOTH, *Times Staff Writer*

WASHINGTON—The Kremlin's decision to stay away from the Olympics represents a deliberate effort to damage President Reagan's reelection prospects, coupled with a desire to retaliate against the United States for boycotting the 1980 Games in Moscow four years ago, U.S. experts on the Soviet Union said Tuesday.

And the overwhelming consensus among specialists in the State Department and in the U.S. intelligence community is that the Soviet announcement is not a bluff. One news report of an equivocal comment by a Soviet diplomat raised hopes briefly but it was soon denied by the diplomat himself.

There is virtually nil chance of them reversing" the decision, one aide to Reagan said in summing up the U.S. government view.

None of the government experts accepted the Soviet assertion that concern over the security of its athletes was the primary reason for its action. Soviet fear of defections by its athletes, however, and a desire to avoid worldwide televised coverage of demonstrations against the Soviet Union, may have affected the move marginally, the U.S. specialists said.

George Kennan, the most experienced Sovietologist in the United States, suggested that Reagan's attacks on the Soviets during his Peking visit last week was a major

Please see OLYMPICS, Page 24

WEATHER

U.S. Weather Service forecast: Today—sunny. Tonight and Thursday—clear tonight and sunny Thursday.

	Highs	Lows
Tuesday	97	66
Today's forecast	near 90	60-65
Thursday's forecast	near 90	low 60s
May 8 last year	74	64

Record high May 8, 1984	97
Record low May 8, 1879	43

Complete details, Part IV, Page 15.

INDEX

Art	Part VI	CALENDAR	Page 1
Astrology	II	VIEW	8
Books	V	VIEW	13
Bridge	V	VIEW	12
Classified	VII	CLASSIFIED	1-20
Comics	V	VIEW	15
Crossword	VII	CLASSIFIED	20
Dear Abby	II	METRO	8
Editorials	II	METRO	6,7
Films	VI	CALENDAR	1-6
Local News	II	METRO	1-5,8
Markets	IV	BUSINESS	1-14,16
Music	VI	CALENDAR	1,5,6
Sports	III	SPORTS	1-12
Stage	VI	CALENDAR	1,2
TV-Radio	VI	CALENDAR	1,7-12
Weather, Deaths	IV		15

Mirror Sport

Wednesday, July 4, 1984   No. 24,997
Telephone: (STD Code: 01) — 353 0246

THE LORD'S PRAYER . .

GOD HELP ENGLAND

DEJECTED: Gower has that sinking feeling

Dossier of defeat

● DAVID GOWER is the first England skipper for 36 years to declare and then lose a Test.

● THE LAST was Norman Yardley in 1948, when Don Bradman's Australians made 404 for 3 at Headingley.

● GORDON GREENIDGE'S unbeaten 214 is the highest international innings by a West Indian at Lord's and only the third double century by an overseas batsman in a Test there since the war.

● IT IS also Greenidge's highest score in 54 Tests.

● HIS UNBROKEN stand of 287 with Larry Gomes is West Indies' best for the second wicket against England.

● IT BEATS the 249 of Lawrence Rowe and Alvin Kallicharran in Barbados in 1973-74.

● IT IS only the tenth time a side has made 300 or more to win a Test.

DEJECTED: Botham looks to the heavens

By PETER LAKER

A CARIBBEAN hurricane called Gordon Greenidge yesterday demolished England in the second Test at Lord's.

With cold-blooded intent, the 33-year-old opener rushed to an unbeaten 214 in five hours as West Indies went 2-0 up in the Cornhill series with nine wickets and 11.5 overs to spare. That one monumental innings—only the third Test double century at cricket's headquarters since the war—was the lethal difference between a world-class side that thinks only in terms of victory and another that tends to have mental blackouts when the chips are down.

After losing 53 priceless minutes through Monday's bad light walk-off by Allan Lamb and Derek Pringle, England skipper David Gower was perhaps 50 runs short of reality yesterday when he challenged West Indies to score 342 to win in five and a half hours.

Greenidge reached his century in 146 minutes (16 fours), 200 in 248 minutes (12 more fours and 2 sixes) and 214 with another fierce four.

His unbroken second-wicket partnership with Larry Gomes (92) added a record 287 in 236 minutes and West Indies' closing total of 344-1 was the fourth highest to win in Test match history.

England's meagre consolation yesterday was the spectacular running out of opener Desmond Haynes by Lamb at 57.

From that moment, Greenidge was in total control. The problem of getting out the legendary Viv Richards that has always bugged England's bowlers never arose.

It hardly mattered when or how Ian Botham, Bob Willis and the rest bowled. Greenidge played them all at will.

His straight-driving, pulling and flicks past cover were vicious, and his over-the-shoulder six off Pringle showed absolute contempt.

It sets England a fearful task for the third test, scheduled to start at Headingley tomorrow week. Mike Gatting, Pringle, Neil Foster and Geoff Miller must all be in danger of being axed.

SCOREBOARD

ENGLAND.—First Inns: 286 (Fowler 106, Broad 55, Marshall 6-85).

Second Innings (Overnight: 287-7)
Lamb, c Dujon, b Marshall 110
Pringle, lbw, b Garner 8
Foster, not out 9
Extras (b4, lb7, w1, nb6) 18
Total (9 wkts dec) 300
Bowling: Garner 30.3-3-91-3; Marshall 22-6-85-2; Small 12-2-40-3; Baptiste 26-8-48-0; Harper 8-1-18-1.

WEST INDIES.—First Inns: 245 (Richards 72, Botham 8-103).
Second Innings
Greenidge, not out 214
Haynes, run out 17
Gomes, not out 92
Extras (b4, lb4, nb13) 21
Total (1 wkt) 344
Bowling: Willis 15-5-48-0; Botham 20.1-2-117-0; Pringle 8-0-44-0; Foster 12-0-69-0; Miller 11-0-45-0.

```
5.41  SCOREBOARD

     WEST INDIES SECOND INNINGS
C G GREENIDGE NOT OUT 214
D L HAYNES RUN OUT 17
H A GOMES NOT OUT 92
TOTAL 344 FOR 1

RESULT: WEST INDIES BEAT ENGLAND BY 9 WICKETS.
```

How the news of England's defeat broke yesterday.

Gower loses his cool

By CHRIS LANDER

ENGLAND'S shell-shocked captain David Gower blew his top last night at the post-match Press conference.

The 28-year-old Leicestershire batsman, who replaced Bob Willis as England skipper this season, came close to walking out.

He got upset when he was repeatedly questioned about the controversial incident on Monday night when batsmen Allan Lamb and Derek Pringle came off for bad light.

Gower said he had

◆ Turn to page 31

◆ Turn to page 31

GOODBYE JO — see Pages 30 and 31

GOODBYE JO — see Pages 30 and 31

ANDY CAPP   by Reg Smythe

Printed and Published by THE DAILY MIRROR NEWSPAPERS Ltd. (01-353 0246) at, and for, Mirror Group Newspapers Ltd., Holborn Circus, London, EC1P 1DQ. Registered at the Post Office as a newspaper.

Olympic Mirror

FRANK McGHEE in Los Angeles

★★★★★★★★★★★★★★★★★★★★★★★★★★★★★★★★★

LEWIS

The man who'll save the Games

ANYONE who isn't yet familiar with the name of Carl Lewis won't be able to avoid it in the next fortnight.

His name—and practically his alone—has saved the Olympic Games from disaster.

His name above others makes millions of sports lovers feel nervously tense with excitement as the Games open in Los Angeles today.

Only this 22-year-old model of symmetrical physical perfection has a chance of winning four track and field medals—at 100 and 200 metres, long jump and sprint relay.

Only Lewis, 6 ft 2 ins and 12½ stone can equal the legendary record set by fellow American Jesse Owens—a record achieved 48 years ago in the hatred of Hitler's Berlin.

Even more importantly, Lewis fufils the real basic requirement of any Olympic gold medallist; that the winner on the day should reign and be recognised as the best in the world.

The boycott by the Eastern bloc and its allies has wiped out belief in a dispiriting majority of events — but not on the track.

It is here that the real appeal of every Games is founded; the real reason why the adrenalin, the arguments, the apprehension are building up.

The boycott cannot tarnish Lewis's achievements if he succeeds—particularly if he shatters the Bob Beamon long jump record most experts thought would survive this century.

There are two types of performer at his explosive events—the muscular "rhino," like our own charging Allan Wells, and the gazelle with its hooves on fire, the image Lewis creates.

The only snag is that even television, with its slow motion replays, cannot make a totally satisfying meal for viewers of Lewis's apparently inevit-

able successes. They simply won't last long enough.

And that throws wide open the exciting possibility that equally lasting and memorable track achievements at these Games will be British.

No nation has ever enjoyed a greater potential domination in any Olympics of the middle distance events—800 metres, 1500 and 5,000—than Britain's feared and famous contingent. Between them Seb Coe, Steve Ovett, Steve Cram and David Moorcroft have dominated all the medals, all the records, all the big occasions for years.

And their longer events provide greater, more detailed opportunities for the drama the eye will enjoy.

There is also, of course, the great Daley Thompson in the decathlon. If you had to bet on the athlete most likely to strike gold Thompson would not rank far behind either Lewis or the greatest certainty of all, America's Ed Moses in the 400 metres hurdles.

They all share another more important certainty that a week after the games, they could line up against the best of the absent athletes from Eastern Europe and still prove their superiority.

Sadly that can't be said for most of the women.

Mary Decker of the USA and Zola Budd who became British at the wave of a wand, perhaps present honourable exceptions, but still can't dispute that victory would be even sweeter if they beat the whole world, not half.

All the competitors may find a similar truth distressing, but it has to be said that the medals have already been devalued.

That doesn't worry the ABC TV company of America, which bought the exclusive rights to screen the Games to more than half the world.

They realise that weaker opposition means more USA winners which is ideal for home consumption.

But it doesn't really console the rest of us.

BLACK STREAK

LEWIS hopes to emulate the great Jesse Owens by winning four gold medals in Los Angeles.

'His name makes millions tense with excitement'

DAILY Mirror

Saturday, August 11, 1984   FORWARD WITH BRITAIN   17p

Daley's bad taste jokes shock fans

WHISTLING: Thompson on the victory rostrum

Miners say NO to peace offer See Page Two

COE

BRITAIN'S Seb Coe coasted into the final of the Olympic 1500 metres in Los Angeles early today. Coe, the 800 metres silver medallist, shrugged off two years of health and fitness problems to finish a comfortable third in his semi-final. He defends his 1500-metres title tomorrow night.

OVETT

WORLD record holder Steve Ovett came second in his 1500 metres semi final, but looked exhausted. Ovett, 28, had clearly not fully recovered from the health problems that have marred his performances. He spent two nights in hospital after collapsing at the end of the 800 metres.

CRAM

WORLD champion Steve Cram eased into the 1,500 metres final with a brilliant last lap run. He raced clear of the field after tracking Ovett for much of the race to give Britain a trio of finalists. The favourite, Brazillian Joachim Cruz, was ruled out of the race by illness.

BUDD

ZOLA BUDD faded on the final lap of the women's 3,000 metres and trailed in sixth behind Rumanian Maricica Puica. But Wendy Sly won the silver medal for Britain. Favourite Mary Decker of America fell after crashing into Zola's heel.

Full Story: Back Page

CHAMP

CONGRATULATIONS: Princess Anne greets Thompson after his Olympic decathlon triumph

OLYMPIC champion Daley Thompson cracked amazing jokes about Princess Anne, and "gay" athletes yesterday.

Thompson, who was appearing at a Los Angeles press conference after winning his second decathlon gold medal, said he wanted to have babies with Princess Anne.

He told newsmen the Princess had said: "I hope the babies are white."

His final comment was: "I haven't been so happy since my granny caught her tit in the mangle."

Buckingham Palace said last night that Princess Anne thought it was "absurd" to see Thompson's remarks as offensive.

A British Olympic Spokesman said it was the athlete's way of telling newsmen to mind their own business.

● Full story— Pages 2 and 3
● Golden glory —Pages 30 and 31

CHUMP

❝I want to have babies with Princess Anne❞   ❝My gran caught her tit in the mangle❞

Mirror Sport

Monday, August 13, 1984   No. 25,031

Telephone: (STD Code: 01) — 353 0246

KING OF HEARTS

KING COE with Princess Anne

GOLDEN MOMENT: Seb Coe crosses the line first in the 1500

From VIC ROBBIE in Los Angeles

SEBASTIAN COE climbed back on top of the world with an historic triumph in his Olympic swansong here and then challenged: "Who says I'm finished now?"

Super Seb, bitterly hurt that some wrote him off last year when a blood disorder left him so weak he could hardly walk, took delight making his critics choke.

He powered to the Olympic 1500 metres crown ahead of world champion and fellow Briton Steve Cram and as the 90,000 Coliseum crowd saluted his genius he turned to the massed ranks of press photographers with the index fingers of both hands raised.

The message was clear. The greatest middle distance runner of all time was back doing what he does best—rewriting the record books.

His 3 minutes 32.5 second victory was an Olympic record, beating Kenyan Kip Keino's 16-year-old-best by 2.38 seconds enabling him to become the first man in Olympic history to win two 1500 metres titles.

Golden

But the 27-year-old Coe will not be persuaded to go for a hat-trick. He said: "I would like to go on for another couple of years until the European championships in 1986 and I don't think I'll be in another olympics."

The triumph of Coe, the golden boy whose electrifying finish captured the hearts of all Britain, spearheaded another Californian medal rush to make this our best-ever Olympics with 15 track and field gongs.

Coe said: "I rate that alongside any of the world records I have broken, that was the best I've felt for two years.

"I'll stay with my plan to move up to the 5,000 next year. I don't want to stay in the sport for ever, but I wouldn't like to leave it without trying another event."

Coe's effort was an action replay of Moscow four years ago when he

'Don't write me off again' —Coe

lost the 800 metres to Steve Ovett and bounced back for the 1500 gold. Last Monday he again picked up silver behind Brazilian Joachim Cruz in the 800. But sadly this time Ovett did not figure in the final scene.

Ovett, who had spent two nights in hospital with respiratory problems after finishing last in the 800 metres, stepped off the track with 350 metres to go a bewildered, worried and tearful man.

He is flying straight home for treatment and tests and said: "I stopped because I was having chest pains and that worried me."

FROM FLAGS TO RICHES—See Pages 26 and 27

ANDY CAPP
by Reg Smythe

SOUNDS LIKE YOUR MUM'S FOOTSTEPS COMING UP THE PATH—

SEE YOU

SEE YOU

I HAVE MY USES, EH, FLO?

DEFINITELY, MUM

SHE'S GREAT FOR HIS HEALTH. WHEN HE HEARS HER COMING HE TAKES A WALK

Printed and Published by THE DAILY MIRROR NEWSPAPERS Ltd.

Daily  Mail

MONDAY, AUGUST 13, 1984 18p

BRITAIN'S LAST MEDAL
—BACK PAGE

World exclusive

MY MOMENTS OF NIGHTMARE -BY ZOLA BUDD

Zola reads a report of her nightmare *Picture: MONTY FRESCO*

ZOLA BUDD told for the first time last night her own story of the nightmare moments on the Olympic track when she became entangled with America's heroine, Mary Decker, in an incident which began the greatest single controversy of the Games.

As Mary Decker again went on American TV to blame the tiny South African-born runner for robbing her of a chance of a gold medal in the 3,000 metres, Zola told the Daily Mail in an exclusive interview how she was leading the field with Decker hard behind her.

'Suddenly from behind I felt a bump,' said 18-year-old Zola. 'I think it was Mary's knee on my left leg.

'Thrown off balance, I lurched a little and felt pain as spikes raked down the back of my left heel. I fought for balance and suddenly I sensed Mary falling, crashing to the track.

'I'm sorry'

'I half turned and glimpsed her roll towards the grass. I couldn't believe it. It was terrible. I wanted to stop. I wanted it all to end. And, in truth, the race for me was already over.'

Zola's grief was intensified by the booing of the fiercely partisan crowd of 90,000 in Los Angeles. Even so her first thought was for the 26-year-old American girl she had always idolised.

But Mary Decker, in her moment of intense disappointment, was implacable. Zola, near to tears, burst out: 'I'm sorry . . . I'm sorry . . . I'm sorry.' The American could only reply in fury: 'Get out of here! Get out! Just go! I won't talk to you.'

Last night Zola said : 'I just stood there. I was frightened and I simply didn't know what to do. I was crying and I just stood there.

'I feel very, very sorry for Mary. It's all so unfortunate and unfair for both of us.

'But I feel that I've learned from what happened and I now understand the way chance can affect things in sport. You have to learn to live with that.

'There's no point in trying to apportion blame but I can understand Mary's frustration and anger. She says it's my fault. I'm not saying it's her fault.

'All I want to say about the whole thing is that I am convinced I didn't do anything wrong.

'I've always admired Mary and this hasn't changed anything. I still do admire her. She's a great runner.

'As for my running right now, I know that what I desperately need is a rest. I need to rest my legs and I need to rest my mind. But once I've had that rest I know my enthusiasm will return.

'I look forward to running and racing again. My first Olympics are over but there are other Olympics to come.'

© *Daily Mail* 1984.

Her interview—Centre Pages
Ian Wooldridge—Page 30

INSIDE World Wide 10, Femail 12, Diary 15, TV, Radio 18, 19, Coffee Break 22, City 24, Letters 25, Antiques & Auctions 26

Essex keep title—at last gasp

Notts fail by four with a ball to go

CHEQUE-MATES! Essex skipper Keith Fletcher and John Lever (right) celebrate last night

By PAT GIBSON

ESSEX retained the county championship last night after probably the most dramatic finish to a season in cricket history.

Notts, with one wicket left and two balls remaining, needed just four runs to beat Somerset at Taunton and pip Essex for the Britannic Assurance title.

Then Mike Bore, a roly - poly Yorkshireman with a career batting average of eight, went for the shot that would have won him immortality at Trent Bridge.

He had already hit the first three balls of the last over from 21-year-old left-arm spinner Steve Booth for 4, 4 and 2 . . . and now his blow for glory soared towards the long-off boundary.

But it did not quite make it. And there was substitute fielder Richard Ollis to take the catch calmly above his head and give Somerset victory by three runs.

Only then were Essex able to pop the champagne corks and celebrate their achievement in becoming the first side to retain the title since Yorkshire won it three years in a row between 1966 and 1968.

They were gathered nearly 200 miles away at Chelmsford to receive the £15,000 champions' cheque—or the £7,500 runners' up prize—as news of the Taunton drama came through.

It had already been the longest day in the life of captain Keith Fletcher, who began it by driving home from Manchester where Essex had beaten Lancashire in two days and left Nottinghamshire knowing they had to win to take the championship.

Close

"I went off to do a bit of fishing when I got home," he said.

"But I couldn't concentrate on that so I went back and painted the garage door and then fiddled about the house for the rest of the time.

"When we won the championhpi last year, I said we could win it again — but I

HOW THEY FINISHED

	P	W	L	D	Tie	Batting Bonus	Bowling Bonus	Pts
Essex (1)	24	13	3	8	0	64	83	355
Notts (14)	24	12	3	9	0	68	81	341
Middx (2)	24	8	7	9	0	63	78	269
Leics (4)	24	8	2	14	0	60	78	266
Kent (7)	24	8	3	11	2	45	65	254
Sussx (11)	24	7	6	10	1	54	79	249
Som (10)	24	6	7	11	0	60	78	234
Surrey (8)	24	6	6	12	0	62	72	230
Warks (5)	24	6	7	11	0	71	60	227
Worcs (16)	24	5	5	14	0	66	74	220
Derby (9)	24	4	6	14	0	72	66	202
Nhants (6)	24	5	9	9	1	58	56	202
Glam (15)	24	4	2	18	0	65	71	200
Yorks (17)	24	5	4	15	0	59	55	194
Hants (3)	24	3	13	8	0	58	62	168
Lancs (13)	24	1	9	14	0	49	72	137
Glouc (12)	24	1	10	13	0	56	61	133

(1983 positions in brackets)

Fletcher salutes his young stars

always thought it would be a close thing between us and Notts because they're a blooming good side.

"Obviously Graham Gooch, with more than 2,500 runs, and John Lever, with well over 100 wickets, have done superbly well for us.

"But I am pleased with the way young players like Neil Foster, Derek Pringle, David East, Chris Gladwin and Paul Prichard have come through since we won the championship in 1979.

"And what pleases me most is that every game we have won we have done it by bowling the opposition out in their second innings.

We haven't won any on a declaration."

In the end, though, it was a declaration that brought the championship to such a pulsating climax . . . with Ian Botham, who apparently cannot keep out of anything, timing it to perfection.

It set Notts a target of 297 in a minimum of 52 overs—which turned out to be 60 with spinners Vic Marks and Booth bowling 53 of them unchanged.

And the beauty of it was that neither Fletcher not Notts' gallant captain Clive Rice could have any complaint.

Thanks Both

By JOHN DAVIES

NOTTS skipper Clive Rice paid tribute last night to the sporting gesture from Ian Botham which set up the grandstand finish at Taunton.

Rice, who led the victory bid with a superb 98, shrugged off the disappointment of defeat to say: "A lot of thanks are due to Ian Botham for making such a fantastic game of it.

"When Ian declared, I thought the target was probably 20 runs too much. But I didn't calculate on the extra overs being bowled by their two spinners.

"With the title going to the last over, nobody could possibly have written this story if they had tried.

"I'm really relieved we've got all winter to recover from it. I'm 35 and I feel 50."

Rice also paid a big compliment to New Zealand all-rounder Richard Hadlee, who has inspired Notts championship challenge throughout and picked up the £500 Britannic Assurance Player of the Year award after the match.

"Hadlee has been unbelievable this summer and achieving the double was a fantastic performance," said Rice.

Mike Bore, whose breathtaking 27 took Notts to the brink of victory, declared : "I'm terribly disappointed to lose out by just three yards with that final blow. I should have had an extra lunch for strength !

"When I went out to bat I didn't think we had a chance, but I started to hit the ball well and we got closer.

"If it had been a longer boundary I would have probably tried for two, but it was there to be hit over the short boundary and I went for it."

Francis out of England shape

By STEVE CURRY

TREVOR FRANCIS is sacrificed by England tonight as manager Bobby Robson unfolds the shape of his team to challenge for the 1986 World Cup.

Francis, who has scored six goals in five games for Italian club Sampdoria this season, is given only a substitute's shirt against East Germany at Wembley.

He remained poker-faced after being told he was out of England's final international before World Cup qualification begins next month.

But his disappointment will be heightened by the fact that seven other members of the team that played in the 1982 World Cup in Spain are in Robson's side.

Consistent

Robson, after two years of changing faces, has decided that only four youngsters can break into the team—Mike Duxbury, Mark Wright, Steve Williams and John Barnes.

"I'm going mainly on last season's form and Trevor was never really fit last year," explained Robson.

"When he is totally fit and on song he is a world class player. But while he's been injured, Mark Hateley has done well and Paul Mariner and Tony Woodcock, as a pair, have hit form.

"There is competition for places. If Trevor has an injury-free year and becomes more consistent and becomes again a proven goalscorer he will be considered for the team."

Southampton's Wright and Williams are back in the side, central defender Wright playing his first Wembley interna-

● Turn to Page 39

PUB DOG Graham Allen Arthur Millington

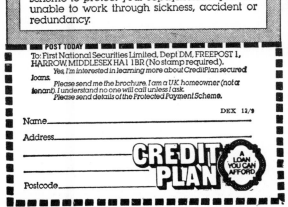

IT STILL HASN'T BEEN INVENTED

SLURP — SCRAPE

MORE IMPORTANT THAN THE WHEEL....

SLURP — SCRAPE

...THE ALL—WEATHER, STAY-STILL, TONGUE-RESISTANT...

LICK SLURP — SCRAPE SCRAPE

...NON-SLIP DOG DISH

305

Ian Wooldridge has written about sport
from Fleet Street — and most other
corners of the world — for 27 years. For
seven of them he was the *Daily Mail's*
cricket correspondent and since 1972 has
been the paper's sports columnist. His
idiosyncratic style and belief that
sportswriting may embrace sparring with
Idi Amin, flying with the RAF's Red
Arrows, driving 6,000 miles through the
Australian Outback and covering a 1,100-
mile sled-dog race across Alaska in mid-
winter, have won him three Sportswriter
of the Year awards and two Columnist of
the Year titles. Despite this he remains a
sports traditionalist and constantly
attacks what he sees as the decline in
manners in so many of the world's
arenas. His appreciation of style, courage
and flair in sport are reflected in his
introduction to this book.